WHITE
WOMEN
IN
RACIALIZED
SPACES

SUNY series in Feminist Criticism and Theory
Michelle A. Massé, editor

WHITE WOMEN IN RACIALIZED SPACES

*Imaginative Transformation
and Ethical Action in Literature*

EDITED BY
Samina Najmi
and
Rajini Srikanth

STATE UNIVERSITY OF NEW YORK PRESS

Published by
State University of New York Press, Albany

© 2002 State University of New York

Chapter 2 was first published in slightly different form as "Category Crisis: South Asian Americans and Questions of Race and Ethnicity" in *Diaspora* 7:3 and is reprinted by permission of University of Toronto Press Incorporated, © 1998. A longer version of chapter 3 was previously published as "Condemned before Trial: The Intersection of Age, Immigration and Race in People vs. Basuta" in *Amerasia* 27:1 and is reprinted by permission of University of California, Los Angeles, © 2001. Portions of poems by Elizabeth Bishop in chapter 10 are reproduced from *The Complete Poems 1927–1979* by Elizabeth Bishop, by permission of Farrar, Straus and Giroux, © 1987.

Printed in the United States of America

For information, address State University of New York Press,
90 State Street, Suite 700, Albany, NY 12207

Production by Cathleen Collins
Marketing by Michael Campochiaro

Front Cover Artwork by Kanishka Raja, *Big Mouth* 1999, oil on canvas on 32 panels, 70x52 inches overall. Image courtesy of the artist.

Library of Congress Cataloguing in Publication Data

White women in racialized spaces: imaginative transformation and ethical action in literature / edited by Samina Najmi and Rajini Srikanth.
    p. cm. — (SUNY series in feminist criticism and theory)
  Includes bibliographical references and index
    ISBN 0-7914-5477-0 (alk. paper) — ISBN 0-7914-5478-9 (pbk. : alk. paper)
    1. American literature—History and criticism. 2. White women in literature.
  3. Women and literature—United States. 4. Ethics in literature. 5. Race in literature.
  6. White women. I. Najmi, Samina. II. Srikanth, Rajini. III. Series.

PS173.W46 W48 2002
810.9'352042—dc21

                                                                        2001055067

10 9 8 7 6 5 4 3 2 1

—for Ammi and Abbu

—for Vaidehi and Nirmala

Contents

Foreword

ELIZABETH AMMONS

The need for this book is real.

Two days ago I attended a faculty workshop on incorporating Asian American material into college courses. The group was small: the leader plus twelve participants, half of whom were Asian American and African American, the other half, white women. We each stated our reasons for coming. We wanted to build on what we were already doing, we wanted to begin a process not yet engaged, we wanted to get beyond a black/white paradigm. The motives varied. Then one white woman declared: "I want to find a different way to think about race. I don't want to talk about whiteness and color." The Asian American leader, a bit startled, asked if the woman could clarify. "I don't want to use whiteness and color as concepts," the white woman said. "I want to find a different metaphor."

As a white woman, I was embarrassed and angry yet also grateful for the nakedness of the statement. Most liberal whites have learned to disguise and hide their longing for race to disappear now that we are starting to be studied, analyzed, implicated, and judged. Yet lurking just below the surface are obvious yearnings and denial. Oh, for the good old days when nice white people like me could simply teach about the race problems of other people—people with dark skin or oval eyes or nonwestern language-heritage. How did whiteness become a race category? Can't race and color—and with them discomfort for me as a white person—just go away? I want some other way to think about all this.

In offering rich, diverse analyses of white women in racialized spaces, this book challenges such white escape-hatching, by which I mean the desire and practice of perpetuating white privilege by exempting whiteness from serious race analysis. That exemption relieves white people from responsibility in the color-based system of racism which currently dominates globalized western world views and power relations. Historically, the socially constructed invisibility of whiteness has served to assert its alleged racelessness, which, of course, is designed to keep whiteness somewhere outside the pervasive system of dominance and subordination that it, in fact, maintains and enforces to keep itself—white power—intact. In this way white entitlement, unearned advantage, and conferred control have remained safe from analysis; and white people, including white women, have remained safe from self-confrontation. To protect this no-analysis zone, whites now propose: Let's get beyond color. Let's talk about something else, like class. Let's find new metaphors. Anything to reduce my discomfort, responsibility, and need to change.

Enabled by the work of race theorists such as Ruth Frankenberg, Ian Haney Lopez, Michael Omi, Howard Winant, and Toni Morrison, this book urges all of us, whatever racial and gender location we occupy, to think critically and deeply about whiteness. Until white people in particular do that, there is little hope of dismantling the color-coded, race-based system of privilege and oppression that governs most of the world, to the detriment of all. As this book shows, focusing especially on white women—a group subordinated by gender yet privileged by race—offers a provocative vantage point on race because, presumably, this group's experience can lead its members to seek systemic change. However, this can happen only if white women give up fantasies of innocence and yearnings for color evasion—the wishful thinking that we are, somehow, beyond implication, analysis, culpability. We are not. The essays in this book are invaluable in demonstrating the key role white women play in the maintenance of global racism and, consequently, the hard work that white women need to do if antiracism is to be anything more than rhetoric.

Acknowledgments

We wish to thank Michael Manson for having welcomed three panels on the topic of this book at the 1997 Northeast Modern Language Association (NEMLA) conference in Baltimore; feminists of color whose probing work inspired our own; the SUNY Press reviewer for posing the complex questions that led us to a rigorous analysis of our own assumptions; Judith Greene, our astonishingly vigilant copyeditor at SUNY Press; and Abbie Goodman, our most efficient indexer.

CHAPTER ONE

Introduction

SAMINA NAJMI AND RAJINI SRIKANTH

At a guest lecture that one of us delivered in Athens, Georgia, a graduate student asked how we academics could avoid essentializing whiteness in the same way that blackness, for instance, has been essentialized. A provocative question in its own right, it becomes all the more so coming from a young black woman in the South, for it highlights the vigilance that people of color have always called for in discussions of race. The woman's question underscores the crucial role of "non-white" voices in keeping whiteness studies from becoming entirely self-reflexive; further, it reminds us of a fact that is easily forgotten amidst the recent avalanche of works by whites on whiteness: that not only has whiteness always been visible to, and analyzed by, people of color, but that contemporary whiteness studies itself was born of the demand by feminists of color, in the early 1980s, that white feminists interrogate their own whiteness.[1] As editors, we offer this book in the tradition of "Third World" feminism: by way of keeping the field of whiteness complicated. Aside from responding to the question of essentializing, we raise similar questions about whiteness at the outset: Why study whiteness at all? Why focus on literature? And why examine the role of white women in particular? We take these up, one at a time.

WHY WHITENESS?

> White racism is a pathology looking for a place to land, sadism
> in search of a story.
>
> —George Lipsitz

In "The White Stuff," Homi Bhabha declares that

1

[s]ince "whiteness" naturalizes the claim to social power and epistemological privilege, displacing its position cannot be achieved by raising
the "gaze of the other" or by provoking the "return" of the repressed or
the oppressed. The *subversive* move is to reveal within the very integu-
ments of "whiteness" the agonistic elements that make it the unsettled,
disturbed form of authority that it is—the incommensurable "differences"
that it must surmount; the histories of trauma and terror that it must
perpetrate and from which it must protect itself; the amnesia it imposes
on itself; the violence it inflicts in the process of becoming a transparent
and transcendent force of authority. (21)

Bhabha voices the assumption underlying white scholars' study of whiteness that
heightened self-consciousness is the first step toward any change. See yourself as
you really are, with your inconsistencies and conflicts; understand the effect of
your actions on peoples and societies; take responsibility for the consequences of
your thoughts and values in the perpetuation of oppression and abetting of injustice, and you cannot help but be aghast at what you have enabled and permitted
to continue. Whether such an assumption is valid remains open to debate, but if
we accept that heightened self-consciousness is a sine qua non of voluntary change,
an essential first step in divesting oneself of arbitrary power, then whiteness studies
would appear to have a purpose, a necessary positive value. But a heightened self-
consciousness resulting from being the subject of unaccustomed scrutiny can also
make many whites uncomfortable. Our book suggests that they work through that
discomfort to see how the practice of whiteness plays itself out in manifestations
of power. As Ruth Frankenberg argues in *Displacing Whiteness*, we need to make a
distinction between whiteness as a bounded, impermeable culture and whiteness
"as practice rather than object" (20). This is certainly a fruitful distinction in that
it promises to keep us from essentializing or reifying whiteness; it is, moreover, a
perspective with a long tradition amongst peoples of color. Even the controversial
Malcolm X, as David Roediger points out, "made a point of connecting whiteness
with the exercise of power, not with biology" (*Black on White* 12). More recently, in
"Brown-Skinned White Girls," Frances Winddance Twine challenges "biologically
essentialist precepts that suggest one must be of exclusive European ancestry to have
access to a white cultural identity" (215)—one which does not involve passing.
Focusing on women of part-African American descent, who were raised by white
or Asian mothers in middle- and upper-class suburbs, Twine shows how they identify as white, and how this identification shifts when they move to a racially politicized, urban college campus. Her analysis thus not only problematizes notions of
biological whiteness—or whiteness as it is understood in common parlance—but
also suggests that the *practice* of whiteness itself needs to be deconstructed.
    Robyn Wiegman, however, has alerted us against a too-ready embracing of
whiteness studies, urging instead an examination of the tension between the

universality of the power of whiteness and the particularities that have given to white racial power its "historical elasticity and contemporary transformations" (118). The trend in whiteness studies, she points out, is to particularize whiteness—that is, to detail its particular manifestations in specific contexts (geographical, historical, cultural, economic locations) and so to make it appear less monolithic, less overwhelming. Such a trend, she argues, can eclipse the universal power of whiteness, a power that persists across its particular manifestations, cuts through specificities, and devastates those who fall within its purview. Thus, to say that whiteness is not monolithic and to demonstrate that it is a nuanced construction reflects a disingenuous refusal to acknowledge the destructive effects of white power, which, in its overwhelming effect on the lives of people, carries the weight of the universal. Many contemporary whites, steeped in Civil Rights ideologies, disaffiliate from segregationist and white supremacist practices to declare themselves antiracist. Wiegman argues, however, that the acceptance of such disaffiliation as the overwhelming mark of antiracism obscures the many myriad ways in which "liberal" whites contribute silently to the economic power of whiteness.

The second equally problematic trend, she points out, is the move in whiteness studies to minoritize the white experience—in other words, to give to it a history of victimhood. Inflecting whiteness with class and stressing the ways in which power and privilege are mediated by socioeconomic conditions, such that poor whites can claim to be every bit as victimized as people of color, represents a strategy of making whiteness appear to be not a threat but a misunderstood phenomenon. Pointing to recent anti-affirmative action moves (spearheaded by academia), Wiegman reveals how these efforts are framed with the rhetoric of "minority" experience: "we" are being unfairly denied our rights because there are too many of "you" who are making claims on available resources. A similar move is the ethnicizing of whiteness in order to deflect attention away from its power and, instead, to illuminate past experiences of discrimination suffered by various groups that fall under the "white" category—Irish, German, Italian, and Jewish immigrants. Wiegman poses provocative questions: "What generates this compulsion for a minoritized whiteness that is not "expensive" to people of color? Or, more precisely, why does the production of a minoritized whiteness become the seemingly necessary precondition for an antiracist project?" The particularizing of whiteness does not necessarily lead to anti-essentialism (and in seeking to anti-essentialize itself, whiteness appropriates one of the basic strategies of antiracist efforts by people of color); "nor does it guarantee the white subject's disaffiliation from the powers of pretensions of universality." Wiegman concludes, rather pessimistically, that there is "no theoretical, historical, or methodological escape from the impossibility of the antiracist white subject, partly because the very focus of the subject has far too much of the universal at stake" (147).

Wiegman's criticism of whiteness studies is trenchant and not without legitimacy. Indeed, self-examination is no guarantee of self-reconstruction, or no guarantee of self-reconstruction that matters. Whiteness studies can become a self-indulgent self-preoccupation, as she warns; more troubling, it can lead to a self-conceptualizing as victim that can result in dangerous reprisals against those who are seen as being responsible for the alleged victimization. We applaud Wiegman's corrective and critical take on whiteness studies and her insistence that it not become a self-congratulatory or self-preoccupied field of inquiry. We share her call that the "political project for the study of whiteness entail[ ] not simply rendering whiteness particular but engaging with the ways that being particular will not divest whiteness of its universal epistemological power" (150). Thus, while we acknowledge that white power can be mitigated by class, gender, and sexual orientation, we maintain that such mitigation does not have an appreciable impact on the power of whiteness over the bodies and lives of people of color.

Our point is not to deny that the power of whiteness can be attenuated by its contexts, but to understand the limits of such diminishments and the motivations of those who propose them. Class, while it may exclude the individual from entry into certain domains, does not usually invite physical or bodily harm. Further, one can acquire new class signifiers—either through wealth or education—and can mask one's original class origins or even entirely erase them. The situation is slightly more complicated with sexual orientation. Such brutalities as the 1998 killing of Matthew Shepherd, a white gay man in Wyoming, attest to the oppression of gays within the white mainstream. Queer studies scholars have made the persuasive argument that the immense hostility directed toward gays and lesbians stems, in part, from the feeling that their sexual behavior inhibits procreation of the race. In this context, the "danger" they pose is akin to the danger miscegenation is purported to pose to advocates of racial purity. Miscegenation taints whiteness; homosexuality diminishes whiteness by undermining its procreation (Nayan Shah). Although homophobia is by no means exclusive to the white community, we do agree with queer theorists that the racial element of homophobia is worth investigating for a nuanced understanding of this attitude. In the same context, pro-choice advocates have pointed out that mainstream antiabortion efforts are largely directed at white women, and that little effort is made to encourage non-white pregnant women to bring their fetuses to term. Such assertions point to the interior fault lines within whiteness and to the necessity of descending into its cracks and crevices, in addition to keeping sight of the larger landscape of whiteness.

But, however its contours may change, the broader landscape of whiteness remains. It is worth quoting white hip-hopper journalist Will "Upski" Wimsatt at some length here to illuminate the kind of vigilant self-interrogation that can prevent the broad theoretical landscape we now call whiteness studies from becoming just another academic fad or just another gesture of white guilt seeking absolution:

I am where I am because of the misfortune of others. While I get paid to write about hip-hop the people who taught me hip-hop are either struggling to get by, in jail, or dead.

I still have a lot to learn from blacks. I still have irrational fears of them. I still slip into degrading white ways of seeing (one of the worst is that I don't expect enough of blacks; another is that I expect too much of them). My speech still slips into a caricature of black speech. As whites, we cannot help blacks without undercutting their self-determination; we cannot be cool without encroaching on their cultural space; we cannot take risks without exercising our privilege to take risks; we cannot integrate without invading; we cannot communicate on black terms without patronizing. Faced with this situation, we need not become paralyzed. We must take the risks necessary to do right, while recognizing that, unlike the black struggle to make it in white America, our effort is not the center of importance.

"I'm confused about what your point of view is," an editor of mine once said. "I can't tell from reading this whether you are a hip-hopper or a racist, an insider in black society or some kind of outside sociologist. Do you love black people or do you hate them?" My answer is that I'm human, meaning that I'm complex enough to be all these things at once.

If only black people could get away with that. (Qtd. in Cornel West 203)

Wimsatt's articulation of the complex motivations and particularized subject positions available to whites—complexities and particularizations that were not perceived to be possible for people of color—reinforces the validity of Richard Dyer's observation that whiteness functions as "infinite particularity" (Wiegman 118). Particularity has always been available to whites, forming refuges that deflect attention from the universality of its power—the universality which imbues the larger landscape of whiteness.

Our book could be seen as abetting the particularization of whiteness, and in a sense that is exactly what it does. However, we make visible these specific manifestations of whiteness over time and in different historical and geographical locations not to undercut the monolithic power of whiteness. Rather, we think of this collection of essays as akin to a prism's operation on white light. The splitting of white light as it passes through the prism reveals the many components of visible light. In understanding the qualities of each of these components—its physical attributes and the uses to which it can be put—we have deepened and complicated our knowledge of white light. We trust our book will perform the same function. With regard to our own relationship to whiteness, as Americans of South Asian descent, our negotiations with the racial landscape of the United States are ambiguous and complex.[2] Positioned between black and white, and often used as a buffer between them, South Asian Americans' encounter with race has been unpredictable, dependent on economic, political, and cultural forces at play at any given moment. Hence our exploration of whiteness represents a means of understanding our own assigned and claimed racial positions within the United States. Our take on whiteness is necessarily complicated by our different experiences with it in the postcolonial nations of Pakistan and India *and* our current experience with it in the United States. Raka Shome makes the point eloquently for us when she describes a "disembodied" whiteness in India, resulting not from contact with white bodies but from a "discursive whiteness" that remains as a residual aftermath of British colonization even after white bodies are no longer present in India. Mindful of her class position, Shome details the impact of discursive whiteness through her indoctrination in Western humanism in Catholic school, in the politics of skin color, and in the tyranny of the English language and literature—to all of which we can relate. Her point that whiteness travels, whether through colonialism or cultural invasion (and now through the demands of global capitalism), reminds us that the effects of whiteness can be felt even in places where there are no white bodies. Similarly, Shome speaks to our own experience when she describes the qualitative difference in the impact whiteness has on her in the United States. Here, whiteness "others" her through racism and anti-immigrant sentiment. The white body being the norm, her brown body "becomes the irreducible sign of difference everywhere [she] go[es]." The difference has been accentuated since the September 11, 2001 terrorist attacks on the World Trade Center buildings and the Pentagon, with many South Asians in the United States becoming the target of racist violence.[3] Our inquiry into whiteness thus stems from multiple interlocking imperatives. We have been guided in our construction of this anthology by the need to foreground the multidimensionality and multicontextuality of whiteness—geographic, historic, cultural, and discursive—even as we keep in mind that such particularizations of whiteness by no means diminish its authority. This contribution to the discourse on whiteness underscores our belief that whiteness studies can not be permitted to cast itself as merely the flip side of ethnic studies, but must be defined as a space in which both whites and people of color can explore constructions of race and representation from multiple dimensions.

WHITENESS STUDIES IN THE UNITED STATES: WHENCE AND WHITHER?

Before turning to the question of "Why focus on literature?" a brief overview of some of the studies that analyze the construction and deployment of whiteness in the United States and elsewhere seems to be in order. It bears repeating that whiteness has always been commented on by people of color—a point amply made by David Roediger's edited volume, *Black on White* (1998). Certainly, many nineteenth-century works, such as the slave narratives of Frederick Douglass and Harriet Jacobs, and Charles Chesnutt's essay, "What Is a White Man?" constitute analyses of whiteness. However, we use the term "whiteness studies" to mark the body of contemporary theoretical works analyzing the process whereby the monolithic power of whiteness came to be constructed.

A social constructionist approach to race first gained ground in 1986 with the publication of Michael Omi and Howard Winant's *Racial Formation in the United States* and the influential collection of critical essays, *"Race," Writing, and Difference*, edited by Henry Louis Gates, Jr. The year 1986 also marks the publication of Virginia Dominguez's *White by Definition*, focusing on legal constructions of whiteness as applied to, and challenged by, Louisiana's Creole population. As such, Dominguez's work represents one of the earliest social constructionist analyses of race to focus specifically on whiteness. Since then, much has been written about whiteness, with differing areas of emphasis: while David Roediger focuses on the formation of the white working class in *The Wages of Whiteness* (1990), as does Noel Ignatiev, Ian Haney Lopez's *White by Law* (1996) expands Dominguez's discussion to illuminate the ways in which U.S. law shapes ideas about race and nationality, determining—by no means consistently—who qualifies as white and American. Our project owes a special debt to Ruth Frankenberg's *White Women, Race Matters* (1993), which broke new ground not only in its theoretical formulations of whiteness but also in its emphasis on how white *women* experience themselves as white, at varying levels of consciousness. Frankenberg's work and Vron Ware's *Beyond the Pale* (1992) complement each other in that the former theorizes white femininity while the latter historicizes it in terms of transatlantic racial politics. Other historical approaches focusing on white women include Kathleen Blee's *Women of the Klan* (1991), a study of white women's roles in the second KKK, and Jenny Sharpe's *Allegories of Empire* (1993), which examines how the construct of white femininity operates in colonial contexts.

In the realm of literary studies, Anna Maria Chupa remains a rare critic to spotlight white women characters (from a Jungian perspective) in *Anne: The White Woman in Contemporary African-American Fiction* (1990).[4] Two more recent works worth mentioning here, though not theoretical in emphasis, are Jane Davis's *The White Image in the Black Mind* (2000), which presents a broad typology of white characters in African American literature, and Renee Curry's *White Women Writing White* (2000), critiquing the poetry of Elizabeth Bishop, H.D., and Sylvia Plath in the context of their whiteness. It is, however, Toni Morrison's *Playing in the Dark* (1992) which may be credited with having catapulted whiteness studies to the center. In this now seminal theoretical work, Morrison argues that white canonical authors like Melville, Poe, Twain, Cather, and Hemingway construct their own white identities and literary expressions vis-a-vis an American Africanist presence. (Euro-Africanism, she suggests, finds similar expression in colonial literature.)

In Morrison's provocative argument, "Whiteness, alone, is mute, meaningless, unfathomable" (59); it derives its associations of freedom and Americanness through the directly oppositional constructions of blackness as the "not-free" and the "not-me." More recently, Valerie Babb's *Whiteness Visible* (1998) analyzes American literature from the seventeenth century to the present to show how whiteness was, and continues to be, formed in response to various hegemonic agendas, particularly by way of establishing a national identity amongst heterogeneous peoples, potentially divided by class.

As Babb has shown, since the earliest white settlements in America, whiteness has served as the binding glue that has defused class tensions and minimized differences in nationality, language, and religion amongst a disparate people. In particular, poor whites have historically not only resisted identification with the poor of other racial groups but have used the whiteness of their skin to prop up their sense of self—a sentiment mockingly echoed in Elma Stuckey's poem, "Enslaved": "'Don't want your food, out of my sight!/ I'm clinging to this—I'm white, I'm white!'" Such assertions of whiteness on the part of white workers have often manifested themselves in violence: from the economically motivated lynchings of African Americans during post-Reconstruction, to the murder of Vincent Chin at the hands of disgruntled autoworkers in 1982, to the barbarous killing of James Byrd in Texas in 1998. Incidents like these reflect not only the white supremacist's sense that America belongs to whites but also the flaunting of white skin in much the same way that other kinds of property are flaunted, to assert superior status.[5] Even outside this violent context, as Du Bois put it, "the white group of laborers, while they received a low wage, were compensated in part by a sort of public and psychological wage" (700).This being the case, to insist on attaching qualifiers to whiteness constitutes an evasion of the privileges that accrue to white skin per se—the kind of privileges Peggy McIntosh has itemized so eloquently in "White Privilege and Male Privilege" (1988).

Two moments in U.S. history highlight the emphasis on skin color as it relates to the construction of a civic polity. The first, as Babb points out, was during the early years of the republic, when the United States as a fledgling nation was articulating its criteria of democratic participation. "The Naturalization Law of 1790 limited the privilege to 'free white persons' and an amendment passed in 1870 extended the right to 'aliens of African nativity or persons of African descent'" (Chandrasekhar 19)—a gesture which was no more than a legality with little substance in practice. The second overt articulation of skin color and its relationship to citizenship occurred during the early decades of the twentieth century, the period when large numbers of immigrants came to the United States from Southern and Eastern Europe and Asia. The Chinese Exclusion Act had been in effect since 1882, in response to widespread agitation by Irish workers, while the Gentlemen's Agreement with Japan (1907) and the Asiatic Barred Zone (1917) were implemented to limit immigration from Japan and to shut out entry of individuals from parts of Asia not covered by the Chinese Exclusion Act or the Gentlemen's Agreement. In the meantime, Asians who were already in the United States attempted to apply for citizenship. Two illustrative cases are those of Bhagat Singh Thind and Takao Ozawa. Prior to 1923, Indians were the only Asians to have been granted citizenship, on a case-by-case basis, on the presumption that Indians belonged to "the same racial classification as the 'Europeans' and to 'the Mediterranean branch of the Caucasian family,' while the Chinese and Japanese belonged to the Mongoloid group" (Chandrasekhar 19–20). Thus, when Takao Ozawa, a person of Japanese descent, applied for citizenship in 1922 he was denied it by Justice Sutherland who justified his decision by stating that "white" was synonymous with "Caucasian," and Ozawa's being Mongoloid precluded his candidacy for citizenship. Emboldened by this reasoning, a year later Bhagat Thind Singh, of Indian descent, applied for citizenship as a Caucasian. The same Justice Sutherland ruled, however, that Thind and other nationals were ineligible for citizenship because the term "white persons" as understood by the common man did not apply to Thind who, although scientifically Caucasian, was clearly not white. In denying Thind citizenship, Sutherland was refuting his own earlier argument in the Ozawa case that equated "Caucasian" with "white person." Thus, Justice Sutherland felt no compulsion to be consistent: while in the Ozawa case he had used race as a criterion of citizenship, in the Thind case his criterion was color.

Ian Haney Lopez's analysis of these and other representative cases aims at establishing three essential points: that the legal system in the United States has stringently demarcated the boundaries of a whiteness that is understood to be inherently superior; that through such demarcations, it has instituted exclusionary laws—like those barring entry into the United States and prohibiting interracial marriage—which have determined what most "Americans" will look like; and that by determining who will be empowered and who will not, the law "translates ideas about race into the material societal conditions that confirm and entrench those ideas" (14). Lopez concludes that whiteness as it has been constructed is of too much value to whites to be given up easily.

A decade prior to Lopez, Virginia Dominguez had taken on the fascinating question of whether one can declare one's racial identity at will, regardless of law or physical appearance. In *White by Definition* (1986), she uses the 1982 case of Louisiana native Susie Phipps, who, at forty-eight years of age, went to court to have herself declared white, challenging thereby a Louisiana law that, despite her white skin, deemed her to be black because she was descended from a black slave. Dominguez argues provocatively that there is a complication embedded in the legal system with respect to racial identity:

> To speak of "what one is" is to imply that some identities are fixed, given, unalterable. A change of phrasing makes this clearer. "Freedom to choose

what one wants to be" would contain an implicit denial of the fixed-
ness of identity in that it suggests that it might be possible to realize
one's wishes. "Freedom to choose what one is becoming" would convey
a similar message. In this case, will and desire seem irrelevant, and extra-
individual forces are patently evident in the very phrase "is becoming";
but the words openly assert a process of becoming. The activity would
be continuous rather than completed. In both of these alternative
forms, there is room for individual choice and action and, thus, room
for conceptualizing freedom to choose one's identity. But how, after all,
can we possibly conceive of freedom of choice if we take identities as
givens? And if there is really no choice, how are we to interpret the
legal granting of "choice"? (4)

Lest we consider Dominguez's argument to be merely a legal or academic exercise,
let us not forget that understanding how race operates is critical to redressing past
wrongs. Dominguez articulates the paradox inherent in a focus on race: "Protecting the rights of blacks require[s] the maintenance of a system for distinguishing
blacks from whites, even though the system had come into existence for the purpose of disenfranchising those identified as black" (5). Indeed, the anti-race-based
initiatives in California and Texas testify to the current reluctance to engage with
the unspoken privileges accruing to whiteness. A focus on race, the anti-affirmative action advocates argue, disenfranchises whites. However, such a perspective
ignores that "white," too, is a race and, specifically, that it confers certain material privileges upon its members. Whiteness, as Cheryl Harris reminds us, is "property" that can be cashed, sometimes in ways not immediately apparent. To treat
whiteness as the unspoken norm is to fail to see precisely how those who are perceived as white have come systematically to acquire this capital, buttressed by the
particularities of the law.

WHY LITERATURE?

> Thinking in terms of scripts has liberatory potential; scripts
> after all can be broken, rewritten, or played subversively out of
> context.
> —Alison Bailey

In his essay, "Reflections on Critical Whiteness Studies," Parker Johnson asks why,
given the pioneering impact on whiteness studies of Toni Morrison's *Playing in the
Dark*, "there has not been a noticeable rise in the study of whiteness in literature
in a manner similar to the social sciences" (3). We believe that one reason for the
relative silence of literature is the 1970s emergence of cultural studies and the
confluence of such phenomena as ethnic studies and feminism. These movements

fueled the drive to examine narratives and testimonies not generally identified as literary and to interrogate the social and political forces operating within the institutions and systems of civic formations. The term "literature" has itself been called into question, with Marxist critics exposing the hegemonic value judgments undergirding the criteria for calling a piece of writing "literature." The challenge to traditional notions of "the literary" has resulted in the application of the practice of literary analysis to "objects" other than literature. Not surprisingly, then, literary scholars find themselves somewhat on the defensive when they focus on material that falls under the traditional understanding of what constitutes literature.

We do not offer this collection defensively, however. Beyond presenting this anthology as a corrective to the literary "silence" in whiteness studies, we eagerly take on the challenge posed to us by one reviewer of this volume: "Why literature, and how are 'literary representations' (as opposed to other discourses?) particularly useful (or obfuscating?) for gaining critical access to 'white women'?" The reviewer observes that most available volumes on whiteness studies follow an inter-disciplinary cultural studies approach, pointing out that "some have argued that 'cultural studies' as a model of 'mixed' or inter-disciplinary knowledge production offers a kind of study inherently consistent with the business of displacing neutral self-reference that is at the heart of critical 'whiteness studies' . . . [S]cholars in cultural studies will reasonably contend that inter-disciplinarity as such is the only likely basis for a properly 'anti-essentialist' . . . interrogation of 'race.'"

Acknowledging the profound usefulness of a cultural studies approach, we nevertheless believe that it need not displace a discipline-specific methodology such as literary analysis. If anything, the sensitizing of those intellectual and emotive muscles and nerves that are called into play when studying the ways in which language can be manipulated is often essential to penetrating nonliterary "texts" and apprehending their impact, as the New Historicists have demonstrated. (We are not analyzing here the term "literary" or the criteria for its applicability, only observing that certain discourses and authors have been more readily identified as literary than others and that these identifications are subject to the social and cultural forces operating at any given historical moment.) Given that knowledge is primarily discursive and that self-consciousness is also discursively experienced, it seems obvious that a heightened ability to "read"—whatever the "object" of our reading—is critical to any project that involves an effort to transform or shift from one set of conditions to another alternative set of conditions. In answering the question "What good is reading literature?" Steven Knapp asks us not so much to engage with our "wildly various relations to literary texts but with the possible ethical and political benefits of literary *interest* . . . —that is, an interest in representations that construct new compositions of thought and value out of pre-existing relations between words and objects and the responses associated with them (where the 'objects' in question are actually types of persons, actions, and situations as well as 'things')" (89).

Before probing the implications of literary interest as Knapp defines it, and discussing its connection to ethical or political matters, let us contemplate what Derrida says about literature: "literature seemed to me . . . to be the institution which allows one to *say everything*, in *every way*" (36). This power, "*in principle* . . . to say everything, to break free of the rules, to displace them, and thereby to institute, to invent and even to suspect the traditional difference between nature and institution, nature and conventional law, nature and history" (37), enables literature to be a subversive instrument or to be a space in which one can simultaneously consider conflicting perspectives, multiple scenarios, and, as Knapp says, "generate *new* possibilities of valuation" (89). Knapp cautions that complexity of perspective is not inherently a "good" thing, for there is no guarantee that such a stance leads to the ethically appropriate response (where what is to be deemed "appropriate" can itself be contested). In a brilliantly argued commentary, Knapp declares that perhaps the

> moral benefit of literary interest lies not in any capacity to tell us which values are the right ones, but far more modestly, in the way it helps us to find out what our evaluative dispositions *are*. Perhaps a complex scenario [such as is constructed by the play of imagination to be found in literature] sets up a kind of experiment in which we test not the moral worth of one scenario against another one, . . . but the relative strengths of our own responses to the alternative scenarios. (100)

Further, Knapp wonders why we should value this self-consciousness generated by our responses to the complex scenarios of literature. His answer, while not entirely satisfactory, points us in a fruitful direction toward making a connection between literary interest and the sphere of politics and civic society: "The kind of person we happen to value—by no means the kind of person valued at every time in every human society—is the kind that wants to check itself out, know how it feels, be aware of its inconsistencies" (101); we value such a person because in a democratic society founded on the principle of pluralism, it is imperative that we all engage in this kind of self-analysis in the context of our relationship with both those like and unlike ourselves. Knapp argues that

> A person who discovers, by reading literature, the conflicts, inconsistencies, and overdeterminations among her own dispositions is a person who can read *herself* as an instance of descriptive representation. She therefore encounters in herself an analogue of the predicament . . . detected in a descriptively representative legislature: how to choose a particular course of action without suppressing the competing interests that all have a right to be registered in the same representational space. She finds herself embodying the ascendancy of information over action, of representation over authority, of "thick description" over simplifying principle, that reappears at various levels of the liberal state. (101–02)

The limitation of Knapp's very fine line of reasoning is that it assumes a reader who is open to the discoveries of conflicts, inconsistencies, and overdeterminations within her/himself. But to dismiss literature's potential as an instrument of self-knowledge within the context of alternative scenarios, and the implications of such knowledge for a civic society, simply because of those readers who do not take advantage of the opportunities an encounter with literature offers, is to discard a tool of immense value. Recently, one of us taught an introductory course in the art of literature, covering short fiction, poetry, and drama. The students were mostly from disciplines other than English and were taking the course to fulfill a humanities requirement. As is typical of most readers unfamiliar with literary analysis, the students entered the course wary of poetry. However, by the end of the semester, a majority of the students commented that the poetry section had been their favorite because in poetry meaning had not been immediately available to them; they liked having to work with the intricacies of language to make meaning and appreciated hearing the different ways in which their classmates engaged the material. On a similar note, Derek Attridge reminds us of "the paradox that reading in the strictest sense is called for by that which is *unreadable* in a text" (3). By "reading" Attridge here means engagement, interpretation, analysis, the act of going beyond noticing the obvious imitative and referential aspects of literature to those elements that cannot be immediately assimilated. Whiteness studies, then, can be seen to involve two steps—first, the making visible of whiteness to those who do not see it even as they wield its power, and, second, having made whiteness visible, to present it as needing to be read, needing to be examined beyond its immediate visible manifestations.

Almost thirty years ago, Roland Barthes in his pioneering work with photographs and other visual images made the distinction between *denoted* message and *connoted* message, in which the denoted message of a photograph (or painting, drawing, cinema, or theatre) is the message without the code, i. e., the imitative reproduction of reality (scene, object, landscape), and the connoted message is the "second meaning, whose signifier is a certain 'treatment' of the image (result of the action of the creator) and whose signified, whether aesthetic or ideological, refers to a certain 'culture' of the society receiving the message" (17). Working with a similar distinction he made between work and text, we can steer ourselves toward an understanding of the particular advantages of literature in the interrogation of a construct such as whiteness. Barthes explains:

> the work is a fragment of substance, occupying a part of the space of books (in a library for example), the Text is a methodological field. The opposition may recall (without at all reproducing term for term) Lacan's distinction between 'reality' and 'the real': the one is displayed, the other demonstrated; likewise, the work can be seen (in bookshops, in catalogues, in exam syllabuses), the text is a process of demonstration, . . . ; the

work can be held in the hand, the text is held in language, only exists
in the movement of the discourse . . . the *Text is experienced only in an
activity of production.* (156–57)

We would argue that literature is the realm that most readily encourages, perhaps
even demands, a textual engagement with its artifacts; in other words, a literary
approach facilitates a nuanced understanding of the ways in which we are constituted and constitute others in language. Thus, social and political institutions,
systems of commerce, frameworks of education, all of the intricate grids of interaction upon which a civic society is founded can be "read." Going back to Barthes's
distinction between display and demonstration, one could say that literature makes
us dissatisfied with mere display; it sharpens in us the appetite to know how and
why things operate in certain ways, it makes us demand demonstration. With
regard to whiteness studies, therefore, we would argue that literature sensitizes
and prepares us to probe the intricacies of current structures of whiteness and to
imagine and envision alternate modes of its manifestation.

WHY WHITE WOMEN?

> As the often-silent benefactors of both white supremacy and
> legal protections that were made possible by civil rights move-
> ments led by people of color, white women in particular have
> a moral and ethical responsibility to place the abolition of
> white supremacy at the forefront of their personal and political
> agendas.
>
> —Dreama Moon

White women occupy an interstitial position in the sociocultural landscape of
the United States, European nations, and those countries in which the residual
effects of colonialism still operate. At once racially privileged and sexually marginalized, their in-between status theoretically should give to white women the
resources and the sensibilities to become a significant mediating force in bringing
together the center and the periphery and eventually blurring the distinction
between the two. But the practices of white women have not always optimized on
this potential. Though they have been energetic in calling for solidarity among
all women in opposing patriarchy, white women have not been equally motivated
to examine their own racial privilege. Feminists of color, including Third World
feminists, have long criticized white women's blindness in this regard. The impas-
sioned articulations of Audre Lorde, bell hooks, Cherrie Moraga, Trinh T. Minh-ha
and Chandra Talpade Mohanty, to name a few, speak to the necessity of a nuanced
examination of the intersection of race and gender. Womanhood does not result
in automatic bonds of shared oppression, they reason, particularly when much of
the oppression is racially inflected. The response to this criticism in Marilyn Frye's

1981 address is relevant to contemporary white feminists who continue to be accused of insensitivity to race:

> It seemed like doing nothing would be racist and whatever we did would be racist just because we [white women] did it. . . . Am I racist if I decide to do nothing? If I decide to refuse to work with other white women on our racism? My deciding, deciding to do anything is poison to her [a feminist of color]. Is this what she knows? . . . It becomes clearer why no decision I make here can fail to be an exercise of race privilege. . . . What is this "being white" that gets me into so much trouble after so many years of seeming to me to be so benign? (Qtd. in Mike Hill 6)

Frye's final question reveals the blind spots that our book seeks to illuminate. While white women have long considered themselves to be the champions of the down-trodden, the essays in our volume complicate this perspective. They do not deny the many instances in which white women have, indeed, labored side by side with racial Others to challenge white male privilege, but the essays probe these instances to uncover the intricate tangle of social, political, and psychological forces underpinning these moments. By displacing attention from race to an exclu-sive focus on gender, white women—and white women writers—abdicate their ethical and moral responsibility in the fight against racism. As Renée Curry observes, "Keeping oneself innocent of racism enables one to write with racially fraught vocabulary and yet to ignore its implications" (16). Curry's book demonstrates "ways to read poetry written by white people as racial works that reflect white worlds and white imaginations" (170). Our collection takes the examination of the white female imagination beyond the realm of poetry into narrative, and beyond the United States into other territories.

Literature, with its ability to render complexity (by creating alternative sce-narios to a particular ethical, political, or emotional problem against which readers and characters test their responses), forms an ideal vehicle for exploring white women's actual and potential roles, and the possibilities and limitations of their agency, in the effort to undercut the oppressive force of whiteness. Indeed, as Nina Baym and others have shown, literature in nineteenth-century America became a powerful vehicle through which white women began to envision new roles for themselves beyond the domestic space and beyond the paternalism of their fathers, brothers, and husbands. Because literature is seen as disconnected from reality, a realm apart, it invites the performance of bold and subversive acts within its pages, the testing of new possibilities of being. These fictive scripts may be seen as preparation for transformative and life-altering moves in the real world. Indeed, Frances Twine underscores the central role of literature in the fight against slavery, pointing to the domestic space as the potential site for subversive prac-tices by white women: "The war over slavery was first fought not on the Civil War

battlefields but in the popular literature of the antebellum period, most of it read
by women; it was through an appeal to the sanctity of motherhood that the evil
of slavery—with its disregard for the holy bond between infant and mother—was
rendered most luridly visible to white America" ("White Mother" 144). One could
debate the extent to which literature was the moving force in the fight against
slavery (notwithstanding Abraham Lincoln's quip to Harriet Beecher Stowe that
she was the little lady who started all the trouble), but Twine is right to remind us
that family/home represents a crucial site for the dismantling of racial oppression.
In discussing the birth of the literary genre of memoirs by white mothers of black
children,[6] Twine writes that these texts can be read in multiple ways—"novellas
of consciousness, parenting guides, antiracist treatises, and feminist autobiographies"—and that they "point to some of the conditions under which an antiracist
consciousness might be formed among white women in the post-Civil Rights
United States" (148). Twine quotes Jane Lazarre's eloquent cry, "'What is this
whiteness that threatens to separate me from my own child?'" and notes that "[l]ike
abolitionist literature, this appeal bases its emotional force on the power of motherhood to speak across difference" (qtd. in Twine 151).

Let us not forget, however, that white women have also used the family/
home not to subvert but to preserve the status quo. Dreama Moon, who focuses
on the production of white femininity as a middle-class bourgeois enterprise, argues
that white girls are "made" at home through certain communicative practices: "The
enculturative process is *racialized* within the cultural space of the white family/
home in that the patriarchal production of 'good girls' within the family is inex-
tricably linked to the racist production of 'good *white* girls.' In short, becoming a
'good girl' within the context of white family relations often takes on a racialized
dimension as what it means to be 'good' is frequently bound up with issues of racial
loyalty and solidarity" (181). Given the centrality of home in the process of creating white girls, and the role of women as primary socializing agents of white
children, Dreama Moon calls on white women to "build 'home' as antihegemonic
spaces in which engagement with the movement against white supremacy is made
a cultural norm" (196).

Similarly, Vron Ware has shown how white women use the domestic space
and their power within it to further racism. Discussing white women's racist reasons for having elected a neofascist party in a racially diverse neighborhood of
England during the elections of 1993, Ware declares that their justifications were
couched in the rhetoric of protecting the home. Their complaints against Bangladeshis and Blacks centered on the defiling of the domestic space through the
smells, spitting, cockroaches, and disease that allegedly accompanied the presence
of Bangladeshis and Blacks. They also pointed to the practice of polygamy among
Bangladeshi Muslims and saw in its unfairness to women the "mark of an inferior
civilization." As Ware observes, ironically, the dutiful young white mother "becomes
a cipher for racial intolerance through the vulnerability and powerlessness that

[white femininity] comes to articulate. . . . [T]he enduring image of a seemingly passive, but wronged, white femininity can be seen to occupy a central place in the contemporary histories of racist domination and female subordination" ("Island Racism" 300). White women give racism a veneer of innocence and of family values; in doing so they invest themselves with a vulnerability that has easily been deployed to oppress men and women of color.

Most glaringly, the institution of American slavery—one of the mightiest edifices of racial oppression anywhere—was constructed on the body of the fragile, pure, and chaste white woman, a strategy that Minrose Gwin compellingly documents. Moreover, eloquent personal narratives by white Southern women testify to the ways in which their supposed vulnerability and innocence continue to be mobilized in the service of racism. For example, Kim Hall writes, "Fear has been central to the meaning of whiteness in my life: fear of miscegenation, fear of non-white others, fear of being disowned" (29). Another Southern white woman, Amy Edgington, credits Civil Rights' warriors with helping to "create a world where [she] ha[s] the chance to become a true adult instead of remaining a child who must do what white men dictate" (43). With regard to white Southern women's fiction, Rebecca Aanerud's reading of Kate Chopin's heroine, Edna Pontellier (*The Awakening*, 1899), demonstrates compellingly the intersections of literature with sociocultural and historical forces. Accounting for the novel's poor reception, Aanerud locates its publication in the historically specific moment of post-Reconstruction, a time marked by widespread lynchings of black men, allegedly for raping white women. In this sociohistorical context, *The Awakening* presented a heroine who threatened the position of the white male in his exercise of power over the black male: "Edna Pontellier is a white woman whose 'immoral behavior' cannot be attributed to black male lust. As such her transgression threatens to destabilize not only the authority of white men over white women, but the authority of white men over black men" (44). Aanerud's analysis reminds us of the skills that we acquire from reading literary texts, and the value of these skills in reading the text of life. Further, it underscores the ways in which certain literary texts have been embraced by white women as celebrations of a "raceless" feminism, with a blind eye to the racial dynamics that are central to their themes and even to the manner of their reception in the literary world.

It would appear, then, that white women have a special responsibility to undo racism, given the benefits they have derived from it and given the deliberate and unwitting ways in which they have abetted it. Echoing Adrienne Rich in "Disloyal to Civilization," Alison Bailey makes the case that rather than feel paralyzed by knowledge of one's racial privilege and the impossibility of disposing of it completely, white women should use that privilege to topple racist institutions. Refusing to use one's privilege in the service of antiracism can amount to a waste of resources, or worse: "Although the master's tools may not be able to successfully dismantle the master's house, they may be just the tools we need to gain access to its contents. . . . Furthermore, refusal to use the tools privilege affords us to break into the master's house may amount to protecting the house" (99). The essays in this anthology explore the extent to which, and the ways in which, white women use the realm of fiction and poetry to acknowledge or ignore privilege, to attack or protect edifices of racism, and to take up arms in, or retreat from, the war against oppression.

THE ESSAYS

Primarily literary in focus, the essays cover extensive historical and geographical ground. They address the early captivity narratives of white women in seventeenth-through-nineteenth-century America and bring us all the way up to the present moment in the trials of Louise Woodward and Manjit Basuta, both British nannies, accused of causing the deaths of their infant charges in the United States, in two separate cases. In addition to the United States, the essays take us to Egypt, South Africa, Cameroon, India, and Thailand. We seek through this collection to understand how the intersection of whiteness and gender manifests itself in different historical and cultural settings. The majority of the essays focus on this intersection as it occurs in literary texts. We have included an essay on film primarily because women are now becoming active players as cinematographers and directors, and so questions of representing racial Others will become as relevant for cinema as they are for literature.

Three of the essays in this volume are nonliterary in focus. We include them in an opening section, "Brown on White," to demonstrate how, as Gayatri Spivak has observed, it becomes necessary to read the world as text if we are to appreciate fully the complexity of what we live and experience. Susan Koshy's essay in this volume, "South Asians and the Complex Interstices of Whiteness: Negotiating Public Sentiment in the United States and Britain," is particularly relevant to a discussion of the "silence" surrounding whiteness. Situating South Asians vis-à-vis whiteness in the United States and Britain, Koshy draws attention to the protean quality of legal definitions of whiteness as they have been applied to South Asians. While in Britain South Asians have been categorized as black, their racial identity in the United States has had a more complex history. Positioned outside the black-white polarity that usually governs race in the United States, South Asians become an ambiguous racial category, whose very ambiguity, legally and socially, provides a nuanced perspective on whiteness. Koshy's essay also draws attention to South Asian American invisibility, resulting from such ambiguity—an invisibility which is, however, quite different from the ways in which hegemonic whiteness is invisible, as South Asian American invisibility serves to silence and erase, rather than empower. Koshy goes on to examine the Louise Woodward case as a focal point for her argument, demonstrating how the white British au pair accused of killing eight-month-old Matthew Eappen could be cast as innocent by public, media, and judge, while the South Asian origins of the victim's father, Dr. Sunil Eappen, and his marriage to the white Dr. Deborah Eappen served to throw that "innocence" into sharp relief. Koshy argues that the highly publicized case "marks the limitations in middle-class South Asian American strategies to claim an identity unmarked by race. The Woodward case dramatizes the ways in which, despite the rhetoric of the American dream, class does not provide access to the immunities and privileges of whiteness for racial minorities."

In a companion piece, titled "Whiteness and Soap-Opera Justice: Comparing the Louise Woodward and Manjit Basuta Cases," Monali Sheth picks up where Koshy leaves off. Sheth demonstrates that while Woodward profited from her own whiteness and the nonwhiteness of the Eappens, Manjit Basuta—a British South Asian day-care provider in San Diego—could not play on the sympathies of the white mainstream in Britain or the United States in the same way, despite strong evidence of circumstances that ought to have operated in her favor. Analyzing Basuta's case in light of Woodward's, Sheth underscores the "highly racialized issues of immigration and nationality" that had tacitly determined the terms of the public debate surrounding the Basuta trial, on both sides of the Atlantic. Sheth contends: "While both Woodward and Basuta were immigrants to the United States, only Basuta was seen as the 'racial other' in the courtroom and the American public consciousness. It is this difference that made Woodward's alien status something that could be overlooked, while it made Basuta the 'perpetual alien.' Similarly, in the U.K., both Basuta and Woodward were British citizens, but Basuta alone, as the 'racial other,' could not achieve the ultimate standard of 'Britishness.'"

If whiteness gave to Woodward the cashable capital of "innocence," then, as Vijay Prashad's essay argues, whiteness conferred upon Mother Teresa the quality of benevolence. She was, in Prashad's words, "the quintessential image of the white woman in the colonies, working to save the dark bodies from their own temptations and failures." His examination of her does not detract from her extraordinary work but shows how her elevation to mythic proportions by the Western media results in two types of silencing: (1) it inhibits an appreciation for the brown-skinned women and men of India who, like her, labor to help the dispossessed and the diseased, and (2) it forestalls a critique of the economic structures that give rise to the conditions which dispossess the Third World in the first place. The essays by Prashad, Sheth, and Koshy, together comprising Part I of our volume, raise the social, political, and economic issues that readers will reencounter in Parts II and III, as textual renditions of white women in racialized spaces.

The essays in Part II, "White American Womanhood," focus on such renditions in an exclusively American context. The first three illustrate the limitations of white women's attempts to break out of the stranglehold of white patriarchy. Rajini Srikanth's essay, "Ventriloquism in the Captivity Narrative: White Women Challenge European American Patriarchy," focuses on white women's articulations of selfhood in the popular genre of the American captivity narrative. Drawing on a few selected texts, Srikanth shows that white women in Puritan, colonial, and nineteenth-century America used the captivity narrative to mount an oblique challenge to Euro-American patriarchy. During their period of captivity by Native American tribes, some white women gradually came to realize aspects of their selfhood to which they had not had access within the constraints of Euro-American femininity and domesticity. Within the context of the racialized Native American Other, these women felt "at liberty" to act in ways that would have been deemed transgressive and unacceptable in "freedom": they exhibited independence, physical violence, boldness, and deception. This new selfhood, Srikanth argues, could be entertained and expressed because the reading public perceived the women's challenge to be directed against the Native American, not against white patriarchy. However, the challenge was at best limited; the captivity narratives were appropriated into the new republic's agenda of nation building and westward expansion. Srikanth's essay discusses the ways in which white women held captive "used" the racialized Otherness of the Native American to enact new ways of being; but cloaking this new self behind the Native American Other enabled the co-optation of the narratives by the nation's leaders to justify their encroachments upon the Native Americans' ways of life.

Similarly, Peter Chvany's essay, "'Those Indians Are Great Thieves, I Suppose?': Historicizing the White Woman in *The Squatter and the Don*," underscores both the potential and the limitations of Maria Amparo Ruiz de Burton's late nineteenth-century critique of U.S. expansionism. Highlighting her insightful linkage of race and class in the oppression of Californios, Chvany argues, however, that situating Ruiz de Burton's novel in the context of white femininity—in terms of both its fictional representations of white women and the author's self-representation as a white Mexican—reveals the limitations of her critique of oppression. As Chvany demonstrates, Ruiz de Burton's focus on the racio-economic oppression of upper-class white Californios casts San Diego as the "prostrate South" of post-Reconstruction politics, at the continued expense of the truly dispossessed Native American and African American population.

Like Srikanth and Chvany, Diana Paulin examines the political potential of white women's narratives. In "'Let Me Play Desdemona': White Heroines and Interracial Desire in Louisa May Alcott's 'My Contraband' and 'M.L.,'" Paulin revisits nineteenth-century domestic fiction by white women like Alcott, to illuminate their subtle but highly-charged politics. She discusses the author's radical depictions of interracial relationships involving white women and light-skinned black men, and her bold challenge to the myth that white women needed protection against "burly black brutes." To this extent, Alcott's white heroines serve as models of transgressive female agency, but, Paulin argues, her stories privilege white women's agency and identity vis-à-vis black male powerlessness. Although, as such, the narratives do not significantly challenge racial hierarchies—indeed, they replicate the racial myopia of nineteenth-century women's rights activists—Paulin's essay explores the ways in which they might "provide space for reevaluating the transformative power of popular and sentimental fiction."

The next two essays in Part II invert the white female gaze, focusing on black authors' representations of white women. They demonstrate two very different—almost antithetical—dimensions of the black gaze, however. In "Getting in Touch with the True South: Pet Negroes, White Crackers, and Racial Staging in Zora Neale Hurston's *Seraph on the Suwanee*," Delia Konzett challenges prevailing critical trends which dismiss Hurston's *Seraph* as a novel pandering to a white audience. Framing her discussion in the context of Hurston's controversial essay, "The 'Pet' Negro System" (1943), and spotlighting the poor white "Cracker" heroine of *Seraph*, Konzett illuminates the novel's engagement with the intersecting and conflicting roles of race, class, and gender in the articulation of the New South. As Konzett argues, Hurston's analysis eschews binary constructions, laying "bare a messy system in which traditional oppositions of perpetrator and victim, master and slave, white and black, overlap and are at times indistinguishable from one another."

Contrasting sharply with Hurston's nuanced politics, Malcolm X and Iceberg Slim form the focus of Terri Oliver's essay, "Prison, Perversion and Pimps: The White Temptress in *The Autobiography of Malcolm X* and Iceberg Slim's *Pimp*." Yoking together these two African American male writers with diverse backgrounds and motivations, Oliver first locates their narratives in what she identifies as a long tradition of "white temptresses" in black male autobiography. She goes on to show how both Malcolm X's and Iceberg Slim's narratives, in particular, challenge the equation of white femininity with innocence, recasting white women as a physical and psychic threat to black manhood. As such, Oliver asserts, their narratives rewrite the classic tragic-mulatta story, in which a light-skinned black woman meets her death through a white male villain. Mindful of black feminist criticism of sexist ideologies of black masculinity, Oliver argues nevertheless that these authors' confessional and cautionary tales about the white, thrill-seeking temptress not only respond to the historical memory of lynching but call attention to the reenactments of that racio-sexual dynamic in the 1960s era of the Civil Rights Movement.

Part II concludes with Zhou Xiaojing's essay, "Subject Positions in Elizabeth Bishop's Representations of Whiteness and the 'Other.'" Zhou takes issue with critics who, interpreting Bishop's poems as voicing a single subject position—that of a privileged white woman—attempt to explain the poet's perspectives on race, gender and class, in that light. Informed by Foucault's theory of subject positionality and Bakhtin's theory of double-voice, Zhou's argument posits that allowing for multivocal subjectivities reveals complex and many-sided perspectives on race, class and gender in Bishop's poems, especially as these affect relationships between women. As a white woman who wrote, often ambivalently, of race- and class hierarchies at home and legacies of colonial oppression in Brazil, Bishop straddles both Part II and Part III of our collection, forming seamless links between the subjugation of nonwhite Others within the United States and abroad.

Part III, "The Global 'Memsahib,'" focuses on imperial and colonial contexts of white women's narratives.[7] The silences embedded in Bishop's poetry—silences surrounding white lesbian sexuality—become the focus of Paula Krebs's analysis in "How Can a White Woman Love a Black Woman? The Anglo-Boer War and Possibilities of Desire." Unlike male homosexuality, sexual relationships between women of different races, within a specifically colonial frame, remain generally uninterrogated. Krebs's essay makes good the omission by locating the 1899–1901 Anglo-Boer War in South Africa within the seldom discussed context of the history of lesbian sexuality. Focusing on an account by Emily Hobhouse (herself a white Englishwoman) of the relationship between a white woman and her female African servants, Krebs's interest lies not in demonstrating evidence of lesbian relationships but in exploring the discursive possibility of lesbianism in a particular colonial context. Referring to Eve Sedgwick's idea of "a powerful unknowing *as* unknowing, not as a vacuum," Krebs argues that the antiwar discourse of the times relied on the inadmissability of interracial lesbian desire to promote a more politically expedient image of same-sex sympathy.

Like Krebs and Paulin, Céline Philibert also explores the implications of interracial desire, using film as text. Her essay, "From Betrayal to Inclusion: The Work of the White Woman's Gaze in Claire Denis's *Chocolat*," explores the ways in which Claire Denis, herself a white woman who grew up in Cameroon, challenges traditional cinematic viewpoints on colonialism. Analyzing the construction of the white female gaze in *Chocolat*—a gaze which she characterizes as both racial and sexual in nature, Philibert sees Denis's film as aligning Cameroon's struggle for national identity with Denis's own attempts at self-definition. As such, Philibert argues, *Chocolat* "constructs, restructures, and transforms viewing strategies as well as gender and racial determinations," both at the personal and public levels, in a colonial context. Philibert's essay takes us to a Francophone location. Her inclusion in this collection is not meant to suggest an undifferentiated whiteness among women in different racialized contexts; rather, because she focuses on the white woman's gaze within the domain of heterosexual and cross-racial desire, her essay offers a valuable comparison to Paulin's and invites an analysis that keeps at the forefront the dimensions of history, culture, and geographical location. Interracial desire in Louisa May Alcott's nineteenth-century United States and in Claire Denis's twentienth-century remembrance of her childhood in colonial Cameroon are both similar and different; we urge readers to find the points of intersection and divergence.

Another angle on gendered colonial discourses forms the focus of Melissa Miller's essay, "The Imperial Feminine: Victorian Women Travellers in Egypt." Miller addresses optimistic feminist analyses of narratives by white Victorian women, arguing that the primary texts do not support the image of "a Victorian heroine who, presumably unlike her male counterparts, displays a greater sensitivity to difference and reluctance to dominate." Miller's analysis focuses on the racialized, distinctly Muslim, space of Egypt—an area too often neglected by race theorists and literary scholars. Standing as it does at the confluence of several cultures and continents, Egypt complicates such categories as "African," "Asian," "Mediterranean," and "Arab." Miller's essay challenges the notion of Victorian women as innocent bystanders in this liminal space, providing a historical link to Sheth's and Koshy's contention that white femininity operates as innocence in contemporary court cases such as Louise Woodward's. Spotlighting texts by Luci Duff Gordon and Amelia Edwards, Miller considers the implications of the terms "mother," "teacher," and "man" in relation to these two women, arguing that Gordon and Edwards assume a "racialized masculinity," as they conflate whiteness with the power of masculinity to dominate the Arab Other in a "feminine" manner.

Part III closes with Susan Morgan's essay, "Chinese Coolies, Hidden Perfume, and Harriet Beecher Stowe in Anna Leonowens's *The Romance of the Harem*," bringing together many of the themes and concerns of the preceding essays. Although Siam (Thailand) withstood official colonization, Leonowens's Victorian subjectivity, and her position as governess-narrator in Siam's royal palace, link her narrative to imperialist discourse. Morgan analyzes a section in Leonowens's relatively obscure second memoir, demonstrating how it interrupts conventional colonial discourse in such "realistic" travel narratives by Victorian women as those discussed by Miller. The racialized space of Siam here also represents the very gendered space of Nang Harm, the royal city whose gates confine the women of the king's harem. Focusing on the British governess-narrator, Anna, and her Siamese friend, Sean Klean, a royal concubine who recreates herself as a Buddhist Harriet Beecher Stowe, Morgan argues that the identities of the three women are fluid, permeable, and overlapping in this female space. As such, they not only represent a seamless connection amongst the history, politics and rhetoric of freedom in Siam, Britain, and the United States, they also overturn racial and colonial hierarchies. In particular, the "teacher" of Miller's discussion gets reinscribed in Morgan's interpretation of Leonowens's narrative as "student," and the text demands a parallel process of (un)learning on the part of the reader. This is not, Morgan argues, a simple reversal still operating within the language of imperialism; it represents, rather, a "politics of metamorphosis" (as opposed to a politics of identity) which favors a plurality of subject positions, making possible narrative moments "when gender works to suspend . . . the veil of imperialist assumptions which drives the narratives of so many nineteenth-century British travel memoirs."

Morgan's critical engagement with Leonowens's Stowe brings us back full circle to the racialized space of the United States. We hope that, collectively, our volume will demonstrate that white women can, if they so choose, alter the hegemonic implications of their whiteness in racialized spaces, preempting any temptation to allow a politicized consciousness to fray into paralyzing guilt. We hope that our collection invites the white woman, instead, to abdicate from "pedestals" of power and privilege, to her own advantage as well as that of others—permitting herself, in the words of a poem by Adrienne Rich, to be "dragged by the roots of her own will/ into another scene of choices."

NOTES

1. Mike Hill, and Chris Cuomo and Kim Hall are among the few whiteness scholars who foreground this fact in their respective Introductions. Cuomo and Hall further note that "White men and African American men seem to listen and respond to each other as if the huge amount of scholarship by feminists of color (and the growing body of work by antiracist white feminists) doesn't exist" (6).

2. See Susan Koshy's essay in this collection. South Asia is a geopolitical label comprising the seven countries of Bangladesh, Bhutan, India, the Maldives, Nepal, Pakistan, and Sri Lanka. South Asian Americans trace their ancestry to one or more of these countries.

3. Visit the websites of the South Asian Journalists Association (SAJA) and the South Asian American leaders of Tomorrow (SAALT) for news reports on the backlash against South Asians. The SAALT report compiles over six hundred separate incidents in the aftermath of September 11: *http//www.saja.org/ tipssources. html#backlash, http://www.saalt.org/*.

4. See also Samina Najmi's dissertation, *Representations of White Women in Works by Selected African American and Asian American Authors*.

5. See Cheryl Harris, "Whiteness as Property."

6. Twine discusses in particular Maureen Reddy's *Crossing the Color Line* and Jane Lazarre's *Beyond the Whiteness of Whiteness*.

7. "Memsahib" (Madam) was the local term for Englishwomen in British India, and has since found its way into English literary texts, as well as the Oxford dictionary. We extend the use of the word here to connote the class- and power relations that inform white female subjectivity in any colonial location or imperialist context.

WORKS CITED

Aanerud, Rebecca. "Fictions of Whiteness: Speaking the Names of Whiteness in US Literature." Frankenberg, *Displacing Whiteness* 35–59.

Attridge, Derek. "Introduction." Jacques Derrida. *Acts of Literature*. New York: Routledge, 1992. 1–29.

Babb, Valerie. *Whiteness Visible: The Meaning of Whiteness in American Literature and Culture*. New York: New York UP, 1998.

Bailey, Alison. "Despising an Identity They Taught Me to Claim." Cuomo and Hall 85–104.

Baym, Nina. *Novels, Readers, and Reviewers: Responses to Fiction in Antebellum America.* Ithaca: Cornell UP, 1984.

———. *Women's Fiction: A Guide to Novels by and about Women in America, 1820–1870.* Ithaca: Cornell UP, 1978.

Bhabha, Homi. "The White Stuff." *Artforum* (May 1998): 21–24.

Blee, Kathleen. *Women of the Klan: Racism and Gender in the 1920s.* Berkeley: U of California P, 1991.

Chandrasekhar, S. "A History of United States Legislation with Respect to Immigration from India." *From India to America.* La Jolla: Population Review Publications, 1982. 11–28.

Chupa, Anna Maria. *Anne: The White Woman in Contemporary African-American Fiction.* Westport: Greenwood, 1990.

Cuomo, Chris, and Kim Hall, eds. *Whiteness: Feminist Philosophical Reflections.* Lanham: Rowman, 1999.

Curry, Renée. *White Women Writing White: HD, Elizabeth Bishop, Sylvia Plath, and Whiteness.* Westport: Greenwood, 2000.

Davis, Jane. *The White Image in the Black Mind: A Study of African American Literature.* Westport: Greenwood, 2000.

Derrida, Jacques. *Acts of Literature.* Ed. Derek Attridge. New York: Routledge, 1992.

Dominguez, Virginia. *White by Definition.* New Brunswick: Rutgers UP, 1986.

Du Bois, W. E. B. *Black Reconstruction.* New York: Kraus Thomson, 1935.

Edgington, Amy. "Growing Up in Little Rock." Cuomo and Hall. 37–44.

Frankenberg, Ruth. ed. *Displacing Whiteness.* Durham: Duke UP, 1997.

———. *White Women, Race Matters: The Social Construction of Whiteness.* Minneapolis: U of Minnesota P, 1993.

Gates, Henry Louis, Jr. ed. *"Race," Writing, and Difference.* Chicago: U of Chicago P, 1986.

Gwin, Minrose. *Black and White Women of the Old South: The Peculiar Sisterhood in American Literature.* Knoxville: U of Tennessee P, 1985.

Hall, Kim. "My Father's Flag." Cuomo and Hall. 29–35.

Harris, Cheryl. "Whiteness as Property." *Harvard Law Review* 106 (1993) 1709–91.

Hill, Mike, ed. *Whiteness: A Critical Reader.* New York: New York UP, 1997.

Ignatiev, Noel. *How the Irish Became White.* New York: Routledge, 1995.

Johnson, Parker. "Reflections on Critical White(ness) Studies." Nakayama and Martin 1–12.

Knapp, Steven. *Literary Interest: The Limits of Anti-Formalism.* Cambridge: Harvard UP, 1993.

Lazarre, Jane. *Beyond the Whiteness of Whiteness: Memoir of a White Mother of Black Sons.* Durham: Duke UP, 1996.

Lipsitz, George. *The Possessive Investment in Whiteness*. Philadelphia: Temple UP, 1998.

Lopez, Ian Haney. *White by Law: The Legal Construction of Race*. New York: New York UP, 1996.

McIntosh, Peggy. "White Privilege and Male Privilege: A Personal Account of Coming to See Correspondences through Work in Women's Studes." Center for Research on Women: Working Paper Series. Wellesley: Center for Research on Women, 1988.

Moon, Dreama. "White Enculturation and Bourgeois Ideology." Nakayama and Martin 177–197.

Morrison, Toni. *Playing in the Dark: Whiteness and the Literary Imagination*. New York: Vintage, 1993.

Najmi, Samina. *Representations of White Women in Works by Selected African American and Asian American Authors*. Diss. Tufts U, 1997. Ann Arbor: UMI, 1997. 9726594.

Nakayama, Thomas, and Judith Martin. *Whiteness: The Communication of Social Identity*. Thousand Oaks: Sage, 1999.

Omi, Michael, and Howard Winant. *Racial Formation in the United States from the 1960s to the 1990s*. 1986. New York: Routledge, 1994.

Rich, Adrienne. "Disloyal to Civilization: Feminism, Racism, Gynephobia." *On Lies, Secrets, and Silence: Selected Prose, 1966–1978*. New York: Norton, 1979.

———. *Your Native Land, Your Life: Poems*. New York: Norton, 1986. 23.

Roediger, David, ed. *Black on White*. New York: Schocken, 1998.

———. *The Wages of Whiteness*. London: Verso, 1990.

Shah, Nayan. "East of California" Conference, New York U, 1996.

Sharpe, Jenny. *Allegories of Empire: The Figure of Woman in the Colonial Text*. Minneapolis: U of Minnesota P, 1993.

Shome, Raka. "Whiteness and the Politics of Location: Postcolonial Reflections." Nakayama and Martin. 107–128.

Stuckey, Elma. "Enslaved." Roediger. *Black on White* 121.

Twine, Frances Winddance. "Brown-Skinned White Girls: Class, Culture, and the Construction of White Identity in Suburban Communities." Frankenberg, *Displacing Whiteness*, 214–43.

———. "The White Mother: Blackness, Whiteness, and Interracial Families." *Transition* 7.1: 144–154.

Ware, Vron. *Beyond the Pale: White Women, Racism, and History*. London & New York: Verso, 1992.

———. "Island Racism: Gender, Place, and White Power." Frankenberg, *Displacing Whiteness*. 283-310.

West, Cornel. "I'm Ofay, You're Ofay: A Conversation with Noel Ignatiev and William 'Upski' Wimsatt." *Transition* 7.1 (1997): 177–203.

Wiegman, Robyn. "Whiteness Studies and the Paradox of Particularity." *boundary 2* 26.3 (Fall 1999): 115-150.

PART ONE

Brown on White

CHAPTER TWO

South Asians and the Complex Interstices of Whiteness

Negotiating Public Sentiment in the United States and Britain

SUSAN KOSHY

The model minority position has increasingly come to define the racial identity of a significant number of South Asian Americans; it depends on the intermediary location of a group between black and white and holds a particularly powerful appeal to immigrant groups.[1] In order to highlight the features of South Asian racialization in the United States, I provide a brief history of the contrasting politicization of South Asians in Britain. The early classification of the group in Britain as "Coloured"/ "Black" offers a contrasting categorization of the same group, and reveals both the contingency of racial categories and their embeddedness in particular histories of colonization and immigration. In concluding, I take up the Louise Woodward au pair case, since the public response to this case highlights the contrasting racial representations of South Asians in Britain and the United States. It also marks the limitations in middle-class South Asian American strategies to claim an identity unmarked by race. The Woodward case dramatizes the ways in which, despite the rhetoric of the American dream, class does not provide access to the immunities and privileges of whiteness for racial minorities; instead, in accordance with the peculiar logic of the model minority prototype, class position is used at once to deny recourse to racial explanations and to generate resentments of extraordinary privileges unavailable to the "average" citizen.

The analysis of aspects of pre- and post-1965 South Asian American identity is an attempt to reopen the debate on the complexities and contradictions of South Asian American racial positioning. Prevailing constructions of South Asian

29

American racial identity tend to simplify the complex hierarchies of color, class, and caste immigrants bring with them from their homeland by collapsing them with the historical patterns of race in the host country. Moreover, the study of South Asian Americans is further complicated by the disciplinary constraints of an emerging field: the archive is only just beginning to be developed; a significant amount of the research so far has been produced by literary scholars, but much empirical work in anthropology, sociology, and history remains to be done on South Asian American racial identification; and finally, scholars working on this subject also face the challenge of working across disciplinary boundaries in unfamiliar fields. Thus, it is vital to exercise care in formulating generalizations, especially since the group is very diverse and has a disjunct history of immigration to the United States. There are striking differences between the early and later immigrants and a continuous narrative of white-identification cannot accommodate either the diversity South Asians bring with them from their homelands or the caste, gender, generation, and class differences that shape their racial positioning in the United States. The study of the racial identification of this group is an urgent one, since the second generation of post-1965 immigrants is just coming of age and has begun to shape a political identity more actively focused on the U.S. context; for them, even more crucially than for their predecessors, the strategies of disavowal of racial identity or the claiming of blackness are inadequate to engaging the transformed racial dynamics of the post-Civil Rights era. Much of the scholarship so far has focused on the first generation and left unexplored the significant differences between the first and second generation in terms of their racialization; or, it has dealt with second-generation identity through the analysis of particular subcultures.[2] It seems likely, though, that the second generation will confront and bring the issue of racial identity to greater resolution, since the strategies of deferral used by the first generation, whether in defining themselves as "postcolonials," "global citizens," or "overseas South Asians" are, for the second generation, inadequate to engaging the daily realities of the country where they were born and live.

SOUTH ASIAN CLAIMS TO CITIZENSHIP
IN THE EARLY NATURALIZATION CASES

Sucheta Mazumdar's frequently-cited essay "Race and Racism: South Asians in the United States," offers the definitive interpretation of Asian Indian claims to citizenship in the early naturalization cases from 1900–1923. Mazumdar contends that the claims to whiteness in the naturalization cases reflect the racist attitudes of South Asians, many of whom (particularly those of the upper-caste), subscribed to theories of their racial genealogy as Aryans. Speaking of the prevalence of the myth of Aryan origins among many South Asians then and now, she states, "They are themselves acutely color-conscious; they see shades of brown in skin color which to any casual observer is black" (25). The purpose of her essay is to explicate "this racialism among a people who *are black*, but have sought to prove over and over again that they *are white*" (italics mine).

What is immediately apparent in these statements is the assumption that racial categories are natural and transhistorical—Indians *look* black and therefore they *are* black; ironically, these assertions run counter to one of the grounding premises of the antiracist position that the article asserts. As Mazumdar herself explains, the anthropological project of defining racial groups in terms of fixed physical characteristics proved an impossible one, and has been almost completely discredited in the present. Moreover, contrary to Mazumdar's claims, the divergent responses of Americans to the appearance of South Asians seem to suggest that they did not always "look black" to outsiders. For instance, Karen Leonard notes that court clerks who had to fill out the blank on race on the marriage licenses of early Punjabi immigrants "sometimes wrote 'brown,' sometimes 'black,' and sometimes 'white,' *depending on the applicants' skin coloring and the county*" (italics mine, 68). Leonard highlights not only the diversity in responses among the clerks, but also the significance of political factors like the particular region where the application was sought. Furthermore, in the 1909 case of Abdullah Dolla, *the only racial prerequisite case involving a South Asian in which the judge relied on ocular proof as a determining test of whiteness*, the court granted his petition. When Dolla, an Afghan born in Calcutta, applied for U.S. citizenship, the government argued that he was a native of India and therefore nonwhite. Dolla contended that he could produce a white doctor who would testify that he was of "pure Caucasian blood," that he was accepted as a white in Savannah, Georgia, and that he even had a burial plot in Savannah's whites-only cemetery. The judge scrutinized Dolla carefully, finally asking him to pull up the sleeves of his shirt. Dolla's pale forearms convinced the judge to grant his petition (Jensen 250).

What, then, does it mean to say that South Asians *are* black? What Mazumdar fails to consider is that, in the United States, the meaning of blackness has been very precisely codified in law and not left to the ocular impressions of casual observers. Cheryl Harris explains that the infamous "one-drop rule" even anticipated the possibility that some blacks did not look black, and was devised as a way to keep them in their place (1740). As numerous examples indicate, the issue of how a particular group "looks" is not easily settled; at the least, it cannot be considered outside a specific context, or apart from the question of whose gaze provides the reference. For instance, Dan Caldwell has described the "Negroization" of the early Chinese immigrants who were frequently identified with native Americans and blacks (53). Ronald Takaki explains that "the Chinese migrants found that racial qualities previously assigned to blacks quickly became 'Chinese' characteristics. . . . White workers referred to the Chinese as 'nagurs,' and a magazine cartoon depicted the Chinese as a bloodsucking vampire with slanted eyes, a pigtail, dark skin, and thick lips. Like blacks, the Chinese were described as heathen, morally inferior, savage, childlike, and lustful" (219). The comparisons to blacks were both moral and physical: "Chinese women were condemned as 'a depraved class' and their depravity was associated with their almost Africanlike physical appearance" which was seen as being "but a slight removal from the African race." Can one then resolve the question of the racial identity of South Asians, as Mazumdar does, by concluding that since most of them do not look white (by the criteria that have come to define whiteness in the contemporary United States), that they are black?

Moreover, to recover intentionality from the claims advanced in a court of law, as Mazumdar does, overlooks altogether the way in which the law frames the terms of argument. Noting that the nearly seventy Asian Indians who gained citizenship did so by proving they were members of the Aryan race and therefore "white," she contends:

> What concerns us here is the premise on which the struggle for citizenship was based. South Asians saw themselves as "Aryan" and, therefore, as "Caucasian" and "white" despite the fact that plenty of evidence already existed to the contrary. This self-perception prevented the immigrants from making common cause with other Asians who were barred from citizenship on grounds of race—such as in the Ozawa case. Instead of challenging racism, the South Asian struggle became an individualized and personalized mission to prove that he was of "pure-blood Aryan stock." Though victimized by white racism, which denied them citizenship, the South Asian response was equally racist. (30)

This conclusion so completely ignores the legal and historical framework of these cases that, by a profound irony, the racism of the law comes to be constructed as the racism of the appellants.

However, an historical analysis of whiteness opens up a completely different perspective on the early naturalization cases.[3] Congress had established racial prerequisites for naturalization through the passage of the Naturalization Law of 1790, later amended after the Civil War, restricting naturalization to "free white persons" and "aliens of African nativity or persons of African descent." Soon after, the 1882 Chinese Exclusion Act explicitly denied naturalization to the Chinese. For all other applicants, the geographical indeterminacy of whiteness opened up the possibility of citizenship. In a superb study, *White by Law: The Legal Construction of Race*, Ian Haney López analyzes the prerequisite cases for naturalization that were argued from 1878–1952[4] in state and federal courts, including the two, *Ozawa* and *Thind*, that reached the Supreme Court. According to López, while most naturalization decisions did not involve formal court proceedings, fifty-two cases construing the racial prerequisite to citizenship reached the courts and worked in shaping the legal definition of whiteness over this period of time. The petitioners for citizenship came from various countries: Syria, Burma, the Philippines, Hawaii, India, Mexico,

China and Japan. All, except one, sought naturalization by trying to prove that he was white.[5] As the terminology "prerequisite cases" itself indicates, the cases reached the courts and were defined by their construal of the racial criteria, which were a prerequisite for naturalization. Thus, an emphasis on the racism of litigants in naturalization cases elides the power of the institutional structures that require the use of racist "truths" as the condition for admissibility into the courtroom and as the framework of address to the law. The courtroom did not provide a forum to mount an antiracist protest or to foster pan-ethnic coalitions around the racist criteria for naturalization; in fact, the terms of the law worked explicitly to undermine such possibilities, prompting various litigants to prove their whiteness by declaring their dissimilarity from other Asian groups or by disavowing their Asianness altogether. However, the arguments offered by various parties in their attempts to prove their whiteness often brought definitions of whiteness and the rationales on which they were based to crisis. *Paradoxically, whiteness was brought to crisis not by challenges to its legitimacy as a prerequisite to citizenship, but by the attempts of diverse appellants to be included within it.*

López notes the striking fact that in the fifty-two prerequisite cases, all but one petitioner sought to claim citizenship by proving his whiteness, when, after 1870, naturalization could also be claimed by those who were black.[6] Why? Preempting the "obvious" but tautological response that it was because there were few "black" immigrants at this time, López inserts the crucial reminder that the various citizenship claimants did not fit neatly into either white or black category within the classification schema of that time. He adds, "some immigrant groups, for example the Chinese, were initially characterized as Black, suggesting that for some, attempting to naturalize as a 'white person' was the more difficult route" (51). In explaining the preponderance of white person cases, he refers to the indeterminacy of the legal category of white person (lacking geographical specificity) as compared to the clarity of the definition of a black person as one of African nativity, or African descent. He concludes:

> The existence of more firmly established racial definitions of who was Black may also have obviated the need for new litigation. The legal definition of Blacks, unlike that of Whites, was already well established at the turn of the century. In addition, however, it seems nearly certain that the social stigma and harsh discrimination imposed on those with Black status discouraged applicants for citizenship from seeking admission on that basis. Immigrants to the country quickly learn the value of being White rather than Black, and thereby learn to cast themselves as Whites. (52)

One of the crucial elements in López's analysis that opens up a very different perspective on these cases is the recognition that too literal a reading of these cases may be the product of our own view of the naturalness of racial categories that are current in our time. As such, it serves as a very valuable caution:

The lengthy categorical debates in the prerequisite cases seem ridiculous only because we have fully accepted the categories these cases established. Decisions about racial identity are complex; they appear obvious only in retrospect, and then only from a vantage point built upon the assumption that races are fixed transhistorical categories. The extent to which the definitional struggles in these cases seems quaint measures on some level the extent to which we have erroneously accepted their simple conclusions. The truly curious, then, is not the typological sophistry of the courts, but our own certainty regarding the obvious validity of the recently fabricated. (55)

Thus, contrary to the view that "the attempt to prove over and over again that they were white" was unique to Asian Indian citizenship petitioners, it is clear that this was the avenue chosen by all but one of the petitioners in the prerequisite cases. If one extends Mazumdar's argument that the claim to naturalization as whites was proof of racist attitudes, then one must conclude that other petitioners like the Japanese, Filipinos, Burmese, or Chinese were also racists. But as López points out, "Like others who directly challenged the legal construction of race, Thind had no choice but to pursue his challenge within the institution, pursuant to the rules, and according to the language that would be used to judge him" (149). In other words, to view the terms of the argument entirely as an active choice on the part of the petitioners is not only misleading, it neglects to consider the extent to which legal discourse structures arguments within its domain.

Furthermore, the contention that Thind and other Asian Indian litigants should have made common cause with Ozawa is difficult to substantiate, especially if the framework of that coalition were to have been its antiracist agenda. The arguments advanced by Ozawa in making his case are as pernicious as Thind's; in addition, they are marked by a fervent assimilationism that is an unambiguous rejection of his Japanese cultural identity. Ozawa, like Thind, based his petition for citizenship on the claim that he was white. He argued that although he was of Japanese descent, his skin color was white, whiter, in fact, than that of many of those who were legally recognized as "white." To support his argument, Ozawa adduced the observations of various anthropologists: "in Japan the uncovered parts of the body are also white"; "the Japanese are of lighter color than other Eastern Asiatics, not rarely showing the transparent pink tint which whites assume as their own privilege"; and "in the typical Japanese city of Kyoto, those not exposed to the heat of summer are particularly white-skinned. They are whiter than the average Italian, Spaniard or Portuguese" (qtd. in López 81). In all except one of the prerequisite cases, irrespective of the national origin or racial mixture of the petitioners, their effort was to prove their whiteness in the terms recognized by the law.

The avenue chosen by the appellants from various parts of the world in proving their whiteness varied according to their national and putative racial origins.

Table 2.1. History of the Classification of Asian Indians by the Census Bureau

Census Year	Census Classification
1910	**Other**/Non-White Asiatic/Hindu
1920	**Other**/Hindu
1930	**Hindu**
1940	**Hindu**
1950	**Other**/Non-White/Asiatic Indian
1960	**Other**/Non-White/Hindu
1970	**Other**/White
1980	**AsianIndian**
1990	**Asian or Pacific Islander/Asian Indian**

Note: Census classifications are taken from the categories listed on the Census form as responses for the question on race or color; these categories are indicated in boldface type. Census classification into subcategories is drawn from the instructions to the enumerators and the definitions and explanations of terms published in the Census.

West Asian and South Asian litigants claimed whiteness by citing their anthropological classification as Aryans; East Asians and other "Mongolian" groups asserted whiteness on the basis of their skin color; mixed-race claimants pointed to varying fractions of whiteness. Forced on a case-by-case basis to articulate the criteria by which whiteness was to be determined, and unable to salvage a rational foundation for the idea of whiteness, the law finally resolved the matter through recourse to a tautology: the 1923 Thind ruling stated that a "white person" was a person "the average well informed white American" knew was white (*U.S. v. Thind*, 211). Viewed within the legal context of these cases, the claim to Aryan origins was part of a maneuver for citizenship, one among the several deployed by the diverse appellants in these cases, but the most viable one within the courtroom for South Asians. Indians who sought naturalization were newcomers to a country in which only citizenship bestowed the right to own or lease land—after the passage of alien land laws in a number of states—and the right to vote. The whiteness they sought, then, was a political status.

If the courts showed some early inconsistency in categorizing South Asians, the Census Bureau, which had the official responsibility for classifying the various groups, was consistent in defining them, from their earliest appearance on its records in 1910, as "non-white Asiatics," except in 1970 (Census, vol. I, 126). As Table 2.1 shows, they were categorized in the 1930 and 1940 Census as "Hindus"; as "Other"/ "Asiatic Indian" in 1950 and as "Other"/"Hindu" in 1960; as "Other"/ "White" in 1970;[7] as "Asian Indian" in 1980; and as "Asian Indian" within the category "Asian or Pacific Islander" in 1990. In fact, instructions to Census enumerators in 1950 specifically state that "persons originating in India should be reported as 'Asiatic Indians'" (Census, vol. II, Part I, 469); and in 1960 the instructions state that "for persons originating in India (except those of European stock), mark 'Other' and specify as 'Hindu'" (Census, vol. I, Part I, cxiii). Thus, it was only once in 1970, in the aftermath of civil rights legislation, that federal agencies decided to count them as "White" in order to deny them minority status. When this decision was challenged by Asian Indian organizations, they were reclassified as "Asian Indians" in the 1980 census.

An umbrella group of Asian Indian organizations launched the campaign for reclassification as minorities in order to become eligible for affirmative action programs and to benefit from civil rights initiatives. The idea provoked strong controversy: the debates were played out in the pages of community newspapers like *India Abroad* and in several conferences sponsored by the major Indian organizations. Finally, in 1977, Asian Indians lobbied for and won reclassification as "Asian Pacific Americans" and were awarded the category "Asian Indian" in the 1980 Census. It is important to note that this debate took place during the recession following the 1973 Oil Crisis, when sharp job cuts hit some immigrants, while others were unable to find the positions for which they were qualified. Uncertainty about the benefits attached to minority status in the United States fed optimistic expectations about its likely advantages derived from their knowledge of such programs in India, which has one of the most extensive caste-based affirmative action programs in the world. There were also significant economic divisions within this group of recent middle-class immigrants. For certain upper strata professionals, like doctors and engineers with advanced degrees, whose jobs were still secure, the main concern was with acceptance by their American peers. In their minds, minority status jeopardized acceptance, already undermined by derogatory labels like FMG (Foreign Medical Graduate). But among a larger number of Indians, some in the lower tier of their professions, often stuck in technical niches and unable to move into managerial and executive ranks, and others, who were overqualified for their jobs, minority status promised better prospects for access and mobility.

The lack of referential density surrounding South Asian American identity, the chameleon quality that has marked its emergence, and its belatedness on the U.S. scene have produced an unusually inchoate formation. Despite their presence in this country for nearly a century, this presence has hardly and then very unevenly registered on the public consciousness. For example, although there are similarities in the number and flow of immigrants from South Asia and Korea, Koreans are more visible today than their South Asian counterparts. Korean immigrants can be incorporated into the "common understanding" of Asianness in a way that South Asians cannot; hence their greater visibility.

The question remains, though: how long will the inchoate status of South Asian Americans continue? Certainly, as time passes, the density of references and associations will accumulate and they will come to be positioned with more fixity in the American symbolic economy. Although their geographical dispersal has allowed them a degree of invisibility, in areas with concentrations of South Asian

Americans like New Jersey and New York, their presence has prompted racist attacks. In September 1998, a young Trinidadian Indian man, Rishi Maharaj, was set upon and beaten by a number of white men in Queens, New York. More recently, in the aftermath of September 11, South Asians have been killed and assaulted because of their identification with Arabs.

In recent years, they have also become the objects of the kinds of racial stereotyping heretofore reserved for other minorities. Although working-class South Asian Americans are in the minority, statistically speaking, the cab driver, the convenience store worker, and the newspaper vendor have come to represent all South Asian Americans in the media. Today, the most visible South Asian in America may well be Apu, the harried Kwik-E-Mart owner on *The Simpsons*. By contrast, the professionals with their degrees, Anglicized accents, and middle-class status fall outside these same stereotypes; they also seem to have disappeared into suburbia. Two exceptions to this class-specific representation of South Asian Americans in the mainstream media are figures who have drawn journalistic attention— the motel owner and the computer programmer—representing the double-pronged threat of "foreign" capital and skilled labor. Computer programmers are usually represented to the public through the genre of the investigative report, where the narrative thrust is to expose their invisibility, which itself becomes a symbol of the surreptitious takeover of U.S. institutions or jobs.

In an ethnic formation where the minority position of South Asian Americans is often constructed around and by business-related concerns (the forming of the Asian American Motel Owners Association, the pressure to form Little Indias in various cities) while South Asian American organizations are largely relegated to the sphere of cultural activities, they have been slow to emerge and respond as a political constituency. Moreover, the professional class, which largely occupies secure positions in fields like engineering, computers, and medicine has been slow to acknowledge or identify problems around which to formulate political solidarity. It is generally maintained within this group that problems of discrimination or access that do crop up can best be tackled on an individual basis. Thus, class stratifications have shaped their capacity and willingness to organize collectively around civil rights issues, particularly as these issues have been strongly marked by color and race in the United States. This deferral of the confrontation with race, particularly among the first-generation middle class, takes many forms from emphasis on cosmopolitanism, the need for assimilation, the assertion of Indian cultural pride, to the affirmation of a color-blind citizenship. When there was an outbreak of racist attacks against South Asian Americans in New Jersey in 1987, Johanna Lessinger reports that the leaders of the immigrant community initially formulated the problem as an issue of cultural misunderstanding rather than racism. The political protests that followed the New Jersey attacks were slow in developing, hesitant in forming cross-racial alliances with other groups, and were also met with apprehension and opposition within the South Asian American community. When demonstrations were eventually organized to protest the racist attacks, critical support to the organizers came from the Committee Against Anti-Asian Violence (140–41). This episode reveals the difficulty of organizing politically around a bourgeois platform of model ethnicity, but it also illustrates the possibility of addressing problems of race through the formation of strategic alliances with other groups. The latter move would involve rethinking the self-image as anomalous minority not in terms of culturalist explanations (our culture equips us to succeed better than other minorities) but in terms of structural explanations (how are we positioned in relation to other groups within American society). It would also involve surrendering the faith in a meritocracy that the successes of South Asian Americans purportedly testify to.

Generally, South Asian Americans negotiate the U.S. multicultural terrain by circumventing a confrontation with race by stressing ethnicity and class position. Many South Asian Americans are positioned in the most hallowed and euphemistic of locations, the middle class. Furthermore, their ready employability as engineers, lab scientists, computer scientists, and doctors is often taken as proof of a color-blind meritocracy, when in actuality it reflects the demand for skilled labor that made possible their entry into the country in the first place. The seduction of the rhetoric of a meritocracy is that it affirms the value of their achievements while simultaneously coding these successes as quintessentially American. Of necessity, such a rhetoric positions their achievements against that of other minorities. The irony here is that America takes the credit for achievements that are partly the product of the subsidized education of many South Asian Americans in their homeland, while highlighting the dismal performance of other minorities, many of whom pass through an underfunded and inadequate public school system in the United States. Within this rhetoric, South Asians can be solicited to think of themselves as value-added Americans. Dinesh D'Souza's arguments in *The End of Racism* are probably a classic example of this position. As long as there are other minorities to wear the sign of race, we have the alibi of ethnicity.

SOUTH ASIAN RACIALIZATION IN BRITAIN

In the United States, Indians were originally classified in the Census as "Hindu," then counted once as "White" in 1970, but after 1980, they have been categorized as "Asian Indian." In Britain, they were originally termed "coloured" or "black" but more recently have been referred to as "British Asian." In Britain, the Census has not played a central role in categorizing and labeling minority populations as it has in the United States, since ethnic group membership has never been recorded in the British Census until 1991. The only question from which ethnic origin could be derived in the 1961 British Census was one on an individual's place of birth. Thus, the early labeling of South Asians and Afro-Caribbeans as "coloured" or "black" derived from political and populist discourse on immigration and social policy in the 1950s and 60s; for instance, in the absence of Census counts, the Home Office published estimates of the numbers of "coloured immigrants." The 1971 Census gave currency to the terms "New Commonwealth" (South Asia, Africa, and the Caribbean) and "Old Commonwealth" (Canada, Australia, and New Zealand) immigrants; figures for these categories were compiled in the Census by adding a question on the parent's place of birth (Fenton 147–48). According to Fenton, this terminology reinforced the "vulgar distinction between white and coloured" (148). Finally, in the 1991 Census, after much controversy,[8] a question on ethnic group membership was added that listed Whites, Blacks (subdivided into several categories), several Asian groups by national origin, and Other categories.

However, even as South Asians were being labeled in the political discourse of the host society, in the late 60s and early 70s, some of them began to mobilize around a political identity as blacks. This self-designation came under critique within the community in the 1980s and was gradually superseded by the notion of a British Asian identity. In Britain and the United States, "Asian" is not merely a geographical referent but a metaphor shaped by particular geopolitical relations. In the United States, since Asia has been historically identified with East and Southeast Asia (an association reinforced by the currency of Pacific Rim discourse), and the image of the Asian American derives from that association, South Asians are often not identified as Asian Americans. But if South Asians are the invisible Asians in the United States, in Britain, the long history of British involvement in the subcontinent and their significant numbers in the minority population have led to the popular conflation of Asian with South Asian identity.[9]

South Asians began to arrive in Britain in substantial numbers only after 1950. Labor shortages in an expanding post-War economy produced an influx of workers from colonial and ex-colonial territories, mainly from the Caribbean and South Asia. These migrants faced discrimination in housing and employment; most were forced to take jobs as dishwashers, foundry and mill workers, domestic workers and streetsweepers (Layton-Henry 44–46). In the late 1960s and early 1970s, their numbers were supplemented by East African Indians, from Kenya, Tanzania, and Uganda (the latter were political refugees expelled from Uganda in 1972, the other two groups had left in the wake of post-Independence Africanization policies). Parminder Bhachu explains that unlike the direct migrants from the subcontinent, who were rural, unskilled workers, "twice migrant" East African Indians were urban, skilled workers, public sector employees, and businesspeople, many of whom had transferred capital out of Africa before leaving. The early subcontinental migrants had been largely male, while the East African Indians arrived in tri-generational family units, unique in international migration (33–37). In Britain, they set up restaurants, grocery shops, and ethnic boutiques or moved into civil service and factory jobs. The East African Indians were similar to the small group of migrants from the subcontinent—doctors, engineers, and teachers—who had entered under the preferences for skilled workers. After 1983, approximately 17,000 Sri Lankan Tamil refugees (McDowell 5), displaced by the effects of war, sought asylum in Britain, joining an established middle-class Tamil community; the refugees formed a heterogeneous group, middle- and lower- middle class, and took jobs as accountants, shop owners, and gas station attendants. To white Britons, however, the arrivants appeared an undifferentiated mass, variously referred to as "coloureds," "blacks," "wogs," and "Pakis." The perception of Afro-Caribbeans and South Asians within a common "blackness" was produced by racist attitudes, their common position as immigrants, and their shared history as colonial subjects. Minorities in an island-nation with little ideological space for nonwhite immigrants, both groups were concentrated in the underclass, lived largely in segregated neighborhoods, and were conspicuous by their dress, food, cultural symbols, religious practices, and accents. To a segment of the public, their mere presence constituted a threat to British national identity.

Public and media hostility to "coloured" immigration rose as the need for cheap labor declined, erupting in racist riots that led to the passage of the Commonwealth Immigrants Act in 1962. This Act reversed the established tradition of treating all Commonwealth and colonial people as British subjects with equal rights of citizenship. The Act restricted the entry of Commonwealth citizens by giving preference to those with a specific job or skill. The entry of Kenyan Indians in the late 60s, a contingency overlooked in the 1962 Act,[10] reignited populist hysteria about Asian immigration. Subsequent legislation systematically targeted and impeded non-white immigration while simultaneously keeping open the immigration of certain whites. In fact, the 1968 Commonwealth Immigrants Act, passed in the wake of the Kenyan Asian crisis, invented a new category of British citizenship—the "patrial," based on parents' or grandparents' British origins, or an individual's birth or naturalization in Britain—that facilitated this racially selective entry to the country (Layton-Henry 71–97). The 1971 Immigration Act cut off further immigration from the "New Commonwealth," with the exception of the Ugandan Asians who were admitted in 1972, and a limited number of immigrants who entered under provisions for family reunification (Mason 29).

The majority of South Asians drew on extensive community networks, often organizing family, work, and cultural life around them, and operating within locales of ethnic concentration. These networks also enabled them to mobilize effectively in local politics. Unlike in the United States, where Asian Indians constitute only 0.33% of the population and rank seventh among the minority groups (U.S. Census, 1990),[11] in Britain, South Asians are the largest minority group forming 2.9% of the total population (Labour Force Survey, 1996).[12] Ethnic minorities comprise just under 6% of the total population, with Afro-Caribbeans, the next largest group, constituting 1.5%. Hence, because of their numbers and concentration, they have been successful in electing candidates for office at the local and national level, and in mobilizing politically.

Responses to British racism have produced other strategic identities. From the late 1960s to the early 1980s, as South Asians increasingly became the targets of racist attacks, were subjected to racist immigration laws, and organized against discrimination in housing, employment, and education, black British identity offered an important vehicle for resistance. The successes of the Civil Rights movement in the United States gave efficacy and power to the label "black" and served as an inspiration to minorities fighting racism in Britain. "Black caucuses" representing both Asians and Afro-Caribbeans sprang up in trade unions and cultural organizations. Feminist groups like the Southall Black Sisters and OWAAD (Organization of Women of Asian and African Descent) also formed cross-racial alliances. Public funding of multicultural projects encouraged the growth of a black identity in independent filmmaking, theater, and literature. Black workshops like Retake and special programming on Channel 4 have been crucial to the emergence of filmmakers like Ahmad Jamal, Pratibha Parmar, and Gurinder Chadha. In the academy, too, South Asians as well as Afro-Caribbeans became the subject of studies on black Britain.

Despite the crucial importance of "blackness" in the politicization of South Asians in Britain—especially among activists, academics, artists, and intellectuals—it was superceded in the eighties by the idea of a British Asian identity. Some have argued that South Asians constitute the largest minority group and, therefore, should not be subsumed within a black identity but should establish a separate identity. Other South Asian critics of blackness argue that Black Power ideology derives from the historical experiences of people of sub-Saharan African descent and, thus, can accommodate a *cultural* and *political* identity for Afro-Caribbeans in Britain. By contrast, within blackness, South Asians gain a political identity but lose their cultural identity (Hazaaresingh, Modood). This shift to culturalist definitions of British Asian identity has been challenged by other South Asian critics. They point out that the institutionalization of multiculturalism by state and local authorities led to a diversion of community struggles from issues of racial oppression to group-specific problems, thus promoting the growth of cultural difference at the expense of race consciousness (Brah, Sivanandan). The valorization of British Asian cultural identity and the rejection of black identity also assumes that British Asian identity is autonomous from Afro-Caribbean cultural forms. But as critics in the recent collection *Dis-Orienting Rhythms* argue, the meanings of British Asian cultural identity cannot be exhausted by defining it as a product of a South Asian "tradition" or as a response to white racism. For instance, British Bhangra draws on Reggae, Dub, and Soul, using Punjabi musical forms and western instrumentation. Since the ongoing struggle against racism requires the formation of multiracial coalitions, the internal contestation of blackness would be more constructive than outright rejection.

It is also becoming clear that British Asian identity can create as many problems as it solves. The use of culture as the primary or exclusive ground for defining a minority position poses particular problems for South Asians, since the emphasis on cultural identity also opens up the prospect of further fission along religious, linguistic, and regional lines. It is not surprising, then, that the 90s have seen a resurgence of ethnic particularisms and signs of growing conflict between various British Asian groups. Since the move to a British Asian identity was linked to the emergence of a South Asian middle class, the claim to ethnicity has also served as a class strategy to dissociate South Asians from the working-class associations of blackness. For this reason, British Asian identity is serviceable to conservative and progressive political agendas.

The mobilization of South Asians and Afro-Caribbeans in Britain around blackness was viable because of their shared structural position in British society, their simultaneous arrival in Britain, and a shared subjection to British colonialism. Moreover, the British racial hierarchy operated around a more straightforward white-colored polarity than its U.S. counterpart. In the United States, however, the history of slavery had developed the meanings of the black-white binary *prior* to the arrival of immigrant groups like South Asians. The subsequent racialization of South Asians, like that of other Asian Americans, was fundamentally shaped by immigration and naturalization legislation and their positioning at an interme- diary level in the racial hierarchy. Moreover, the distinctive histories of racializa- tion of other groups such as Mexican Americans and Native Americans have further complicated patterns of racial stratification within the United States. Thus, in the United States, the appropriation of blackness by South Asians is politically problematic because it obscures the important differences in the trajectory of the two groups. On the other hand, the South Asian American strategy of using ethni- city and class to resist racial identification leaves no avenue for identifying and mobilizing around problems of race, when they occur. Since their small numbers and settlement patterns work against the formation of an efficacious independent political bloc as in Britain, a major question that faces South Asian Americans is what kind of coalitions they will form. Unlike in Britain, where ethnicity has offered a viable though still problematic means of politicization, in the U.S. the emphasis on ethnicity, in the absence of other affiliations, tends to become an isolationist and apolitical move.

THE LOUISE WOODWARD CASE:
RACIAL INVISIBILITY AND PUBLIC SILENCE

Finally, I will examine a case that brings out the differences in the racialization of South Asians in Britain and the United States and highlights the limitations in the middle-class minority strategy of refusing racial identification within the United States. Speaking of South Asian racialization, critics define the problem by citing instances of racial violence like the beating death of Navroze Mody on September 27, 1978 in Hoboken, New Jersey, and the related Dotbuster incidents (Misir).

More recently, the events of September 11 and the war in Afghanistan have created another charged context for the equalization of South Asians. One publicized case has, however, never been discussed in this context. But the very invisibility of race in this case involving a South Asian American is as revealing as the swirl of publicity surrounding it and the hysterical emotions generated by some of the major protagonists.

On February 4, 1997, Louise Woodward, an English au pair, dialed 911 and told the dispatcher that an eight-month-old infant in her care was barely breathing. The following day, Woodward was arrested, and when the baby died of head injuries a few days later, was charged with murdering the child. The victim was eight-month-old Matthew Eappen, the son of two suburban doctors from Massachusetts. The baby's mother Deborah Eappen was a white American, and the father Sunil Eappen was of Indian origin.

When the case went to trial, the defense opted for an all-or-nothing strategy. They rejected the prosecution's offer to add manslaughter to the indictment, deciding instead to give the jury the option of either finding Woodward guilty of murder or of acquitting her. Judge Hiller Zobel warned Woodward she would get no second chance if her strategy failed. The prosecution's medical experts argued that Woodward had killed the baby by shaking him violently or hitting his head against a hard surface, resulting in a 2 1/2 inch skull fracture and brain swelling. The defense's medical experts contended that the skull fracture was probably an old one and that Woodward's "rough handling" may have only restarted a bleeding in the old wound, leading to the infant's death.

On October 30, 1997, the jury found Woodward guilty of second-degree murder; the charge carried a mandatory life sentence, with no possibility of parole for fifteen years. A few days later, in an astonishing turnaround in the case, Woodward was set free. On November 10, Judge Hiller Zobel, exercising a rarely used judicial power, set aside the jury's verdict and reduced Woodward's charge to manslaughter. Involuntary manslaughter carries a maximum sentence of twenty years and no minimum sentence. He then set her free, sentencing her only to the 279 days already served.

From the outset, the au pair's cause mobilized supporters in her hometown of Elton in England. The hometown crowd raised money for her and congregated at the local pub to follow the televised court proceedings; they turned her ordeal into a compelling national symbol. After the murder conviction, sympathy for Woodward reached a fever pitch, and outrage at the murder verdict found voice in printed pages and on the airwaves in the United States and Britain. In a surreal reversal, the convicted au pair became the center of an outpouring of public support, while the bereaved young couple were vilified for pursuing their careers and leaving their two children in the care of a nineteen-year-old.

To many in Britain, the Woodward case signified the inversion of colonial order. The same immigration laws that made it difficult for an unskilled English woman like Louise Woodward to move to the United States, except as an au pair, had enabled the entry of highly skilled Indians like Sunil Eappen's parents. Sunil Eappen himself represented a kind of Indian unfamiliar to many in Britain, where immigration restrictions had created a less affluent Indian community. An article in The *Los Angeles Times* noted that "the case came to symbolize . . . a resentment in England over a class system that exports working-class girls to serve in the homes of upwardly mobile Americans" (Mehren A1). Eappen's ability to employ a young English woman to care for his mixed-race children overturned colonial relationships, and this inappropriateness was displaced onto media representations of the U.S. legal system in Britain. Within this narrative, Woodward's innocence became a metaphor for pristine English goodness framed by the media-driven legalities of an errant ex-colony. This perversion was racialized by characterizing the American legal system as the system that set O.J. free, despite the fact that the flamboyant Simpson lawyer Barry Scheck was leading Woodward's defense team: "many people have seized on the conviction as a national affront to Britain by the same justice system that acquitted Simpson" (Montalbano A6).[13]

The perverse coupling of two former colonies and the incoherence it engendered was embodied in the figures of the Indian male reincarnated as an affluent American citizen and his white American wife. Interviews with a former au pair of the Eappens were used to suggest that Sunil Eappen ogled the young white women he employed, resurrecting the familiar figures of the lecherous Indian man and the innocent English rose. Unlike the specter of threatening hypermasculine sexuality associated with stereotypes of Afro-Caribbeans, stereotypes of South Asian masculinity are often linked to furtiveness, treachery, and sexual repression in Britain. At the center of many stories was Deborah Eappen's unnaturalness, her failures as a mother. Although she had cut back her working hours to three days a week and came home to nurse Matthew at lunchtime, she was accused of not loving her children enough. Supporters of Woodward carried signs reading "Free Louise, Jail the Mother" and "One Less Kid, One More Volvo." By contrast, when the Zoe Baird nomination for Attorney General was dropped because she had not paid taxes for her nanny, there had been widespread support in the United States for Baird's difficulties in balancing maternal responsibilities and professional ambitions. Deborah Eappen's motherhood was certainly the site of scandal, but not the one that was named. Speaking of the unnaturalness of her motherhood in terms of her class was a way of not talking about the unnaturalness of her motherhood in terms of her racial transgression.

In Britain, the Woodward case was widely read as a national allegory pitting English against American ways: Alice Thompson, the conservative columnist opined, "we invented the concept of the efficient Mary Poppins, so it's obvious we would feel insulted when an American mother accused a sweet-looking British girl of murdering her child. The coverage of the trial has gone beyond mere anger of America seemingly snubbing the motherland. This is war" (qtd. in Montalbano A1). Across the Atlantic, however, many Americans took up the Woodward cause and denounced their own national institutions when the jury found her guilty of murder ("Americans Apologise for Judicial System"). In a highly unusual move, the *Boston Globe* and the *New York Times* ran editorials urging Judge Zobel to reduce the charge to manslaughter. Why was the public so vociferous in their support of the convicted killer of an American baby—a foreigner who showed little contrition? The British embraced Woodward as British, but Americans seemed aloof from the idea of the Eappens as Americans. Where, Larry King asked Sunil Eappen, did he come from? From Chicago, replied Eappen. No, where was he originally from? King persisted. His parents were from India, Eappen answered. As an interracial couple, too, the Eappens mobilized no constituency.

According to a news report that appeared prior to Zobel's ruling, Woodward's best hope for having the verdict set aside lay in the personality of the judge "who is known for his independence of spirit and pronounced anglophilia" (Varadarajan 3). Interestingly, Judge Zobel's ruling largely accepted the version of events offered by Woodward and the defense's medical experts.[14] Since the defense's medical evidence was inconclusive and the prosecution's medical evidence was very strong, Zobel's decision to favor the defense's version of events clearly rested on his judgment of Woodward's personality.[15] The judge's ruling offers extraordinary extenuation for her culpability in the infant's death: "Frustrated by her inability to quiet the crying child, she was a 'little rough with him' under circumstances where another, perhaps wiser, person would have sought to restrain the physical impulse. The roughness was sufficient to start (or restart) a bleeding that escalated fatally."[16] Then he concluded: "I view the evidence as disclosing confusion, fright and bad judgment, rather than rage or malice." Zobel's benign reading of the events stresses her youth, inexperience, and incapacity for violence.

The Woodward case reveals the extraordinary protection available to whiteness within the legal system and the multiple levels at which it operates in presumptions about behavior, capacity for malice, and susceptibility to suffering. Responding to the judge's ruling, Deborah Eappen said: "I think there is something in him [the judge] in all of us, that does not want to believe people who look like Louise could do what Louise did. But the truth is Louise killed Matty and Judge Zobel at once admits that and does not make her take responsibility for what she did. Would he do that for a poor black or Hispanic defendant?" (Coles 5). But framing the issue in this way avoided another equally salient question: Would Woodward's responsibility be so mitigated if the dead baby and both its parents had been white?

The popular vilification of the Eappens cannot be understood apart from their racial identities, and yet no discussion of the case highlighted the issue. On the contrary, Sunil Eappen's affluence not only turned public sympathy against him but was also viewed as exempting him from the problems of race. Moreover, his racial identity as a South Asian carries an ambiguity that requires public naming in the United States, or else its effects operate invisibly. But the Eappens themselves never invoked race in relation to his identity, only to Woodward's. It is significant that when Deborah Eappen talks of hypothetical defendants who may have received a different ruling from the judge, the two categories she cites are "black" and "Hispanic." Is the category "Asian American" not perceived as negatively racialized within the justice system? Can an Asian American identity not support such a rhetorical appeal? Or is it that "Asian American" is the same category occupied by her husband? The Eappen case elicited charged and polarized public responses in the U.S. and Britain and generated innumerable letters to the editor in leading newspapers. But while other Americans were vociferous in stating their opinions, people who were identifiably South Asian by name remained curiously silent about this case in the press. This is in strong contrast to other issues such as Hindu nationalism, the Kashmir issue, and misrepresentations of South Asian culture that invariably provoke a rash of letters to the editor. Watching the story unfold on TV, I knew there must have been many other South Asian Americans like me across the country, following it closely, but as a public, voiceless about its racial meanings. A silent, spectatorial community. The Eappen's story as a racial story disappeared in the public arena; if it lived briefly as a racial story, it was in the hidden spaces of private conversations and silent witnessing. Thus, if the Eappen case offers a parable about race for middle-class South Asian Americans, it is precisely because of the absence of reference to race.

NOTES

1. Several scholars have discussed the effects of the model minority position on South Asian Americans (Bhattacharjee; George; Rajagopal; Visveswaran).

2. Maira examines the emergence of an Indian American youth subculture through music and fashion.

3. For a more detailed elaboration of this argument, see Koshy, "Morphing."

4. In 1952, legislation was passed removing all racial prerequisites for naturalization. Immigration and Nationality Act of 1952, § 311, ch. 2, 66 Stat. 239.

5. The reason that women did not show up as petitioners in the naturalization cases is that their claims to citizenship or naturalization derived from the status of their husbands. According to an 1895 treatise, "A woman partakes of her husband's nationality; her nationality is merged in that of her husband; her political status follows that of her husband." However, the Supreme Court had ruled in 1868 that only "white" women could gain citizenship by marrying a citizen. Moreover, if a noncitizen woman was married to a man racially ineligible for citizenship, she herself was similarly debarred, whatever her own racial qualifications for naturalization. Similarly, American women were stripped of their citizenship if they married an alien after 1907, or in a partial retraction of this law, if they married an alien ineligible for citizenship after 1922. This provision was only finally repealed in 1931 (López, 46–47).

6. *In re Cruz* was the only reported case where a plaintiff sought naturalization as a person of African nativity. The petitioner had an African-Native American mother and a Native American father, but the court rejected the petition stating that a person who was one-quarter African and three-quarters Native American was not eligible for citizenship as a person of "African descent."

7. In the 1970 census, most South Asians self-classified in the category "Other," but these entries were subsequently edited in compiling census data and added to the tally for the "white" category.

8. Controversy broke out over the framing of the question and because of suspicion among some minority groups over the reasons for soliciting this data. As a result, the question was dropped from the 1981 Census. However, the Labour Force Survey, which was started in 1979, had regularly included a question on ethnic group identity (Fenton 149).

9. South Asians constitute 49.5%, Afro-Carribeans 26.46%, and Chinese and Other Asians 8.68% of the total non-white population. Other ethnic minorities, which include those of mixed origin, make up the remainder of the nonwhite population (Labour Force Survey 1996).

10. The 1962 Act controlled the entry of Commonwealth *citizens*, but there were a significant number of British passport holders living abroad, who were not covered by the Act. Among them were people of Indian origin, whose forbears had lived in British East African colonies for several generations. When the African countries gained independence, they were given the choice of citizenship in either Britain or the African state. Those who chose British citizenship gained the right of entry and abode in Britain (Mason 28).

11. These percentages are based on population figures listed in the *Statistical Record of Asian Americans*, 569.

12. See *Social Trends* 27.

13. The report by Frances Gibb, the legal correspondent for *The Times*, presents numerous negative comments by British lawyers about the U.S. legal system.

14. Zobel posted his sixteen-page ruling on the website for the *Massachusetts Lawyers Weekly* (http://www.lawyersweekly.com), making it the first time a court decision has been handed down on the Internet.

15. A day after Woodward was set free, the Massachusetts Society for the Prevention of Cruelty to Children circulated a letter signed by fifty medical experts in child abuse challenging the defense's medical evidence supporting Woodward's claim of innocence: "The prosecution put forward well-established medical evidence that overwhelmingly supported a violent shaking/impact episode on the day in question." Dr. Jan Bays, chairwoman of the American Academy of Pediatrics Committee on Child Abuse and Neglect stated that the symptoms displayed by Matthew Eappen were characteristic of shaken baby syndrome, "It's violent shaking, so violent that anyone witnessing it would know that this was very dangerous to this baby" (qtd. in Goldberg A1).

16. Woodward's lawyers had called on the medical community to establish a blue-ribbon panel to investigate the possible over-diagnosis of shaken-baby syndrome, the alleged cause of Matthew Eappen's death. Dr. Randall Alexander, a leading expert on the syndrome, responded by saying that it was a well-established syndrome that had been the subject of over two hundred research papers (qtd. in Goldberg). In an article published in the *New England Journal of Medicine*, Duhaime et. al. call for renaming "shaken-baby syndrome" as "shaking-impact syndrome" to clear up misapprehension and ambiguity about the cause of the injuries in such deaths. They state that nearly all, if not all, of the injuries in these cases are the result of a violent impact to the head. The theory that Matthew's death was caused by somewhat rough handling was accepted by Judge Zobel, although Duhaime et al. note that the kind of impact necessary to produce the injuries associated with shaking-impact syndrome are equivalent to a fall from a two-story building.

WORKS CITED

"Americans Apologise for Judicial System." *The Times* 1 November 1997: 5.

Bhattacharjee, Annanya. "The Habit of Ex-Nomination: Nation, Woman, and the Indian Immigrant Bourgeoisie." *Public Culture* 5.1 (1992): 19–46.

Bhachu, Parminder. *Twice Migrants: East African Sikh Settlers in Britain*. London: Tavistock, 1985.

Brah, Avtar. "Difference, Diversity and Differentiation." *"Race," Culture and Difference*. Eds. James Donald and Ali Rattansi. London: Sage, 1992. 126–45.

Caldwell, Dan. "The Negroization of the Chinese Stereotype in California." *Southern California Quarterly* 53 (1971): 123–31.

Coles, Joanna. "I Did No Harm to Matthew, Au Pair Tells His Parents." *The Guardian* 12 November 1997: 5.

D'Souza, Dinesh. *The End of Racism: Principles for a Multiracial Society*. New York: Free Press, 1995.

Duhaime, Ann-Christine et al. "Nonaccidental Head Injury in Infants—The 'Shaken-Baby Syndrome.'" *New England Journal of Medicine* 18 June 1998: 1822–29.

Fenton, Steve. "Counting Ethnicity: Social Groups and Official Categories." *Interpreting Official Statistics*. Eds. Ruth Levitas and Will Guy. London: Routledge, 1996.

Gall, Susan B. and Timothy L. Eds. *Statistical Record of Asian Americans*. Detroit: Gale Research, 1993.

George, Rosemary Marangoly. "'From Expatriate Aristocrat to Immigrant Nobody: South Asian Racial Strategies in the Southern Californian Context." *Diaspora* 6.1 (1997): 31–60.

Gibb, Frances. "Trial Exposes Worst Traits of US Justice." *The Times* 31 October 1997: 4.

Goldberg, Carey. "Pediatric Experts Express Doubt on Au Pair's Defense." *New York Times* 12 November 1997: A1.

Harris, Cheryl I. "Whiteness as Property." *Harvard Law Review* 106 (1993): 1709–91.

Hazareesingh, S. "Racism, Cultural Identity: An Indian Perspective." *Dragon's Teeth* 24 (1986): 4–10.

In re Cruz. 23 F. Supp. 774 (E.D.N.Y. 1938).

Jensen, Joan. *Passage from India: Asian Indian Immigrants in North America.* New Haven: Yale UP, 1988.

Koshy, Susan. "Morphing Race into Ethnicity: Asian Americans and Critical Transformations of Whiteness." *Boundary 2* 28.1 (2001): 153–94.

"Labour Force Survey 1996." *Social Trends* 27 (1997). Ed. Jenny Church et al. London: Govt. Statistical Service, 1997.

Layton-Henry, Zig. *The Politics of Immigration.* Oxford: Blackwell, 1992.

Leonard, Karen. *Making Ethnic Choices: California's Punjabi Mexican Americans.* Philadelphia: Temple UP, 1992.

Lessinger, Johanna. *From the Ganges to the Hudson: Indian Immigrants in New York City.* Boston: Allyn and Bacon, 1995.

López, Ian Haney. *White by Law: The Legal Construction of Race.* New York: New York UP, 1996.

Maira, Sunaina. "Identity Dub: The Paradoxes of an Indian American Youth Subculture (New York Mix)." *Cultural Anthropology* 14.1 (1999): 29–60.

Mason, David. *Race and Ethnicity in Modern Britain.* Oxford: Oxford UP, 1995.

Mazumdar, Sucheta. "Race and Racism: South Asians in the United States." *Frontiers of Asian American Studies.* Eds. Gail M. Nomura et al. Pullman, WA: Washington State UP, 1989. 25–38.

McDowell, Christopher. *A Tamil Asylum Diaspora.* Providence, RI: Bergahn Books, 1996.

Mehren, Elizabeth. "Au Pair Freed; Conviction Cut to Manslaughter." *Los Angeles Times* 11 November 1997: A1, A16.

Modood, Tariq. "'Black' Racial Equality and Asian Identity." *New Community* 14.3 (1988): 397–404.

Montalbano, William D. "The Land of Mary Poppins Stands Behind Its Nanny." *Los Angeles Times* 10 November 1997: A 1, A 6.

Rajagopal, Arvind. "Better Than Blacks? Or, Hum Kaale Hain To Kya Hua." *SAMAR* (Summer 1995): 4–9.

Sharma, Sanjay, John Hutnyk and Ashwani Sharma. Eds. *Dis-Orienting Rhythms: The Politics of the New Asian Dance Music.* London: Zed, 1996.

Sivanandan, A. "RAT and the Degradation of Black Struggle." *Race and Class* 26.4 (1985): 1–33.

Takaki, Ronald. *Iron Cages: Race and Culture in 19th-Century America.* New York: Oxford UP, 1979.

U.S. Bureau of the Census. *Thirteenth Census of the United States Taken in the Year 1910*. Vol. I. *Population: General Report and Analysis*. Washington D.C.: U.S. Govt. Printing Office, 1913.

U.S. Bureau of the Census. *U.S. Census of Population: 1950*. Vol. II. *Characteristics of the Population*. Part I. United States Summary. Washington D.C.: U.S. Govt. Printing Office, 1953.

U.S. Bureau of the Census. *U.S. Census of Population: 1960*. Vol. I. *Characteristics of the Population*. Part I. United States Summary. Washington D.C.: U.S. Govt. Printing Office, 1964.

United States v. Bhagat Singh Thind. 261 U.S. 204 (1923).

Varadarajan, Tunku. "'He Will Not Strike Down Jury Verdict.'" *The Times* 3 November, 1997: 3.

Visweswaran, Kamala. "Diaspora by Design: Flexible Citizenship and South Asians in U.S. Racial Formations." *Diaspora* 6.1 (1997): 5–29.

Zobel, Hiller B. "The Louise Woodward Judgment." *The Times* 11 November 1997: 12.

CHAPTER THREE

Whiteness and Soap-Opera Justice

Comparing the Louise Woodward and Manjit Basuta Cases

MONALI SHETH

On June 14, 1999, Manjit Basuta, a British South Asian day-care provider, was found guilty of shaking thirteen-month-old Oliver Smith to death in her San Diego home. In accordance with California penal law, Basuta was sentenced twenty-five years to life for "assaulting a child under the age of eight, causing great bodily injury resulting in death." (Penal Code 2–3). The specific timing of the case had pushed the issue of child abuse to the forefront of public discourse. The Basuta trial took place merely a year and a half after another British au pair Louise Woodward was found guilty of shaking eight-month-old Matthew Eappen to death. Since they shared British citizenship and faced similar charges, Basuta was compared to Woodward in a variety of media accounts. According to Hemant Shah, Professor of Journalism and Mass Communications at the University of Wisconsin, the manner in which the Woodward and Basuta cases were handled indicate a prodigious "double standard" whereby the race of each defendant heavily influenced the public reception of their cases. (Guilty 2). As member of a marginalized group, Basuta became the subject of racist, stereotypical depictions in the media and racially inspired attacks in the courtroom which Woodward, as a white woman, did not contend with. This essay reviews the case both as a legal matter and as a matter of public opinion, investigating the ways in which Basuta was criminalized on the basis of race. Using the Woodward case as a point of reference, I will examine how the racial anxieties the American and British public harbored against Basuta were eventually projected onto the trial and its media coverage, powerfully shaping the conclusion of the case.

Specific controversies surrounding Basuta's immigration history, nationality, and religion brought these racially charged sentiments underlying the case to the foreground. It was discovered that she had submitted a false petition for political asylum to immigration authorities and that she had employed an undocumented Guatemalan helper at her day care. It was also alleged that Basuta had threatened to deport the helper if she did not corroborate her version of the story, claiming that Oliver Smith was injured when another child pushed him onto a concrete surface. While these developments were relevant to the case at some level, the prosecution and the local media tended to represent them in a completely disproportionate manner. In fact, sensationalized portrayals of Basuta as a "flight risk" to her "native" India and other xenophobic slurs often overshadowed the actual content of the case. Although these depictions may have been intended to incite a critical discussion around the defendant's credibility, they ultimately encouraged the public to condemn Basuta on the basis of a racialized representation of her immigration history.

Basuta's national identity also developed into a point of contention. In the local media, she was continually referred to as "Indian" even though she had never lived in or visited the country, and her citizenship and strong familial ties to Britain had obviously indicated otherwise. The British press expressed a similar ambivalence toward her national identity. Despite her British citizenship, she represented the "racial other" and "perpetual foreigner" in the public consciousness, and therefore did not qualify for the sympathy and support that Woodward had successfully garnered as a white woman. The general public in both countries also became fixated on Basuta's Sikh background. Several times in the context of the case, Sikhism was racially stereotyped in a similar fashion as Islam, branded a religion of turban-clad "fanatics" and "terrorists."

Both the overt and indirect attention given to Basuta's racial identity ultimately produced a racially polarized response from her local and international communities, casting South Asian Americans and British South Asians on one side, and the larger, predominantly white American and British constituencies on the other. In contrast to their response to the trial of Louise Woodward, the white American and white British communities demonstrated a racially motivated distrust and suspicion of Basuta. Some went so far as to express an outright confidence in her guilt even before the case was tried in a court of law. South Asian Americans and British South Asians, however, were generally outraged by the conclusion of the case, asserting that racial prejudice and xenophobic sentiment interfered with the fairness of the legal proceedings and the press coverage.

TRIAL BY RACE:
COURTROOM IMMIGRATION POLITICS IN *PEOPLE VS. BASUTA*

While the American judicial system is generally perceived as untainted by social and political prejudices, the realities of the legal process tend to contradict this popular notion. According to sociologist Richard Gelles, author of *Behind Closed Doors: Violence in the American Family*, the length of an offender's sentence will greatly depend upon "the age of the victim, the sex of the offender, the relationship of the offender to the victim, and the *race* of the offender *and* the victim."[1] Gelles suggests that judges, who are often depicted as impartial mediators, are also vulnerable to socially constructed stereotypes about age, sex, and race. Similar studies have been conducted by psychologists and legal scholars that investigate how jurors frequently formulate verdicts on the basis of certain facial stereotypes in which race can form a major factor. These stereotypes supposedly serve as "intuitive" guidelines, which somehow assist jurors in differentiating "guilty" defendants from "innocent" ones (Zebrowitz 104). Loaded with racially charged issues of immigration, the legal proceedings in the Basuta case reflect these unfortunate realities of trial by race.

The prosecution's case consisted of two main components: a scientific argument grounded in the medical opinion of some pathologists, and a character assessment of Basuta based on her Guatemalan helper, Cristina Carillo. The immigration politics imbedded in the second portion of the argument wielded significant ideological power. Prosecutor Dan Goldstein ingeniously crafted a "good immigrant/ bad immigrant" dichotomy, whereby Carillo fit the first category and Basuta represented the latter. The following comments Goldstein made during the trial illustrate his attempt to depict Carillo as the "good immigrant" to members of the jury:

> When [Carillo] came forward, she became vulnerable. She took this stand and she testified she was an illegal immigrant in our country, that she didn't have papers. . . . She knows what that means to her and she's stepping up at the plate and she's answering up.[2]

Goldstein asserted that Carillo, out of a sense of civic duty, risked deportation to tell the truth while Basuta told horrific lies in order to save herself and avoid taking responsibility for the death of Oliver Smith. Making vicious attacks on Basuta's character, based on her immigration history, Goldstein suggested that her dishonesty with her application for political asylum had somehow confirmed her ability to kill Oliver.

When Carillo took the stand, she claimed that Basuta threatened to deport her if she did not agree to her version of the story, and that, contrary to what she initially told the police, Basuta had shaken Oliver Smith and banged his head on the floor because he did not come for his diaper change. Throughout the course of the trial, however, the defense had proven that Carillo had altered the details of Oliver's injury at least twelve times, lying to people she had no reason to, including her brother and her attorney. Her credibility was further marred when she admitted in court that she had been dishonest with the police on several occasions (Goodwin 4).

Carillo's ties with the prosecution became increasingly questionable. When she testified before the Grand Jury, she mentioned that Oliver Smith had a bruise on his forehead. However, the bruise did not materialize until after his death in the hospital, to which Carillo was not a witness. How then did she become aware of its existence? Iredale and the defense team suggested that Carillo's undocumented status made her extremely vulnerable and that she may have restructured her testimony at the request of the prosecution, or perhaps she was offered an opportunity to stay in the United States legally if she tailored some of her comments to strengthen their case against Basuta. The defense also proposed the theory that Carillo was afraid she would face serious criminal charges, and changed her testimony to avoid becoming a suspect herself (Goodwin 4).

While the jury claimed to have discarded Carillo's testimony when formulating the verdict because it had been discredited in court, the damage had already been done. Goldstein successfully pitted Carillo against Basuta. Carillo might have lied "out of confusion," but Basuta had done so "deliberately" in order to "conceal" her role in Oliver Smith's death. And with the vulnerability around her immigration status, class background, and racial identity, Carillo's willingness to step up to the role of the "good immigrant" portrayed by Goldstein was understandable. As Iredale suggested, had the sequence of events taken a slightly altered course, Carillo, as a poor immigrant woman of color, could have easily been deported or targeted as a suspect by the prosecution. As it was, however, Goldstein exploited Carillo's weak position in order to advance his own agenda, placing immigration politics as the ideological centerpiece of his legal strategy.

Judge William H. Kennedy, who presided over the trial, also played into the immigration politics surrounding the case. According to the penal statute under which Basuta was convicted and under the conditions specific to her trial, the judge could either give her probation or the full-term sentence of twenty-five years to life. At the first hearing, he was ambivalent about imposing the sentence required by law and considered the possibility of going with probation on the grounds that the punishment could be "cruel and unusual" as applied in her case. Kennedy commented on his receipt of "hundreds if not thousands of letters" on behalf of Basuta and asserted that he did not believe she committed "an intentional, malicious act." He postponed the sentencing to another hearing two months later, and requested that the attorneys analyze and compare penalties for more severe crimes and then re-examine the various kinds of sentences assigned by judges in other states for similar crimes (Krueger B–1).

At the second hearing, even before the attorneys presented their arguments, the merciful, sympathetic attitude Kennedy held toward Basuta had completely disappeared. He ultimately chose to hand her the sentence of twenty-five years to life. He justified his decision primarily with a series of arguments pertaining to Basuta's lack of credibility. The arguments were linked directly to her false application for political asylum. Kennedy told the court that he had been "quite disturbed" by the petition Basuta submitted to immigration authorities in 1994, in which she claimed she was being persecuted by Indian officials for her practice of the Sikh faith (Stote 1). While this document proved Basuta capable of lying, the judge followed prosecuting attorney Goldstein in a faulty line of reasoning, lumping "liar" with "child killer." Stephen Jakobi, a British attorney currently aiding the defense team in Basuta's appeal, argues there was no substantial connection between the two charges and that they should have been dealt with separately:

> I must say as a commentator I was concerned…I can't see how lying on an immigration paper has anything to do with this particular offense. It's a separate matter. I was somewhat surprised [Kennedy] took that into account.[3]

In addition to being unrelated to the charge at hand, Kennedy's argument had also been selectively applied. Carillo, too, had been dishonest with her immigration status and had, in fact, admitted to lying during the trial while under oath. Did that make Carillo as culpable as Basuta? What had perturbed Kennedy was not merely the fact that Basuta had lied. Carillo had lied too and with matters directly related to the case. Why, then, should Kennedy be more bothered by Basuta's lie? The premise behind political asylum is that an immigrant is fleeing the oppressive conditions of home (usually somewhere in the Third World) in order to acquire freedom in America (Trend 61). Basuta contradicted this narrative of journey on all terms. She was an illegal immigrant from England, not India, who was residing in a nice home in a good neighborhood, and seemingly living the "American Dream" which perhaps many believed she did not deserve (Onono 1999). Basuta's profile did not fit the California stereotype of an illegal immigrant or refugee. The incongruence between who Basuta actually was and the idea of an illegal immigrant in the popular imagination threatened the public's faith in its ability to distinguish "illegal immigrants" from "legal immigrants." Kennedy's decision to deliver the twenty-five-year-to-life sentence was rooted in the public's adverse reaction to the image of an illegal nonwhite immigrant, whose "criminal traits" were not recognizable by any "standard" definition, killing an innocent white child.

According to Amarjit Singh, Basuta's brother, the full-term sentence the judge assigned to Basuta was chiefly intended to "placate white California society" (Honigsbaum 14). And Kennedy's decision had clearly reflected the current of broader public sentiment. In a web poll conducted the day of the sentencing, San Diego's KFMB Channel 8 posed the following question: "Do you agree with the judge's decision to sentence Manjit Basuta twenyt-five years to life in prison?" While 40% did not agree and a small 6% voted not sure, a 54% majority agreed with the terms of the judge's sentencing.[4] San Diego radio host Roger Hedgecock conducted a similar poll, asking his listeners: "Was Manjit Basuta's sentence fair?" Only 36% voted no with an overwhelming 64% majority approving of the judge's decision.[5]

With a sizable overseas audience for the case and the presence of the British press at the hearing, the judge was also obligated to discuss what distinguished the circumstances of Basuta's sentencing from the conditions of Woodward's sentencing. While the jury had convicted Woodward of second-degree murder, the judge presiding over her case ultimately reduced her charge to manslaughter and shortened her fifteen-year sentence to the 279 days she had already served in jail. The judge in Woodward's case described the nineteen-year-old au pair's actions as those "characterized by confusion, inexperience, frustration, immaturity and some anger, but not malice" (Rogers 6). Playing on similar stereotypes about age, Kennedy explained that he imposed a harsher penalty on Basuta because of the wisdom and maturity she should have acquired by her age, and implied that that was precisely what differentiated Basuta's situation from Woodward's. During the final sentencing hearing, he made the following statement:

> There is no question in my mind that the actions of the defendant caused the death of a 13-month-old boy. She is in her forties. She is not a teenager who doesn't know right from wrong.[6]

Although there is undoubtedly a substantial difference in age between Woodward and Basuta, Kennedy's line of reasoning conceals a major double standard. For instance, if Woodward were a nineteen-year-old woman of color, would her youth excuse her of convicted criminal behavior (especially when anyone eighteen years of age and older is legally considered an adult)? The judge's emphasis on age as the primary disparity between Basuta and Woodward masks the saliency of race in the different outcomes of each case.

Kennedy's discussion of age in the context of the sentencing hearing serves as a good point of departure as it leads into a discussion of the media and its framing of the case and the public reaction it evoked. Like the judge, the press also emphasized age as a primary factor explaining Basuta's inability to attract broader public support. By citing the overwhelming attention that young Woodward received during the height of her trial, members of the media attempted to reinforce this claim. But at some point, the press could no longer avoid commenting on how racial difference had ultimately distinguished the content and quality of the media coverage in the Basuta and Woodward cases and the nature of the public responses to them.

THE CULTURAL MANIFESTATIONS OF TRIAL BY RACE: "ALIENNESS" AND THE "RACIAL OTHER" IN THE MEDIA COVERAGE OF *PEOPLE VS BASUTA*

According to Asian American Studies scholar Robert Lee, the "alienness" of immigrants materializes on two particular platforms, "a formal political or legal status" and "an informal, but no less powerful cultural status." Lee then argues that alien legal status and the processes by which it can be discarded are often determined by " the cultural definitions of difference."[7] The disparate treatment of the Basuta and Woodward cases by the media and the public illustrates how cultural notions of difference, specifically race as it is popularly defined, can characterize Basuta as an alien criminal threatening the American cultural landscape, and Woodward as a friendly visitor.

Both Basuta and Woodward are British citizens. Both were convicted of similar crimes. Basuta has lived in the United States for ten years while Woodward endured a short stay through an au pair exchange program. With these circumstances laid out, it is important to ask what allowed Woodward to garner the support of the masses and sustain their interest that did not allow Basuta the same. Like Kennedy, many journalists and media commentators answered the question by briefly mentioning supposed "universal" stereotypes about age. It was simply that Woodward was able to extract more public sympathy because she was considered a young woman with a promising future and not a middle-aged mother like Basuta. Sarah Graham, one of the first British reporters to bring attention to the Basuta case, made the following assessment about the British media and their perceptions of Basuta and Woodward:

> The [British media] were saying that [the Basuta case] wasn't interesting enough. And it's because Manjit is a devout Sikh. She is middle-aged. There's nothing glamorous about her really. Louise Woodward was a more interesting person to look at. Somebody described her as "sexy." And that's why she got the media attention she did.[8]

As a "middle-aged" woman and a "devout Sikh," Basuta evidently failed to earn the titles of "glamorous," "interesting," and "sexy," epithets that had previously been used to describe young Woodward by all her fans. Many British and American journalists claimed that Woodward appealed to the masses in spite of her faults because she possessed a "televisual face" (Riddell 21), or, as one popular magazine noted, she was "cherubic" and "well-groomed" (McCarthy 67). In a law journal article titled "Faces of Innocence," psychologist Leslie Zebrowitz asserted that Woodward fit the "baby face" stereotype near perfectly:

> [Woodward] . . . [has a] "baby face"- round visages, large eyes, small noses, and small chins. Such an appearance creates the impression of naiveté, warmth and honesty, traits that could yield a negligent offense but not an intentional one. Woodward does not look like a murderer . . . We simply refuse to believe [Woodward] capable of such crime. (104)

Using Zebrowitz's mode of analysis, it can be concluded that Basuta undoubtedly fell outside this facial stereotype and instead was identified with its opposite or what the psychologist refers to as a "mature face." The term "baby face" implies innocence, especially when contrasted to the expression "mature face" which indicates experience and even an inclination towards guilt. The "baby face/mature face" paradigm is problematic because of the universalistic sentiment attached to it, suggesting it is imbued with some sort of objective standard. Yet the physical description which Zebrowitz provides is highly racialized. "Large eyes" and "small noses" are features which tend to be more prevalent among whites than any other ethnoracial group. "Baby face" also becomes a racial construct in that it distinguishes "harmless citizens" from "dangerous criminals," a group typically associated with people of color in the popular imagination. By a mere process of elimination, "harmless citizens" can then only be equated with white people. In this racialized equation, Woodward matches the latter description and Basuta qualifies for the former, leaving the white British au pair a beneficiary of "soap opera justice" and the British South Asian child-care provider its unfortunate victim (Riddell 21).

The media's emphasis on the age difference between Basuta and Woodward, however, eventually shifted to a discussion of the racial difference between them and its impact on the public response to their cases. While the South Asian constituencies in the United States and United Kingdom that supported Basuta were relatively small in comparison to the masses that rallied on Woodward's behalf, they persistently pressured the media to investigate the ways in which issues of race and immigration directed the course of the case. The British press was more willing than the American press to examine the pivotal role race played in producing such disparities in the media coverage and public interest in the two cases. Two possible reasons may account for this. First, the British South Asian constituency that rallied together on behalf of Basuta was a larger political force to reckon with than their South Asian American counterparts in San Diego.[9] Secondly, the racially charged issue of Basuta's false application for political asylum was virtually absent from public debate of the case in the U.K. These conditions may have facilitated a more open, critical discussion of race and its influence on public opinion towards the case.

British tabloids and papers began to print headlines which acknowledged the impact Basuta's racial identity had on the public response to the case: "The Unknown Killer: This British Woman Has Been Convicted of Killing a Toddler, but the UK Press Has Ignored Her Case. Would Things Have Been Different if She Were White?" (Gentleman & Campbell 4). Even top British press agent, Max Clifford, publicly asserted that racism ultimately caused the Basuta case to draw such minimal coverage in the media and greatly contributed to her "unknown status" in the larger British community. According to Clifford, stories about Asians, like the Basuta case, do not interest the masses in Britain:

> Most editors are not interested in Asian people. If I have four clients and one of them is Asian, I have to work 100 times harder to get the same amount of coverage for the Asian client. Being Asian is a huge stumbling block particularly for the tabloids.[10]

Suresh Grover, coordinator of the National Civil Rights Movement in Britain, made a comment similar to Clifford's:

Only about 0.5% of the cases involving Asian individuals we have on our books ever get any publicity. The other 99.5% fall by the wayside because the Asian community is not seen as something that will fill pages or sell papers.[11]

As both Clifford and Grover testify, Basuta's racial identity prevented her from securing broader public support. The media's reluctance to report on the Basuta case, or other stories involving Asians, reflects popular British attitudes toward issues of race and citizenship—particularly, that race supersedes nationality. Being Asian, Basuta lacked a shared racial identity with the larger community and her citizenship alone did not provide access to "Britishness." A great deal of Woodward's success in attracting public support lay in her ability to appeal to the "racial bonding" among white Britons.[12] Basuta's inability to partake in this white racial camaraderie made her legal plight in the U.S. of little concern to the majority of the British public.

In addition to the racial identity of the defendants, the racial identity of the families of the victims influenced how the press represented the Woodward and Basuta cases. According to sociologist Richard Gelles, had Woodward been from Barbados or Trinidad, her manslaughter sentence of 279 days would have actually been "ten years, with five to serve." He also concluded that a nonwhite offender with a white victim would receive a harsher sentence and less public sympathy than a white offender with a nonwhite victim (Scarf 15).

The Woodward case presented the second scenario, with Woodward as the "white offender" and the parents of Matthew Eappen as the "racial other." In the media, Drs. Deborah and Sunil Eappen were publicly scrutinized because of allegations made by the defense that they abused their child. On several occasions, both the British and American media portrayed the Eappens as cold parents, capable of hurting Matthew and then concealing their abuse of him. Their suspicion of the Eappens was often grounded in either the interracial marriage between Deborah, a white woman, and Sunil, a South Asian American, or sometimes solely in Sunil's racial identity, pinpointing his parents' upbringing in India's caste stratified society. One writer contrived the following convoluted theory about the Eappens' motives in hiding their involvement in their own son's death:

There has to be a reason why [the Eappens] thought they had to hide [their abuse of Matthew] . . . If there is a racial or national origin prejudice against one, that is another reason for one to avoid suspicion, thus a reason to hide the injur[ies]....Further, the Drs. Eappens are a racially mixed couple. This too may have caused them to fear prejudice . . . Further, India has caste system. Sunil's parents may have been raised to be more racially conscious than they would have been had they been raised in non-caste system. (Purkiss 62)

In the Basuta case, the parents of Oliver Smith, both white, were not subject to such a racially charged character assassination in the media, and were often given the benefit of doubt. Even though Oliver Smith's father, Jeffrey Herbert Smith, formally accused the mother, Audrey Amaral of abusing the child on police record, the larger local community rarely considered her a suspect. Smith's decision to retract earlier statements he made to the police in order to join Amaral in a one-million-dollar civil suit against the Basuta family also failed to incite suspicion. As a divorced white mother, Amaral was often a recipient of public support and sympathy. In the local media, she was portrayed only as a victim "stripped of her motherhood" as a result of her child's untimely death (British Nanny 2). Although Amaral's only criteria in her day-care search for Oliver had been spending the least amount of money possible,[13] she was depicted as an activist championing the cause of shaken baby zealots, and an advocate of child protection in day care. Amaral was commended for helping draft "Oliver's Law," a piece of legislation enacted by Governor Gray Davis on January 1, 2000, which mandates that child-care licensing facilities provide parents with verbal notice of their right to review a provider's records.[14]

According to British attorney Stephen Jakobi, if more emphasis had been placed on the parents' potential involvement in Oliver's fragile medical condition, then "a lot of sympathy would have been forfeited."[15] But journalists, particularly at the local level, dismissed the allegations made by the defense that Amaral was abusive and careless with Oliver as defamation. San Diego's "Radio Mayor" Roger Hedgecock, made the following comment during his program: "Judge Kennedy is a law-and-order guy. He was not swayed by . . . [the defendant's] slander of the dead boy's parents."[16] Despite evidence that indicated otherwise, Hedgecock absolutely refused to acknowledge that the allegations put forth by the defense against Oliver Smith's parents had any validity.

Hedgecock's attitude toward the case, although perhaps extreme, was emblematic of the sentiment held by most other members of the local press. They were wary of introducing the issue of race to the public debate surrounding the case, often dismissing the possibility that racial prejudice could have influenced important aspects of the trial. In one instance, Hedgecock openly mocked British reporters who probed the issue of race in the Basuta trial, labeling them "full of indignation." He responded to a question posed by a journalist from the British Broadcasting Corporation (BBC) about the role of race in the court proceedings in the following manner:

> Basuta is a Sikh, and her family is here (illegally?) from India . . . race is always a possible factor, but the jury was primarily influenced by evidence that Basuta had killed a baby in her care and then lied to cover it up.[17]

His comments here contradict a basic premise he initially establishes, namely that the law is a supreme force immune to racial prejudice. In his response, Hedgecock first identifies Basuta by her religion and then follows up with a slur involving her immigration status. In the process, he misnames the sending country (which is actually Britain, but he assumes it to be India despite the fact that BBC is interviewing him). All three identity markers Hedgcock uses to identify Basuta are conflated with race, two of which are employed in a derogatory manner. Yet, he is convinced that the judge and the jurors, possibly sharing his attitudes toward Basuta, could hardly be persuaded by their racist convictions in a trial which, he maintains, was determined on the basis of "evidence."

British Public Relations Advisor, Max Clifford, disagrees with the likes of Hedgecock, asserting that race was inextricable from the outcome of the Basuta case, especially when compared to the conclusion of the Woodward trial:

> Basuta has not had as much interest as Louise Woodward because she's Asian . . . If she had the kind of support Woodward had, I have no doubt her chances of acquittal would have improved.[18]

Basuta's racial identity evidently prevented her from acquiring even remotely the same degree of public support and sympathy that Woodward had garnered in both the U.S. and the U.K. With the majority of the British community unaware of her trial, and the larger San Diego community confident of her guilt even before her trial began, the public pressure tactics applied by Basuta campaigners lacked the same force and potency which was present in the efforts of Woodward's supporters. Unlike Basuta, the young white nanny secured almost unanimous support in Britain. Over $600,000 were raised by British citizens and then donated to Woodward's parents to cover expenses for the legal battle. The Woodward case hit the front pages of all major American and British newspapers and tabloids, and even displaced regular television programming on all the major networks as the jury approached a verdict (Guilty 2). While Woodward claimed the presence of television cameras was harmful to her, it was ultimately the international attention her case drew which influenced the judge to reduce her charge from second degree murder to manslaughter and then restrict her sentence to the nine months she had already served (Norman 31). In a special Gallup Poll taken in November 1997, immediately after her sentencing hearing, an overwhelming 52% of the public approved of the judge's decision to reduce her charge to manslaughter, compared with 30% who disapproved, and 18% who had no opinion on the matter (Newport 7).

Basuta, who drew minimal press attention and even less public support, hardly benefited from the presence of the media. The Basuta case seldom picked up national headlines in the American press and failed to interest the British press until its concluding stages. And even when it did manage to grasp the attention of the British tabloids and papers, it hardly compared to the media frenzy the Woodward trial created. Although the local media followed the Basuta case closely, it rarely provided fair coverage and was often inclined to a pro-prosecution viewpoint.

While a strong political network mobilized on Basuta's behalf, it did not include a broad cross section of the population. The support she received primarily consisted of what many referred to as an "ethnic following" of British South Asians and South Asian Americans, concentrated in the cities of London and San Diego.[19] While British South Asians are the largest racial minority in London, the South Asian Americans in San Diego make up a much smaller group and, consequently, would have benefited from coalition building with other groups. With the controversies surrounding the testimony of Cristina Carillo, it was difficult for campaigners to solicit support from a Latino constituency in San Diego. Fears related to their occupational status and their immigration status might have also discouraged many Latina women in day care from offering their support. With a large portion of the child-care industry in San Diego consisting of immigrant women from Russia, Somalia, and Vietnam, as well as Mexico,[20] language barriers as well as similar anxieties about immigration and job security may have posed obstacles to potential efforts at coalition-building. The limited presence of African Americans in the Del Mar area where Basuta ran her day care, and the small number of African American women employed in San Diego's child-care industry[21] perhaps made it difficult for campaigners to draw support from a black constituency. The campaign in San Diego was able to secure the backing of some Turks and Iranians, who had been friends of the Basuta family, but the size of the group was relatively small and the extent of their involvement was limited (Sikh Foundation 1).

Yet, even with the full-fledged support of these groups, the Basuta campaign unfortunately would not have gathered the same political strength of the Woodward case because, in addition to garnering the interest and support of the majority white communities in the U.S. and the U.K., Woodward had secured the interest and the support of the majority white legal system and media in both countries. While Basuta and Woodward were British citizens and therefore foreigners in the U.S., only Woodward was able to shed her "alien" legal status. Applying Robert Lee's "alieness" theory mentioned earlier in the section, it is evident that the cultural definitions of difference were set up so that as a white woman, Woodward could participate in the white "racial nepotism" that ultimately produced her acquittal.[22] Even if she did not file a false petition for political asylum, as a racial minority, Basuta could not have been a beneficiary of the white privilege in the United States and the United Kingdom that had sustained and supported Woodward. And it was this distinction between Basuta and Woodward that caused the course of each case to diverge at a critical juncture.

CONCLUSION

Analyzing the Basuta trial in the context of the Woodward trial draws out some of the highly racialized issues of immigration and nationality that initially were not openly acknowledged or discussed in the United States or the United Kingdom, but nevertheless had monopolized the terms of the public debate surrounding the case from the very beginning. While both Woodward and Basuta were immigrants to the United States, only Basuta was seen as the "racial other" in the courtroom and the American public consciousness. It is this difference that made Woodward's alien status something that could be overlooked, while it made Basuta the "perpetual alien." Similarly, in the United Kingdom, both Basuta and Woodward were British citizens, but Basuta alone, as the "racial other," could not achieve the ultimate standard of "Britishness." As a result of these opposing racial dynamics, it was only the white Woodward who could emerge as a victor in the court of law as well as the court of public opinion, in spite of being convicted. A close examination of the racial elements imbedded in the Basuta trial, both as a legal matter and as a subject of public discourse, clearly indicates that the case was not merely an issue of shaken baby syndrome or an earnest mission to seek criminal justice. Basuta was ultimately tried, convicted, and sentenced on the basis of her racial identity and her immigration history, and not on charges involving child abuse or murder.

NOTES

1. Qtd. in Maggie Scarf 15.
2. Qtd. in "Closing Arguments Begin in Murder Trial" 1.
3. Stephen Jakobi, telephone interview, 17 Jan. 2000.
4. KFMB San Diego Channel 8, "Do You Agree with the Judge's Decision to Sentence Manjit Basuta 25 Years to Life in Prison?" 1 Oct. 1999 <http://www.kfmb.com>.
5. Roger Hedgecock, 1 Oct. 1999 <http://www.sandiego.insider.com/news/roger/basuta/html>.
6. Qtd. in Deborah Collcutt 4.
7. Qtd. in Paul M. Ong 163.
8. Sarah Graham, personal interview, 5 Aug. 1999.
9. South Asians comprise the largest Asian subgroup and largest racial minority in the United Kingdom. See Ong 366.
10. Qtd. in Gentleman and Campbell 4.
11. Qtd. in Gentleman and Campbell 4.
12. See Derrick Bell 9.
13. Katie Kenchur, telephone interview, 16 Jan. 2000. Kenchur is Public Relations Officer for the San Diego Family Child Care Association.
14. Debbie Bowles, personal interview, 19 Jan. 2000. Bowles is President of the San Diego Family Child Care Association.
15. Interview with Stephen Jakobi.
16. Hedgecock, <http://www.sandiego.insider.com/news/roger/basuta/html>.
17. Hedgecock, <http://www.sandiego.insider.com/news/roger/basuta/html>.
18. Qtd. in "Guilty, and No Glamour" 2.

19. Interview with Stephen Jakobi.

20. Dana Lovelace, personal interview, 4 Jan. 2000. Lovelace is Child Care Advocate at the Day Care Licensing Office in San Diego.

21. Interview with Dana Lovelace.

22. See Derrick Bell 47.

WORKS CITED

Bell, Derrick. *Faces at the Bottom of the Well.* New York: Basic, 1992.

Bowles, Debbie. Personal interview. 19 Jan. 2000.

"British Nanny Sentenced 25 Years for Baby's Death." *Agence France Presse* 1 Oct. 1999: 2.

"Closing Arguments Begin in Murder Trial against Day Care Provider." *Associated Press* 9 June 1999: 4.

Collcutt, Deborah. "Why Nanny Deserves No Mercy by Judge." *Daily Mail* 2 Oct. 1999: 4.

"Do You Agree with the Judge's Decision to Sentence Manjit Basuta 25 Years to Life in Prison?" KFMB San Diego Channel 8. 1 Oct. 1999 <http://www.kfmb.com>.

Gentleman, Amelia, and Duncan Campbell. "The Unknown Killer: This British Woman Has Been Convicted of Killing a Toddler, but the UK Press Has Ignored Her Case. Would Things Have Been Different If She Were White?" *Guardian* 16 June 1999: 4.

Goodwin, Jo-Ann. "Framed? Can Any British Nanny Now Find Justice in America?" *Daily News* 5 Aug. 1999: 4.

Graham, Sarah. Personal interview. 5 Aug. 1999.

"Guilty, and No Glamour." *The Week* 17 Oct. 1999: 2.

Hedgecock, Roger. 1 Oct. 1999 <http://www.sandiego.insider.com/news/roger/basuta/html>.

Honigsbaum, Mark. "'I'm Not Guilty,' Insists Nanny." *Observer* 3 Oct. 1999: 14.

Jakobi, Stephen. Telephone interview, 17 Jan. 2000.

Kenchur, Katie. Telephone interview. 16 Jan. 2000.

Krueger, Ann. "Basuta Sentencing Delayed: Judge Is Weighing Day Care Operator's Fate in Boy's Death." *San Diego Union-Tribune* 6 Aug. 1999: B–1.

Lovelace, Dana. Personal interview. 4 Jan. 2000.

McCarthy, Terry. "A Stunning Verdict." *Time* 10 Nov. 1997: 67.

Newport, Frank. "Mixed Reaction from Public to Judge's Decisions in Au Pair Case." *Gallup Poll Monthly* (Nov. 1997): 7.

Norman, Ken. *The Lynch Mob Syndrome.* Carlisle: The Portia Campaign, 1999.

Ong, Paul M. *The State of Asian Pacific America: Transforming Race Relations, A Public Policy Report.* Los Angeles: LEAP Asian Pacific American Public Policy Institute and the UCLA Asian American Studies Center, 2000.

Onono, Erika. *The Real Story of the Forgotten Nanny*. London: 20/20, 1999.

"Penal Code Chapter 2. Abandonment and Neglect of Children." *Deering's California Codes Annotated*. San Francisco: Lexis Law Publishing, 1999. 2-3.

Purkiss, Dianne. "The Children of Medea: Euripedes, Louise Woodward, and Deborah Eappen." *Cardozo Studies in Law and Literature* (Summer 1999): 62.

Riddell, Mary. "If You Commit a Crime, You Can Become a Star and Get Asked on to Chat Shows. But It Must Be the Right Sort of Crime." *New Statesman* 4 Sept. 1998: 21.

Rogers, Charles G. "Found Guilty of Bad Judgement." *Los Angeles Daily Journal* 19 Nov. 1997: 6.

San Diego Sikh Community Monthly Newsletter. *Sikh Foundation News* 2.6 (July 1999): 1.

Scarf, Maggie. "Lock 'Er Up." *New Republic* 30 Mar. 1998.

Stote, Martin. "Tears As Killer Nanny Is Jailed for 25 Years." *Birmingham Post* 2 Oct. 1999: 1.

Trend, David. *Socialist Review* 24.4 (1994): 61.

Zebrowitz, Leslie. "Faces of Innocence." *ABA Journal* (Apr. 1999): 104.

CHAPTER FOUR

Mother Teresa as the
Mirror of Bourgeois Guilt

VIJAY PRASHAD

Growing up in Calcutta, I was privy to three kinds of white people: the tourists (whether of the hippie or the Five-Star variety), the Soviets (the only whites who attempted to mingle with people), and Mother Teresa. The hippies always tried to sell us jeans in exchange for dope, the Five-Star folks attempted to take pictures of our less fortunate from their air-conditioned cars and secure hotels. The Russians sold us cheap copies of Marxist classics, children's folk tales, and Tolstoy, as they tried to engage us in banter not altogether easy given the barriers of language. The last type of white person was entirely unique, as she trod the pavements in search of misbegotten souls, followed in many cases by well-dressed Indians who wanted so much to help the Mother do good in their own city. These well-heeled Indians started to take interest in the Mother, I think, only after the famous painter M. F. Husain painted a series of portraits of her in 1979–80. (He continued to paint her until her death.) I saw her only once, from a distance, when my school visited Nirmal Hirday (Home of the Pure Heart, where the dying come to be comforted). She passed by us, without speaking, but with a big smile, as some of my fellow preteens called out to her. I was able to go home and brag that I had been near a celebrity in the heart of our dear but tormented city. When Mother Teresa died on 5 September 1997, I remembered that brief encounter to remind myself of the unusual path taken by this Albanian woman who decided to settle in the city of my birth and tend to those not born with my privileges. But my reflections drowned in the bile of the media, portraying her as a saint sent by providence to tend to the otherwise forgotten peoples of India. This was a mockery, one that was not entirely outside the self-presentation offered by Mother Teresa.

. Despite herself, Mother Teresa is the quintessential image of the white woman in the colonies, working to save the dark bodies from their own temptations and failures. One thinks of the images of Florence Nightingale or Josephine Butler. Butler came to India to assist the "helpless, voiceless, hopeless" whose "helplessness appeals to the heart, somewhat in the same way in which the helplessness and suf-fering of a dumb animal does, under the knife of the vivisector" (qtd. in Ware 159). The Euro-American-dominated international media continue to harbor the colo-nial notion that white peoples are somehow especially endowed with the capacity to create social change. When nonwhite people labor in this direction, the media typically search for white benefactors or teachers, or else, for white people who stand in the wings to direct the nonwhite actors. Dark bodies cannot act of their own volition to stretch their own capacity, for they must wait, the media seem to imply, for some colonial administrator, some technocrat from IBM or the IMF to tell them how to do things. When it comes to saving the poor, the dark bodies are again invisible, for the media seem to celebrate only the worn out platitudes of such as Mother Teresa and ignore the struggles of those bodies for their own libera-tion. To open the life of someone like Mother Teresa to scrutiny, therefore, is always difficult. First, one has to overcome the colonial overdetermination of her image, her compassionate sacrifice on behalf of those whose charred skin damns them to an uncomfortable life. There is a temptation to see her as one of those earnest white women who come to the colonies to save brown women from brown men (in the manner of Katherine Mayo) and to protect brown children from the callousness of brown parents. Second, an aura surrounds her image, one that seems to disallow any form of criticism. When a figure is rendered blessed, it becomes hard to con-duct an analysis of those elements of life that are not enshrined in the divine. Third, we all feel inadequate in relation to her spartan life, filled with a genuine sense of service. She shares some similarities with Gandhi, who also made criticism seem absurd as he sat amongst the poor in their clothes and with a smile on his ineffable face. Certainly, Mother Teresa was an extraordinary person, or else there would not be such attention at her death. Our critique of Mother Teresa is not intended to downplay her role in the amelioration of suffering amongst some of the world's poor. We are interested in the limitations of her work, not in the intri-cacies of her theology or of her efficacy in her own terms. Lenin, in 1905, urged Marxists not to be dogmatic towards religion. "Unity in this really revolutionary struggle of the oppressed class for the creation of paradise on earth," he wrote, "is more important to us than unity of proletarian opinion on paradise in heaven." (Lenin 87). This essay will analyze the ways in which Mother Teresa's work was part of a global enterprise for the alleviation of bourgeois guilt, rather than a genuine challenge to those forces that produce and maintain poverty.

Mother Teresa died in the same week as Lady Diana Spencer. Both women appeared to the world as icons of charity: Diana as the arbiter of fashion and as the vanguard of compassion (notably toward AIDS survivors and those maimed by landmines), and the Mother as the savior of the world's poor. Whatever one might say of Diana,[1] a year before she died she established herself as a major spokesperson against the international arms industry. In January 1997, Diana traveled to Angola, to speak out against the 110 million landmines that currently litter the world. At a gala to raise tens of thousands of dollars, she noted that "these mines inflict most of their casualties on people who are trying to meet the elementary needs of life. They strike the women gathering firewood for cooking. They ambush the child sent to collect water for the family" (qtd. in *Seattle Times*). It is a mark of our relatively undemocratic public culture that the struggles of so many nameless and faceless people against landmines carries so much less weight than that of a celebrity, but nevertheless, Diana used her credibility to champion the issue. (However, she did not go after the large "conventional" arms industry, whose profits enable the buoyancy of the United States and British economy, and of the British Royals.) The Mother and the Lady provided easy symbols of charity rather than social change as they promoted forms of altruism well suited to privatized social action rather than to substantial social change. The masses wept before Buckingham Palace and along the streets of Calcutta, but they did not use the example of these figures to continue the fight for social justice.

HOW THE MOTHER BECAME A SAINT

Our problem with Mother Teresa begins with her glorifiers who removed her from the realm of history and deposited her, during her lifetime, in the realm of myth. It all began with Malcolm Muggeridge's 1969 documentary and 1971 book, *Something Beautiful for God*, which transformed a local social worker into a saint. Muggeridge first came to southern Asia in 1925 as a teacher, then in 1934 as an assistant editor of *The Statesman* of Calcutta (during which time he had an affair with painter Amrita Sher-Gill), and once again in the 1960s to cover the Mother's life. A typical disillusioned imperialist, Muggeridge hated India as much as its "smells and tinkling sounds" entranced him (qtd. in Wolfe 48). Muggeridge's biographer captures his sense of guilt at British imperialism in India, and clearly, Muggeridge sought some easy way to salve this sense of guilt. His theological ruminations allowed for some escape, and his meeting with Mother Teresa enabled him to put his faith in line with his sense of guilt at British rule in India. Anything from the Mother was capable of being rendered in trans-human terms by London's gossip columnist. For example, struck with bad light during the making of the documentary in 1969, Muggeridge claims Mother Teresa performed a "miracle" and allowed for wonderful footage.

Soon, the entire panoply of media and professional mendicants descended upon Calcutta and put the city down in order to lift Mother Teresa up. Calcutta became the ahistorical emblem of distress.[2] Its imperial past and communist present did not enter into this representation of the city. There was no sense of the destruction wrought by the East India Company (few question, for instance, its responsibility for the 1769–70 famine, wherein one third of Bengal's population perished) or by the British Empire (few, indeed, question its role in the 1943 famine, wherein 3 to 5 million people died).[3] These are examples from famines, the more graphic marker of imperialism's practice. Further, there was no interest in the events in East Pakistan (Bangladesh, after 1971), whence 12 million refugees descended upon West Bengal. In short, Muggeridge and his ilk paid little heed to the production and maintenance of poverty in Bengal. At the dawn of independence, Muggeridge returned to India for a brief stopover, and wrote in his diary, "Twilight of Empire. Now the Night" (qtd. in Wolfe 239). The white ruler was to depart and end a form of rule that decimated this part of the globe. Yet, for Muggeridge that rule was still the light, and Indian rule was to be the "night." Racist imperialism redux.

Of Calcutta's poor, the anthropologist Claude Levi-Strauss noted that "they are more like a natural environment which the Indian town needs in order to prosper." India, for him, is a "martyred continent" whose people are not poor for any reason other than demography (Levi-Strauss 133–34). Levi-Strauss, like Lapierre and Muggeridge, relied upon Malthusianism ("overpopulated"), a theory which cannot grasp the structural problems of the region, but which offers cheap slogans in the service of callousness (with very sharp misogynist effects, as in population control policy).[4] These writers turn Calcutta into a vile pit, oppressed by its teeming millions, rather than exploited by the forces of international capital; the salvation of the city is not to be found in anti-capitalist movements, but in the intercession of the proto-saint.

During the period of Muggeridge's visit to Calcutta, the Communist Party of India (Marxist) [CPM], the Communist Party of India [CPI], and the Bangla Congress formed a United Front experiment. They pledged to "govern and mobilize" the people, not simply to perform the tasks of a state in crisis, but also to organize the peasantry and the proletariat, and to devolve power in their hands. During these experiments, the ruling Congress Party and its U.S. allies conducted a reign of terror against the Communists.[5] The work of the United Front was consistently disrupted and the police eliminated many young people for their belief in equality and freedom. (Twelve hundred communist cadres died at the hands of the establishment, to be exact.) The Congress Party, in fact, conducted a dress rehearsal for its Emergency regime (1975–77) in Bengal (1972–75) as it urged the repressive forces to arrest the communists and to harass their organizations. Speaking of the authoritarian Emergency, Mother Teresa told Eileen Egan that "people are happier. There are more jobs. There are no strikes" (qtd. in Egan, *Such a Vision* 405). The trains, as the fascist slogan goes, run on time. Mother Teresa was joined by another "saint," Vinoba Bhave, the Gandhian (of the Mahatama variety), who also supported Mrs. Gandhi's Emergency. Bhave camped out in the center of Delhi, called Mrs. Gandhi's suspension of civil liberties an *Anushasan Parva* (Era of Discipline), and even congratulated her scheme for compulsory sterilization toward population control.[6] Both Bhave and Mother Teresa earned support and goodwill from the political elite, and the Mother was even rewarded with a sentimental "autho-rized" biography by Navin Chawla (an Indira Gandhi loyalist and bureaucrat).

Mother Teresa's sanction of the Emergency glossed over some striking political and economic realities. In 1977, the Left Front (of the CPM, CPI, and other Left allies) won their first of five consecutive elections and, in the past two decades, the Left has enabled significant changes in rural Bengal. West Bengal has only 3.58% of the cultivatable land in the Indian Republic and yet it has contributed over 20% of the total surplus land that falls under the land ceiling laws. Of the 4.8 million acres distributed in the country as a whole, West Bengal contributed 920,000 acres. Further, of the 2 million landless cultivators who received land, 56% came from socially oppressed communities (37% to Scheduled Castes and 19% to Scheduled Tribes). Apart from land reform, the Left Front initiated Operation Barga in 1978 which registered 1.4 million tenant farmers and provided them with legal instruments to stave off eviction and to struggle for shares of the harvest. These initiatives provided an atmosphere in rural areas for the betterment not only of those millions directly affected by the policies, but also for all of rural West Bengal. Now, peasants recognize that they have a friendly government and they are able to bargain more effectively for wages (annual growth rate of real wages from 1980 to 1991 was 5.7% per year) as well as work hard to ensure a steady rise in output (annual growth rate of output from 1980 to 1991 was 5.6% per year). West Bengal now has the highest agricultural growth rate in the country. Two scho-lars note that an important consequence of the Left Front-led "agrarian struggles and the mass mobilization of some of the poorest people for their economic rights has been the raising of political awareness. The poor, therefore, are no longer pli-able clients of local elites, but assertive and vigilant participants in local democ-racy."[7] It serves the anti-Communist pundits well to ignore these developments and to concentrate on saintliness instead. Once the Left is erased, the only hope for the poor appears to be Mother Teresa. Her own history (her past and present) was rapidly superseded by her myth. This was compounded after the Indian govern-ment awarded her the Padma Shri or Order of the Lotus (1962), the Vatican gave her the John XXIII Prize for Peace (1971), the United States honored her with the Good Samaritan prize (1971) and the J. F. Kennedy Award (1971), the British bestowed upon her the Templeton Prize (1973), the United Nations struck a medal in her honor (1975), and she received the Nobel Prize for Peace (1979). These awards removed Mother Teresa from secular history and into a sacred time wherein it became impossible to be rational toward her role in my city.

HOW AGNES BECAME TERESA

To return Mother Teresa to history is to start with her real name and her place of birth. Few know her as Agnes Gonxha Bojaxhiu of Albania (born in Skopje,

Macedonia, 16 August 1910), a young girl who joined the Institute of the Blessed Virgin Mary (the Sisters of Loreto) and came to India in 1929 to teach at one of Loreto's many schools for elite girls. The Loreto order was founded in 1609 by an Englishwoman, Mary Ward (1585–1645), who wished to create an organization parallel to the Society of Jesus, but who had to be content, under Church authority, with an educational order pledged to train the elite across the globe (Peters). Agnes taught for close to two decades in the Loreto schools of Calcutta before she gained exclaustration from the Vatican and founded the Missionaries of Charity (1950) in independent India to continue "Christ's concern for the poor and the lowliest" (as the 120-page constitution of the Missionaries puts it).

The Missionaries set up Homes for the Dying, a leper village, and a Children's Home. They brought relief for many people, if not in medical terms, then certainly in terms of love and affection. Mother Teresa's sisters attempted to soothe the ill and the dying with the balm of love, since many had only rudimentary training in the arts of allopathic medicine (or any medical tradition, for that matter). The Mother herself had spent a few months in 1948 training as a medical missionary with the Medical Missionary Sisters in Patna (founded by Mother Anna Dengel [1892–1980] in 1925 in the United States), but her own sisters did not avail themselves of medical education. In 1994, Dr. Robin Fox visited the Missionaries of Charity in Calcutta and found that the sisters did not utilize modern technology, notably the study of blood to determine such common ailments as malaria from other illnesses. The sisters used no procedures to distinguish the curable from the incurable. "Such systematic approaches are alien to the ethos of the home. Mother Teresa prefers providence to planning; her rules are designed to prevent any drift towards materialism." On the question of pain and its alleviation, the sisters offered no relief for the dying. "I could not judge the power of their spiritual approach," Dr. Fox wrote, "but I was disturbed to learn that the formulary includes no strong analgesics" (807–8).[8] In his mischievous appraisal of Mother Teresa, Christopher Hitchens argues that "the point is not the honest relief of suffering but the promulgation of a cult based on death and suffering and subjection" (*Missionary* 41). Further, he notes, "helpless infants, abandoned derelicts, lepers and the terminally ill are the raw material for demonstrations of compassion. They are in no position to complain, and their passivity and abjection is considered to be a sterling trait" (*Missionary* 50). This is a far cry from the communist experiments.

"Blessed are the poor in spirit," says the Gospel of Matthew, "for theirs is the kingdom of heaven." Poverty is the condition of saintliness, an idea shared by the Christianity of Mother Teresa and the nondenominational saintliness of Mahatma Gandhi. Both identified the poor as the blessed and they both sought not to abolish poverty, but to valorize the poor and suggest that only amongst the poor can one find happiness. Gandhi wrote extensively of the "dignity of poverty" and he urged people to see the joy of poverty. In 1931, he noted in London that those who are in an ideal state of poverty "possess all the treasures in the world. In other words, you really get all that is in reality necessary for you, everything. If food is necessary, food will come to you" (52). Along these lines, Mother Teresa noted that poverty is "beautiful," or, indeed, that "poverty is freedom" (*No Greater* 96). Poverty, then, ceases to be bad, becoming instead something to celebrate. The poor can be treated with condescension as those who will redeem the world by their acceptance of charity. "The poor do not need our compassion or our pity; they need our help," the Mother wrote. "What they give us is more than what we give to them . . . The poor are our prayer," she argued (*No Greater* 102). Or, indeed, the poor are "Christ in his distressing disguise" (qtd. in Muggeridge 97). The poor are, therefore, important for their presence, since the missionaries require their existence to conduct their good works. The causes of poverty and the eradication of poverty are both eclipsed by the condition of patronage demanded of the poor by the charity industry.[9] Upon Mother Teresa's death, her successor Sister Nirmala noted that "poverty will always exist. We want the poor to see poverty in the right way—to accept it and believe that the Lord will provide" (qtd. in Crossette 14). The Missionaries of Charity preach subservience and fatalism, two habits that hold back any hope of the politicization of the poor towards genuine social change. Their approach, fortunately, does not exhaust the wide-ranging positions taken within the Catholic community.

LIBERALISM OF THE CROSS

Pope John XXIII (1958–1963) offered an important encyclical to the Catholic world on 15 May 1961 ("Mater et Magistra"). He urged the church to concern itself with "man's daily life, with his livelihood and education, and his general, temporal welfare and property" (para. 3). The Pope looked back to an historical 1891 encyclical of Pope Leo XIII (1878–1903), which "defended the worker's natural right to enter into association with his fellows" (para. 22). Further, he revisited Leo XIII's criticisms of capitalism as immoral. "Enormous riches accumulated in the hands of the few," John XXIII wrote, "while large numbers of workingmen found themselves in conditions of ever-increasing hardship. Wages were insufficient even to the point of reaching starvation level, and working conditions were often of such a nature as to be injurious alike to health, morality and religious faith" (para. 13). This document, among others, formed the basis for the Second Vatican Council (1962–65), which overturned the conservatism of John XXIII's predecessors. Mother Teresa was consistently opposed to Vatican II and to John XXIII. She welcomed the current Pope, whose fundamentalism and anti-communism on a number of issues came closer to her own brand of Catholicism. Mother Teresa walked in step with Pope John Paul II, who was not only opposed to abortion and women entering the priesthood, but was also not too keen on the radical edge of Liberation Theology. John Paul II invited the "good nun" to the 1980 synod on marriage to denounce abortion and contraception and on 5 February 1994, at the National Prayer Breakfast in Washington D.C., she announced extraordinarily that "the greatest destroyer of peace today is abortion" (qtd. in *National Catholic*). Of both Mother Teresa and Diana Spencer, Katha Pollitt rightly notes that they are "flowers of hierarchical, feudal, essentially masculine institutions in which they had no structural power but whose authoritarian natures they obscured and prettified" (9).

Many believe that Vatican II refounded Catholicism on social justice and radical action in favor of the poor. John XXIII did not, however, champion total engagement with the roots of poverty, for he urged his followers to preserve the right of big capital to hold onto the means of production (what he called "property," but which could hardly mean the meager belongings of the proletariat and the peasantry). Along with Pope Pius XI (1922–39), John XXIII argued for a distinction "between Communism and Christianity," since socialism is "founded on a doctrine of human society which is bounded by time and takes no account of any objective other than that of material well-being" (para. 34). From this caricature of socialism, the Pope urged his flock to eschew making alliances with the Left and he noted that the church must work to ameliorate conflict and to stop "a widespread tendency to subscribe to extremist theories far worse in their effects than the evils they purport to remedy" (para. 14). Many Catholics, however, do work without Vatican sanction, in fact with the "direct disapproval" of the Pope (Vanaik 12). This is the path of Liberation Theology, of some who follow Dorothy Day within the *Catholic Worker*, of those radicals emboldened by the struggles of the figure of Jesus to fight against the causes of poverty, notably in our epoch, the capitalists.[10] Such a tradition includes within it the assassinated Archbishop Oscar Romero of El Salvador who engaged with the structural causes of suffering and did not glorify pain in any way. It includes Daniel Berrigan S. J., who, in 1967, wrote that "killing is disorder[;] life and gentleness and community and unselfishness is the only order we recognize. For the sake of that order, we risk our liberty, our good name. The time is past when good men can remain silent, when obedience can segregate men from public risk, when the poor can die without defense" (qtd. in Zinn 479). It further includes those Catholics in Latin America about whom the Guatemalan military wrote that they saw "no difference between Catholics and the Communist subversives" (qtd. in Dunkerley 494). Mother Teresa was more than scornful of such Catholics, of whom she said, "You have not become priests to be social workers" (*Loving* 46).

If Mother Teresa did not praise the Liberation Theologists, she did find some merit in the argument that our contemporary world tends to dehumanize most people and turn them into so many instruments for the creation of profit. "Poverty doesn't only consist of being hungry for bread," she noted, "but rather it is a tremendous hunger for human dignity. We need to love and to be somebody for someone else. This is where we make our mistake and shove people aside . . . The world today is hungry not only for bread but hungry for love, hungry to be wanted, to be loved"(*No Greater* 93). Mother Teresa recognized the many forces that con-duct anti-capitalist work, a struggle that she did not consider antithetical to her own work. "In the world today there are those whose struggle is for justice and human rights. We have no time for this because we are in daily and continuous contact with people who are starving for a piece of bread and for some affection." Under pressure to make some gesture towards these activists, Mother Teresa declared, "I want to state clearly that I do not condemn those who struggle for justice" (*No Greater* 152). "If people feel it is their vocation to change structures, then that is the work they must do" (qtd. in Egan, "Blessed" 19). Mother Teresa, in other words, worked to provide some basic necessities in the lives of the people although she recognized that she did not address the causes that produced more and more people who would need her care. But if poverty is eradicated, the basis for the Mother's religiosity is put in doubt, for she is clear that the poor are not a symbolic representation of Jesus, "*they are* Jesus" (*In My* 30).

When it comes to an assessment of the structures that produce poverty, Mother Teresa unequivocally distanced herself from those Liberation Theologists and others whom she tactfully did not dismiss directly. "We have no right to judge the rich," she said in a most un-Christian fashion. "For our part, what we desire is not a class struggle, but a class encounter in which the rich save the poor and the poor save the rich" (*No Greater* 97–98). Charity is the only means to salvation, not any funda-mental structural change that might liberate the poor from degradation. Sound-ing almost like Deepak Chopra,[11] Mother Teresa cautioned that "a person who is attached to riches, who lives with the worry of riches, is actually very poor. How-ever, if such a person puts her money at the services of others, then she is rich, very rich" (*No Greater* 47). If one gives money and if one meets the poor, then one is capable of grace and salvation. The poor, on the other hand, are already filled with grace, a state of bliss that they cannot see since they are blinded by a false consciousness of misery. Mother Teresa is able to discount social transformation by recourse not only to the Matthewian idea of poverty as beautiful, but also to the Schumacherian idea that small is beautiful. "If someone feels that God wants from him a transformation of social structures," the Mother wrote, "that's an issue between him and his God . . . I never think in terms of crowds in general but in terms of persons" (*No Greater* 69). The individual person is the atom of her activism, not the social totality that might provide some clues towards exploitation, but that is now rather under pressure from the micro-theory that privileges the local (the individual) over the general. Such an argument allows the Mother to avoid the practice of social change. When asked about injustice, she declines to partici-pate in its abolition, but takes refuge behind those very "large organizations" that she otherwise feels cannot be personal in their actions (*No Greater* 175). The strug-gles of the people are less important than local charity and global transformation —both means to further reduce the power of the people and their capacity to act with dignity and strength.

THE INCORPORATION OF MOTHER TERESA

Perhaps the most disturbing thing about Mother Teresa is the company she kept, partly, I think, for raising money to do her work. She is, of course, not alone, since many nongovernmental organizations (NGOs) are prone to cavort with the rich and famous from whom they secure funds to do their work. The NGO phenomenon raises substantial questions about democracy and the tendency to abandon the state as the site of struggle (that is, to abandon the instrument of the state as a redresser of social wrongs). With the withdrawal of the state from intervention for social justice, notably since the economic downturn from 1967–73, NGOs entered those vacated zones (such as health care, primary education, nutrition). The World Bank, under Robert McNamara, championed the NGO as an alternative to the state, leaving intact global and regional relations of power and production.[12] McNamara made his famous statements about NGOs at the annual meeting of the World Bank's Board of Governors in Nairobi in 1973, about the time when the monetarists (under Milton Friedman and F. A. Hayek) dethroned a watered-down Keynesianism to end faith in state engineering (and to withdraw the state to its role of guardian of property, both as police and as law courts). The monetarist attack on state intervention allowed the NGOs to emerge as a nonstate instrument, to be funded privately, for development. Therefore, NGOs allowed states to reduce taxes and abdicate the creation of social equality. Now, the proletariat and peasantry had to wait upon the charitable benevolence of the rich and the NGOs rather than demand redress from a democratic state. NGOs rely for their sustenance not only upon accountable sources of finance (state funds), but on private donations (such as foundations or from individuals). For the latter, there are many motivations for donation, charity being only one among them. Another, perhaps dominant, strand seeks to rein in the actions of those who are politically organizing the poor towards an eventual confrontation with congealed power.[13] Think of those with whom Mother Teresa was often photographed: Diana Spencer, Michèle Duvalier (wife of the notorious Baby Doc Duvalier), Nancy Reagan, Hilary Clinton, Robert Maxwell, and, finally, Charles Keating.

Charles Keating is remembered as the emblem of the Savings & Loans fiasco, wherein his own Lincoln Savings & Loan Association required a $2 billion bailout by the federal government, due to its licentious expenditure of the public's money.[14] In 1992, Keating was charged with seventy counts of racketeering and fraud, and he spent a brief period of his ten-year sentence in prison before a federal judge found him innocent due to a procedural problem during the trial. Keating not only ripped off U.S. workers of millions of dollars, but he bribed five U.S. Senators (the "Keating Five," which included Senator John McCain) to prevent his prosecution. During his halcyon days, under the false hope of Reaganism, he donated $1.25 million to the Missionaries of Charity and lent his private jet to Mother Teresa for her travels. At the same time, he lent $8.5 million to save his friend Jerry Falwell's ailing organizations; Falwell was an ally from the days when Keating served on a Nixon-appointed anti-pornography commission. When Keating was brought to trial in 1992 (before the court of none other than Judge Lance Ito), Mother Teresa wrote the good judge a letter on behalf of her friend (18 January 1992).[15] The first sentence smacks of hypocritical humility: "We do not mix up in Business or Politicts [sic] or courts." Of course, this is just what the letter attempts to do, since the Mother notes that "Mr. Keating has done much to help the poor, which is why I am writing to you on his behalf." Then, in a Reaganesque manner, Mother Teresa offers ignorance as a cover for her plea on behalf of Keating. "I do not know anything about Mr. Charles Keating's work or his business or the matters you are dealing with. I only know that he has always been kind and generous to God's poor, and always ready to help whenever there was a need." She asks Ito to go inside his heart, pray, and follow the example of Jesus. Either the Mother was naive, which is unlikely, or she did not evince any concern for the means by which Keating made that money (against "God's poor"), only a fraction of which was returned as charity to earn the prestige of Mother Teresa's name.

Mother Teresa, like other "non-political" service organizations, ended up compromising her principles for her benefactors. During the referendum in Ireland to end the constitutional ban on divorce and remarriage in 1995, Mother Teresa traveled around the Emerald Isle, preaching against the feminists for whom this was an important battle. (They won by a narrow 50.3% against 49.7% on 24 November 1995.) At the same time, Charles and Diana Windsor spoke of moving from separation to divorce, as Diana's interview with BBC on 20 November suggested. Mother Teresa, in an interview to *Ladies Home Journal*, noted of that marriage that "no one was happy" (qtd. in Hitchens, "Throne" 7). For those in power, one has one set of principles and for those who are powerless, one has another. The examples are numerous of this form of reversal of principle, but one more will suffice here.

During the night of 2–3 December 1984, methyl isocyanate left the environs of a Union Carbide factory and poisoned thousands of people in Bhopal, India. The Bhopal massacre at the hands of Union Carbide was but the most flagrant example of a transnational corporation's disregard for human life for the sake of its own profit. In 1983, Union Carbide's sales came to $9 billion and its assets totaled $10 billion. Part of this profit came from a tendency to shirk any responsibility towards safety standards, not just in India, but also in Union Carbide's Virginia plant. After the disaster, Mother Teresa flew into Bhopal and, escorted in two government cars, she offered Bhopal's victims small aluminum medals of St. Mary. "This could have been an accident," she told the survivors; "it is like a fire [that] could break out anywhere. That is why it is important to forgive. Forgiveness offers us a clean heart and people will be a hundred times better after it" (qtd. in Jones 32). John Paul II joined Mother Teresa with his analysis that Bhopal was a "sad event," which resulted from "man's efforts to make progress" (qtd. in Jones 298). There is something terrifying about these statements—about the way both religious figures are able to step away from what is widely recognized as a flagrant example of corporate greed.

THE FUTURE'S HARVEST (*THERIZEIN*)

Bengal's proletariat and peasantry are, each day, in the midst of a process of politicization. As a balm, some have taken shelter in the embrace of Mother Teresa (just as they do in the arms of the Ramakrishan Mission or such organizations, less visible to the Euro-American media), and others are mystified by her ceaseless activity. Unlike the bourgeoisie, she remains dressed in simple garments and continues, in a humble fashion, to tread a self-admittedly endless path. Her Sisyphian labor is meaningful to the proletariat, the peasantry, and the unemployed, whose own labor appears in this light. Some of it is meaningful for her kindness in the face of poverty, but there is also the aspect of her being white and yet concerned for the wretched of the earth that plays upon the sentiments of all people. A white woman abandons her country and comes to tend to the refuse of capitalism: this is itself worthy of attention, just as the life of Madeleine Slade (who became Mirabehn to Gandhi) is to those who reflect on modern Indian history.[16] All white women in nonwhite spaces are not, however, the same, since they must also negotiate other political structures such as class and imperialism. There are white women, such as Janet Jagan (former President of Guyana) and Agnes Smedley (a radical who was a communist partisan in China), who are revered for the stands they took in nonwhite places, stands that lost them the privileges of whiteness even as they used these towards radical goals. Mother Teresa is nothing like Janet Jagan or Agnes Smedley, but she is certainly also miles away from Diana Spencer and Cindy Crawford. Her remove from those who revel in privilege, however, should not blind us to the limitations of her own activities.

As lines of demarcation become distinct, as the Communists make clear the different approaches to poverty, the admiration of the people for Mother Teresa will lessen. But this is not an essay about Mother Teresa only. It has attempted to provide a sense of the charity industry, a trough for bourgeois guilt. There will be many Teresas in the future to assuage this sense of guilt, itself unresolvable under the cruel rule of capital.

NOTES

Thanks to Joe Sims who first asked me to write this piece, to Sister Pat Byrne for our conversations, to Rosy Samuel for her faith, to Krishna Raj, Kanak Dixit, Deepak Thapar, Eddie D'Sa, and others who asked me to rewrite this for their journals, to John Hutnyk for his Calcutta, and to Mridul De for his, to Christopher

Hitchens for his book, and to Rajini Srikanth and Samina Najmi for this one. This essay has appeared, in different forms, in *Political Affairs*, vol. 76, no. 9, September 1997 (New York), *Economic and Political Weekly*, 8–14 November 1997 (Mumbai), *Himal South Asia*, December 1997 (Kathmandu), and *Goan Overseas Digest*, vol. 6, no. 1, January-March 1998 (London).

1. And the very best book for this is *After Diana: Irreverent Elegies*, ed. Mandy Merck and Sara Maitland.
2. Without a doubt, Dominique Lapierre's bestseller, *The City of Joy* (1985), and the popular Hollywood movie contributed to this image. See John Hutnyk's excellent *The Rumour of Calcutta*.
3. On the 1943 famine, see Sen.
4. See Naila Kabeer, *Reversed Realities*.
5. On the issue of the United States, most people are unaware of Daniel P. Moyniham's revelation from 1978: "We had twice, but only twice, interfered in Indian politics to the extent of providing money to a political party. Both times it was done in the face of a prospective Communist Victory in a state election, once in Kerala and once in West Bengal, where Calcutta is located" (*A Dangerous Place* 41).
6. See *Amrita Bazar Patrika* and my "Emergency Assessments."
7. Sunil Sengupta and Haris Gazdar, "Agrarian Politics and Rural Development in West Bengal," 159. This is also the verdict of G.K. Lieten and Neil Webster.
8. See also S. E. Kellogg, 5–11.
9. This is despite Mother Teresa's enigmatic comment that "poverty has not been created by God. We are the ones who have created poverty. Before God, we are all poor" (*In My Own Words* 30).
10. An excellent introduction is provided in Michael Lowy, *The War of Gods*.
11. For Deepak Chopra, see my *Karma of Brown Folk* 47–68.
12. See *World Bank's Partnership*.
13. See Prakash Karat, *Foreign Funding*.
14. See Michael Binstein and Charles Bowden, *Trust Me*.
15. Qtd. at length in Hitchens, *Missionary Position* 64–71. Also see Hitchens's and Tariq Ali's documentary *Hell's Angels*, for Channel 4, in 1994.
16. Much could be written about Mirabehn, who came to Gandhi's ashram in 1925 and lived in India till her death. When Mirabehn first wore Indian clothes, Gandhi was "definitely displeased, but he restrained the expression of his feelings." There was a fear that a white woman may not know what to do if assaulted as an Indian. When Mirabehn, dressed as an Indian, was insulted in a racist manner at the Taj Mahal hotel in Bombay, Gandhi "laughed heartily and said, "That was a fine experience for you." As a white woman, Mirabehn earned certain privileges, but she was willing to risk these for the cause, something that earned her the respect of Gandhi and the other nationalists (Madeleine Slade 80–87).

80 Prashad

WORKS CITED

Binstein, Michael, and Charles Bowden. *Trust Me: Charles Keating and the Missing Billions*. New York: Random House, 1993.

Crossette, Barbara. "Pomp Pushes the Poorest from Mother Teresa's Last Rites." *New York Times* 14 Sept. 1997: 14.

Dunkerley, James. *Power in the Isthmus: A Political History of Modern Central America*. London: Verso, 1988.

Egan, Eileen. "'Blessed Are the Merciful': Mother Teresa (1910-1997)." *America* 20 Sept. 1997: 19.

———. *Such a Vision of the Street: Mother Teresa, the Spirit and the Work*. Garden City: Doubleday, 1985.

Fox, Robin. "Mother Teresa's Care for the Dying." *Lancet* 344.8925 (17 Sept. 1994): 807–8.

Gandhi, M. K. *Socialism of My Conception*. Ahmedabad: Navajivan, 1966.

Hitchens, Christopher. *The Missionary Position: Mother Teresa in Theory and Practice*. London: Verso, 1995.

———. "Throne and Altar." *Nation* 29 Sept. 1997: 7.

Hutnyk, John. *Rumour of Calcutta: Tourism, Charity, and the Poverty of Representation*. London: Zed, 1996.

Jones, Tara. *Corporate Killing: Bhopals Will Happen*. London: Free Association, 1988.

Kabeer, Naila. *Reversed Realities: Gender Hierarchies in Development Thought*. London: Verso, 1994.

Karat, Prakash. *Foreign Funding and the Philosophy of Voluntary Organisations*. New Delhi: National Book Centre, 1988.

Kellogg, S. E. "A Visit with Mother Teresa and the Missionaries of Charity in Calcutta." *American Journal of Hospice and Palliative Care* 11.5 (Sept. 1994): 5–11.

Lapierre, Dominique. *The City of Joy*. Garden City: Doubleday, 1985.

Leiten, G. K. *Continuity and Change in Rural West Bengal*. Delhi: Sage, 1992.

Lenin, V. I. "Socialism and Religion." *Collected Works*, volume 10. Moscow: Foreign Languages Publishing House, 1962.

Levi-Strauss, Claude. *Tristes Tropiques*. Harmondsworth: Penguin, 1992.

Lowy, Michael. *The War of the Gods: Religion and Politics in Latin America*. London: Verso, 1996.

Merck, Mandy, and Sara Maitland, eds. *After Diana: Irreverent Elegies*. London: Verso, 1998.

Mother Teresa. *In My Own Words*. Ed. Jose Luis Gonzalez-Balado. New York: Gramercy, 1996.

———. *Loving Jesus*. Ed. Jose Luis Gonzalez-Balado. Ann Arbor: Servant, 1991.

———. *No Greater Love*. Novato: New World Library, 1989.

Moynihan, Daniel. *A Dangerous Place*. London: Secker & Warburg, 1979.

Muggeridge, Malcolm. *Something Beautiful for God: Mother Teresa of Calcutta*. New York: Harper & Row, 1971.

National Catholic Reporter 19 Sept. 1997.

Peters, Henriette. *Mary Ward: A World in Contemplation*. Leominster: Gracewing, 1994.

Pollitt, Katha. "Thoroughly Modern Di." *Nation* 29 Sept. 1997: 9.

Prashad, Vijay. "Emergency Assessments." *Social Scientist* 24.9-10 (Sept. 1996).

Karma of Brown Folk. Minneapolis: U of Minnesota P, 2000.

Sen, A. K. "Famine Mortality: A Study of the Bengal Famine of 1943." *Peasants in History: Essays in Honour of Daniel Thorner*. Ed. E. J. Hobsbawm. Calcutta: Sameeksha Trust and Oxford UP, 1980.

Sengupta, Sunil, and Haris Gazdar, "Agrarian Politics and Rural Development in West Bengal." *Indian Development: Seclected Regional Perspectives*. Eds. Jean Dreze and Amartya Sen. Delhi: Oxford UP, 1996.

Slade, Madeleine. *The Spirit's Pilgrimage*. New York: Coward-McCann, 1960.

Vanaik, Achin. "No Sense of Proportion." *Hindu* 12 Sept. 1997: 12.

Ware, Vron. *Beyond the Pale: White Women, Racism, and History*. London: Verso, 1992.

Webster, Neil. *Panchayati Raj and the Decentralization of Development Planning in West Bengal*. Calcutta: K. P. Bagchi, 1992.

Wolfe, Gregory. *Malcolm Muggeridge: A Biography*. Grand Rapids: Eerdmans, 1995.

World Bank's Partnership with Nongovernmental Organizations. Washington, D.C.: World Bank, 1996.

Zinn, Howard. *A People's History of the United States*. New York: Harper, 1990.

PART TWO

White American Womanhood

CHAPTER FIVE

Ventriloquism in the Captivity Narrative

White Women Challenge
European American Patriarchy

RAJINI SRIKANTH

Captivity narratives were extraordinarily popular in America between the mid-seventeenth and mid-nineteenth centuries. If we are to believe the figures, it would appear that tens of thousands of men, women, and children were held captive for varying periods of time by Indian tribes (Derounian-Stodola and Levernier 2). There were between 450 and 500 narratives of these captivities published in over 1,200 editions (Kestler xiii). In this paper, I focus on a subset of these narratives—those written by white women, specifically those of European ancestry.[1] Much scholarship has been devoted to the role of captivity narratives in serving, for a period of three hundred years, the Puritans, revolutionaries, and westward-moving settlers to establish their moral claim to American soil over what they believed to be the "indolent," "savage," and "barbaric" Indians;[2] it is not my intention to rehearse these nation-building functions of the captivity narratives. Rather, I seek to explore specific rhetoric within selected white female captivity narratives so as to demonstrate that the captives' focus on the Indian as the racial Other permitted a surreptitious challenge to European American patriarchy. I wish to examine the importance of the captivity narrative as a forum for female expression and empowerment and to explore to what extent this empowerment was made possible by the racialized nature of the captivity experience. I argue that the captivity narrative provided a safe and acceptable space in which to articulate a new version of European American womanhood. Admittedly, the challenge to patriarchy was obliquely delivered, but the value of the narrative is that it permitted the woman, returned from captivity, the opportunity to reflect upon the extraordinary enlargement of her capacity for thought and action.

Mary Rowlandson, the most famous of the North American white female captives and the one most frequently studied, views her telling as a form of enhanced self-knowledge: "that I may the better declare what happened to me" (12). Barbara Rodriguez examines Rowlandson's narrative as the self-enabling move of a woman who during her captivity was seen and saw herself as an object that could be priced and traded (50–95). Speaking of seventeenth-century women and their captivity narratives, Tara Fitzpatrick declares that "as the primary tellers of their tales, the women captives became the active authors of their own histories, defying if never escaping the traditionally masculine authority and authorship central to the Puritan sexual order" (5). For those women who did not write the narrative themselves (frequently, because of lack of education),[3] and who, therefore, spoke their narratives to scribes, the captivity tale was the first attempt at a public voice, delivering a message that would be taken seriously and that would not endanger them for presuming to speak in the heavily patriarchal *zeitgeist* of colonial, revolutionary and postrevolutionary America.[4] It is not clear to what extent the process of constructing the captivity narrative enabled women to effect changes in their restrictively gendered roles post-captivity, but for those who chose to speak about the experience, these narratives frequently served as the texts in which they were able to erect and preserve an image of themselves as resolute survivors and skillful strategists.

VENTRILOQUISM AND CHALLENGE

It might be helpful to consider ventriloquism in attempting to understand the means by which the captivity narrative served women as a nonthreatening medium in which to test out the limits of transgression, challenge, and resistance. Ventriloquism enables the "projecting" speaker to subvert without appearing to do so, because the transgressive message is disembodied, that is, appears to be coming not from the speaker but from some "figure" out there. That "speaking" figure is, not surprisingly, some inanimate representation of a lifelike form. The ventriloquist can channel the most radical messages through this obviously doll-like and essentially voiceless figure and so permit the audience/reader to "toy" with the subversive idea. I would suggest that the captivity narrative served the seventeenth, eighteenth, or nineteenth-century women a function similar to the ventriloquist's disruptive message spoken through some figure "out there," removed, and at a distance from the real speaker. Steven Connor, in his *Dumbstruck: A Cultural History of Ventriloquism* (2000), uses the word "ventriloquism" "to designate all of the many forms of "sourceless" or "dissociated" or "disssimulated" voices, and links ventriloquism with "divine annunciation, oracular utterance, [and] the voices of those seemingly possessed by the spirits" (23–24). The history of ventriloquism, from as early as the Greeks to the nineteenth century "reveals the complex alternations between . . . two contrasting possibilities"—one, "the power to speak through others" and, the other, "the experience of being spoken through by others" (Connor 14). In both cases, women used ventriloquism as a vehicle to express themselves against the authority of the Church and against patriarchal dictates, and, especially in the eighteenth and nineteenth centuries, ventriloquism came to be located within the context of resistance to and transgression of authority. In an earlier version of the discussions contained in his book, Connor argues that the

> dissociated voice is a recurrent source of excess, menace and awe. Because it is a category of excess, a figure of nonfigurability, it has no one meaning. . . . [L]ike the neurotic symptom, it is both wound and cure, enigma and explication, trauma and therapy. But we can also see . . . that the dissociations and resituations of the voice are always a matter of power. Firstly, the dissociated voice of ventriloquial fantasy mediates between the body and language, which is to say also between the body and culture. The variability of the voice's origin, whether magically detached from the body, or erupting from illegitimate orifices, means that the ventriloquial voice is both an attempt to imagine and pit the speech of the body against the speech of culture, and an attempt to control that illegitimate speech, to draw it into discourse. It is for this reason that the ventriloquial voice is associated both with challenges to political authority, and with their reassertion. For the voice is the mark both of the self's presence to and its estrangement from itself; *the ventriloquial voice enacts the strangeness of the self's self-presence.* (internet entry, "A Cultural History of Ventriloquism"; emphasis added)

I quote at length from Connor because his argument helps to illuminate the paradox of the captivity narrative—how it is both an assertion of the white woman's strength and power and, at the same time, a reminder/remembrance of her powerlessness. In the writing of the narrative, the "redeemed" woman re-creates a time of an alternate selfhood even as she now, in the voice of the woman safely returned to the European American community, underscores the difference between that subjectivity and her present one. My contention is that the evocation of that alternate subjectivity was made possible in large part as a consequence of the racialized context in which that new subjectivity first came to be. The white woman was permitted to display behavior contrary to what was deemed desirable in order to survive in an environment of racial Others. The racial Otherness of her captors may have, in fact, been seen as the "corrupting" influence that made possible the transformation of her "essential" character.

CAPTIVITY, POST-CAPTIVITY, AND GENDER ROLES

Many women carried into their post-captivity lives aspects of that transformation from obedient helpmeet to independent thinker. Lyle Koehler, in his study of seventeenth-century New England women, observes that

> Indian warfare worked against the orthodox Puritan sex role by virtu-
> ally requiring women to assume a rather "masculine" energy and spirit.
> Forced to endure long marches by summoning up every ounce of courage,
> captive women sometimes held themselves ready to flee into the unfami-
> liar wilderness if a suitable opportunity arose. (429)

Women who had endured such an experience, says Koehler, "could hardly have
found it easy to be deferential, passive wives" (429). Referring to women in Massachusetts, he declares that their challenge to Puritan patriarchy was augmented by
widows and orphans from Maine who, during the 1690s, fled to the Bay Colony
to escape Indian attacks. Many of these women

> were more joy-loving, more assertive, and quicker to abuse the authori-
> ties than were their Massachusetts counterparts. Through the refugees'
> personal example and their zealous search for employment, they too
> helped to accelerate the process of change, particularly sex-role change,
> in places like Boston, Charlestown, and Salem. (430)

I do not by any means wish to give the impression that women who escaped from
captivity or were ransomed back to their communities suddenly became empowered and unproblematically transgressive. Quite the contrary. Many were viewed
with suspicion, believed to have had their sexual purity tainted; many suffered
from "captivity neurosis"—a condition Koehler describes as being characterized
by insomnia, extreme guilt, and perpetual watchfulness. Post-captivity life underscored the *difference* between women who had endured captivity and those who
had not undergone the same experience.

It is precisely to this difference, however, that I wish to draw attention. The
cataclysmic upheaval of the women's pre-captivity lives made possible a radical
restructuring of their own consciousness. The language of twentieth-century anthropological fieldwork—fieldwork being an experience that is at one level akin to and
at another level dramatically different from captivity—might help one to appreciate the extent to which many of these women had to reorder the most basic
conceptions of their European American world view. The female captive found
herself in a situation in which she was thrown entirely upon her own resources.
The experience of captivity made of the captive a participant-observer of the highest degree. The immediate immersion in another culture forced a reconsideration
of how she would survive; she had to learn how to decode the new space and
function within its parameters. Her survival depended on her being able "to become"
Indian, to discard the inhibitions that served as a barrier between herself and her
captors. Her interactions could not, therefore, be controlled encounters with another
culture, could not be characterized by the quality of immersion-yet-detachment
that has traditionally marked the ethnographer's involvement with the culture/
group being observed and studied (see Trinh T. Minh-ha's critique of Western

anthropology).[5] In her position of becoming, by necessity, fully involved with the activities of the tribe whose captive she was, the white woman exhibited a "crossing over" into a reality different from the one she had hitherto known. The "crossing over" whether made temporarily until release or permanently, in the case of trans-culturated captives was undertaken with volition, a conscious decision that survival depended on learning quickly the social nuances of American Indian life. (Mary Jemison and Eunice Williams were among the most famous of women who prefer-red not to be "rescued" and chose to remain with the Indians.)[6] There is little evi-dence to tell us the extent to which this newly acquired understanding of another culture, this reorientation of world view, manifested itself in the women's thinking once they escaped or were released from captivity. But the record of transculturated captives indicates that for some, at least, return to their pre-captive lives was an unwelcome prospect. Thus, what is surprising is not that the captured women were able to reorient their thinking, but that they chose to reject a once-familiar world when given the opportunity to return to it. Mary Jemison, in fact, attained the status of a leader in her adopted tribe.

There is evidence to suggest that in some Native American tribes women enjoyed far more liberated roles than European American women did in their communities. The story of Benjamin Hawkins, an agent for the Creek Indians in 1797, is illustrative. Hawkins was approached by an elderly Creek woman with the request that he wed her widowed daughter. Wanting to ensure that he would wield complete control over his wife and children after the marriage, he drew up a contract, which, in part, read: "The ways of white people differ much from those of the red people, . . . white men govern their families." He insisted that his wife would have to agree to his raising the children (even hers by a previous marriage) as *he* pleased, and that no one in her family would oppose him. He added, "The red women should always be proud of their white husbands, . . . should always take part with them and obey them, should make the children obey them, and they will be obedient to their parents and make a happy family." When the old Creek woman understood his conditions, she withdrew her request to him, unwilling to let her daughter enter a situation in which "the women and children would be under the direction of the father" (Norton 94).

In 1833, J. & J. Harper of New York published *Sketches of the Lives of Distin-guished Females* as part of its series Library of Useful and Entertaining Knowledge for Boys and Girls. I use this work as a springboard into a gender-based discussion of possible reasons for overwhelming male interest in the captivity narrative, an interest separate from the obvious agenda of nation-building against the backdrop of the conquered racial Other. Preceding the title page of the book are two illus-trations—on the left-hand page, a portrait of Ann Judson, a woman who went with her husband to India as a missionary. On the facing page appear the title of the book and, below it, an illustration captioned "Burning of a Widow in India." It is entirely possible to see this illustration as a logical accompaniment to Ann Judson's portrait; after all she did "distinguish" herself in India. Perhaps one could also attribute the illustration to the penchant for the exotic and the sensational, an inclination that would explain the enormous popularity of the captivity narrative and its rapid development in the nineteenth century into the "penny dreadful" genre. However, I want to push the implications further and suggest that widow burning held a particular perverse fascination for the male gaze because it so graphically underscored the woman's helplessness and victimization, at the same time that it privileged her eternal loyalty and allegiance to her deceased husband. In choosing to grace this particular text with this illustration, the publishers perhaps wished to offer to their readers an example of female servitude even while condemning such a practice, and in the condemnation to remind their female readers of how much they had to be thankful for in being spared the necessity of making such an extreme sacrifice in honor of their husbands. The narrative of Ann Judson within the book makes merely a cursory reference to widow burning; it is part of a list of self-destructive practices that the Hindus are said to follow.[7] Therefore, the prominent placement of the illustration seems entirely gratuitous unless one understands it within the larger context of the book's agenda: "written for girls with a view to their mental and moral development" (title page). The young girls were being instructed to emulate women who were accomplished but ultimately subservient, adventurous but always within the limits of womanly restraint. Referring to the ancient Arab queen Zenobia, the female narrator of the text says,

> Ambition, my dear children, . . . was the cause of her downfall. Had she been content with a small kingdom, she might have died, as she had lived, a great queen, and a great woman; but she grasped at too much, and lost all. She was not satisfied with being queen of Palmyra, but she aimed to become the rival of Rome, in the extent of her dominion, and in the number of her conquests; and this competition was fatal both to her and to her country. (35–36)

Lata Mani, in her analysis of nineteenth-century British texts on bride burning in India, points to the curious voyeurism evident in these colonial accounts: the women are given no voice and rendered entirely powerless, while the male eyewitness of the British empire gazes at her helplessness, stricken with pity for the beautiful young woman, observing her victimization. Watching as a widow is being led to the funeral pyre, one of the officers of the British empire's government tells us that he

> stood close to her, she observed [him] attentively. . . . She might be about twenty-four or five years of age, a time of life when the bloom of beauty had fled the cheek in India; but she still preserved a sufficient share to prove that she must have been handsome. Her figure was small, but elegantly turned; and the form of her hands and arms was peculiarly beautiful. (Mani 400)

Mani remarks that "[s]uch 'tender' descriptions of the personal appearance and beauty of widows suggests the voyeuristic pleasure of a specifically male gaze, contemplating what it constructs as the wife devoted to her husband in death as in life" (400).

Notwithstanding the obvious differences between captivity narratives and British accounts of widow burning, it is possible to detect a parallel between the two types of texts. The overwhelming male interest in the publication and widespread distribution of captivity narratives (after all, men, not women, controlled access to publishing and distribution) perhaps indicates a desire to experience vicariously the pleasure of keeping women in their appropriate places, of underscoring their helpless and subordinate positions.

VICTIMHOOD VERSUS
DISPLAYS OF STRENGTH AND CUNNING

June Namias notes incisively that three particular archetypes of white female captives span the centuries in which the genre was immensely popular and that the three archetypes of Survivor, Amazon, and Frail Flower correspond roughly to three identifiable eras of American history: colonial, revolutionary, and the westward-expansion period between 1820 and 1870 (Namias 24). In describing the Frail Flower type, Namias writes that

> the most complete renditions of the Frail Flower do not appear until the 1830s and 1840s, and they correspond to the rise of True Womanhood and the mass marketing of sentimental fiction. . . . Th[e sentimental] heroine turns frailty, motherhood, cleanliness, and disgusting Indians into highly salable works. The Frail Flower appears frequently in such narratives. She is the poor, hapless woman who is taken unawares. She is shocked and distressed by her capture and by the deaths and dislocations that go with it. What makes her a candidate for Frail Flower status is that she rarely emerges from her shock, distress, and misery. Frail Flower narratives include brutality, sadomasochistic and titillating elements, strong racist language, pleas for sympathy and commiseration with the author's suffering, special appeals for her sad lot as a distressed mother. (36–37)

The helpless white female captive enables a construction of the American Indian male as demonic, and therefore to be feared and aggressively resisted. Minrose Gwin has pointed to a similar deployment of the image of the frail, pure, and chaste Southern white woman in the construction of the image of the bestial and dangerous African American male slave. Thus, the portrayal of weak or helpless white females against the backdrop of undesirable racial Other males suggests the desirability of white males and reinforces Euro-American patriarchy.

Subtexts of various captivity narratives give the lie to the Frail Flower image, even during the nineteenth-century expansion of the nation (the historical period in which Frail Flower depictions abound). Mary Kinnan's brief narrative offers a melding of resourceful and strong woman on the one hand and sentimental and melodramatic victim on the other. First published in 1795, Kinnan's account of her three-year captivity among the Shawnees alternates between the rhetoric of helplessness and that of clear-minded and cautious pragmatism. The same woman who early in her captivity becomes "indifferent to [her] existence" and contemplates killing herself (VanDerBeets 323), "who yielded [herself] up entirely to despondency, and endeavored to stifle the few scattered rays of hope, which faintly twinkled, like the glimmerings of a lamp just ready to expire" (VanDerBeets 328–329), becomes the woman who can summon up enough energy and resources to effect her escape. In describing the circumstances of her escape Kinnan's prose is unadorned and rather businesslike, in contrast to the heavy sentimentality of the language that recalls her weakness:

> I heard from my brother, who had joined a party of British traders, and was coming down to the Rapids that he might see me, and perhaps assist me to escape. . . .
>
> In order to concert some means of escape, my brother sent a friend to exchange bread for milk. After performing this errand, he opened to me his real business, and appointed a tree where I might meet my brother that night. According to these directions I went, and how great was my surprise and disappointment to find nobody there. But the person who had previously appointed the tree as a place to meet, explained to me the next day the reason why we missed of each other, we having gone to different trees. The next night, however, the Indians having fallen asleep, I stole out about eleven o' clock. (330)

I would argue that the sentimentalized and weakened captive that emerges in portions of Kinnan's narrative serves to mask the woman of fortitude, an individual capable of surviving disappointment and disaster and resilient enough to persist in her efforts to gain freedom. Frail Flowers served as useful disguises (not only to mislead the Indian captors but also the white male reader) behind which a resolute and quick-thinking woman was carefully planning her escape (not only from the experience of physical captivity but also from the psychological captivity within which she was being held by Euro-American patriarchy).

Languishing victims, they were not. In 1864, Fanny Kelly was captured by Sioux Indians while she and her family were journeying from Kansas to Idaho. She was a prisoner for five months before being released to a United States garrison at Fort Sully in the Dakota territory. Mrs. Kelly, a skillful and resourceful woman, was largely responsible for crafting the strategy that ultimately made possible her release. The Indians had intended to use her as a type of "Trojan Horse" to enter the fort and once inside to kill the soldiers there. But Fanny Kelly foiled that attempt, employing an ingenious mix of manipulation, ruse, and deceit. She used a young Indian by the name of Jumping Bear as her courier, cajoling him to deliver a letter from her to the commanding officer at the garrison. Jumping Bear had developed a passion for Fanny Kelly, and she exploited his feelings, telling him that he could prove his devotion by carrying a letter from her to the fort. It was in this letter that she warned the garrison of the impending attack. With great pride, she declares the importance of that letter: "A written statement from Lieutenant Hesselberger, setting forth the fact of my writing and sending the letter of warning, and that it undoubtedly was the means of saving the garrison at Fort Sully from massacre, is on file in the Treasury Department at Washington" (201). Fanny Kelly duped the naïve Jumping Bear to establish herself as a formidable agent for her nation.

This same Fanny Kelly is rendered in quite different terms in a poem written by a soldier in dedication to her. Describing her life with the Indians, he observes,

> . . . you, a captive, stand among the dead;/ For months in bondage to this savage band,/ With none to rescue from his cruel hand,/ To rove with them o'er prairies far and wild,/ Far from thy husband and thy murdered child./ No star of hope, nor sun's resplendent light,/ Sends down one gleam upon this fearful night;/ No power to pierce the dark and hidden gloom,/ That veils the heart while in this earthly tomb./ But, lo! A change, a wondrous change, to thee!/ Once held a captive, but now from bondage free. (269)

Notice the miraculous nature of the rescue in the words, "But, lo! A change, a wondrous change, to thee!" Fanny Kelly is granted no agency, her rescue in its fantastical quality curiously echoing the fairy tales of Sleeping Beauty, Cinderella, and Snow White, in which passive and silenced women are rescued from bondage to spells or other evil influences by men active in the pursuit of their freedom.[8] Fanny Kelly's captivity narrative, *My Captivity Among the Sioux Indians*, fills the gap, the silence, between the "earthly tomb" predicament and the "But, lo!" exaltation of the rescue. Published in 1871 and in length approximately 63,000 words, her narrative gives voice to her acumen, daring, resourcefulness, fortitude, and quick-thinking. The racialized nature of the experience—the racial Otherness of her captors—underscores the intensity of the test, the rigor of the challenge. Even a cursory glance at randomly selected captivity narratives will reveal the frequency of such epithets as "savage," "demonic," "bestial," and "wily" to describe the American Indians. The Indian captors provided the foil to the white woman's reconceptualization of herself as courageous, inventive, and powerful. The "weaker sex," in these narratives, surprised herself, exhibiting characteristics far removed from the domain of womanhood as it was then conceived.

THE RACIAL OTHER AND
ACCEPTABLE WHITE FEMALE VIOLENCE

Several captivity narratives are marked by displays of ferocious violence on the part of white female captives, even by those who initially portray themselves as help-less and utterly distraught. These descriptions of white female aggressive behavior are frequently so graphic that they can only be comprehended and assimilated within the context of the Indian's racial Otherness. In emphasizing race, I depart slightly from Michelle Burnham who, in her brilliant analysis of Hannah Dustan's violent massacre of her captors, makes the point that people accept Dustan's uncha-racteristically violent act because it takes place within the gendered context of motherhood and female chastity. Dustan was seized in 1697 when her husband was absent from home. She had only recently given birth to a child and was made to watch the Indians kill the infant and then forced to walk miles through the wilderness. Fearful of being raped and as an act of revenge for her murdered child, Dustan convinces her fellow captives (her midwife and a young boy) to assist her in killing ten sleeping Indians. As Burnham points out, Dustan used a very "Indianized" form of aggression—massacring her erstwhile captors with tomahawks and then scalping them (52). While I agree with Burnham in her claim that Dus-tan's obviously gendered impulses of motherly love and protection of sexuality made it possible for Cotton Mather and his contemporaries to accept and even extol her extreme violence, I would argue that it was also the race of the victims that miti-gated the threat to Euro-American patriarchy contained in Dustan's murderous rampage.

Gary Ebersole reminds us that even in nineteenth-century America, almost two hundred years after Dustan's axing of her captors, female violence generated great anxiety. In the

> plethora of nineteenth-century prints, etchings, paintings, sculptures, and stage performances based on the captivity theme [. . .] the woman who used violent (normally male) means to save herself or her family mem-bers was frequently associated with the figure of the Amazon or of mar-tial queens, such as the African Zenobia. Such women, though, usually were portrayed as finally subdued and in chains themselves." (221–22)

That the anxiety was lessened when female violence was directed at Indians is evident in the following 1849 document, "A White Man's Rationale for Killing Indians on the Overland Trail":

> One evening, after camping, a scout of the Oregon party rode in and reported a party of Indians camped about five miles ahead, about twenty in number; . . . All were up in arms in a few minutes, and ready to start for them. *The women were as much excited as the men.* But the captain put

a stop to their haste; told them the better plan would be to wait till night and crawl carefully out and bag the whole party. His plan was adopted, and guns were cleaned and ammunition looked after. It was arranged that some should remain with the women and children, and the rest to start about eleven o' clock, surround their camp, and at a signal rush in and surprise the ferocious native. Three of our party volunteered —there was no lack of volunteers, the trouble was, all wanted to go, which would leave the homeguard too small. But the women were not afraid to remain alone; *they wanted the "red devils rubbed out," as they expressed it*. (286, emphasis added)

One could minimize the impact of race on the emergence of female violence and trace it back to fears of violated sexuality or protective motherhood. Certainly, it would be impossible to disentangle the relationship between the racialized Other and the perceived threat to one's womanhood from that racialized Other. But the captivity narrative genre offers us at least one example of violence which resists easy explanations along the axis of womanhood. Race and gender intersect in complex ways in an incident recounted in Rachel Plummer's captivity narrative. Plummer was captured in 1836 in Texas by Comanches and spent two years in captivity. Having grown despondent at the length of her capture and not wishing to live any longer, Plummer informs her reader that she decides to be disobedient in the hope of inviting violence upon herself from the Comanches. Consequently, when she is ordered by her mistress to go back to town to get an implement used in the digging of roots, Plummer refuses to comply. A spirited fight, remarkable for its physicality, ensues between the two women, at the end of which a victorious Plummer exhibits compassion for her antagonist:

I told her I would not go back. She, in an enraged tone, bade me go. I told her I would not. She then with savage screams ran at me. I knocked, or, rather pushed her down. She, fighting and screaming like a desper- ado, tried to get up; but I kept her down; and in the fight I got hold of a large buffalo bone. I beat her over the head with it, expecting at every moment to feel a spear reach my heart from one of the Indians; but I lost no time. I was determined if they killed me, to make a cripple of her. . . . I had her past hurting me, and indeed, nearly past breathing, when she cried out for mercy. I let go my hold of her . . . She was bleed- ing freely; for I had cut her head in several places to the skull. I raised her up and carried her to the camp. (353)

The text is noteworthy for the various underlying messages it contains. First, it draws attention to a dormant yet potent aggressiveness within the white woman. Second, that the violence is called into play not in the defense of sexual purity or the pro- tection of one's child is also significant, suggesting that there are other conditions under which women can be moved to aggressive behavior. Finally, in displaying her aggression at an American Indian woman, Plummer renders her violence less threatening, more acceptable, to the Euro-American male. It is as though she warns of her capacity for violence while, almost in the same breath, tempering the warning by inscribing it within the context of the racialized Other female.

Plummer's display of physical aggressiveness and compassion for her victim win her the praise of one of the big chiefs of the tribe:

> You are brave to fight—good to a fallen enemy—you are directed by the Great Spirit. Indians do not have pity on a fallen enemy. By our law you are clear. It is contrary to our law to show foul play. She began with you, and you had a right to kill her. Your noble spirit forbid you. (353–54)

Here, too, Plummer both identifies with and sets herself apart from her captors. She has fought like an Indian but, in withholding the final blow, she has displayed her whiteness. At least, that is the message one can glean from her narration of this incident.

The body of the Indian male—in the case of Hannah Dustan—and the body of the Indian female—in Plummer's story—become the sites upon which the two white female captives enact a new version of self. The majority of captivity narratives begin with a graphic description of the destruction of home—even when that home consists only of a train of wagons moving westward. The physical destruction of home marks the onset of a psychological journey away from notions of womanhood associated with that home. Connor's phrase "the strangeness of the self's self-presence" is a particularly useful way of understanding the relationship between the narrator of the captivity narrative and the captive of whom she speaks. The racialized nature of the captive's experience underscores the strangeness of that other self. Her narrating voice, its discourse firmly grounded within the body politic of the Euro-American world, evokes a body and voice out there that is part of that Other world of the un-Christian wilderness. While that captive body appears to be powerless, the subtext of the captivity narratives suggests otherwise.

ALLURE OF THE RACIAL OTHER

A slightly different trajectory of patriarchal challenge than that found in the subset of captivity narratives discussed thus far manifests itself in the suggestion—both in captivity narratives and in works of fiction—that the racial Other, that is, the Indian male, might actually be more appealing than the Euro-American patriarchs would have one believe. Mary Rowlandson speaks of her captors' solicitousness for her comfort and feelings on several occasions: for example, in "The Fifth Remove," when they ensure that her feet do not get wet when they cross a river even though several of the Indians are themselves knee-deep in water; in "the Eighth

Remove," when they comfort her, tell her that no harm will come to her, and offer her spoonfuls of meal; and also in "The Eighth Remove," when King Phillip pays her for her seamstressing services and treats her with friendship. Rowlandson, of course, attributes their good treatment of her to God's intervention and his constant watchfulness over his flock (53). Elizabeth Hanson, who was taken captive in Dover in 1724, recounts the kindness of her Indian master who was "humane enough to carry [her] babe in his arms; which [she] looked upon as a singular favor, because he had besides a very heavy burden, and considerably more than he could take up without the help of his men (134). She declares that she found in him "more civility and humanity than [she] could have expected (135). Although, like Rowlandson, Hanson attributes the Indians' kindness to God's hand, these suggestions of Indian goodwill and empathy are significant interventions in the patriarchal narrative of the uncivilized savage. Yet, the extraordinary nature of the captivity experience, the mind-altering qualities of the tumultuous disruption of the women's pre-captivity lives, gives to these accounts of Indian gentleness the otherworldly outer body characteristics of the ventriloquist's message.

A bold challenge to the patriarchal depiction of the undesirable Indian male is offered by Lydia Child in her 1824 fictional narrative, *Hobomok*. But she, too, tempers her alternative vision, as will become evident below. Her work is significant not only for the prospect of interracial marriage that it presents but also because it offers a convincing demonstration of ventriloquism (as defined by Connor) as a mode of resistance and subversion. In Child's novel, a Puritan maiden weds an Indian male.[9] Mary Conant, the daughter of a rigid Puritan patriarch marries the Indian Hobomok when she receives news (false, as it ultimately turns out) of her fiance's death at sea. Note closely the language Child uses to describe the moment of Mary's "consciously" made decision:

> There was a chaos in Mary's mind;—a dim twilight, which had first made all objects shadowy, and which was rapidly darkening into misery, almost insensible of its source. The sudden stroke which had dashed from her lips the long promised cup of joy, had almost hurled reason from his throne. What now had life to offer? . . . In the midst of this whirlwind of thoughts and passions, she turned suddenly towards the Indian, as she said, "I will be your wife, Hobomok, if you love me." (121)

Clearly, Mary is not in full possession of her senses. Child continues to emphasize the abnormality of her demeanor, and in doing so appears to be capitulating to the prevailing patriarchal vision even as she critiques it: "Mary, so pale and motionless, might have seemed like a being from another world, had not her wild, frenzied look revealed too much of human wretchedness" (123). During the Indian ceremony in which she is asked to declare her love for Hobomok, "Mary raised her head with a look, which had in it much of the frightful expression of one walking in his sleep, as she replied, 'I love him better than any body living'" (125). Child's presentation of Mary's adult decision to wed cross-racially as the act of a mind temporarily unbalanced, of a woman not quite herself, makes of Mary a doll-like figure, not in complete control of herself, a "being from another world," who speaks the transgressive message of the ventriloquist, in this case Child herself.

More than a 150 years after Child's *Hobomok*, Zebra Books of New York published a series of historical romances in which white women use Native American male captors for feminist purposes. The title of each book in the series (published in the 1980s), bears the word "savage," reproducing the penny-dreadful "marketing" ploy of the nineteenth-century texts, but differing dramatically from them in presenting this savage milieu as the preferred abode of the white captive. Kate McCafferty, who sees in these modern pulp romances the "reemergence" of the captivity narrative, writes that the heroine of these romances

> finds in the Native American male . . . "the green world guide," who brings her through unknown and dangerous space in safety, away from an oppressive patriarchy. He offers . . . a utopian society in which women are valued for their social contributions; where they are sexually assertive members of a group distinctive for cooperation and solidarity; where women and men are helpmates within a (fictionalized) fairly androgynous division of labor. (51)

I would argue that these narratives, written in the late-twentieth century but harking back to the distant past, display the devices of ventriloquism. The transgressive message is located in a time and place so obviously removed from present-day reality that its implications are no longer threatening. The genre of the historical romance provides the ready-made framework within which the subversive protagonists are marked as being outside the realm of the white woman's twentieth-century world.

In relying so heavily on Connor's description of ventriloquism as a mode of challenge, I do not mean to suggest that all captivity narratives can be seen through this lens. However, I do believe that this perspective enables us to understand the often puzzling contradictions in these narratives—the victimized woman who surprises with her acumen, the helpless captive who frees herself with cunning. The racialized nature of the captivity experience—the white woman's sojourn in a context so unlike her own Western milieu—releases her from conformity to conventions and opens up a space in which, among racial Others, she, too, can become an Other, a being unlike herself. The captivity narrative was the stage upon which race and gender, issues central to the social and political landscape, were being enacted. From their positions of ostensible powerlessness, white female captives spoke their transgression, the disruptive force of their words carefully hidden within the cloak of their captors' race. The captives' utterances gave form to an enlarged vision of womanhood and enabled women to conceive of new possibilities of thought and action. The experience of captivity among the Indians generated in some women the confidence to resist their captivity to their husbands, brothers, and fathers.

EPILOGUE

A contemporary captivity experience of white women in a racialized space is that of Shelter Now International workers Dayna Curry and Heather Mercer. The two women, aged 30 and 24, respectively, were part of a group of eight individuals imprisoned by Afghanistan's then Taliban government for the crime of preaching Christianity. They were captives of the Taliban for approximately three months, from August 5, 2001 to November 15, 2001. In rhetoric similar to that of Mary Rowlandson, they attributed their safe release to their faith in God and said that the Taliban "treated them with respect and allowed them to pray and sing hymns regularly in jail" (Frantz B3). Perhaps what is most astonishing about their rescue is the symbolic and ironic quality of it. With a fire they started with the head scarves worn by six women in the group, they were able to draw the attention of U.S. Special Forces Heliocopters to their location. The head scarves, which had served as markers of their forced enslavement to the Taliban, became the very means of their release.[10]

NOTES

1. In addition to Anglo men and women, Mexican and African American men and women were also taken captive. The most numerous were the white captives, however. This preponderance seems perfectly logical when we consider that one of the reasons that Indians took captives, according to Derounian-Stodola, was revenge: "Angry at Europeans who stole their lands and massacred them in wars, Indians sometimes retaliated by subjecting enemy captives to ritualistic ceremonies of torture and death" (2–3).

2. These three adjectives occur most frequently in characterizing the Indians. The negative rhetoric to describe Indians is so pervasive in the extant material of the period between the early seventeenth and mid-twentieth centuries that it is difficult to identify specific texts. A good place to begin, however, is Albert Hurtado and Peter Iverson's edited volume *Major Problems in American Indian History*, which includes primary documents from as early as 1492.

3. Nancy Cott writes that in the eighteenth and early nineteenth centuries, only about half of New England women could sign their names. See Cott's chapter on Education in her book *The Bonds of Womanhood*.

4. See especially Linda K. Kerber, *Women of the Republic*; Mary Beth Norton, *Liberty's Daughters*; and Janet Wilson James, *Changing Ideas about Women*.

5. See especially her chapter "The Language of Nativism: Anthropology as a Scientific Conversation of Man with Man" in her book *Woman, Native, Other.* On the matter of "becoming Indian" to survive, it is interesting to note that the Spaniard Alvar Nunez Cabeza de Vaca, whose narrative of captivity is the first recorded document of this North American genre, survived his captivity "by acculturating to the point where they [he and his three fellow captives] were allowed to move freely among the tribes" (Bruce-Novoa, 129).

6. Derounian-Stodola offers synopses of both captives' lives: "Eunice Williams was taken captive during a raid on Deerfield, Massachusetts, on 29 February 1704. With her parents and two brothers, she was forced to march to Canada. Two younger sisters were killed during the attack, and her mother died shortly after the journey began. While her brothers and her father, who was the Puritan minister of Deerfield, were later ransomed, Eunice remained among the Indians, converted to Roman Catholicism, and married into the tribe. In later life, she and her Indian family returned to Massachusetts, but legend has it that she refused to enter her brother's house because her father had remarried" (7). "Mary Jemison was approximately 12 years old in 1775 when Shawnees attacked her home near Gettysburg, Pennsylvania, killing her parents and taking her captive. After an initial period of lament and regret, she embraced the culture of the Seneca family that adopted her. Remembered as the 'white woman of the Genesee,' she grew up in the Genesee River Valley of western New York, was twice married to Indian chiefs, and became a leader of her adopted tribe" (6).

7. "Self-destruction and self-torture are considered by them as the best means of pleasing their gods, and atoning for their sins. Many drown themselves in the Ganges, whose waters they worship as sacred; widows burn themselves in the funeral pile of their husbands; some stand for years on one foot, others hold their arms or heads in one position, until they become so fixed that they cannot alter it; sometimes they remain for life in a hole dug in the earth, barely large enough for them, and entirely covered up, except a small aperture left for air" (198).

8. Jules Zanger points also to the parallel between "the European captivity fairy tale" and the Indian captivity narrative: "A persistent motif in traditional fairy tales describes a young man who stumbles into or is tricked or seduced into a fairy world where he spends a brief time in revelry: dancing, drinking, making love. When he emerges, however, he discovers that he has been 'Under the Hill' for many years or even centuries, that all he loved have died, and that he has grown old" (124).

9. Child began a fascinating "conversation" in early American letters. James Fenimore Cooper would respond to her proposed worldview with *The Last of the Mohicans* (1826), offering an "acceptable" version of a relationship between whites and Indians and dispelling any possibility of miscegenation between the Indian man and white woman. In 1827, Catherine Maria Sedgwick, in her novel *Hope Leslie*, modified the vision delineated by Cooper by seeking "to develop rather

than foreclose the possibilities Child had opened up" (Karcher xxxv). Sedgwick portrays the only cross-racial (Indian-white) marriage in the nineteenth-century "frontier novel" (Karcher xxxvi). However, I would argue that both Sedgwick and Child employ the art of indirection in order to make palatable to readers their challenge to patriarchy and its segregationist vision of the nation. In Sedgwick's text, Faith is captured by Indians in her early childhood and raised by them; thus, her marriage to an Indian man can be read as a logical outcome of a young girl's transformation into an Indian because of her extreme youth at the time of her capture. I suggest that it would have been problematic to have an *adult* Faith make the conscious decision to wed an Indian. Child, however, does just that, although she, too, as I argue makes her challenge indirectly.

10. In addition to Douglas Frantz, "A Nation Challenged: The Captives; U.S. Relief Workers Tellof Fear and Faith," see articles by other *New York Times* reporters—Ross E. Milloy, "A Nation Challenged: Relief After Release; Hometown is Jubilant Aid Workers are Free,'" Norimitsu Onishi, "A Nation Challenged: The Rescue; 8 Aid Workers' Ordeal Ends Happily in Pakistan," and John F. Burns, "A Nation Challenged: Hostages; U.S. Flies Aid Workers to Safety in Pakistan."

WORKS CITED

Bruce-Novoa, Juan. "Alvar Nunez Cabeza de Vaca." *The Heath Anthology of American Literature*. Ed. Paul Lauter. Vol. 1. Lexington: Heath, 1990. 128–129.

Burnham, Michelle. *Captivity and Sentiment: Cultural Exchange in American Literature, 1682–1861*. Hanover: UP of New England, 1997.

Burns, John F. "A Nation Challenged: Hostages; U. S. Flies Aid Workers to Safety in Pakistan." *The New York Times* (Nov. 15, 2001): A1.

Child, Lydia Maria. *Hobomok and Other Writings on Indians*. New Brunswick: Rutgers UP, 1991.

Connor, Steven. "A Cultural History of Ventriloquism." Internet address: http://rs306.ccs.bbk.ac.uk/Departments/English/Staff/skcvent.htm.

———. *Dumbstruck: A Cultural History of Ventriloquism*. Oxford: Oxford UP, 2000.

Cott, Nancy F. *The Bonds of Womanhood: "Woman's Sphere" in New England, 1780–1835*. New Haven: Yale UP, 1997.

Derounian-Stodola, Kathryn Zabelle, and James Arthur Levernier. *The Indian Captivity Narrative, 1550–1900*. New York: Twayne, 1993.

Ebersole, Gary L. *Captured by Texts: Puritan to Post-Modern Images of Indian Captivity*. Charlottesville: UP of Virginia, 1995.

Fitzpatrick, Tara. "The Figure of Captivity: The Cultural Work of the Puritan Captivity Narrative." *American Literary History* 3.1 (1991): 1–26.

Frantz, Douglas. "A Nation Challenged: The Captives; U. S. Relief Workers Tell of Fear and Faith." *The New York Times* (Nov. 17, 2001): B3.

Gwin, Minrose. *Black and White Women of the Old South.* Knoxville: U of Tennessee P, 1985.

Hanson, Elizabeth. "An Account of the Captivity of Elizabeth Hanson, Now or Late of Kachecky, in New-England." VanDerBeets 130–150.

Hurtado, Albert, and Peter Iverson. *Major Problems in American Indian History.* Lexington, MA: D. C. Heath and Company, 1994.

James, Janet Wilson. *Changing Ideas about Women in the United States, 1776–1825.* New York: Garland, 1981.

Kelly, Fanny. *My Captivity Among the Sioux Indians.* New York: Corinth Books, 1962.

Karcher, Carolyn L. "Introduction." *Hobomok and Other Writings on Indians.* New Brunswick: Rutgers UP, 1991. ix–xxxviii

Kerber, Linda K. *Women of the Republic: Intellect and Ideology in Revolutionary America.* New York: Norton, 1986.

Kestler, Frances Roe, ed. *The Indian Captivity Narrative: A Woman's View.* New York: Garland, 1990.

Kinnan, Mary. "A True Narrative of the Sufferings of Mary Kinnan, who was Taken Prisoner by the Shawnee Nation of Indians on the Thirteenth Day of May, 1791, and Remained with them till the Sixteenth of August, 1794." VanDerBeets 319–32.

Koehler, Lyle. *A Search for Power: The "Weaker Sex" in Seventeenth-Century New England.* Urbana: U of Illinois P, 1980.

Mani, Lata. "Cultural Theory, Colonial Texts: Reading Eyewitness Accounts of Widow Burning." *Cultural Studies.* Ed. Lawrence Grossberg, Cary Nelson, and Paula A. Treichler. New York: Routledge, 1992. 392–408.

McCafferty, Kate. "Palimpsest of Desire: The Reemergence of the American Captivity Narrative as Pulp Romance." *Journal of Popular Culture* 27.4 (Spring 1994): 43–56.

Milloy, Ross E. "A Nation Challenged: Relief After Release; Hometown is Jubilant Aid Workers are Free." *The New York Times* (No. 16, 2001): B4.

Minh-ha, Trinh T. *Woman, Native, Other: Writing Postcoloniality and Feminism.* Bloomington: Indiana UP, 1989.

Namias, June. *White Captives: Gender and Ethnicity on the American Frontier.* Chapel Hill: U of North Carolina P, 1993.

Norton, Mary Beth. *Liberty's Daughters: The Revolutionary Experience of American Women, 1750–1800.* Ithaca: Cornell UP, 1996.

Onishi, Norimitsu. "A Nation Challenged: The Rescue; 8 Aid Workers' Ordeal Ends Happily in Pakistan." *The New York Times* (Nov. 16, 2001): B1.

Plummer, Rachel. "A Narrative of the Capture and Subsequent Sufferings of Mrs. Rachel Plummer, Written by Herself." VanDerBeets 333–66.

Rodriguez, Barbara. *Autobiographical Inscriptions: Form, Personhood, and the American Woman Writer of Color.* New York: Oxford UP, 1999.

Rowlandson, Mary. The Captive: *The True Story of the Captivity of Mrs. Rowlandson Among the Indians and God's Faithfulness to her in her Time of Trial.* Tucson: American Eagle, 1990.

Sketches of the Lives of Distinguished Females. New York: J. & J. Harper, 1833.

"A White Man's Rationale for Killing Indians on the Overland Trail, 1849." Hurtado and Iverson. 286–88.

VanDerBeets, Richard. Ed. *Held Captive by Indians: Selected Narratives, 1642–1836.* Knoxville: U of Tennessee P, 1994.

Zanger, Jules. "Living on the Edge: Indian Captivity Narrative and Fairy Tale." *CLIO* 13.2 (1984):123–32.

CHAPTER SIX

"Those Indians Are Great Thieves, I Suppose?"

Historicizing the White Woman in The Squatter and the Don

PETER A. CHVANY

Reading *The Squatter and the Don* encourages us to historicize and contextualize the term "white woman" in both the late nineteenth century and the late twentieth by linking it to class, situating it within modern capitalism, and recalling that U.S. forms of racism, though they have largely become the world standard, have never been the only modes of racial oppression, and thus are neither naturally given nor impossible to abolish.

María Amparo Ruiz de Burton's 1885 text, one of the earliest known novels by a woman of Mexican descent writing in the United States, makes a sophisticated critique of racist oppression directed by "Anglo" Americans against Mexicans in California in the 1870s.[1] Contrasting the affluent, educated, and refined Alamar family of the San Diego area with newly arrived "squatters" led by the nouveau-riche Darrell family, Ruiz de Burton exposes both Anglo racist assumptions and the corrupt mechanisms by which Californios are legally disinherited of land that had been part of Mexico only a generation before. As individual Darrells of the younger generation begin to see the Alamares as equals and romantic partners, Ruiz de Burton turns her focus to the further crisis engendered by railroad expansion into southern California and the devastating effect of shady monopoly-capitalist economic practices on both Anglo and Mexican communities. Thus the novel links racism not only to mere bigotry but also to one group's abuse of economic power over another, liminally connecting racism to capitalist class oppression.

However, Ruiz de Burton's linkage of racism to class breaks down in the gap between her portrayals of the text's white women and its people of color. The Alamares compare favorably to the Darrells precisely because they are represented as "white" people of unmixed European stock. They are rescued from economic ruin by Clarence Darrell, who marries the "dimpled and white and soft" (151) Mercedes Alamar and provides for his in-laws from his own investments. Those investments include not only his participation in the expanding Gilded Age stock market but his stake in mines which, in historical terms, were often sites of labor exploitation of Mexican workers. Elsewhere in the text, Ruiz de Burton (herself the daughter of upper-class Mexicans, the widow of a U.S. Army officer, and a California landowner) stereotypes "Indian" ranch hands, "squaw" domestics, and the Darrells' black "mammy."[2] Her appeals for justice against the railroad monopolists portray San Diego as part of the "prostrate South" of Reconstruction, calling for "redemption" of "the white slaves of California." Her Californio protagonists are indeed victims of Anglo racism, but they are also former racist oppressors of Native people during their own period of rancher capitalism. They now seek to join the white ruling class of the post-Reconstruction United States. Ruiz de Burton's admirable refutation of racist stereotypes thus leaves upper-class Mexican privilege intact and is silent about the oppression of Mexican mestizos and other people of color. Understanding her text's identification with (and as) the "white woman" allows us to carry her critique of racism forward into the twenty-first century without reproducing its class-based displacement of racist oppression onto other peoples on the text's margins.

WHITE WOMEN

There are several white women in *The Squatter and the Don*. Mary Moreneau Darrell, matriarch of the title "squatter" family, opens the novel attempting to remind her husband of both the immorality and the typically bad business outcome of squatting. "To be guided by experience," she tells him, "is to profit by wisdom of our own" (55). She wants William Darrell to ensure that he only "takes up" land around San Diego which is definitely not involved in a title dispute. Their "sad experience in Napa and Sonoma valleys" (57) resulted from losing previous disputes. Mary Darrell also insists that he must "not go on a Mexican grant unless you buy the land from the owner" (57). Ruiz de Burton carefully presents Mary Darrell as both ethically conscientious and an economically astute member of modern bourgeois society. Because she knows land-grabbing's real drawbacks, she intends the "profit" of her experiential wisdom and moral vision to lead directly to profits of the ordinary economic kind. For her, nonracist behavior unifies pragmatism with rectitude.[3] To the extent that William ignores her—he fails to inquire about the status of the Alamar title, taking the word of his lower-class squatter friends that it has been settled, and then stonewalls when his errors are revealed—he never does profit. To the extent that Clarence Darrell, Mary and William's eldest son, follows both his mother's explicit desires and her implicit example (he secretly pays Don Mariano Alamar for both his father's claim and his own, supports the Don's agricultural plans, and steers clear of the other squatters), he meets dramatic economic and personal success. By the end of the novel he is "worth twelve million dollars" (364) and is happily married to Mercedes Alamar.

Mary Darrell's counterpart, Doña Josefa Alamar, wife of the title Don, closes the novel with a speech of similar moral authority, in which she rails against the abuses of monopoly capitalism in California. "God of Justice," she muses, observing a gala wedding in a nearby mansion, having moved to San Francisco and given up the rancho forever, "is this right, that so many should be sacrificed because a few men want more millions?" The text explains:

> To her, rectitude and equity had a clear meaning impossible to pervert. No subtle sophistry could blur in her mind the clear line dividing right from wrong. She knew that among men the word BUSINESS means inhumanity to one another. . . . but the illustration, the ocular demonstration, had never been before her until now in that gay house. (363)

Warned by fair-weather friends that "you will give great offense. . . . you cannot speak against rich people; San Francisco society will turn against you," Doña Josefa replies "I slander no one, but shall speak the truth" (364). This affirmation of fundamental truthfulness introduces the final chapter, Ruiz de Burton's direct authorial summation of the novel's lessons. She proposes that *"the people of California take the law in their own hands,* and seize the property of [millionaire capitalists], and confiscate it, to re-imburse the money due *the people"* (366, author's italics). At points such as this, the radicalism of Ruiz de Burton's vision of what it will take to refashion the U.S. political landscape, including its racism, is evident.

That radicalism is, of course, expressed in terms common to other texts of the nineteenth century. Throughout the novel, Ruiz de Burton employs the generic conventions of sentimental melodrama to frame her social protest. African American feminist critic Claudia Tate's recent work on black women's post-Reconstruction novels of "genteel domestic feminism" (4) describes how such novels critique dominant society. Tate explains that their "domestic plots rely on a tradition of politicized motherhood that views mothers and the cultural rhetoric of maternity as instruments of social reform" (14). Stowe's *Uncle Tom's Cabin*, with its famous final appeal to the mothers of (white) America to support abolition, is one well-known example. *The Squatter and the Don* affiliates itself with a genteel feminist tradition in several ways, especially by giving these two women protagonists a decisive moral view whose wisdom is borne out by the novel's events.

But what justifies our calling Doña Josefa a "white" woman, when contemporary Chicana/Latina discourse usually insists on pride in the mestiza background of Mexican peoples as a necessary component of progressive antiracist politics? The answer is that Ruiz de Burton herself persistently identifies the Alamar family as a "white" family, and wants her readers to understand that the Anglo denial of "white" status to Mexican Californians is a primary indicator of Anglo racism. The men of the Alamar family impress a newly arrived Clarence not only with their gentlemanly behavior but also with the fact that "They look like Englishmen"; another young squatter agrees, exclaiming, "particularly Victoriano; he is so light he looks more like a German, I think" (89). The Don has "mild and beautiful blue eyes" (64). His daughter Elvira is referred to as the "*rosa de Castilla*" (151). His daughter Mercedes, the romantic heroine, is repeatedly identified by the "golden threads" of her hair, her "white throat," or her hand, "so dimpled and white and soft" (151).

Though such depictions depend on the fact that some Mexican people do come from predominantly European backgrounds, they also indicate Ruiz de Burton's sophisticated understanding of her Anglo target audience's prejudices. She understood white Americans' deep-seated investment in whiteness as both a symbol of spiritual and sexual purity and as the political sign which subsumed class antagonisms in a shared racial identity, as studies of "whiteness" like those by David Roediger have recently shown.[4] Ruiz de Burton's first novel, *Who Would Have Thought It?*, opens with the recovery from an Indian tribe of a young Mexican girl of pure European blood, whose dark skin proves to be the effect of dye used by the Indians to prevent anyone from wanting to rescue her, and whose beautiful white skin eventually returns.[5] That novel's satirical exposés of the hypocritical racism and naked greed of white Northerners during the U.S. Civil War indicate how compelling Ruiz de Burton found the topic of racial injustice. It may also draw on her residence in the North during her marriage, leading one to wonder what kind of racist mistreatment she herself may have experienced there.

But in both novels, the possibility arises that Ruiz de Burton is not arguing against racial injustice per se, or refuting racism as a system of beliefs. An insistence on white purity does not arise only in Anglo culture, to be sold back to it by a canny author. Race and class divisions took different forms and meant different things in Mexican culture than in the Anglo system, as several writers have argued, but strong similarities existed.[6] Even today, Chicana critic Ana Castillo writes, "for all the lip service in Mexico given to indigenismo, Mexic Amerindians remain on the bottom of the social strata and depending on one's *color* and class, so do many mestizos/as" (2, author's italics). The similarity between Mercedes Alamar's story and Ruiz de Burton's own biography suggests that Ruiz de Burton may have identified as a white woman herself. Such an identification has consequences for her novel's political argument, insofar as the author comes to figure as a white woman in the racialized space of her own text. If Ruiz de Burton is arguing that racism is misdirected at certain people who should really be regarded as white, the possible corollary is that racial oppression is not inappropriate when directed elsewhere.

To understand how Ruiz de Burton's use of whiteness critiques racism but may also perpetuate it, we must look more closely at both her antiracist pronouncements and her depictions of other people of color.

FORMS OF RACISM

Clearly, Ruiz de Burton portrays the Alamares as she does in order to challenge stereotypes about Mexicans living in the United States. Examples of antistereotyping abound. Early on, the squatter Mathews observes that "Those greasers ain't half crushed yet" (73) when a "young Spaniard" denounces the squatters' shooting of cattle in the San Diego region. The contrast between the description of the youth—"Spaniard" highlighting his European nationality—and Mathews's imputation of greasiness is ironically reinforced by the fact that Mathews himself is "noticeable for . . . ugliness," due to "his long, oily, dusty, hair [which] dragged over his neck in matted, meshy locks" (71).

Anglo Americans also claimed that Mexicans were tradition-bound and backward-looking, ignorant of modern culture, and thus stood in the way of progress and prosperity. At the end of a squatter meeting about Don Mariano's proposed solution to the title dispute, the squatter Pittikin sums up the Alamares' problems by claiming that "you can't teach 'an old dog new tricks.' Those old Spaniards never will be business men" (87). Yet Don Mariano advances a pragmatic plan for mutual profit. He promises to acknowledge the squatters' land claims and advance them investment capital at no interest, provided they give up their ambitions as grain farmers and change to a ranch, vineyard, and orchard economy, incidentally sparing his cattle in the process. He bases this plan on his accurate assessment of the squatters' economic motives, on his understanding of weather conditions which make their plans impractical, and on an explicitly capitalist social ethic which breaks with outmoded traditions and seeks to maximize profitable production. He suggests building dams in nearby ravines to trap rainwater for vineyard and orchard irrigation, something neither squatters nor prewar Mexicans had ever considered.[7] "The foolishness of letting all of the rainfall go to waste, is an old time folly with us," he explains:

> Still, in old times, we had, at least, the good excuse that we raised all the fruits we needed for our use, and there was no market for any more. But we were not then, as now, guilty of the folly of making the land useless. We raised cattle and sold hides and tallow every year, and made money. (93)

The opposition between "making money" and "uselessness" or "folly" sketched here recurs throughout his offer. It is conditioned by the fact that where once "there was no market" to support a more profitable system, now there is. In typical

late-nineteenth-century fashion, profit making has the force of a moral imperative in the Don's plea: "In my humble opinion," he concludes, "we *ought* to prefer
cattle raising and fruit growing for our county. We *should* make these our specialty"
(93, my italics). Thus when the squatters reject his plan, the narrative not only
reveals them as the old dogs who can't learn but also sets them against modern
economic common sense. Mexican stereotypes fall like this throughout the novel,
often in equally bravura ways. Yet other stereotypes, noticeably those that apply
to groups Ruiz de Burton is not trying to defend against Anglo racism, persist.

Her treatment of the squatters is certainly understandable, given the real historical depredations arriving Anglos wrought on California. The problem with the
squatter families, other than the Darrells, is their membership in the lower classes.
The novel racializes their class status in ways reminiscent of many other texts
published in the era of "social Darwinism." Bodily marks of lower-class status appear
throughout the text: one squatter has a "broad, vulgar" face (71); a corrupt lawyer
is "a little yellow haired man with a very red neck" (108) and "dull, fishy eyes" (332).
The pseudo-evolutionary essentialism of these representations includes claims that one
squatter is "a cut-throat by instinct" (82), while another is "of the genus *hoodlum*
. . . it must be natural to him to act like a monkey" (109, italics in original).

But rhetorical strategies which succeed as satires on Anglo pretensions to a
higher standard of civilization feel less appropriate when applied to groups likewise oppressed by the Anglo racism Ruiz de Burton ably decries. The absence of
Chinese from a novel set in California and concerned with railroad building is
startling, especially since Chinese laborers did the dangerous construction of the
California Southern Railroad through the Temecula gorge between 1880 and 1883,
an area Ruiz de Burton would have been intimately familiar with.[8] Still more
problematic are her depictions of the Darrell family "mammy," Tisha. "[D]evotedly
attached" to Mary Darrell for years, Tisha is referred to throughout the novel as a
"servant" (59), not a slave. But in a flashback to Mary and William's courtship,
which takes place around 1847, Mary's home is given as Washington, D.C. She
has family in both Maryland and Virginia, which were slave states at the time.
Free or bonded, Tisha thus stands for both the social position of Mary Darrell's
family and for an unproblematized master-servant relationship, which persists past
Emancipation into the 1870's. Tisha is also a stereotype, with her emotionally
flighty "flapping steps" and breathless servant-class bad grammar (61). It sounds
like praise when the Alamares guess that Mary prefers Tisha's cooking to a male
squatter's, but mammies are almost always excellent cooks, both in narratives which
argue for freedpeople's rights and in those which call for continued, romanticized
bondage. The Darrells' proprietary feelings for Tisha and the comic figure she cuts
show up when she rides from the San Diego harbor to the new homestead with
"the boys" rather than "the women folks"; this is described with genteel mockery
as "Tisha in the back in state" (110, 111). She is also delighted at seeing "her favorite
Massa Clary" after an absence because "He was the best, sweetest baby I ever saw,

and so beautiful" (234). This reaction draws on the familiar trope of the servant who puts the Mistress's children ahead of her own. One would never guess that Tisha's social status might have changed since the U.S. Civil War, or that such changes touched on important questions of freedmen's rights or sectional conflict and compromise. "Who," the text asks, "more humble than Tisha?" (181).

Perhaps most disturbing of all, however, are the novel's portrayals of the California Indians. Indians typically appear as undisciplined *vaqueros* on the ranchos, unindividuated figures silently trailing their masters, requiring constant supervision: "those stupid Indians who keep letting the cattle turn back" (260). When performing their labors well, as when they help the Alamares save cattle from a blizzard, they are deferentially silent. Occasional longer representations echo contemporaneous portraits of "the Negro" in U.S. literature. When he is worth singling out, an Indian *vaquero* turns out to be "lazy" (278), like the stable boy Chapo, the only Indian given a name. Chapo is so intent on rolling a good cigarette and getting a good dinner that he fails to put some horses away when Victoriano Alamar tells him to. His inaction allows Clarence to drive away from the Alamar rancho in despair after his father publicly insults Mercedes Alamar's honor. Since subsequent events keep Clarence absent for nearly three years, preventing him from aiding the Alamares as their fortunes dwindle, Chapo's shiftlessness is indirectly to blame for the tragedies that follow. Ruiz de Burton does not press the point, but nothing in the text contradicts its portrait of Indian character.

In another scene, two *vaqueros* aggravate William Darrell's irrational anger toward the Alamares. When the other squatters discover that someone in the Darrell family has paid the Don for the Darrell claims, Darrell confronts the Alamares, makes slurs, and must be lassoed to prevent his striking the Don. His mount bolts, and Gabriel Alamar must ride alongside him to prevent his being unhorsed and injured. The *vaqueros* follow the chase "in high glee" (249), taunting Darrell in Spanish. But although Darrell is flawed, Ruiz de Burton redeems him near the novel's conclusion to show that genteel domestic feminism can address the crises of racism and monopoly expansion, and so he is consistently defined in opposition to the squatters and any other objects of her outright ridicule. The *vaqueros*, cracking jokes and addressing him by the familiar Spanish pronoun "te," display a lack of proper respect for his social position (249). Victoriano Alamar rebukes them indignantly. But within moments Victoriano and Everett, Darrell's own son, are "convulsed with laughter" (251) as they help Darrell from his horse. The text thus implicitly holds the *vaqueros* accountable, not for an ignorance of what constitutes a humorous situation, but for not recognizing the social position that makes it inappropriate for them to show their reactions openly.

That social position is, of course, a racial one. In a casual exchange between Mercedes and Elvira, Ruiz de Burton alludes to the material and historical circumstances underpinning the Indians' position. Mercedes is late dressing for a party. Elvira reminds her: "You have never dressed yourself without someone to help you at home, whether it was my squaw, your squaw, or Mamma's or the other girls, or whether it was your own Madame Halier—you always had an attendant" (198). Mercedes agrees, bemoaning the fact that "I am so utterly useless" (198). Both French governesses and Indians did serve ranchero families, and dependence on their labor might indeed have rendered a young girl occasionally "useless." Yet it is not only Elvira, but also Ruiz de Burton who identifies some servants as "squaws," others by their European rank and name. The difference between a named servant and an unnamed group of them is one of the differences of racism. In historical terms, such racial differences had led to genocidal drops in the Native population of California before and during the rancho period.[9] Eloquently as Ruiz de Burton explodes Anglo myths and argues for justice for Californian Mexicans of the landholding classes, racist ideologies structure her understanding of who is affected by racism and how racism can best be addressed.

THE SQUATTER AND THE DON AS A NOVEL OF ITS TIME

Traditional humanist accounts of racial prejudice typically see it as resulting from a lack of education, a lack of exposure to people from different racial backgrounds, or a simple lack of intelligence. Yet Ruiz de Burton was clearly a brilliant student of the costly injustice of racial oppression. She had hardly lacked for contact with people of mixed-race backgrounds: a friend of the family, Pío Pico, was among the prominent Californios who would have been recognized as having African ancestry. Robert Carlton finds that a Spanish census explicitly identified Pico's grandmother as a "mulata" (11). Since Pico was the governor of California just before the U.S. conquest and later sold the Jamul Rancho to the Burtons, it is unlikely that Ruiz de Burton was unaware of his origins. The consequences of racial injustice were also quite personal for her: she turned to fiction writing in part to raise money to fight later attempts by Anglo interests to take the Jamul Rancho away from her. The Squatter and the Don is nothing less than a loud, clear protest against the racist legal system which made such attacks possible. And the novel's implicit linkage of the racist oppression of Mexican Californians with the economic oppression of Californians of all backgrounds feels startlingly modern.[10] At other points, however, the novel remains a work of its time, and its blind spots are significant.

Yet rather than faulting The Squatter and the Don for participating in the very racism it seeks to overturn, we can understand its "blind spots" productively. They are not simple lapses in judgment, conscious expressions of inter-"minority" hostility, or instances of inattention to the real issues. Instead, Ruiz de Burton's focus on issues of economics, class, and power, precisely the qualities that make her analysis of racism so powerful, also drew her attention to contemporary historical issues whose relevance is less clear to us today than is the fate of the disempowered communities she stereotypes. Ruiz de Burton linked economic, class, and racial issues from a complex position as a white-identified woman, and in a particular racialized space, namely the post-Reconstruction United States. Though her concerns both enabled and disabled her critique of racism, we may empower ourselves to undertake better negotiations in our own time, when issues of whiteness and white women's place in structures of power are no less complex, by understanding precisely how her antiracist project stumbles.

Ruiz de Burton's economic ideology is best understood as antimonopolist, but thoroughly capitalist. Midway through the novel, the Don and his friends meet with Leland Stanford, the (historical) governor of California. They ask him to support the construction of the Texas Pacific railroad, which is slated to terminate in San Diego and thereby bring new prosperity to the region. Stanford, however, is a member of the Big Four, a cabal of railroad monopolists who use their control over the U.S. Congress to thwart competing companies.[11]

After outlining the losses of cattle which have brought them to the brink of economic ruin—"Those Indians are great thieves, I suppose," Stanford guesses, although Don Mariano replies, "not so bad to me as the squatters" (315)—the Don and his friends attempt to convince Stanford that his business dealings are bad for both business and for public morality by quoting Herbert Spencer at him. This may seem ironic to twenty-first-century readers who associate Spencer with defenses of laissez-faire capitalism and the phrase "survival of the fittest." But Spencer scholar J. D. Y. Peel suggests that Ruiz de Burton's portrayal of Spencer as an ethicist was justified. The Spencerian vogue in America—at its height when Ruiz de Burton wrote—largely took him as an apologist for unbridled, ethically disinterested competition. But Peel shows that Spencer represented a middle-class politics of genteel radicalism. It was, specifically, the radicalism of the anti-aristocratic bourgeois industrialists of the English North in the 1830s and 1840s, who sought greater freedom for the expansion of their markets without the democratic excesses of Jacobinism.[12]

By the 1870s, that form of capitalism was being fast superseded by Stanford's brand of monopolist exploitation. Profit imperatives had thrust genteel competition aside. Yet Spencerian radicalism also echoed the political ideology of many New World national liberation movements of the early nineteenth century: the ideology of the Don's generation of bourgeois revolutionaries or Ruiz de Burton's parents. That generation had won independence from Spain and secularized the California missions, creating the same rancho system which is under threat in the novel upon lands wrested from the Church. Ruiz de Burton is thus quite serious when a character tells Stanford that "commercial honor, business morality, should be based on strict rectitude, on the purest equality," and that "monopolies should not exist when they have become so powerful that they defy the law. . . . The fundamental principle of morality is then subverted" (317-18). The problem is that, from a capitalist perspective, ethics and morality are rarely the main point. Ruiz de

Burton, writing from within an avowedly capitalist position herself, has little recourse but to note that the current situation is unfair and oppressive, as if the rancho system had not been.

A similar ideological double bind is at play in Ruiz de Burton's use of the historical romance genre to organize the novel. Rosaura Sánchez and Beatrice Pita, her modern editors, draw on critic George Dekker's work to define this genre, in which "typical characters and conflicts are viewed in relation to social and histori- cal phenomena" (14). Dekker, in turn, traces the American historical romance to the model instituted by Walter Scott in his Waverley novels. From Scott, Ruiz de Burton appropriates a generic form that sympathetically portrays groups of noble counterrevolutionaries bucking the trend of historical "progress." According to Dekker, "In Waverley and its successors Scott created a readily adaptable model for the fictional or historiographical portrayal both of revolution (in this case an unsuccessful one by reactionary Catholic Jacobites) and imperialistic conquest (by the British Protestant armies of progress)" (8). Furthermore, American "histori- cal romance[] . . . translat[es] . . . the conflict between reaction and progressivism into a conflict between regional loyalties and the federalizing, colonizing drives of British and, later, American imperialism" (9).

Clearly, Ruiz de Burton is precisely concerned with American imperialism in so far as she writes from a region conquered by the United States. Just as clearly, the railroad monopolists figure as imperialism's latest exponents, nor would any- one familiar with the history of railroads have much cause to argue with her. Yet Ruiz de Burton again exhibits a typically "American" failure to, as critic Juan Bruce- Novoa puts it, "conceive of the U. S. A. as a product of *multiple and simultaneous* national colonization efforts, all of which ruthlessly displaced Native American nations" (19, my italics). She mistakes the Californios only for imperialism's vic- tims, when they had also been its beneficiaries. This misrecognition leads her to sympathize with a similarly situated group: white Confederate southerners. The conflict over "regional loyalties and federalizing drives" to which Dekker refers translates, in the specific case of the 1870s setting of The Squatter and the Don, into a polarization of the political landscape which puts Ruiz de Burton's land- holding Californians (whatever their race) on the side of racist oppression.

In the 1870s, monopoly capitalism and federalism were associated with the U.S. North, whose coalition of abolitionist and federal-capitalist interests had emerged victorious over the U.S. South, which had represented an agrarian, decen- tralized capitalist economy of gentleman landholders and small industries. The South had also relied on intense labor exploitation based on race, where "white- ness" identified those free from bondage, much as in Mexican California. But the 1870s also witnessed an intense reaction to the radical reforms enacted under Reconstruction, especially those directed at improving the legal, social, and eco- nomic status of people of color. This reaction was often called "redemption," the process by which federally controlled Reconstruction governments of southern states were replaced with locally elected bodies, most of which began a de facto reversal of Reconstruction policy.

The crucial trope Ruiz de Burton uses to frame the political conflict in California is, indeed, the opposition between North and South. Her identification of "the South" as a unified geographic, cultural, and political space seems only liminally meaningful in the opening chapters, even when she uses the potentially loaded term "carpet-bags" to describe the squatter families' luggage as they migrate from San Francisco to San Diego (71). But the novel's last paragraph speaks bitterly of "the blight, spread over Southern California, and over the entire Southern States" by "the great and powerful monopoly" (372). She describes railroad-building schemes which would be "good" if they were undertaken not for profit but "for the sake of the southern people" (204) of San Diego, "to help the impoverished South to regain her strength wasted in the war" (207). She makes frequent references to the South's "sad condition" (216) and its "exhausted" state (296). The South is "the poor South" (297), "the trusting South" (308), its people "those unfortunate, betrayed Southerners" (306). San Diego's ruin by Northern monopolists is put down to the treachery of their hireling, Senator Guller, who is "sent South [by the competing Southern Pacific] to *persuade* the Southern people into believing that the Texas Pacific would be injurious to the South" (305, author's italics), because he "had espoused their cause during the war of the rebellion, and had always held Southern sentiments" (305).

These statements render San Diego conquered Confederate territory. Of course, it was not. But Ruiz de Burton's anti monopolist, pro-agrarian-capitalist sentiments may well have made it seem so. Historian Leonard Pitt points out that California was regionally divided, even before the Anglos came, between Northern *arribeños* and Southern *abajeños*, groups with different political goals arising from different economies.[13] The drier and less gold-rich "cow counties" of the South were often at the mercy of both the Mexican and the Anglo North, even before the U.S. Civil War. And real conditions did sometimes motivate the South's claims of Northern exploitation. The tendency of Southerners of the next generation to blame "Negro misrule" and the "failure" of Reconstruction policy should not obscure how sectional rivalry and the expansion of Gilded Age capitalism created widespread hardship. But Ruiz de Burton concludes the novel with specific, resonant statements: not only are the South's troubles "historical facts," but "Congress, knowing full well the will of the people, should legislate accordingly. If they do not, then we . . . must wait and pray for a Redeemer who will emancipate the white slaves of California" (372).

This invocation of "redemption" and its linkage to the "emancipation" of whites echoes arguments of the day which represented white Southerners as the nation's primary victims. We now know that such arguments were used time and again to re-oppress African American freedmen. Invocations of "white slavery" had the special force in the 1870s of concealing dramatic losses of rights, livelihood, and life suffered by African Americans and other people of color. The term justified extremes of violence, such as Klan activity, under the white supremacist theory that any hardship whites experienced must be the fault of "nonwhite" races rather than class or systemic inequities. Dangerously, white supremacy demanded solutions to this misunderstood situation by any means.

Far from simply expressing an individual Mexican genteel feminist's analysis of U.S. social injustices, or even a collective Mexican American, "minority" perspective on Anglo racism and political economy, Ruiz de Burton's North-vs.-South conclusion thus also participates in a widespread reaction to Reconstruction. Characteristically of American political thought, her proposed solutions to California's problems likewise confuse racial and class issues in ways which leave both racism and class oppression intact. But she was hardly alone in these mistakes. For example, Rickey D. Best, discussing the rhetoric employed by the mostly white San Diego boosters of the Texas and Pacific Railroad in the real history Ruiz de Burton drew from, shows that they invoked the "prostrate South" trope frequently: in this, "San Diego was no different from a score of other cities across the nation that hoped to cash in on the economic benefits of the Reconstruction era" (253). In literary terms, too, *The Squatter and the Don*'s use of the American historical romance, given that genre's frequent debt to white supremacy, provisionally links *The Squatter and the Don* with a questionable tradition including Dixon's *The Clansman* and Mitchell's *Gone with the Wind*. Such texts are often powerfully invested in white womanhood. And usually, as here, white womanhood's travails are fetishized in ways that suggest that the continued exploitation of people of color is either inevitable, or actually desirable.

But we would do well to recall also the biographical facts of Ruiz de Burton's life. Her later years were apparently spent in repeated struggles to defend her title to the Jamul ranch; Crawford notes a court brief in which Ruiz de Burton "described two separate incidents of violence intended to drive her off" (208). That such incidents had apparently not taken place when Henry Burton was still alive indicates how oppressive it could be to be both a woman and a person not considered "American," even if white, in that time or our own. That Ruiz de Burton also started a handful of new businesses to bolster her sagging fortunes may likewise indicate both her strength and the circumstances racism put her in. If the argument of *The Squatter and the Don* breaks down over the question of whether racial justice is intended to benefit people of color in general or merely some relatively privileged, "white" Mexicans of the wealthy classes, we must also recall that Anglo racism *did* affect Mexicans of *all* classes, impoverishing many who might have begun with privilege, perhaps rendering them in fact the outcasts they were already believed to be. The overt lesson of *The Squatter and the Don*, its linkage of racial and economic oppression, remains crucial to an understanding of the racial dynamics of both Ruiz de Burton's day and our own. Its implicit message, that such an insight can be difficult to pursue to its full ramifications, likewise remains crucial to any analysis of white women and racialized spaces which might hope to make racialized space safe not only for white women, but for the others already living there.

NOTES

1. I use the term "Anglo" here, in keeping with Ruiz de Burton's own usage, to refer to white-identified immigrants to California from the rest of the United States. The corresponding term for the novel's Mexicans is "Californio."

2. For information on Ruiz de Burton's biography and entrepreneurial activities, see the Introduction by Sánchez and Pita and the article by Crawford.

3. Mary Darrell's characterization may also critique Anglo-American society on religious grounds. In contrast to the presumably Protestant majority of the squatters and her own New Englander husband, Mary is Catholic, and the Darrells' children are "baptized and brought up Catholics" (62) as well. This links them provisionally to the Alamares.

4. See David R. Roediger, *The Wages of Whiteness: Race and the Making of the American Working Class.* (New York: Verso, 1991).

5. See María Amparo Ruiz de Burton, *Who Would Have Thought It?*, ed. and intro. by Rosaura Sánchez and Beatrice Pita (Houston: Arte Público, 1995).

6. See, for example, Ralph H. Vigil, "The Hispanic Heritage and the Borderlands," *Journal of San Diego History* 19.3 (Summer 1973): 32–39. The racial status of the Californios is a matter of some dispute, though since there were a few hundred families it probably was not uniform. In the late nineteenth century, the Californios tended to claim *criollo* status (that is, pure European blood, or "sangre azul"); historian Leonard Pitt has observed that their descendants still maintained the claim in the early 1960s. Most modern writers agree that most Californios were *mestizos* to some degree.

7. See Crawford 207 for information on Ruiz de Burton's own attempts to build irrigation systems.

8. See Kurt Van Horn, "Tempting Temecula: The Making and Unmaking of a Southern California Community," *Journal of San Diego History* 20.1 (Winter 1974): 26–38. Temecula was the site of Helen Hunt Jackson's *Ramona*, the famous novel about the mistreatment of Native Americans in California; it had also been the site of a property owned by Henry Burton, Ruiz de Burton's husband, in 1860.

9. See Albert Camarillo, *Chicanos in a Changing Society: From Mexican Pueblos to American Barrios in Santa Barbara and Southern California, 1848–1930* (Cambridge: Harvard UP, 1979) 7–8; and Antoniette May, ed. *The Annotated Ramona*, (San Carlos: World Wide Publishing/Tetra, 1989) 31, for estimates of the Native population decline.

10. See, for example, Roediger, or Theodore Allen, *The Invention of the White Race*. Vol. 1: *Racial Oppression and Social Control* (New York: Verso, 1994), for analyses of racism, as opposed to simple group prejudice, as a specifically capitalist form of oppression.

11. Ruiz de Burton's text is largely quite accurate about the details of the historical situation she depicts, particularly when she deals with the racism of the California legal system and the corruption of Gilded Age railroads.

12. This reading of Spencer's political position extends several remarks Peel makes throughout the early chapters of his study. Peel writes that Spencer was associated with the Anti-Corn Law radicals, "against first the 'ruling-class' and later the working class" (11); that "the political radicalism of this provincial Dissenting and manufacturing leadership . . . had not yet been turned aside by their absorption into the upper classes after 1850" (12); and that Spencer began to look old-fashioned as early as the 1860s because his type of liberalism had in effect already carried the day; "his argument rested on the assumptions of the radicalism of 1832–48" (19).

13. See Leonard Pitt, *The Decline of the Californios: A Social History of the Spanish-Speaking Californians, 1846–1890* (Berkeley: U of California P, 1966) 7.

WORKS CITED

Best, Rickey D. "San Diego and the Gilded Age: The Efforts to Bring the Texas and Pacific Railroad to San Diego." *Journal of San Diego History* 34.4 (Fall 1988): 252–80.

Bruce-Novoa [Juan]. *RetroSpace: Collected Essays on Chicano Literature Theory and History*. Houston: Arte Público, 1990.

Castillo, Ana. *Massacre of the Dreamers: Essays on Xicanisma*. Albuquerque: U of New Mexico P, 1994.

Carlton, Robert L. "Blacks in San Diego County: A Social Profile, 1850–1880." *Journal of San Diego History*. 21.4 (Fall 1975): 7–20.

Crawford, Kathleen. "María Amparo Ruiz Burton: The General's Lady." *Journal of San Diego History* 30.3 (Summer 1984): 198–211.

Dekker, George. *The American Historical Romance*. New York: Cambridge UP, 1987.

Peel, J. D. Y. *Herbert Spencer: The Evolution of a Sociologist*. New York: Basic, 1971.

Ruiz de Burton, María Amparo. *The Squatter and the Don: A Novel Descriptive of Contemporary Occurrences in California*. 1885. Ed. and intro. by Rosaura Sánchez and Beatrice Pita. Houston: Arte Público, 1992.

Sánchez, Rosaura and Beatrice Pita. Introduction. In Ruiz de Burton: 5–51.

Tate, Claudia. *Domestic Allegories of Political Desire: The Black Heroine's Text at the Turn of the Century*. New York: Oxford UP, 1992.

CHAPTER SEVEN

"Let Me Play Desdemona"

White Heroines and Interracial Desire in Louisa May Alcott's "My Contraband" and "M.L."

DIANA R. PAULIN

In this essay I examine how Louisa May Alcott's sensational short stories, "My Contraband"[1] and "M.L.," function as "safe" sites for the articulation and exploration of cross-racial desire, specifically white women's forbidden desire for black men. In order to situate my analysis of Alcott's texts within a broader discussion of abolitionist women's fiction, I use Karen Sanchez-Eppler's readings of nineteenth-century antislavery and miscegenation[2] stories in "Bodily Bonds: The Intersecting Rhetorics of Feminism and Abolition" as a point of departure. Complicating Sanchez-Eppler's model, which postulates that the metaphorical linking of slave women and bourgeois ladies in feminist and abolitionists texts allowed nineteenth-century white women writers to conflate the position of slaves with their own and to inscribe their prohibited desires on the body of the light-skinned mulatta,[3] I argue that Alcott's stories reassert white womanhood as the center of the social and political imagination while relegating "blackness"—and everything that it stands for in the narrative—to the margins of their liberating narratives. Comparing "My Contraband" and "M.L." enables me to investigate how Alcott employs moments of miscegenation (interracial mixing) and the actual embodiments of white and black contact, in the form of racially mixed light-skinned black men, to examine the possibilities and results of transgressing heavily guarded racial, gender, and sexual boundaries that were in place in the nineteenth century.

My close readings of these representations of cross-racial desire identify how they simultaneously contain and explode conventional constructions of race ("blackness" and "whiteness"), sexuality, and gender, thus complicating the tendency to read these "domestic" feminized stories as nonpolitical, nonthreatening, and unrelated to national identity formation. The narratives themselves provide the most immediate evidence of the destabilizing impact of this type of fiction. The white heroines in these stories act according to their own sense of morality rather than conforming to the strict codes of their contemporaries. They function as models of female agency, albeit in relation to black male powerlessness, by choosing to align themselves with black men.

* * *

In "Bodily Bonds," Karen Sanchez-Eppler asserts that, to her knowledge, "no antislavery fiction admits to the possibility of a white woman loving or wedding a black man."[4] Instead, she argues, fictional mulattas (women who are mixed-race) serve as figures through which white women play out their "forbidden desire" for black men. For it is only in these fictions—where the mulatta stands in for the white woman—that "the love of a white-skinned woman and a black-skinned man can be designated, and even endorsed, without being scandalous" (44).

Louisa May Alcott's short stories, "M.L." and "My Contraband," disrupt Sanchez-Eppler's formulation by replacing the conventional mulatta with a white woman who willingly transcends racial and social boundaries in order to maintain a meaningful relationship with a light-skinned black man. In contrast to depictions of white male/black female liaisons that were accepted as part of the legacy of slavery, Alcott's representations of white female/black male liaisons articulate desires that were considered taboo and dangerous.[5] Her works portray the forbidden status of these relationships in a manner that challenges white supremacist claims that white women were in need of protection from uncivilized free black men.[6] Alcott takes advantage of the dramatic rupture that these transgressive liaisons produce by creating white female characters who enact their womanhood differently from the norm[7]. At the same time, she also capitalizes on the emblematic status of the light-skinned black male characters (mulatto) by juxtaposing their proximity to and distance from both the sanctioned white world and the forbidden black one. The liminal racial status of the black male characters enables them to play multivalent roles in the narratives and to invite multiple readings about various issues that their presence invokes (like property rights, gender roles, threat of the recently emancipated black male), rather than reinforcing didactic conclusions.

Ultimately, Alcott's explorations focus more on white middle/upper class women's identity than on the antislavery issue or even the fate of freed black male slaves. Similar to Sanchez-Eppler's description of the mulatta figure whose very existence, despite her complex role as a proxy for white women, upholds the "delicacy," supremacy and morality of white womanhood, Alcott's black male characters provide the impetus for articulation of white female agency and transformation.[8] The interracial relationship remains "safe" as long as the black male character occupies a nonthreatening position. In fact, the black male characters either transcend race or reinscribe blackness as "inferior" in order to sustain their relationship with the central white female characters. As the black male characters fade into the background of the narratives, the white women assert themselves as fully developed subjects. Although Alcott's depictions of interracial relationships, where white women freely choose to engage in relationships with black men, do not deconstruct racist conceptions of blackness, they do provide a rich site for exploring the complexities of interracial desire and the rigid racial and gender hierarchies that were in place in the 1860s.

Both "My Contraband" and "M.L." describe the experiences of independent white women whose platonic relationships with light-skinned black men (mulatto) develop into meaningful life-transforming engagements. Although the men in both texts are recently liberated slaves, they continue to provide services for white patrons. "My Contraband" is the story of Nurse Faith Dane who is put in charge of a wounded Confederate officer and assigned the help of Bob, a recently liberated slave who turns out to be the Confederate officer's illegitimate half brother. "M.L." is the story of an independently wealthy white woman, Claudia Tate, who shocks her community by falling in love with and marrying her music teacher, Paul Frere, who is also an ex-slave. For both Nurse Dane and Claudia, these men represent something passionate, exotic, and admirable that neither woman seems to have access to in her own life. Nurse Dane, aware of Bob's racial identity and former enslavement from the beginning of the story, expresses her curiosity about black men:

> Feeling decidedly more interest in the black man than in the white. . . I glanced furtively at him as I scattered chloride of lime about the room to purify the air. . . I had seen many contrabands, but never one so attractive as this. All colored men are called "boys," even if their heads are white; this boy was five-and-twenty at least, strong-limbed and manly. . . I wanted to know and comfort him; and, following the impulse of the moment, I went in and touched him on the shoulder. (75–6)

Intrigue, compassion, and desire fuel Nurse Dane's initial attraction to Bob. He functions as both an object of pity and awe for her. Although she valorizes his charming appearance and pride, she also imposes her authority over him by reducing him to the level of a boy. However, this infantilization provides her with the opportunity to interact with him in a more intimate manner. (Here, it is important to note that one half of Bob's face is disfigured while the other half has no scars. Apparently, the scars were inflicted while he was still enslaved.) She also claims that Bob's past suffering and embattlement are what inspire her passion and sympathy rather than admitting that she is attracted to him. Similarly, Claudia, who has no knowledge of Paul's racial background until the middle of "M.L.," responds to what she and her friend Jessie Snowden describe as Paul's mysterious magnetism. His music stirs "her blood like martial music or heroic speech" (131) and his dark features appeal to her:

Claudia saw a face that satisfied her eye as the voice had done her ear, and yet its comeliness was not its charm. Black locks streaked an ample forehead, black brows arched finely over southern eyes as full of softness as of fire. No color marred the bronze of the cheek, no beard hid the firm contour of the lips, no unmeaning smile destroyed the dignity of the countenance, on which nature's hand had set the seal wherewith she stamps the manhood that no art can counterfeit. (133)

For Claudia, part of Paul's allure lies in his stoic exoticism. She views him as an aesthetically pleasing piece of artwork whose beauty is unsurpassable. In fact, her friend, Jessie Snowden, echoes this sentiment when she refers to Paul as a "great ornament" and invites Claudia to descend from her "Mount Blanc"[9] to look at him. Even before Paul's black heritage is revealed, he represents a dark "other" in contrast to their (Claudia and Jessie's) unmarked whiteness. But, instead of fearing his mysterious origins, Claudia and Jessie attribute his difference to blue-blooded Spanish ancestry and elevate him to the level of a noble prince.[10] Like Nurse Dane in "My Contraband," Claudia locates the source of Paul's "exceptional" manhood in the darkness of his body. Both women identify this racial "otherness" as an integral component of masculinity and beauty. This racialized sex appeal both invokes and refutes the stereotypical associations of the black male body with an oversexed predator.[11] For Alcott represents these light-skinned black men as both manly and lovely, attributes usually categorized as masculine and feminine, respectively. By blurring more conventional notions of gender and race in her depictions of these black-identified men, Alcott distances them from more common characterizations of black men, allowing them to take on multiple roles in her narratives. Alcott's portraits of these men also avoid the conventional "old happy darkey" (like Uncle Tom) formulations that would clearly categorize these men as black and, by extension, mark their desire transgressive and criminal.

In addition to occupying a position of exoticism, these dark men represent a certain nobility of character to Nurse Dane and Claudia, which, to some extent, erases their racial difference. For, as Sanchez-Eppler argues in "Bodily Bonds," in order for either of these "black" men to become heroes, their blackness must be separated from "the configuration of traits that in the bodily grammar of sentimental fiction signals revulsion" (38). In other words, in order to create sympathetic black characters, writers often muted any characteristics that might have been associated with negative stereotypical images of black men (like the uncivilized or hypersexual brute). In the case of "My Contraband," Bob distinguishes himself from other black people by calling them "niggers" and by refusing to associate with them. Nurse Dane reinforces his superiority by attributing his "comeliness" to "his mixed race" ancestry (76) and by lamenting that "he belonged to neither race" (78). In fact, Nurse Dane eventually raises Bob to the level of aristocracy when she states that "[t]he captain was the gentleman in the world's eye, but the contraband was the gentleman in mine" (79). She also insists on calling him Robert instead of Bob because she considers it a more appropriate and ennobling name. Ironically, Bob shares the same blood as the captain, for he is the son/ex-slave of the captain's father. By foregrounding the primacy of Bob's "aristocratic" blood, Nurse Dane relegates his blackness to the margins. Later on, when Nurse Dane discovers that the captain raped Bob's wife while he was still enslaved, she transforms him into a martyr: "He was no longer a slave or contraband, no drop of black blood marred him in my sight, but an infinite passion yearned to save, to help, to comfort him" (84).

In a similar manner, Claudia's emphasis on Paul's honorable qualities lifts him to hero status that renders his black (read inferior) ancestry invisible. Even before Paul reveals his history, Claudia considers him saintly because he shows "no bitterness of spirit," lives "to some high end unseen by human eyes" and possesses a "valiant spirit" (136). Since Paul can do no wrong in Claudia's eyes, his disclosure of his true identity—son of a Cuban planter and an Octoroon slave—only increases his value in her eyes. For she considers his endurance of slavery another marker of his strength and moral fortitude. Similar to Bob in "My Contraband," Paul's superior character masks his racial identity. In fact, he is referred to as a minstrel several times in "M.L." This reference to his musical talent also invokes his ability to perform and to entertain, a role frequently assigned to blacks in the United States (because of slavery and blackface minstrelsy).[12] Ironically, Paul performs as a white man. It is also no accident that both Paul and Bob closely resemble white men and that both women identify them as Spaniards, commenting on the fact that the men's skin is only a few shades darker than their own "authentic" white skin. This simultaneous proximity to and distance from whiteness enables these characters, as well as those who come into contact with them, to either recognize or disregard their blackness.

Despite these gestures of erasure, Bob's and Paul's black identities and slave status do not disappear. Both Nurse Dane and Claudia gaze at their (Bob's and Paul's) exposed dark bodies, marked by their experiences as slaves. Whenever Bob turns his head to expose the disfigured side of his face, Nurse Dane must confront her own prejudices about black men:

> In an instant the man vanished and the slave appeared. . . any romance that had gathered around him fled away, leaving the saddest of all sad facts in living guise before me. Not only did the manhood seem to die out of him, but the comeliness that first attracted me. . . my purpose was suddenly changed; and, though I went in to offer comfort as a friend, I merely gave an order as a mistress. (76–7)

Here, Nurse Dane acknowledges her earlier romanticization and eroticization of the "beautiful side" of Bob by responding with repulsion to his painful-looking scars.

Her description transforms him from a man into a thing by invoking his slave status. She dismisses any possible desire she has for Bob when she is forced to view
the deformations that slavery has inscribed on his body. Instead, she reasserts her
authority and disregards his manhood, enabling her to interact with him in a
detached and impersonal manner. But the emphasis on his body here also disrupts this role-playing by literally incorporating the materiality of his experience
as a slave. Moreover, as Nurse Dane and Bob continue to interact, this distance
breaks down and, in order to maintain an intimate relationship with him without
entering into a sexual liaison, she assumes a sanctioned maternal role. In this
position of power and compassion she can behold his marked black body as
though it belongs to a child, or "boy" in need of her ministration.[13] In this manner,
Nurse Dane redefines her relationship with Bob so that she does not have to sever
her ties with him. By occupying the role of caretaker she can continue to engage
with him intimately without arousing suspicion.

Claudia, on the other hand, identifies the "shadow of some past despair" as a
sign of strength and nobility. And, when she discovers that the "wide purple scar"
on Paul's hand represents the initials of his former slave owner, Maurice Lacroix,
she openly embraces his pain. Even when Paul expresses his anguish by striking
"his scarred hand on the chimney piece with a force that left it bruised and bleeding" (143), Claudia does not shrink from this dramatic display. Instead of distancing herself, Claudia releases her "purer passion" and adopts Paul's suffering as part
of her own. For Claudia, his racial identity, as well as the scars of slavery, reinforce his humanity and his moral superiority.

However, neither of the black male characters attains his sacrificial hero status independently of the white female characters. In fact, Nurse Dane and Claudia
define Bob's and Paul's roles in relation to their own subjectivity. Because Nurse
Dane and Claudia function as self-motivated, educated, and strong moral characters, they possess the independence to judge Bob and Paul according to their merits,
rather than blindly defining them according to a reductive racial hierarchy. In
contrast to depictions of white women whose positions in the established patriarchal structure remain subservient and fixed, Nurse Dane and Claudia assert their
mobility and agency by acting as self-governing subjects. They enact their independence from white male authority (*or exhibit their autonomy*) and their freedom
to make their own choices about love and friendship in a way that most white
women at that time experienced only vicariously. In contrast to white women
who lived out their "forbidden desire" for black men through "vicarious reading[s]
of the body of" the mulatta/slave in antislavery fiction, Nurse Dane and Claudia
represent white female self-ownership because they choose to align their (white)
bodies with the bodies of black men.[14] Their choice to use their bodies "elsewhere"
(rather than conforming to the rigidly prescribed roles for upper/middle class white
women) reemphasizes their self-empowerment.[15] In fact, this assertion of authority and agency, read along with the somewhat feminized characterizations of Bob

and Paul, could indicate that they are performing masculinity. Conversely, Bob and Paul, who become their dependent partners, could be read as performing female conventions. This subtle gender inversion challenges normative masculine and feminine roles. By attributing feminized traits to her black male figures, Alcott disrupts stereotypes of black men as hypermasculine at the same time that she reinforces racist notions that mixed-race black men are somehow less manly because of their contaminated blood. And, although she offers white women a more active role, it is valid only when juxtaposed with the dependence of these black-identified male characters.

In "My Contraband," Nurse Dane demonstrates her independence by her chosen profession, for few women were willing to leave families, travel alone, and nurse the bodies of sick and wounded men. She also treats Bob with a certain amount of respect by addressing him by his first name rather than as "boy" and by showing a genuine interest in his history. When Bob has locked the captain, Nurse Dane, and himself into the hospital room so that he can kill the captain (who is his half brother), Nurse Dane uses her facility with language and her persuasive powers to subdue Bob. In fact, Nurse Dane takes on what would be considered a masculinized role by assuming a position of power and forcing him to submit to her. She recalls that "[h]e let me take from him the key, let me draw him gently away, and lead him to the solitude which was now the most healing balm I could bestow" (87–8). At the same time that Nurse Dane responds forcefully, she also slips in and out of her role as a caretaker. This juxtaposition of feminized maternal behavior and masculinized fortitude, enables Nurse Dane to occupy an unconventional position, not only for a white woman but also for a white woman involved in an intimate relationship with a black man.

Similarly, Claudia remains unconstrained by societal rules in "M.L." Contrary to gender conventions of her time, Claudia initiates her love relationship with Paul. She possesses money and property and it is she who risks social condemnation for marrying a black man and former slave.[16] And, even though she has previously refused to marry because her "master had not [yet] come" (135), she endures public scorn in order to marry the black man whom she loves. After undergoing communal ostracism, which is represented as more horrible than Paul's experiences as a slave, Claudia reassures Paul that "there is no anguish in that brand [his scar], no humiliation in that claim, and that," like him, she accepts only "the bondage of the master who rules all the world" (151).[17] And, for a disturbing moment, Paul looks like "a happier, more contented slave, than those fabulous captives the South boasts of, but finds it hard to show" (151). Distinguishing herself from Southern slave owners, Claudia functions as the most benevolent mistress of them all. For she is willing to drop "down on her knee before" Paul, as if proposing to him, in order to convince him of her moral fortitude and of her loyalty to him. In the same way that Nurse Dane assumes a masculinized role as she ministers Bob, Claudia assumes a conventionally masculinized role as she rescues

Paul and symbolically carries him off into the sunset. It can also be argued that Claudia's relationship with feminized Paul, in some ways, stands in for lesbian desire, since she and her friend Jessie Snowden negotiate their own competing passions through Paul. They vie over him and express their own powerful emotions in relation to him; however, they place him in the traditionally feminized role of the damsel in distress who must be wooed and protected by a suitor. Moreover, since same sex unions would have also been considered transgressive, Alcott negotiates the sex/gender codes by invoking lesbian desire indirectly through the triangular relationship of Paul, Claudia, and Jessie. In this way, her representation of heterosexual interracial marriage may also function as a surrogate for same sex liaisons, which articulates another alternative desire that challenges naturalized (or normative) heterosexual middle/upper-class models. By demonstrating Claudia's assertive pursuit of an intimate relationship with a forbidden object of desire (black man or another woman), Alcott's story provides a model for articulating and fulfilling white female desire and sexuality.

Claudia's role as a heroic savior is, perhaps, reinforced by the fact that Paul was literally liberated from slavery by his white half sister and may function as a sort of allegory for white women's participation in the abolitionist movement. Furthermore, both women are also constructed as morally superior and liberal-minded white women who undergo terrible hardships in order to liberate vulnerable black men.

Although Bob and Paul are the ones who are literally emancipated from slavery, Nurse Dane's and Claudia's liberatory experiences occupy the center of both narratives. For them, Bob and Paul function as serviceable black bodies employed to produce transformation and discovery in their lives.[18] In "My Contraband," Nurse Dane describes Bob as though he is her possession—her contraband—and, in the final scene, he completely submits to her and to the traditional abolitionist solution to racism and slavery—death.[19] (He dies after killing the captain at the Battle of Fort Wagner, which culminated in the victory of the Union over the Confederacy.) Similar to a slave who adopts his/her master's name, Bob literally takes Nurse Dane's name, becoming Bob Dane. In contrast to the master/slave relationship and, to some extent, traditional nineteenth-century matrimony, this symbolic marriage inverts traditional marital conventions and asserts Nurse Dane's position of power.[20] At his dying moment, Bob gives Nurse Dane one final look, "one murmur of submission" and finds "wife and home, eternal liberty and God" (93).[21] As in other sentimental abolitionist fiction, Bob's death is described as a tragic but necessary result of the horrible institution of slavery. Ironically, it is also at the moment of death that Bob has finally liberated himself from slavery and his past (having expressed his manhood in combat). Although Bob is now free to engage in a more substantial relationship with Nurse Dane, his death forecloses any possibility for a prolonged relationship. However, it is Nurse Dane who completes the narrative and who describes Bob's death as a romantic attainment of freedom.

Similarly, in "M.L.," Claudia's betrothal transports her into another world where "she cared little for its [her old world's] censure or praise" (139). Leaving her old life and joining the brotherhood of the Samaritans, Claudia and Paul escape, "[l]ike . . . child[ren] in a fairyland" (154). Once she and Paul enter this world of spiritual "equality," his race no longer matters—it is invisible—and Claudia effortlessly transcends those whom she leaves behind. Like Nurse Dane in "My Contraband," Claudia reinscribes the final moment of liberation in terms of her own subjectivity, stating: "'I cannot give the substance for the shadow, —I cannot leave my world for yours. Put off the old delusions that blind you to the light, and come up here to me'" (155). Claudia surpasses earthly matters so that slavery and racism no longer provide an obstacle to her happiness. This sentimental conclusion creates an idealized world where Paul's race is literally erased and reaffirms the beneficence and integrity of white womanhood, once again reinforcing the centrality and significance of white women's positions. However, at the same time that both women's romanticized roles place them at the center of the narratives, they also suggest that white women's desire and ability to transform relationships between blacks and whites, men and women, can only be explored to its fullest potential in the realm of the imagination (fiction).

* * *

Even though "My Contraband" and "M.L." revise the mulatta woman as surrogate for white womanhood and the white male/black female formulation of interracial liaisons so that the woman is white and the man is black, it is important to consider how this model represents race and gender. Why is it that in these representations of cross-racial relations Alcott can imagine white female agency only in relation to black male powerlessness? Do Alcott's representations challenge the racial/gender constructs of the mid-nineteenth century or do they merely reproduce the hierarchy where blackness remains outside or "other" and whiteness remains in the center?

Although Alcott's models certainly complicate Sanchez-Eppler's formulation of interracial erotics, they don't redefine "blackness" in relation to "whiteness" in any significant way. However, close rereadings of Alcott's fiction do, in fact, provide space for reevaluating the transformative power of popular and sentimental fiction. Despite the fact that her work does not overturn the era's racial/gender hierarchy, its introduction of alternative choices for white women and of expanded definitions of white womanhood, modeled by aspects of Alcott's own life, certainly disrupts limiting hegemonic discourse demanded by such directives as the Cult of True Womanhood. In fact, her stories, while exploring the impacts of cross-racial love and desire, can also be read as reformulations of white upper/middle class women's identities, which would have been increasingly significant and in contestation as women became more active in defining their societal roles in the late nineteenth-century United States.

NOTES

1. Contraband is the term used for property (including slaves) confiscated during the Civil War.

2. The term miscegenation refers to cross-racial mixing but it is not a generic term. It was popularized in 1863 by pro-slavery journalists who wanted to generate fear and anger about sexual relations between whites and blacks. See George Fredrickson's *Black Image in the White Mind*, 171–172.

3. Although I use the term mulatta/mulatto to describe mixed-race individuals, there were different labels that implied different proportions of black and white blood. For example, a quadroon was the label for someone with one-fourth black blood and octoroon was the category for someone with one-eighth black blood. Since these characters were usually described in terms of their proximity to whiteness or some other ethnic category, like Portuguese or Italian, it is more likely that they would have been considered quadroons or octoroons.

4. See Sanchez-Eppler's "Bodily Bonds" 44.

5. It is important to note, however, that some of these stories were rejected because they were considered too controversial for publications like *The Atlantic Monthly*, because its editors feared that the stories would offend the magazine's Southern readership. Alcott's use of a pseudonym also suggests that she did not necessarily want to be identified as the author of such a potentially explosive topic.

6. See Martha Hodes's, *White Women, Black Men: Illicit Sex in the 19th Century South* for numerous examples of the threat that these relationships posed to white patriarchy and the racial hierarchy of the plantation South, especially during and after the Civil War.

7. The image of white womanhood which dominated during the nineteenth century directed women (especially Southern women) to maintain the domestic realm and to limit themselves to assisting their husbands and families. Activist and abolitionist Northern women were often juxtaposed with this idealized definition of womanhood. See Ann Firor Scott's *The Southern Lady: From Pedestal to Politics, 1830–1930.* (Chicago: The U of Chicago P, 1970) esp. 18, 225.

8. This is similar to Morrison's discussion of the Africanist presence which ignites moments of discovery, liberation, and change for whites—black people are present but they are relegated to the background (*Playing in the Dark*).

9. Mont Blanc takes on more significance at the end of the story but it is important to note its multivalence here. It can refer to the symbolic power of whiteness and the superior position that Claudia assumes. It is also a possible reference to Shelley's poem, which meditates on the interchange between nature and the human mind (1817).

10. It was very common in narratives about mixed-race characters for others to identify them as Spanish or as part of some other ethnic/racial group.

11. This image of black masculinity was used to justify lynchings and to support racist oppression of blacks after the Civil War.

12. Eric Lott discusses the emergence and development of blackface and minstrelsy in *Love and Theft*.

13. It is quite evident, however, that Nurse Dane does distinguish between Bob and other black contraband when she meets him again in a hospital after the battle at Fort Sumpter. This time, all of the soldiers that she nurses are black and she distinguishes him from all of the "sable heroes" and from his companion who is "as black as the ace of spades" (90–1).

14. Sanchez-Eppler 43.

15. Harriet Jacobs also demonstrates this self-ownership and this choice to use her body elsewhere in *Incidents in the Life of a Slave Girl*, when she chooses to enter into a relationship with Mr. Sands instead of her owner, Dr. Flint.

16. The fact that her legal marriage to Paul would have given him legitimate access to property and money would have made their marriage more of a threat to white men.

17. Alcott's use of the term "master" to describe both a husband and God is interesting here, particularly in relation to the limited roles of women. It might indicate an attempt to align white womanhood with the condition of slaves, subject to the rule of husbands reinforced by the patriarchal authority of Christianity.

18. Toni Morrison describes this concept in *Playing in the Dark*.

19. Karen Sanchez-Eppler discusses this convention in "Bodily Bonds" 50.

20. In Elaine Showalter's introduction to *Alternative Alcott* she suggests that Bob's adoption of Dane's surname is a kind of marriage to her.

21. It is important to note that Bob's death is the result of a wound he suffered at the Battle of Fort Wagner. This battle culminated in the victory of the Union over the Confederacy. It is significant in relation to Nurse Dane's description of the black bodies of "boys" who have now been transformed into men in the battle for emancipation.

WORKS CITED

Alcott, Louisa May. "M.L." *Louisa May Alcott: Selected Fiction*. Ed. Daniel Shealy, Madeleine B. Sterne, and Joel Myerson. Boston: Little, 1990. 131–154.

———. "My Contraband." *Alternative Alcott*. Ed. Elaine Showalter. New Jersey: Rutgers UP, 1992. 74–94.

Frederickson, George. *The Black Image in the White Mind: The Debate on Afro-American Character and Destiny, 1817–1914*. New York: Harper & Row, 1971.

Hodes, Martha. *White Women, Black Men: Illicit Sex in the Nineteenth-Century South*. New Haven, CT: Yale UP, 1997.

Lott, Eric. *Love and Theft: Blackface and Minstrelsy and the American Working Class*. New York: Oxford UP, 1993.

Morrison, Toni. *Playing in the Dark: Whiteness and the Literary Imagination*. Cambridge: Harvard UP, 1992.

Sanchez-Eppler, Karen. "Bodily Bonds: The Intersecting Rhetorics of Feminism and Abolition." *Representations* 24 (Fall 1988): 28–58.

Showalter, Elaine. Introduction. *Alternative Alcott*. Ed. Elaine Showalter. New Jersey: Rutgers UP, 1992. ix–xliii.

CHAPTER EIGHT

"Getting in Touch with the True South"

Pet Negroes, White Crackers, and Racial Staging in Zora Neale Hurston's Seraph on the Suwanee

DELIA CAPAROSO KONZETT

In her provocative essay "The 'Pet' Negro System" (1943), Hurston describes the complex racial dynamics of the post-Reconstruction South. While upholding racism and its values of white supremacy and black inferiority, this system, Hurston claims, nevertheless establishes mutual individual interests and friendships across racial lines. Unlike the North, whose interest lies in the promotion of justice for blacks as a race but not as individuals, the South, Hurston asserts, is concerned solely with the promotion of black individuals while maintaining the inferiority of the black masses. Quoting from the South's unofficial doctrine, the imagined "Book of Dixie," Hurston explains tongue in cheek this seemingly divine right of white men to possess a pet Negro:

> And every white man shall be allowed to pet himself a Negro. Yea, he shall take a black man unto himself to pet and to cherish, and this same Negro shall be perfect in his sight. Nor shall hatred among the races of men, nor conditions of strife in the walled cities, cause his pride and pleasure in his own Negro to wane. (156)[1]

Blacks who attain the status of pets, says Hurston, are generally seen by whites as "truthful and honest, clean, reliable and faithful," that is, "as white inside as anyone else" (PNS 158). Blacks outside the confines of the pet system fall into the class of "stray niggers" and "nobody gives a damn about them" (PNS 158). As these remarks make evident, Hurston's deliberately provocative language at once polemically advances and questions the pet system as the paradigmatic unofficial social doctrine of the South.

131

Similarly, blacks, says Hurston, have their pet whites, generally whites of high social standing with whom they want to be associated. Hurston gives the example of the Negro servant who, in order to preserve his own class prestige, chastises his master and mistress whenever they fall off their pedestal of whiteness. Exempted from this category of whiteness are "pore white trash" and "strainers" who due to their lower class and economic standing are seen by blacks as undeserving of the label "white" (PNS 158). This complex and contradictory system of racial hierarchy, claims Hurston, came into being during slavery and "symbolizes the web of feelings and mutual dependencies spun by generations and generations of living together and natural adjustment" (PNS 157). Fulminating against well-meaning Northerners making racial policy "in some New York office" (particularly black thinkers), Hurston points out how their seemingly perfect plans are doomed from the start since they do not consider the Southern everyday experience of race as regulated by this entrenched system (PNS 156–57).

Certainly Hurston's essay provokes much discussion and criticism, raising disconcerting and uncomfortable questions about race (as well as Hurston's own stance on race) that cannot be easily answered. Perhaps the most unsettling of these is Hurston's controversial belief that the Jim Crow system somehow works to establish harmony in the South and is therefore justified. In addition, her implication of blacks in this racial system of patronage equally offends conventional race perceptions operating with clear demarcations between victims and victimizers. Insensitive to the fact that the South systematically disenfranchised its entire black population and committed atrocities on "erring" blacks unwilling to conform to the system, Hurston's essay makes the unnerving claim that Southern blacks have in reality been collaborators in the upholding of white supremacy. She deliberately chooses not to condemn the pet system but to reveal alongside its expressions of racial hatred and violence those of genuine care, loyalty, and affection.

In *Seraph on the Suwanee* (1948), published five years after "The 'Pet' Negro System," Hurston elaborates on this system, revealing the central and overlapping roles that race, class, and gender play in the production and representation of the New South. While it is easy to dismiss Hurston's political views expressed in her later works as reactionary, naïve, or self-serving (as has often been done), it is more challenging to attempt to understand her idiosyncratic manner of intervention in the predominant discourse of race in a pre-Civil Rights era.[2] Because of Hurston's controversial politics, her later works have been disregarded or marked off as an embarrassment and we are instead given a one-sided portrait of the author based on her most popular works, *Their Eyes Were Watching God* and *Mules and Men*. The aim of this essay is to trace the workings of this pet system as put forward in *Seraph*, to analyze Hurston's complex and contradictory stances on race which place her work at once at the rear and at the vanguard of her time. As I will argue, Hurston's ambivalence illustrates not simply the self-evident shortcomings of the author but, more significantly, America's pathological and contradictory discourse of race with its fundamental inability to explain the institutions of slavery and second-class citizenship from within the context of democracy. Hurston's writings reflect this pathological situation, exposing the inevitability and impossibility of writing as an African American woman.

It is precisely, however, the ambivalence generated by Hurston and her situation that has enduring value for the cultural and literary study of her work. The tensions and contradictions under which Hurston had to labor are also expressed in her work. At its best, Hurston's work is not merely symptomatic of a nation's pathological ideology of race displaced onto black culture, but it also stages and exposes its inconsistencies. In *Seraph* Hurston articulates what she sees as the unspoken golden rule of the South and thus lays bare a messy system in which traditional oppositions of perpetrator and victim, master and slave, white and black, overlap and are at times indistinguishable from one another. Neat binary distinctions, Hurston realized, are not operable in the context of race: "It happens that there are more angles to this race-adjustment business than are ever pointed out to the public, white, black or in-between" (PNS 156).

I will begin by reviewing Hurston's discussion and exploration of the contradictory and schizophrenic form of Southern racial relations, tracing in particular her analysis of whiteness as a ubiquitous frame of reference in the construction of Southern identity. Examining specifically Hurston's representations of her white female heroine and her relation to other characters, I will show how Hurston maps a complicated network of private and social interactions informing racial self-perception and identity. Unlike the work of her contemporary Richard Wright, Hurston's depiction of race accepts no simple binaries but shows racial identity as a realm that is more negotiable than heretofore traditionally perceived.

If, as Walter Benn Michaels provocatively claims, Hurston is a nativist modernist whose work reinscribes a racial ideology even more insidious than that it sought to replace, we will also see that Hurston believed that race played a primary role in imagining and creating a modern American identity *in a pre-Civil Rights era.* The nation's emerging cosmopolitan multicultural or pluralistic identity, Hurston acutely understood, did not transcend racialized concerns as many believed but instead represented an evolving yet persistently troubled American identity. To gauge Hurston's modernism solely from a post-Civil Rights perspective, as is usually done by contemporary critics, not only is ahistorical but fails to appreciate the partial progress towards racial justice and equality achieved in this particular period with its unique context and limited repertoire of solutions.

Dismissed by many critics as a failure and a classic example of a minority author pandering to white mainstream concerns, *Seraph* is in fact one of Hurston's most compelling texts with its detailing of this messy "race adjustment business."[3] Never one to avoid controversy, Hurston deliberately provokes at all levels. Like her other work, especially *Tell My Horse* (1938) and *Moses, Man of the Mountain* (1939), *Seraph* has proved a bane to feminists, particularly black feminists. These critics find it difficult to come to terms with a xenophobic, insecure, and whimpering heroine, seemingly the exact inverse of her most popular character, the vital and towering Janie Crawford of *Their Eyes Were Watching God* (1937).[4] To complicate matters further, the husband of the heroine establishes his dominance in their relationship through rape and violence, acts the novel does not condemn but depicts as motivated by love.

Similarly, as Hazel Carby has pointed out, *Seraph* has created distress among critics and readers who view Hurston as an ethnic writer attempting to portray and preserve the difference of a distinct African American ethnicity (Foreword viii–ix). Not only is the linguistic difference between her white and black characters virtually unnoticeable in the novel, but Hurston also has whites in *Seraph* repeat the same folk sayings and aphorisms of her earlier black folk characters (Foreword ix). Carby refers specifically to Hurston's letter to Burroughs Mitchell, her editor at Scribner's, in which the author revises her earlier linguistic theories: "I think that it should be pointed out that what is known as the Negro dialect in the South is no such thing . . . What is actually the truth is, that the South, up until the 1930s was a relic of England . . . . and you find the retention of old English beliefs and customs . . . They did not get it from the Negroes. The Africans coming to America got it from them" (Hurston qtd. by Carby in "Foreword" viii–ix). Whereas *Mules and Men* depicts an independent black folk community that produced unique cultural artifacts, *Seraph* upholds the view that white Southerners and black Southerners ultimately share the same cultural heritage. It appears that, in writing a novel about poor white Southerners or Florida "crackers," Hurston did not believe she was leaving her black folk culture behind, as many critics have accused her of doing. Instead, she saw herself as depicting and imagining a New South in which the sociocultural bonds between blacks and whites are staged and thereby acknowledged, leading to a better understanding of the complex relationships between these two races.

Contrary to claims accusing her of pandering to white interests, Hurston draws no flattering portrait of her white heroine but exposes her as a woman of petty prejudices, acting in complicity with social, racial, and patriarchal oppression. *Seraph* is the story of Arvay Henson born into a shiftless, poor, and no-account white family. (The Hensons are more realistic counterparts of Faulkner's infamous Snopes and Bundren families.) Hurston's narrative opens in turn-of-the-century Sawley, Florida, a rural town on the banks of the famous Suwanee River plagued with "malaria, ignorance, poverty and the ever-present hookworm."[5] Its inhabitants are mainly poor white sawmill and turpentine workers cut off from the land on which they live. The few fields that are cultivated have only "scratchy plantings" and the scant flowers in front yards are placed in homely tin cans and buckets (SS 1). Sawley's haggard and pinched landscape, one that reflects the character of the town and people, reveals absolutely no traces of the noble and elegant agrarian lifestyle stereotypically associated with the antebellum South.

Indeed, Hurston's narrative opens with a chronicle of Sawley that elides this glorious era, stressing instead the region's diversity and constantly changing cultural topography:

> Few [in Sawley] were concerned with the past. They had heard that the stubbornly resisting Indians had been there where they now lived, but they were dead and gone. Osceola, Miccanope, Billy Bow-Legs were nothing more than names that had even lost their bitter flavor. The conquering Spaniards had done their murdering, robbing and raping and had long ago withdrawn from the Floridas. Few knew and nobody cared that the Hidalgos under De Sota had moved westward along this very route . . . The Reconstruction was little more than a generation behind. Men still living had moved into west Florida after Sherman had burned Atlanta and made his triumphant march to the sea. A dozen or more men who had worn the gray of the confederacy were local residents. Damn Yankees were suspect [sic] of foraging around still looking for loot; and if not that, gloating over the downfall of The Cause. (SS 2–3)

In making the antebellum period merely another event of the past in Sawley's varied and multicultural history, Hurston does away with the timeless, ahistorical myth of The Old South and "The Cause" with its attempts to repress other historical claims of precedence (those of the Native Americans and colonizing Spaniards). Thus in the opening pages of Hurston's narrative, any claims to original belonging and nativism are challenged along with their accompanying myths of cultural and racial supremacy. Sawley is instead presented as a degenerate community of "white crackers" desperately clinging to the Old South's grand myth of whiteness based not on an actual belief in white superiority but on white resentment, insecurity, and anxiety. Against this setting of cultural poverty and degradation, Hurston's novel unfolds its at once sympathetic and parodistic narrative of the unacknowledged Other within white culture. The focus of Hurston's analysis lies with the fate of a poor white woman, complicating the notion of oppression as being perpetrated only from a position of power and strength. Hurston's heroine, though weak and subservient, is ultimately shown to assert her racial privileges albeit in a passive and indirect fashion.

At the age of twenty-one, Arvay Henson, the novel's protagonist, is well on her way to becoming, according to Southern terms, an old maid when the ambitious Jim Meserve of an upstanding family that has lost its plantations and wealth in the Civil War begins to court her. Having already lost an earlier suitor to her designing older sister, Arvay had instead chosen to devote her life to God. Before Jim's arrival in Sawley, she had stood before her congregation on Communion Day, "young and white, and teasing to the fancy of many men" and announced vague plans to become a missionary and "take the Word to the heathens" in China, India, and Africa (SS 4). However young, unschooled, and impoverished Arvay may be, she, like the rest of the townspeople, nevertheless instinctively understands the unquestioned value of her whiteness, one that enables her to imagine herself in a superior cultural and moral position vis-à-vis nonwhites. While her marriage to Jim does away with her dream of becoming a missionary, Arvay continues to indulge in its underlying myth of whiteness, along with the resentment, insecurity, and fear that feed it, causing her marriage and family life to founder and hindering her own self-growth.

Unable to adjust to the quick changes going on around her and intimidated by the new middle-class lifestyle eagerly sought by her enterprising husband and children, Arvay instead takes solace in an illusionary past that glorifies her heritage:

> Arvay tossed her head defiantly and rhymed out that she was a Cracker bred and a Cracker born, and when she was dead there'd be a Cracker gone. . . . Let Jim and them have their ways. She would go back and let Jim strain with his house and his impudent, biggity niggers his ownself . . . The corroding poverty of her childhood became a glowing virtue, and a state to be desired. Arvay scorned off learning as a source of evil knowledge and thought fondly of ignorance as the foundation of good-heartedness and honesty. Peace, contentment and virtue hung like a rainbow over turpentine shacks and shanties. There love and free-giving abided and not on decorated sun-porches . . . Arvay felt eager to get back in the atmosphere of her humble beginnings. God was showing favor to His handmaiden. (SS 272)

Arvay's nostalgic perspective on the antebellum South conflates race and class into the quasi-Christian virtue of humility with its "humble beginnings" where God "[shows] favor to His handmaiden." Poverty and whiteness, in contrast to Jim's social ambition built on the work of his black servants, become an untainted natural expression of God's grace. Hurston unmasks this onto-theological recovery of a pure cultural origin as an anachronistic illusion in the face of overwhelming economic decline and cultural disintegration.

Even though Hurston uses the same linguistic idiolect in depicting the white rural South as she had used in her depiction of black folklore, she nevertheless treats the two cultural contexts very differently. Unlike *Mules and Men* and her folk novels where poverty permitted its own poetic and imaginative forms of redemption, it appears here as a falsely inflated myth lacking empowerment, thriving instead on resentment and a sense of inadequacy. Whereas Hurston's black folk could nevertheless lead enriched lives from within their restricted condition, the "white crackers" in *Seraph* displace the negative values of poverty onto black culture and embrace an illusion embodied by the Old South. As handmaidens to God, poor whites or "crackers" in Arvay's perspective are not impoverished because they are shiftless, lazy, and dishonest, as she believes is the case with black folk, but are so due to external causes such as greedy Yankees and foreigners as well as traitorous blacks demanding equality.

W. E. B. Du Bois has pointed out how low-paid white workers "were compensated in part by a public and psychological wage" of whiteness that made them feel racially and culturally superior to nonwhites and thus able to deal better with their economic inequality and the contradictions of their situation as poor whites. (700).[6] Similarly, Anne McClintock has discussed how national and imperialist pride compensated white British workers for their class subordination(58–59). As Hurston's work likewise suggests, this compensation of whiteness allowed Southern whites, especially poor whites, to cope with the reality of the New South as a structurally backward and impoverished region in the face of rapid transformations and modernization impinging upon traditional Southern lifestyles and attitudes.

In her depiction of Arvay as a "cracker," Hurston ultimately complicates the traditional perception of whiteness as a seemingly undisturbed hegemonic force and entity. Instead, she focuses on the ambivalent position, perhaps even double-consciousness, of impoverished whites that are at once, as Annalee Newitz and Matthew Wray claim in their analysis of "white trash," "inside and outside whiteness, becoming the difference within, the white Other that inhabits the core of whiteness" (170). In their discussion of stereotypes concerning poor whites, Newitz and Wray argue how terms such as white trash, redneck, cracker, and hillbilly point to the seemingly oxymoronic position of "subordinate white":

> Unlike unmarked hegemonic forms of whiteness, the category of white trash is marked as white from the outset. But in addition to being racially marked, it is simultaneously marked as trash, as something that must be discarded, expelled, and disposed of in order for whiteness to achieve and maintain social dominance. (169)

In their understanding of terms like "cracker" as representing a defective whiteness, Newitz and Way point specifically to that which white compensation covers up or hides, namely the inability of poor whites to live up to ideal and privileged standards of whiteness. A pathological form of Du Bois' black double-consciousness, Hurston's depiction of poor white Southerners traces a schizophrenic whiteness that is divided against itself, a myth of supremacy concealing a sense of economic and cultural inadequacy, anxiety, and degradation.

Gender and its production of sexual identity, or more precisely, the powerful ideology of white Southern womanhood further defines and complicates our heroine's perspective. Hazel Carby has convincingly argued that the relationship between the two different but interdependent ideologies of white Southern womanhood and black Southern womanhood is based mainly on a negative dialectic that disguises or mystifies social relations in order to keep a racial system in place (*Reconstructing Womanhood* 20–22). In antebellum times, the dominant image of white Southern womanhood was based on the "four cardinal virtues [of] piety, purity, submissiveness and domesticity" that placed white women on saintly pedestals (*Reconstructing Womanhood* 23). As its antithesis, the image of black Southern womanhood was based on stereotypes of overt sexuality and brutish physical appetites that excluded female slaves from the category of "humanity," recreating them into breeders and perpetrators of their own rape committed by their white masters. While white women were oppressed in certain significant ways, they nevertheless shared in the power of their husbands, fathers and sons and thus in the oppression of blacks. The apparent fragility and purity of the ideal white woman, like the brutishness of her black counterpart, ultimately worked to keep a system of enslavement functioning smoothly and efficiently as well as to affirm the power of the white patriarch.

In her nostalgic outlook and bearing, Arvay retains the antebellum image of white Southern womanhood with its expected social privileges and compensations. Hurston reinforces this image in the description and portrait of her heroine. Unlike her lusty and well-built sister Larraine,

> [Arvay] was pretty if you liked delicate-made girls. Her shape was not exactly in style in those parts, but that could easily be overlooked. She had breasts to her bosom, but elsewhere Arvay was lean-made in every way. No heavy-hipped girl below that extremely small waist, and her legs were long and slim-made instead of the much-admired "whiskey-keg" look to her legs that was common. She had plenty of long light yellow hair with a low wave to it with Gulf-blue eyes. Arvay had a fine-made kind of a nose and mouth and a face shaped like an egg laid by a Leghorn pullet, with a faint spread of pink around her upper cheeks. (SS 4)

This delicate refinement is also revealed in Arvay's unusual and refined musical talent, her sexual priggishness, her seeming piety, reserved bearing, and her overall incompatibility with the crudeness of Sawley and its people, her father and sister in particular. Like the stereotypical white mistress, she is condescendingly kind to her assumed inferiors when they are dependent on her. At the same time, Arvay is unable to escape from her "degenerate" white background, represented by the birth of her deformed first child who takes after her family, and she is also unable to live up to the ideal of whiteness projected by her husband and other successful children. At once white mistress and white cracker, Arvay reflects the schizophrenia of Southern whiteness with its ideals and suppressed deficiencies.

The overlapping dynamics of gender, class, and race are most interestingly given in the mimetic triangular relationship between Jim, Arvay, and Joe Kelsey, Jim's pet Negro. Uncertain if Arvay is marrying him out of duty and in love with someone else, Jim turns to Joe who advises him: "Most women folks," Joe tells Jim, "will love you plenty if you take and see to it that they do. Make 'em knuckle under. From the very first jump, get the bridle in they mouth and ride 'em hard and stop 'em short. They's all alike, Boss. Take 'em and break 'em" (SS 46). Heeding Joe's advice, Jim "rapes" Arvay and then elopes with her. In this conversation Hurston foregrounds a complex cross-racial patriarchal bond that upholds the oppression of women and places Joe in a position of complicity. Joe does not simply affirm Jim's position of patriarchal power but shares it as a male. He not only encourages Jim to make Arvay "knuckle under" but also explains to him in the manner of a teacher how this act is to be performed. In Joe's statement "They's all alike, Boss," Hurston captures the complex sociocultural dynamics of the modern pet Negro system that at once places Joe in an equal and subservient position to Jim.

Similarly, as a white woman and the spouse of Jim, Arvay is simultaneously an accomplice and victim of the South's white patriarchal ideology. This ambivalent situation is depicted in Arvay's rape in which Jim's violent offense is transformed into an act of love and becomes the basis of their marriage:

> Jim was gritting his teeth fiercely on encountering the barrier of her tight-legged drawers, seeking an opening. Finding none, Arvay felt one hand reach up and grasp the waistband. There was a "plop" and the girl knew that the button was gone. A tearing sound of starched fabric, and the garment was being dragged ruthlessly down her legs. Arvay opened her mouth to scream, but no sound emerged. Her mouth was closed by Jim's passionate kisses. . . . Not until Jim lay limp and motionless upon her body, did Arvay return to herself and begin to think. . . . She was terribly afraid. She had been taken for a fool, and now her condition was worse than before . . . What was to become of her now? Where would she turn for refuge? Not to her folks, certainly . . . Unconsciously, Arvay's own arms went up and were locked around Jim's neck . . . Some unknown power took hold of Arvay. She pressed her body tightly against his, fitting herself into him as closely as possible. A terrible fear came over her that he might somehow vanish away from her arms, and she sought to hold him by the tightness of her embrace and her flood of kisses . . . She must eat him up, and absorb him within herself. Then he could never leave her again. (SS 51–53)

Hurston's careful description of the event plots the course of this transformation, revealing how Arvay's fear of abandonment turns an initial act of violence and mastery into one of consensual seduction and intimacy. Rather than yell rape, an act that would place her in the clear position of victim, Arvay realizes that by conceding to the upper-class Jim she will be compensated socially, economically, and racially, thereby possibly escaping the degenerate whiteness of her family. As Hurston demonstrates, however, the compensation of whiteness, based on anxiety and deficiency, can never be sated and requires constant reaffirmation and expansion. Its supremacy must always be affirmed because it is forever in danger of slipping into inadequacy. Thus Arvay is especially threatened by those she views as nonwhite and thus undeserving of social privileges, namely Joe and white outsiders like her Yankee son-in-law and her husband's foreign white assistant and his family.

In Hurston's modern complex grid of overlapping racial class and gender identities, both Joe and Arvay are deeply implicated in the perpetuation of racism, classism, and sexism. Hurston is careful, however, to delineate the differences in their respective situations. As Jim's pet Negro, Joe plays the role society has assigned to and expects of him. The historian David Goldfield describes Southern racial etiquette and its elaborate attempt to preserve the feudal hierarchy of the antebellum period into the modern period:

> An act of bad manners was not merely a regrettable faux pas, but a major social transgression that threatened order, violated expectations, called into question the rectitude of social and racial givens, and challenged integrity. The players assumed their roles carefully, especially the blacks. The code of etiquette governed every social situation from hunting to casual meetings in the street. For blacks encountering whites, the code demanded, among other things, "sir" and "ma'am," averted eyes, preferably a smile, never imparting bad news, never discussing other whites, and always exhibiting a demeanor that would make a white comfortable in believing that this deferential mien was not only right but the way things ought to be. The white, in turn, would almost always address the black by a first name or by generic terms such as "boy," "uncle," or "aunty," regardless of age . . . From this etiquette flowed an array of assumptions whites held about blacks that reinforced the inferior role of black southerners. Blacks were childlike; they were prone to steal and prone to violence; they were oversexed, stupid, lethargic, dependent on whites, and, above all, happy. (2–3)

Certainly Joe retains the mannerisms of the "old-time Negro." He always refers to Jim as Mr. Meserve, Mr. Jim or "Boss," while Jim simply calls Joe by his first name. Similarly, Joe never brags about his economic successes to Jim but instead delights in telling him entertaining and exaggerated stories about his many failures.

Hurston suggests, however, that this publicly staged and official racialized behavior is only the veneer of a much stronger and deeper bond that both men acknowledge and confirm in private actions. As Jim tells Arvay: "Joe knows where he stands with me. I would trust Joe Kelsey quicker than any man on earth I know of, and Joe knows it" (SS 60). Indeed, it is precisely because Jim is able to see through racial stereotyping of blacks as being childlike and shiftless that he is able to reap economic benefit. Jim's entire economic success is founded on business deals made with blacks and other outsiders whose skills other Southerners, including Arvay, are unable to discern. "That shows the difference between me and you," Jim tells Arvay. "I see one thing and can understand ten. You see ten things and can't understand one. A person can have very good eyesight, Arvay, and even wear glasses on top of that, but if they get in the habit of butting around with their eyes shut tight, they won't be able to see a thing" (SS 261). As Hurston's representatives of the "true South," both Jim and Joe are able to negotiate and to subvert prevailing social structures due to their comprehension that the South's complex racial and social conventions are not set in stone but involve an ongoing performance of Southern racial staging. While restricted in his social maneuverability as a black man, Joe is nevertheless able to empower himself through racial staging. The pet Negro system for Hurston is not simply that which reinforces white supremacy as Goldfield explains above but also, and more importantly, a strategic intervention which enables blacks like Joe to survive and even to flourish under oppressive Jim Crow laws. Both Jim and Joe benefit socially and economically from this unofficial and private association.

To further complicate Joe's position as a pet Negro, Hurston also foregrounds its transitional and changing nature in Joe's son, Jeff, who represents a new generation of Southern blacks. Unlike his father, Jeff does not tell entertaining stories about his failures but carefully notes the reason behind them so as not to repeat the same mistakes. Whereas Joe's playful demeanor seems to confirm negative black stereotypes, Jeff's behavior reveals a quiet self-reliance and confidence. In the most telling scene of the novel, Jeff becomes the moral enunciator and passes judgment on Arvay's cowardly outlook and her inability to act and think for herself. When Arvay becomes paralyzed with fright and is unable to save her husband, Jeff not only rescues Jim but also lets Arvay know she has failed:

> But Jeff gave her a look that halted her where she was . . . The look held. Jeff wanted her to know that she had been judged . . . In that moment Arvay realized what fear had done to her, and how she looked to those who knew it. (SS 256)

This look is later repeated when Jim separates from Arvay, leaving her in the care of Jeff:

> She went to sleep one afternoon on the sleeping porch with her face turned towards the wall. When she somehow woke up suddenly and turned her face over her shoulders, there was Jeff . . . [with] his face pressed against the screen wire, staring at her. His face was pressed so hard against the screening that his nose was flattened, and his lips were distorted into purple blobs. His eyes were fixed on her and unmoving. Neither did he jump away when he saw her see him. Traditionally, Arvay immediately thought of rape and murder. That look was so powerful and intense. But as she studied Jeff's face and eyes she got another shock. Jeff was not longing after her body. It was anger and dislike. If only he had his hands on her, he would tear her to little bitty pieces like a ragdoll. (SS 269)

In these crucial passages, Hurston endows Jeff with the returning gaze of the black Other that displaces whiteness in its refusal to authorize its superiority. Arvay's attempt to fix Jeff as the black rapist and savage comes undone and instead she becomes the object of his gaze and repressed hatred. Arvay can neither escape his look nor his judgment by conveniently falling back onto petty racial stereotypes, and in the end must admit to her own cowardliness and inadequacy. Ultimately, it is Jeff's moral gaze that shocks Arvay into recognizing who she is.

Returning to Sawley, she recognizes her resentment and anxiety in the house of her family that has come to represent her entire Southern heritage:

> Now Arvay looked at it with a scrutiny and darkened . . . it was no house at all. It was an evil, ill-deformed monstropolous accumulation of time and scum. It had soaked in so much of doing-without, of soul-starvation, of brutish vacancy of aim, of absent dreams, envy of trifles, ambitions for littleness, smothered cries and trampled love, that it was a sanctuary of tiny and sanctioned vices. Its walls were smoked over with the vapors from the dead souls like smoky kerosene lamps.
>
> By a lucky chance, she had been carried away from it at a fairly young age, but still, its fumes and vapors had stuck to her sufficiently to scar Jim and bruise her children . . . How much had it blinded her from seeing and feeling through the years! (SS 306–07)

In a symbolic act she burns down her family's house and attempts to patch together her marriage. However, she must first gain Jeff's approval, for it is only after she accepts him on his terms that she is able to win back her husband. In the character of Jeff and his difference to his father, Hurston depicts the ongoing transformations in the Southern racial hierarchy and suggests the real possibility of the pet system becoming, like the Old South, an anachronism.

However, whereas Hurston offers a pointed analysis of whiteness in the characters of Arvay, Joe and Jeff, she is not as successful in her characterization of Jim. Because he remains a one-dimensional character used mainly to gauge Arvay's growth, Jim falls outside of Hurston's critique of whiteness. His privilege and power as an upper-class white male remain unchecked throughout the novel. Embodying Hurston's ethical model of the New South, Jim espouses a liberal perspective that would seem to transcend racism and provincialism but that ultimately proves more insidious. Jim's race-neutral ideologies of liberalism and humanism are in fact invisible norms of whiteness that in the end re-inscribe gender, class, and race and thus rightly make us suspicious of Arvay's self-development. In addition, Hurston's privileging of private face-to-face contact as given in her concern with folk communities is often done at the expense of the public realm, ignoring how institutions and their traditions shape and produce racial identity alongside the private encounters.

Despite these obvious shortcomings, however, Hurston's novel offers a highly sophisticated depiction of frequently interchangeable and overlapping discourses of power in the complicated maze of race, gender, and class relations. These discourses of power function as "articulated categories," to borrow Anne McClintock's term. They represent "not distinct realms of experience, existing in splendid isolation from each other but come into existence *in and through* relation to each other—if in contradictory and conflictual ways" (6–9). In this light, *Seraph* specifically analyzes a form of whiteness divided against itself in the outlook of the "Cracker." From the perspective of a poor white Southern woman, Hurston reveals how whiteness presents itself as the natural center of privilege and power and manifests itself in daily domestic life. In foregrounding Arvay's social position as a "Cracker" unable to live up to the imagined norms of whiteness, Hurston undermines this centrality of white identity and exposes the myth of white supremacy as one of ambivalence and inadequacy.

In this context, the pet Negro system is more clearly presented in all its complex, conflicting, and messy relations to whiteness, doing away with the reductive oppositions of black and white, master and slave, oppressor and victim. In the pet system, then, Hurston depicts a pre-Civil rights institution in which social identities, however constrained, were nevertheless negotiable. Pet Negroes are able to pass as white and white strainers become "white Negroes." While the pet system is also without doubt an institution of inequality serving the purposes of racial oppression, it also contains within its social and symbolic realm of negotiation the possibility, however limited, for change and advancement regarding the cultural and socioeconomic status of African Americans. In this way, Hurston was able to claim that black Southerners did not live merely in oppressive and degraded circumstances but could and did lead productive, if not happy, lives. Black Americans did not simply survive in an atmosphere of institutionalized racism but through strategic intervention were able to turn subordination into affirmation. And as Hurston claims, the pet system also allowed for cross-racial expressions of affection and care that society did not otherwise encourage.

Far from being simply an attempt to win a white mainstream audience or to serve as a spokespiece for assimilationist and universalist discourses, *Seraph* offers a compelling analysis of Southern race relations and whiteness that reveals the contradictions at the core of racial identity. This ambivalence is deliberately staged in Hurston's dedication of the novel. Co-dedicated to Mrs. Spessard L. Holland, the wife of Senator Spessard Holland, who was the former Governor of Florida and a staunch advocate of segregation, *Seraph* is a deliberately double-edged or ambivalent account of race that in typical Zoraesque fashion at once flatters and parodies Mrs. Holland. In attempting to understand Hurston's articulation of Southern race relations, we cannot adhere to the conventional linear and progressive narrative of racial emancipation. Such a model ultimately prevents us from appreciating the significant albeit limited advances made within the context of a historical epoch of racial inequity situated between the era of slavery and civil rights. Instead, Hurston gives us a synchronic perspective, rather than one that is concerned with a heritage of slavery or a future of racial equality.

A modernist in outlook, Hurston is concerned with the performative present of racial staging that enabled Southerners, black Southerners in particular, to repro- duce and to reimagine their racial identities. Southern culture, Hurston demon- strates, is ultimately a racialized tradition that continually reenacts and reimagines America's racial drama with its attendant codes of whiteness and blackness. And if, as Walter Benn Michaels argues, writers like Hurston replaced biological per- spectives of race with a nativist, pluralist modernism that celebrated cultural dif- ference by grounding it in essentialized notions of race-specific cultural practices, we can also see how Hurston understood race as a stubbornly persistent phenom- enon of culture that ultimately cannot be transcended since it remains the defining core of modern America's subjective and collective identities.

NOTES

1. From "The 'Pet' Negro System." Hereafter referred to in text as PNS.

2. For a discussion of how literary critics have made a deliberate effort to dismiss and ignore the political stance that frames all of Hurston's work, see David Heading, "'Beginning to See Things Really': The Politics of Zora Neale Hurston."

3. Robert Hemenway, for example, says that in *Seraph*, "a story of white south- erners, with only random mention of black people," Hurston "largely turned her back on the source of her creativity." See Robert Hemenway, *Zora Neale Hurston: A Literary Biography*. Darwin Turner and Robert Bone accuse her respectively of pan- dering to market tastes and assimilationism. See Darwin Turner, *In A Minor Chord: Three Afro-American Writers and Their Search for Identity*. See Robert Bone, *The Negro Novel in America*. More recent essays have been much more sympathetic to *Seraph*. Lillie Howard notes that while Hurston may have changed the color of her characters, she nevertheless remains firmly in the Southern folk milieu, retaining her earlier themes. Like other Hurston heroines, Arvay Henson, claims Howard, "searches for self-actualization and love, for life-affirming rather than life-denying experiences. White folks, Hurston perceptively realized, must want those things, too." Howard suggests, however, that *Seraph*, in its focus on universal themes, transcends race rather than complicates it, as I would hold. See Lillie Howard, "Ser- aph on the Suwanee." Hazel Carby's astute foreword to *Seraph* discusses Hurston's revisionism in which she repudiates her belief in a unique black culture. *Seraph*, notes Carby, is "a vehicle for Hurston's theories on the relations between black and white culture," and the formation of a national expression. See Hazel Carby, "Foreword."

4. Recently, however, feminist critics such as Mary Helen Washington have begun to question the popular interpretation of Janie as a pre-feminist, noting prob- lematic episodes in *Their Eyes* that reveal Hurston's ambivalence towards her hero- ine and women in general. See Washington's *Invented lives: Narratives of Black*

Women 1860–1960. Here, Washington returns to Robert Stepto's earlier criticism that Janie's power to speak is illusionary, noting disturbing moments in the text when Hurston subverts her protagonist's voice.

    5. *Seraph on the Suwanee* will hereafter be referred to in the text as SS.

    6. See also David Roediger's *Wages of Whitenss: Race and the Making of the American Working Class.* Roediger's compelling study draws upon DuBois's conception of the race-class dialectic, analyzing the paramount role that race played in conjunction with capitalism to form an American working-class identity hostile to blacks.

WORKS CITED

Bone, Robert. *The Negro Novel in America.* New Haven: Yale UP, 1958.

Carby, Hazel. "Foreword." *Seraph on the Suwanee.* New York: Harper Perennial, 1991. vii–xviii.

———. *Reconstructing Womanhood: The Emergence of the Afro-American Woman Novelist.* Oxford: Oxford UP, 1987.

DuBois, W. E. B. *Black Reconstruction.* New York: Kraus-Thomson, 1935.

Goldfield, David R. Black. *White, and Southern: Race Relations and Southern Culture.* Baton Rouge: Louisiana State UP, 1990.

Heading, David. "'Beginning to See Things Really': The Politics of Zora Neale Hurston." *Zora in Florida.* Ed. Steve Glassman and Kathryn Lee Seidel. Orlando: U of Florida P, 1991. 28–37.

Hemenway, Robert. *Zora Neale Hurston: A Literary Biography.* Urbana: U of Illinois P, 1977.

Howard, Lillie. "Seraph on the Suwanee." *Zora Neale Hurston: Critical Perspectives Past and Present.* Ed. Henry Louis Gates and K. A. Appiah. New York: Amistad, 1993. 267–79.

Hurston, Zora Neale. "The 'Pet' Negro System." *I Love Myself When I Am Laughing . . .: A Zora Neale Hurston Reader.* Ed. Alice Walker. New York: Feminist Press, 1979. 156-62. Originally published in *American Mercury* 56 (May 1943): 593–600.

———. *Seraph on the Suwanee.* New York: Harper Perennial, 1991. Originally published in 1948 by Charles Scribner's Sons.

McClintock, Anne. *Imperial Leather: Race, Gender and Sexuality in the Colonial Contest.* New York: Routledge, 1995.

Michaels, Walter Benn. *Our America: Nativism, Modernism, and Pluralism.* Durham: Duke UP, 1995.

Newitz, Annalee and Matthew Wray. "What is 'White Trash'? Stereotypes and Economic Conditions of Poor Whites in the United States." *Whiteness: A Critical Reader.* Ed. Mike Hill. New York: New York UP, 1997. 168–84.

Roediger, David R. *Wages of Whiteness: Race and the Making of the American Working Class.* New York: Verso, 1991.

Turner, Darwin. *In a Minor Chord: Three Afro-American Writers and Their Search for Identity.* Carbondale: Southern UP, 1971.

Washington, Mary Helen. *Invented Lives: Narratives of Black Women 1860–1960.* London: Virago Press, 1989.

CHAPTER NINE

Prison, Perversion, and Pimps

The White Temptress in The Autobiography of Malcolm X and Iceberg Slim's Pimp

TERRI HUME OLIVER

As we enter the new millennium, public discourse concerning young, African American males has reached deafening levels. Often this sound (and fury) has been quite literal; the huge popularity of rap groups has revitalized the music industry while simultaneously guaranteeing that only those profoundly deaf to popular culture would be unaware of the association of the gangster persona with these artists. Other factors are at work to fuel this discussion, including the dismayingly large proportion of African American men who have been involved in the penal system. Obviously, the concern about the future of black men in America has ranged from the most serious sociological and political work to the most trivializing sound bites on the local evening news; however, mainstream attention has centered largely on the transgressive lyrics that seem to celebrate misogyny, violence, and criminal activity. Very real problems of police brutality, urban poverty, and inter- and intraracial violence sometimes collapse into the court battles of celebrities such as Ol' Dirty Bastard and Puff Daddy. At the same time, the largest numbers of consumers of hip hop and rap music are middle-class, white teenagers who sometimes appropriate "gangsta" mannerisms to signify universal, youthful rebellion. Or not so youthful rebellion. At this writing, Madonna, at forty-two, is nominated for a Grammy and has received awards from MTV and *Rolling Stone* magazine for her "Music" video in which her transgendered version of a pimp (complete with big hat, furs, jewelry, and limousine) sings dance music while pouring champagne for a phalanx of beautiful, sexy women. More controversially, Eminem and Kid Rock (white male performers in their twenties) feature songs that insist

upon their authenticity as outlaw figures while adopting styles generally associated with African American youth.

Despite the future uses of these phenomena in popular culture, interest in
the gangster and pimp role increased throughout the 1990s in a way that demands
a linkage back to its antecedents in the late 1960s and early seventies. Robin Kelley
in *Race Rebels* both expertly outlines the history of gangsta culture (through "the
dozens," "toasts," and "baaadman (sic) narratives" throughout the twentieth century)
and sensitively confronts the gender and racial politics underlying what he defines
as an "everyday resistance" to the hegemonic power structure (214). This essay
will not attempt to repeat ongoing, complicated arguments about the effects of
rap music or the cultural meaning of this renewed interest in gangster life. However, I do want to view another influence of pimp narratives upon both old school
and contemporary rap music (215). For Kelley, the question of the pimps' "exalted
status" in 1960s popular culture was a Black Power response to "the image of female
dominance created by the Moynihan report," a way of "turning matriarchy on its
head" (216). While this scholar's reading of the gender politics of pimp narratives
within the community seems correct, he does not unfold the importance of the
white woman as a sexual object to the outlaw figure (especially the pimp, the "mack
daddy"). The following pages attempt to provide a literary history of one of the
strongest American taboos: sexual liaisons between black men and white women,
as depicted in African American texts, with special emphasis on the narratives of
Malcolm X and Iceberg Slim.

Between 1965 and 1967, during the height of the Black Arts and the Civil
Rights movements, two autobiographies were published by two very different
African American men, previously unknown as authors. The first of these was
Malcolm X, already famous across the nation as the public persona for the Nation
of Islam. While continuing his high profile political activities, Malcolm X dic-
tated his autobiography to Alex Haley with the proviso that "Nothing can be in
this book's manuscript that I didn't say, and nothing can be left out that I want in
it."[1] The other aspiring author was Robert Beck, who used his street name, Iceberg Slim, to pen his gritty tale, *Pimp: The Story of My Life*.[2] At the time of publication of his first book, Iceberg Slim was known only to those who remembered
his exploits as a hustler on the streets of various Midwestern cities and to state and
federal law enforcement authorities. Now, more than thirty years following their
initial publications, both books are still widely read despite their very different
audiences. *The Autobiography of Malcolm X* is now canonical in American letters,
and the text has gained even greater fame since the Spike Lee movie was released
in 1992. In contrast, Robert Beck's death the same year received little attention
from the American public, even among scholars of African American literature.
However, at the time of his death, Iceberg Slim was the best selling African
American writer of all time, having sold six million copies of his seven books
(Muckley 18). According to his publisher, Holloway House, *Pimp* alone has sold

over one million copies, with the distribution being largely concentrated in Europe, American prisons, and universities.

Despite the great disparities in their impact on the public, these two men (and their texts) share many characteristics, including very problematic relationships with white women. Both narratives begin with difficult early lives. Malcolm X calls the chapter on his early childhood "Nightmare," while Iceberg Slim names his "Torn from the Nest." Other similarities include urban crime involvement, prison stays, renaming to indicate life changes, a picaresque narrative structure, and a critically important conversion story. Moreover, an important theme, miscegenation, complicates the narrator's attempt to define himself in the white world. In both accounts, the white woman functions as a temptress whose image has been so internalized by the black male that he lusts after her despite societal sanction. These relationships typically end with the male being victimized by the liaison, thus reversing the nineteenth-century fictional prototype of the tragic mulatto in which the victim is female.[3] Further, in both autobiographies, the thrill-seeking white woman actively seeks out the black male, becoming the white huntress who stalks her prey in his own territory. Ironically, in the same decade that these two narratives reinscribe cautionary tales against black/white sexuality, the most liberal portion of American white liberalism was congratulating itself upon its tentative acceptance of interracial romance, exemplified by the film *Guess Who's Coming to Dinner?* Yet, for the majority of America, and certainly for hustlers and pimps, white women were "regarded as stolen property, booty seized from the ultimate hustle" (Kelley 176). However, the white women in *Autobiography* and *Pimp* are neither romantically involved with nor ever really possessions of the black men. Attempts to commodify the white temptress ultimately fail, and as Iceberg Slim declares, "They laying to swindle chump Niggers outta their youth" (*Pimp* 128).

Critics have noted that, beginning with St. Augustine's *Confessions*, the most interesting portion of the conversion narrative is the life of sin which antedates spiritual enlightenment and moral rectitude.[4] In both narratives considered here, the more mundane phases of their lives, before or after their criminal years, are subsumed by the more dramatic years in the urban underworld. Actually, in the *Autobiography*, the reader's fascination with the zoot-suited, lindy-hopping, gangster phase of Malcolm X's narrative often overshadows what Malcolm X points to as the first major turning point in his life: his English teacher's advice that he abandon his ambition to be a lawyer ("no realistic goal for a nigger") and become a carpenter (MX 43). When the young Malcolm Little realizes that, despite being one of the three best students in the class, he had no future beyond that of skilled laborer, he gradually abandons his efforts at achieving the American dream.[5] Malcolm X's descent into a life of crime offers the reader an inverted Horatio Alger story, much of whose popularity proceeds from the natural voyeuristic appeal of the outlaw life.[6] In a similar manner, the continuing popularity of *Pimp*, from its publication until the present, has always been based on readers' preferences for the forbidden that sustains the popularity of the rogue novel, "the picaresque, the adventures of underclass operators, hustlers and survivors from Defoe to Fielding to *Fanny Hill*" (qtd. in Muckley 76).[7] Although Iceberg Slim, in contrast to Malcolm X, had the opportunity to attend college—the young Robert Beck was a student at Tuskegee Institute at the same time—he is expelled when the college administration discovers that he sold moonshine and seduced local girls. The lure of easy money pulls this intelligent young man back to the streets. Describing Iceberg Slim's autobiography, D. B. Graham names it as an example of "negative glamour" (Muckley 18). Through these narratives, readers who live average, possibly boring, existences can vicariously participate in such risky business as drug use, pimping, and hustling, without exposing themselves to danger.

However, for Malcolm X and Iceberg Slim, among the actual life-threatening temptations accompanying street life, the white temptress appears in the landscape of these urban scenes as an additional threat. White women, through an interesting reversal of the black mulatto stereotype, pose a threat to black masculinity by being able to wield more power in their relationship. While white women historically have been present in black male autobiography as a physical danger, in *Pimp* and the *Autobiography*, the seductress becomes a psychic danger as well by compromising the black male's gender identity. Anticipating Franz Fanon's influential explanation of black sexual attraction to whiteness in *Black Skin, White Masks* as potentially neurotic, these narratives portray the emasculating effects of white women.

In the classic tragic mulatto story, a fragile, light-skinned black woman is pursued by a white villain whose obsession with her generally ends with her tragic death. As Werner Sollors points out: "The mulatto or half-breed themes were inevitably tragic or horrifying . . . The cause for the mulattos' tragic roles may be found in the sin of "miscegenation" or in social prejudice, but the life expectancy of mulatto characters in American literature is low" (224–25). Very popular in nineteenth-century novel and theater, these sentimental stories were meant to provoke outrage at the injustice of slavery by presenting an attractive, powerless victim. Despite violent deaths, these heroines always fought for their virtue and maintained their ideals, thus winning a moral victory over their pursuers. *Pimp* and the *Autobiography*, written over a century later, contain odd inversions of the tragic mulatto figure. In these texts, it is strong, male narrators who are targeted as sexual objects by the white world. However, this reversal is not as simple as it would seem because their victimizers are themselves, as women, victims of white patriarchy. Although the white women in these books are generally portrayed unsympathetically, some also suffer fates ranging from paternal rage to imprisonment as a result of their attraction to black men. Further, Malcolm X and Iceberg Slim obviously do not die gloriously virtuous deaths. Their accounts are confessionals, written after years of virtue, but using the figure of the white woman to condemn what they see as the immorality of their past lives. While tragic mulatto stories are intended (at least ideally) to provoke political action that would lead to more equality between the races, the *Autobiography* and *Pimp* were both written as cautionary tales by men who were, after their conversions, largely segregationists in regard to white women. Despite their radical stances, they have reinscribed, through their own ideologies, the very separation of white women and black men that white racists have always urged.

While the purpose here is not to valorize any traditional patriarchal models, the anomalous role reversal of black males and white females in *Pimp* and the *Autobiography* must be addressed in relation to the usual presentation of masculine identity in African American autobiography. Gender roles in male autobiography have been examined frequently for their problematic political import, particularly by black feminist writers.[8] For example, Deborah E. McDowell, in her consideration of Frederick Douglass's autobiographies, reports that this genre is considered by many feminists to be androcentric. Discussing Douglass, McDowell points out that the genre has as its focus "the public story of a public life, which signifies the achievement of adult male status in Western culture" and valorizes "the myth of the self-made man" (44). Speaking more generally concerning black, male slave narrative, Valerie Smith contends that "by mythologizing rugged individuality, physical strength, and geographical mobility, the narrative enshrines cultural definitions of masculinity" (34).

Black feminist critics also find it necessary to respond to the famous controversy inspired by Stanley Elkins' work, *Slavery: A Problem of American Institutional and Intellectual Life* (1959). McDowell briefly outlines Elkins's Sambo thesis which suggests that the emasculating effect in slavery resulted in a "half-man," "half-child." Although the dialogue about this work was both immediate and highly charged, it remained for the publication of John Blassingame's *The Slave Community*, some twenty years later, to argue convincingly that, despite the efforts of the slave owner, "slaves attempted to build monogamous families with the male as the authority figure" (McDowell 40–41). Blassingame's concept of slave family formation still does not address feminist concerns about these models of black, masculine identity formation, such as bell hooks's devastating critique:

> To suggest that black men were dehumanized solely as a result of not being patriarchs implies that the subjugation of black women was essential to the black male's development of a positive self-concept, an ideal that only served to support a sexist order. (hooks, 20–21)

In their desire to emphasize their manhood, black men may have, especially when writing in the autobiographical mode, inserted the white patriarchal model into black letters at the expense of black women. However, the historical reality of the struggle of black men to achieve recognition as men must be addressed, and, as Elizabeth Fox-Genovese convincingly argues, "Slavery had stripped black men of the social attributes of manhood in general and fatherhood in particular" (188).

It is possible, then, to agree upon the harmful impact of the general, "social unmanning" of black men while neither accepting Elkins's idea of personal emasculation (188) or the need for black women to serve as subjects to their patriarchy.

Although the discussion above only briefly introduces the problematics of identity formation in black male autobiography, it underscores the threat of role reversal associated with white women. The literary antecedents of such scenarios have deep roots in the nonfiction writing of African American men. Due to the historic white male anxiety about black male sexuality, white female sexuality has always been associated with physical danger for black men, especially in America. As far as I can determine, the first mention of such a dangerous liaison occurs in the 1789 London edition of Olaudah Equiano's slave narrative. Although Equiano, or Gustavus Vassa, eventually becomes a Methodist and marries a British woman, he reports of seeing, while still in slavery, a brutal mutilation: ". . . I have seen a negro-man staked to the ground, and cut most shockingly, and then his ears cut off bit by bit, because he had been connected with a white woman who was a common prostitute . . . the most abandoned woman of her species" (Equiano 104). Earlier in the autobiography, Equiano assures the reader of the exemplary modesty and chastity of the women of his village; obviously, this prostitute attests to the degraded state of white society as well as to the victimization of the black male. Further, the "abandoned" prostitute reveals the white woman's curiosity about black sexuality, a curiosity that is always fraught with the danger of white male retaliation. Without doubting the truth of these occurrences, it is useful to note that even Equiano's very early African American autobiography (and slave narrative) is a mediated construction as well as a firsthand memory. For example, Carl Pedersen points out that "his recollection of his Ibo childhood is informed by his reading of the works of the Quaker antislavery writer Anthony Benzet" (46).

As a fervent convert to Christianity, Equiano expresses, at the end of his narrative, the twin ambitions of becoming a missionary to Africa and of helping to end the slave trade. In order to fulfill this mission, like many slave narrators, this author uses biblical references to expose the injustices of slavery. In the shocking passage of torture related above, Equiano invokes the figure of the Great Whore of Babylon,[9] the hereditary temptress leading the chosen people away from God and into death and destruction. African Americans have traditionally identified with the Israelites in their search for safety and a homeland, and, in this account, a white American whore takes on the mantle of Lilith.[10]

In 1829, "David Walker's Appeal," a political tract specifically addressed to "Coloured Citizens," continues these biblical references by comparing unfavorably Christian America's laws against intermarriage with the Pharaoh of Egypt: "he gave him to wife Asenath the daughter of Potipherah priest of On" (Walker 183). However, Walker, fearing that this critique would be seen as indicative of his attraction to white women, rushes to declare, "Do they not institute laws to prohibit us from marrying among the whites? I would wish, candidly, however, before the Lord, to be understood, that I would not give a pinch of snuff to be married to any white person I ever saw in all the days of my life" (184). The use of "person" instead of "woman" is interesting here, but, to clear up any gender confusion, Walker goes on to say that to be married to a white woman is "to be a double slave to her" and suggests that a black man who would intermarry "ought to be treated by her as he surely will be, viz: as a NIGGER!!!!" (Walker 184). Amazingly, in the middle of this paragraph about intermarriage, Walker apologizes for even bringing up the subject, "I only made this extract to show how much lower we are held, and how much more cruel we are treated by the Americans, than were the children of Jacob, by the Egyptians" (Walker 184). Walker's prophetic language transforms the "fleshpots" of Egypt[11] into the more mundane, but also more dangerous, American Christian woman.

Later in the century, a few black luminaries, such as Frederick Douglass and Charles Chesnutt, tried to make a case for intermarriage as a solution to America's racial problem; most did not. By the late nineteenth century, lynching had become widespread throughout the South, with rape often being the charge that initiated violence. Between 1889 and 1899 the average number of lynchings was 187.5 per year. W. E. B Du Bois wrote in 1917 that he "was particularly bitter at the attitude of white women" who assumed that the "height" of the black male's ambition "is to marry them" (qtd. in Marable 86). Earlier, while still at Harvard, his hostility toward white women is more pronounced. Du Bois wrote a scathing essay on the American girl in which he compared the white woman to "the American Hog in its native simplicity" (qtd. in Marable 15). And his suggestion "to cure this eyesore" was that the white woman should "obtain an education and, lastly, go to work" (qtd. in Marable 16). Later, while studying in Germany, Du Bois changes his mind about white European women, if not American women, when he tells of his holiday in Eisenach, Germany:

> I emerged from the extremes of my racial provincialism. I became more human; learned the place in life of "Wine, Women, and Song"; I ceased to hate or suspect people simply because they belong to one race or color. (Du Bois 160)

Included in this new openness was his flirtation with the blond Dora Marbach, a German woman with whom Du Bois exchanged confessions of love. However, when Dora suggests that they marry, he responds, "But I knew this would be unfair to her and fatal for my work at home, where I had neither property nor social standing for this blue-eyed stranger" (Du Bois 161). In a contemplation on his twenty-fifth birthday in Berlin, Du Bois mentions another German woman, Amalie, for whom he fears he has been "the (perhaps) life ruin which is cruel" (*Against Racism* 28). W. E. B. Du Bois seems to have, indeed, overcome his "racial provincialism."

In his nonfiction writing (as opposed to *Autobiography of an Ex-Colored Man*, 1912), James Weldon Johnson does not disclose his personal feelings about white women but does investigate the matrix of desire and taboo that leads to violent reactions against interracial couples. He writes in his 1933 autobiography, *Along This Way*, that he was arrested and nearly lynched in Florida for escorting a light-skinned black woman who was taken to be a white woman by a crowd of white men. Later in this book he writes:

> A situation which combines the forbidden and unknown close at hand could not do less than create a magnified lure . . . It is possible that Dame Nature never kicks up her heels in such ecstatic abandon as when she has succeeded in bringing together a fair woman and a dark man together; and vice versa. (Johnson 390)

Unfortunately, this mischievous mixing of the races, for Johnson, leads inevitably to disaster. While excited by what he saw as positive changes in racial relations, Johnson's autobiography includes a cautionary tale about an old friend who married a white, Southern woman. Although this couple had several children, prospered, and appeared happy, his friend's financial losses led him, in 1930, to kill himself. In this story, the black man kills himself by a gunshot wound to the heart and declares, in his dying words, "I'm just tired of life" (Johnson 394). The struggle to maintain an interracial relationship, particularly in the face of poverty, proves to be overwhelming. If this story were fiction, the gunshot wound to the heart would appear too flamboyantly artificial.

Not surprisingly, Richard Wright's experiences with the dangers of white women are more personal, dangerous, and graphic. In his 1937 essay, "The Ethics of Living Jim Crow: An Autobiographical Sketch," Wright reports on the risks accompanying his job as a bellboy in Jacksonville, Mississippi. When called upon by the prostitutes to run errands, the bellboys often encountered the undressed prostitute who felt unashamed because "you were not regarded as human" (Wright 295). However, while waiting on a "huge, snowy-skinned blonde," the young Wright allowed his gaze to linger too long upon the naked woman. Observed by the prostitute's customer in the act of observing, Wright is warned by the "thick-set man" to, "Keep your eyes where they belong, if you want to be healthy!" (Wright 295). While, in 1789, Equiano reports of the mutilation of a black man's ears for the transgressive act of consorting with a white prostitute, in twentieth-century Jacksonville, the sentence was more severe:

> One of the bell-boys was caught in bed with a white prostitute. He was castrated and run out of town . . . We were given to understand that the boy who had been castrated was a "mighty, mighty lucky bastard." We were impressed with the fact that the next time the management of the hotel would not be responsible for the lives of "trouble-makin' niggers." We were silent. (Wright 296)

Following this threat, it took some years for Wright to express his voice in his powerful fiction. Mary Dalton's death and dismemberment in *Native Son* expresses

Wright's fictional revenge on all of the careless white women who entrap black men in dangerous, forbidden relationships.

James Baldwin provides his own anecdote about a relationship with a white woman, which, while totally asexual in content, was perceived as threatening and potentially evil by his father. In "Notes of a Native Son," Baldwin refers to a young, white schoolteacher who, in addition to encouraging his reading and writing, took him to see a play. Although his father disapproved of plays, he allows the youthful Baldwin to go because he is influenced by the authority that the teacher holds. Still, Baldwin's father is suspicious of the teacher's intentions, as Baldwin recounts:

> Before the teacher came my father took me aside to ask why she was coming, what interest she could possibly have in our house, in a boy like me. I said I didn't know, but I, too, suggested that it had something to do with education. And I understood that my father was waiting for me to say something—I didn't quite know what; perhaps that I wanted his protection against this teacher and her "education." (91)

In this passage, the only interest that Baldwin's father can accept as understandable from a white woman is sexual. Further, Baldwin's age at the time (nine or ten) would make this "education" particularly perverted. Despite Baldwin's assertion that this schoolteacher was guileless and actually helped his family financially, the father's fears were never totally allayed. In the four or five years that the unnamed teacher continued to mentor Baldwin, his father "never trusted her and was always trying to surprise in her open, Midwestern face the genuine, cunningly hidden, and hideous motivation" (Baldwin 92).

To judge from the autobiographies referred to above, the only safe love affair with a white woman is, for a black man, one that happens away from American soil. Miscegenation, while conspicuous in some other countries, holds its most virulent resonance in the United States. In *I Wonder as I Wander* (1956), Langston Hughes alludes to a Du Boisian sort of affair with a white woman, Natasha, in Russia. In a much more detailed account than Du Bois's, Natasha follows the model of the white huntress by surprising Hughes at 2 a.m. by appearing in his bed at the New Moscow Hotel. Although Natasha had been bom and educated in Moscow, she was an actress who often played peasant parts, and, according to Hughes, "she just liked peasants—and Negroes" (Hughes 224). When Natasha offers to leave her husband and follow Hughes back to America, his reflections include the following:

> There were enough troubles just trying to earn a living in the land of Jim Crow without having a white wife on my hands. My father had married a German woman in Mexico, but I had no idea of marrying a Russian in Moscow unless I were intending to stay in the Soviet Union. And to take one back to America with me! (Hughes 225)

With the possibility of returning to America, Hughes escapes this temptress unvic-timized, with only a thorough cursing in a combination of English, French, and Russian as negative consequences of the liaison.

With their travels confined to the United States, both Malcolm X and Ice-berg Slim are confronted with the lure of the white temptress in their own neigh-borhoods. In Malcolm X's own words, "in any black ghetto in America, to have a white woman who wasn't a common whore was—for the average black man, at least—a status symbol of the first order" (MX 78). While Iceberg Slim learns to negotiate the streets, he makes friends with a hustler called Party Time, who declares, "Two sights I ain't never seen and that is a pretty bulldog and an ugly white woman" (*Pimp* 35). As Slim becomes more sophisticated, he realizes that Party Time's observation is merely a rusty cliché, although as an inexperienced youth, he finds the comment to be "as witty as Hell."

Of course, this fascination with the sexuality of the "other" is not a one-way street. In these autobiographies, it is the desire of white women to experience the eroticism of the exotic that leads them into the downtown areas and clubs in search of black sexuality. The nightclub is the perfect modernist space in which traditional social structure can unravel in anonymity. Both of these texts begin their consideration of street life in the mid-thirties through World War II, follow-ing the formative impact of the Harlem Renaissance, when America's interest in black life flourished. However, this curiosity about the black male doesn't lead neces-sarily to a more egalitarian attitude among white women. Malcolm X recounts his conversations with a white madam who made her living supplying Negro males to well-to-do white women. According to this madam, white women generally had a complexion preference:

> She told me that nearly every white woman in her clientele would specify
> "a black one"; sometimes they would say "a real one," meaning black,
> no brown Negroes, no red Negroes. (MX 139)

In order for the sexual experience to be "authentic," these women demand some-one whose physical attributes reflect most strongly their African heritage. Despite their physical attraction, Malcolm X points out the irony that:

> those white women had no more respect for those Negroes than white
> men have had for the Negro women they have been "using" since slavery
> times. And, in turn, Negroes have no respect for the whites they get in
> bed with. (MX 140)

As proof of this assertion, Malcolm X recounts his experience with his own white temptress, Sophia, whom he says he did not respect despite their long term affair (MX 140).

Iceberg Slim often drops slighting references to white women in the midst of his larger narrative, as in the following passage. While in Chicago, Iceberg Slim glances into a nightclub, tellingly named "The Devil's Roost." In five sentences, the author emphasizes the predatory nature of the white woman in a black nightclub:

> The joint was jumping. Pimps, whores, and white men crowded the circular bar [. . .] Silk broads itching for forbidden fruit sat in booths lining the walls. Their faces glowed starkly in the red dimness. Their long hair flopped around their shoulders as they threw their heads back. They laughed drunkenly with their black lovers. (*Pimp* 95–96)

As in Malcolm X's description above, these, "silks" are desperately in search of what they consider to be the "authentic" sexual experience, which they believe can come only from a black man. Again, the white women generally prefer black men with a darker complexion. Iceberg Slim describes a friend as "short, powerful, and shiny black" who was "ugly enough to break daylight with his fist," yet who was irresistible to many of the thrill-seeking white women who believed in the myth of black male sexual superiority. Contemptuously, Iceberg Slim describes the white women who "sneaked into the black side of town panting as they chased after that hoary myth, 'Nigger men do it so good it thrills you to your toe nails . . .'" (*Pimp*, 34). In these scenes, white women are willing to transgress societal mores for sexual excitement, without any personal interest in their partner or the courage to appear with black men in the white side of town. As well as scorning their hypocrisy, Iceberg Slim inverts racist language to make the white women into hypersexual animals who "itch" and "pant" while inebriated. Further, the "red dimness" provides a hellish cast for the sinning women who do not require a serpent to induce them to lust after "forbidden fruit." As the first woman to succumb to temptation, Eve was seduced; however, these daughters of Eve not only give in to the allure of the proscribed, they actively seek it out. Further, with his description of these women's wild, long hair and glowing faces, Iceberg Slim's "silks" appear otherworldly, evil, and almost witchlike.

The use of the term "silks," with the attendant quotation marks, reflects Iceberg Slim's distancing of these women from the social realities of black inner city life. Since a portion of this author's agenda is to educate about street life, he includes a glossary at the back of his autobiography. Although "silks" is not listed there, his use of quotation marks alerts the reader to the fact that this term was one used as shorthand to indicate a variety of characteristics. Part of the power that these white women wield is financial; they are able to dress in silk, an expensive, natural fabric. However, sick of "that half-ass screwing at home," they "laying to swindle chump Niggers outta their youth" in their search for the "authentic," the natural, sex experience (*Pimp* 128). In Iceberg Slim's career in the sex trade, one of the worst things that could happen is being "Georgiaed," defined in his glossary as "to be taken advantage of sexually without receiving money" (*Pimp* 315). Much of this narrative's disdain for the "silks" is their reluctance to spend money for sex; however, looming over this annoyance is the threat of retaliation by white men who attempt to assure their racial and sexual hegemony through control of white female sexuality.

Glass Top, a friend of Iceberg Slim's declares, "Shit, if you stripped and searched all of 'em you wouldn't find a 'C' note. They ain't nothing but square housewives" (*Pimp* 128).

This acting out of sexual attraction between black men and the white temptress would be, in and of itself, of limited interest except for the negative consequences of the behavior for the black participant. Malcolm X claims that he was taught in "a thousand ways" that "most white men's hearts and guts will turn over inside of them, whatever they may have you otherwise believe, whenever they see a Negro man on close terms with a white woman" (MX 109). According to Katrin Schwenk, he had a lot of empirical proof to support this "gut feeling." Schwenk quotes James Cutler's 1905 assertion that "our country's national crime is lynching" and cites the following footnote: "Deb Friedman has demonstrated that between 1930 and 1979, 455 men were executed for rape; 405 of them were black. This statistic already gives food for thought; matters appear even more sinister when one realizes that although some black men were executed for raping black women, the overwhelming majority of victims were white, and no white man was executed for raping a black woman" (322).

For Malcolm Little, at this point referred to as Detroit Red, the life-threatening possibilities of an affair with a white woman came not from a lynch mob, but a jealous husband. When his white girlfriend's husband found out about her affair with a black man, he went to Malcolm's Harvard Square apartment with a gun to kill him (MX 172). Fortuitously, at the time he is being hunted by the angry husband, Detroit Red is being taken to a police precinct to be charged for running the burglary ring that he had formed with the same girlfriend, Sophia, her sister, and her sister's black lover. Even in this arrest, Malcolm X is nearly shot, prompting him to declare, "I have thought a thousand times, I guess, about how I so narrowly escaped death twice that day. That's why I believe everything is written" (MX 172). Although Malcolm X always admitted that his imprisonment saved him from an early death on the streets and led to his conversion to Islam, his remembrance of the way he was treated during his trial and conviction seethes with anger. Not only was his bail higher than Sophia's, the court machinery was both fascinated and appalled by his relationship with an upper-middle-class white woman. Social workers and his own court-appointed lawyers were more interested in his sex life than his theft. His own lawyer declares, "You had no business with white girls!" (MX 173). When sentenced in 1946, his jail term was ten years rather than the usual two-year burglary sentence, and Malcolm X always believed that his real crime, for the Commonwealth of Massachusetts, was having a white lover (MX 173).

Iceberg Slim, while never imprisoned as a result of a sexual relationship with a white woman, includes a cautionary tale about one such victim. When only seventeen years old, Iceberg Slim was sent to the state reformatory for pimping his fifteen-year-old girlfriend. While there, he met a "square," a religious, young black man named Oscar, who was incarcerated on a charge of statutory rape. In this cautionary tale, the white woman was really a girl, and certainly not a tempt-ress; yet, through his relationship with her, Oscar's life is devastated. After being discovered "smooching" with Oscar, a "crippled Irish girl of seventeen" is interro-gated by her family until she confesses that "old black Oscar had indeed trespassed the forbidden valley" (*Pimp* 52). Once in the reformatory, Oscar is beaten viciously with a steel cane by a guard, a "dummy." Again, it is his crime of miscegenation which causes this beating, as Iceberg Slim explains: "I remembered the murderous force of the blow the dummy had struck. I remembered the pleased look on his face. I knew from the con grape-vine that he was from Alabama . . . The dummy knew about that crippled Irish girl" (*Pimp* 55). Iceberg Slim reports that after beating and confinement, Oscar was "shipped to the funny farm where perhaps he is today, thirty years later" (*Pimp* 57). Although Iceberg Slim doesn't report ever having kept a white woman in his stable of prostitutes or even having a white mistress, ironically, his final imprisonment in 1960 (rearrested for being an escaped fugi-tive) stems from a federal charge of "White Slavery" based on his movement of black prostitutes across state lines (Muckley 21). As Peter A. Muckley points out: "White Slavery" under American law is not equivalent to a charge of "Pandering," but rather has to do with the movement of minors across state borders (21). Ice-berg Slim, objecting to charges of "White Slavery," insisted that he was never once "put in prison for the right reason" (Muckley 21).

As well as actual victimization, the gender role reversal in these books deserves further analysis. In both autobiographies, the protagonists, in their first meeting with white women, cede power to them. The symbol for the transfer of power in both books is the automobile, the ubiquitous phallic symbol for twentieth-century America. When the young Malcolm Little meets the blond Sophia in a dance hall, he notes her affluence as well as her physical attraction, "shoulder-length hair, well built, and her clothes had cost somebody plenty" (*MX* 78). This assessment of her wealth is confirmed when she takes him for a ride in her expensive con-vertible:

> She knew where she was going. Beyond Boston, she pulled off into a side road, and then off that into a deserted lane. And turned off every-thing but the radio. (*MX* 79)

Of course, Malcolm is more than happy to be along for the ride, as Sophia turns off everything but the radio and, presumably, him. However, due to the twin attrac-tions of whiteness and money, the woman is in the driver's seat in this reversal of the classic American make-out scene.

Iceberg's Slim's account of a similar scene occurs when he is already an ex-con-vict and a pimp. Hardly a naive young boy, Iceberg Slim (known as Youngblood at this stage in his career), after his evening ritual in which he "dressed and pow-dered his face" (*Pimp* 141), wanders into a bar called The Fun House. The gender reversal continues as he literally runs into a white woman whom he describes as "a perfumed line-backer," Melody (*Pimp* 144). Feigning car trouble, Melody asks for mechanical assistance in her odd and affected parlance:

> As a matter of fact my car is disabled. I was going inside to call for help when our heavenly bodies collided. Is it possible that you're not oblivious to the esoteric aspects of car repair? (*Pimp* 144)

While the reader, at this point, has many reasons to doubt Melody's identity, Youngblood is impressed by her, and, especially, by her car:

> My eyes followed her manicured finger to the sparkling new Lincoln sedan. Everything about her hollered class and affluence. (*Pimp* 144)

Melody also takes her conquest for a ride, but Iceberg Slim, unlike the less graphic Malcolm X, informs the reader about her seduction technique:

> The pulse on her satin throat was maniacing [sic]. She slid close to me. She zippered her scarlet mouth to mine. That confection tongue flooded my mouth with sugar. Her nails dug into my thighs. She gazed at me. (*Pimp* 146)

This seductress is very physically aggressive; the use of the neologism "maniacing," presumably indicates her almost insane passion. I will return to her story later in this essay, but even this introduction shows the role reversal made possible by whiteness and affluence. By contrast, in his many other accounts of cars, Iceberg Slim is the driver, and his passengers are his black prostitutes.

These two stories, of Sophia and Melody, also connect the figure of the white woman to homosexuality, a practice that both authors condemn. Malcolm X expresses deep and continuing guilt about a young, innocent, black girlfriend, Laura, in the fourth chapter of his book. In his excitement at being boldly picked up by the blond, affluent Sophia in Roxbury's Roseland dance hall, Malcolm unceremoniously dumps Laura. Believing that this disappointment in young love has ruined her life, Malcolm claims:

> She started going out late and drinking liquor. This led to dope and that to selling herself to men. Learning to hate men who bought her, she also became a Lesbian. To have treated her as I did for a white woman made the blow doubly heavy. (*MX* 80)

Whether the reader believes in Laura's slide into prostitution and lesbianism, or their causation, Malcolm X's cautionary tale is clear.

Iceberg Slim's meeting with Melody, not surprisingly, contains more than simple gender role inversion. After Melody takes him to her plush, suburban home, Iceberg's thoughts are as follows:

> This beautiful white bitch has class. Maybe I can string her out and get all the scratch she's got, then make a whore outta her. With her rear end, this bitch is sitting on a mint. (Pimp 144)

However, to his disappointment, the beautiful woman he has tied to her bed wears a custom made, flesh colored jock strap under her black panties. Discovering the truth, his indignant response is, "I'm a pimp, not a faggot. I'm getting the hell out of here." Angry and abusive, Iceberg Slim leaves Melody bound to the bed. After an expensive cab ride back into the city, he reflects, "It had been like a nightmare Halloween all the way. All trick and no treat" (*Pimp* 151). His indignation, given his intentions for Melody, is amazing, but, even in this situation, the question of a black male's vulnerability arises. Fearing that Melody could send him to jail, he thinks:

> What if he couldn't free himself by the time his folks got home? He was a cinch to cover himself. He'd say a Nigger burglar or holdup man had robbed him and trussed him up. (*Pimp* 151)

Even when the white temptress is not a woman, s/he signals danger for the black man.

Force and violence pervade Iceberg Slim's stories of pimp life. However, when referring to white women, he again portrays the black male as the victim. Commenting on some white women's obvious appreciation for his friend Glass Top, Iceberg Slim asks, "Jack aren't you afraid those 'silk' broads behind you will rape you?" (*Pimp* 125). Although this comment is made in jest, just a few pages earlier he recounts an incident that occurs while he is visiting an older, powerful pimp, Mr. Jones, to get advice. While there, one of the white prostitutes, Peaches, wants to have sex with him and begs her "Daddy" to force the issue:

> Mr. Jones, make this pretty punk freak off with your baby. You don't let nobody say no to you. Force him, Daddy, force him. Show him who's boss. Sic Miss Peaches on him. (*Pimp* 122)

Although Iceberg Slim escapes this scenario unharmed, his real fear is that he will, by offending Miss Peaches, end up shot by her pimp.

By contrast, Malcolm X focuses more on the moral depredation of white women. While helping his brother, Reginald, find his hustle on the streets, Malcolm X suggests to his brother that he find a white woman:

> I'd point out Negro-happy white women to him, and explain that a Negro with any brains could wrap these women around his fingers. But I have to say this for Reginald: he never liked white women. (MX 130)

Although some black men, like Reginald, did not respond to white women, enough did that, "during World War II, Mayor LaGuardia officially closed the Savoy Ballroom" (MX 131). Malcolm X suggests that the reason for this action was the desire of the white patriarchy to keep white women away from the attractions of black men: "Harlem said the real reason was to stop Negroes from dancing with white women. Harlem said that no one dragged the white women in there" (MX 131). In this passage, Malcolm X ascribes to the community a voice that, despite its difference on other issues, agrees about the erotic fascination of black men for white women. Also, the cost to the community, economically and socially, from the closing of the Savoy stems from the lust of white women and the fear of white men.

Later, at the time he dictates this book, Malcolm X is still appalled by white immorality, especially that of the upper classes, which has "the world's lowest morals" (MX 140). As proof of this, he offers a contemporary newspaper story about "white housewives and mothers" who were operating a call-girl ring in suburban New York City. Reacting to stories of wife-swapping "key parties," Malcolm X declares: "I have never heard of anything like that being done by Negroes, even Negroes who live in the worst ghettos and alleys and gutters" (MX 141). Long reformed from his life of sin, Malcolm X still warns of the dangers of the white temptress. Exempt from the pressures of "the worst ghettos and alleys and gutters," the sexual license of white women is inexplicable to the moralist since it ultimately speaks simply to the reality of female sexuality. Despite his clear aversion to white patriarchy, Malcolm X is appalled by the lack of self-control of the white female and the ineffectiveness of the social control exerted by the white male.

Eventually, in these autobiographies, the white temptress is not a temptation at all. After their conversions and regained self-respect, both authors marry black women, have children, and work for the future. The hard-edged, cynical Iceberg Slim actually becomes sentimental when crediting his children for keeping him straight. Malcolm X preaches to other black men that a central part of Islam is learning "to shelter, protect, and respect black women." Speaking to Alex Haley, he declares his disdain for interracial marriage by stating that the only thing he likes integrated is his coffee. Obviously, the choices of Malcolm X and Iceberg Slim to reject women outside of their race, made at a time when interracial romance was slowly becoming more accepted, can not be universalized or seen outside their contexts. However, for these popular authors, the decision to shun white women was based on the predatory figure of the white temptress, a manifestation of America's racist value system, and reflects, for them, an increased political awareness, and pride in their own racial identity.

NOTES

1. *Malcolm X*, 445. All future references to *The Autobiography of Malcolm X* will be indicated by "MX."

2. All future references to *Pimp: The Story of My Life* will be indicated by *Pimp*.

3. Werner Sollors notes that William Wells Brown, the first African American novelist, uses the mulatto story as the plot of his abolitionist book, *Clotel; or The President's Daughter* (1853). He notes, "She dies as a Christ-like martyr with arms outstretched upon a bridge across the Potomac" (Sollors 225). Clotel is the

unacknowledged mulatto daughter of a president, and her death, so near the capi-tal, is meant to inspire shame for the injustices of slavery. The exremely popular play, *The Octoroon* (1859), by the Irish American dramatist Dion Boucicault, ends with another tragic mulatto committing suicide by poison (Sollors 225).

4. In *The Autobiography of Malcolm X*, the conversion takes place roughly at the midpoint of the book; Iceberg Slim, on the other hand, doesn't see the light until the last chapter "Dawn," just before his epilogue. Of course, Malcom X's conversion to Islam is known even by those who have not read his narrative. Ice-berg Slim, following his decision to return to "straight" life becomes first a pesti-cide salesman, then a successful author and lecturer in schools. Attracted to the Black Panthers, Iceberg Slim adopted many of their political ideas.

5. The lindy-hop is a dance form which emerged in the mid 1920s. It is the original form of swing dancing/jitterbug, and is generally associated with Harlem and the Savoy Ballroom. In a footnote in his article, "Malcolm X and the Limits of Autobiography," Paul John Eakin describes the critical response to the stages of Malcolm X's conversion experience: While Sidonie Smith, in *Where I'm Bound: Patterns of Slavery and Freedom in African American Autobiography*, empha-sizes a series of disillusionments with American life, Stephen Butterfield, in *Black Autobiography in America*, sees the narrative in the context of a series of develop-mental moves towards a revolutionary persona (Eakin 155).

6. As early as 1966, Robert Penn Warren comments that Malcolm X was a success in the Horatio Alger tradition. In contrast, Carol Ohmann, in 1970, reads the narrative as a parodic inversion of the American success story (Eakin 154).

7. From D. B. Graham's "Negative Glamor," quoted in Muckley.

8. Among the critics McDowell cites are bell hooks' *Ain't I a Woman* (Boston: South End, 1981), Deborah Gray's *Arn't I a Woman* (New York: Norton, 1985), and Mary Helen Washington's, "These Self-Invented Women: A Theoretical Framework for a Literary History of Black Women," *Radical Teacher* (1980): 148–176.

9. As Northrop Frye explains, "The demonic counterpart of the Bride who is Jerusalem and the spouse of Christ is the Great Whore of Babylon of Revela-tion 17 who is Babylon and Rome, and is the mistress of the Antichrist. The word 'whoredom' in the Bible usually refers to theological rather than sexual irregulari-ties, the term was adopted not simply as abusive but because of the practice of maintaining cult prostitutes in Canaanite temptes . . . Jezebel, Ahab's queen, is treated as a whore not because she was believed to have cuckolded Ahab, but because she introduced the worship of Baal into northern Israel" (Frye 141). Sexuality and otherness are therefore inscribed into the typology of the Whore of Babylon.

10. Lilith, a night monster probably originating in Sumeria, is said in Jewish folklore to have been the first wife of Adam. This story is probably an effort to reconcile the Genesis 1:27 account of the creation of woman with that of Genesis

2:24. Lilith was allegedly the mother of the demons or false spirits (Frye 140–141). Interestingly, this account also makes her the mother of the first mixed progeny, having transgressed by having sex with a demon.

    11. Malcolm X calls Harlem for whites, "their sin-den, their fleshpot" (*MX* 137). This reference is reminiscent of Exodus 16.2–4, when the people of Israel, "murmured against Moses and Aaron in the wilderness, and said to them, 'Would that we had died by the hand of the Lord in the land of Egypt, when we sat by the fleshpots and ate bread to the full.'" In the Hebrew Bible, the fleshpots are literally seasoned meat but the term has come to indicate the dangerous allure of easy living, especially tainted by the Egyptian captivity.

WORKS CITED

Baldwin, James. "Notes of a Native Son." *Notes of a Native Son*. Boston: Beacon Press, 1983.

Du Bois, W. E. B. *Against Racism: Unpublished Essays, Papers, Addresses, 1887–1961*. Ed. Herbert Aptheker. Amherst: U of Massachusetts P, 1985.

———. *The Autobiography of W. E. B. Du Bois*. International Publishers, 1968.

Eakin, Paul John. "Malcolm X and the Limits of Autobiography." *African American Autobiography: A Collection of Critical Essays*. Ed. William L. Andrews. New Jersey: Prentice Hall, 1993. 151–161.

Equiano, Olaudah. *The Interesting Narrative and Other Writings*. Ed. Vincent Carretta. New York: Penguin, 1995.

Fox-Genovese, Elizabeth. *Within the Plantation Household: Black and White Women of the Old South*. Chapel Hill: U of North Carolina P, 1988.

Frye, Northrop. *The Great Code: The Bible and Literature*. New York: Harcourt, 1982.

Fanon, Frantz. *Black Skin, White Masks*. Trans. Charles Lam Markman. New York: Grove, 1967.

Gates, Henry Louis, Jr. and Nellie Y. McKay. "Preface." *The Norton Anthology of African American Literature*. Ed. Henry Louis Gates, Jr. and Nellie Y. McKay, New York: Norton , 1997.

hooks, bell. *Ain't I a Woman?* Boston: South End Press, 1981.

Hughes, Langston. *I Wonder As I Wander*. New York: Hill and Wang, 1956.

Iceberg Slim (Robert Beck). *The Naked Soul of Iceberg Slim*. Los Angeles: Holloway House, 1971.

———. *Pimp: The Story of my Life*. Los Angeles: Holloway House, 1967.

Kelley, Robin G. *Race Rebels: Culture, Politics, and the Black Working Class*. New York: Free Press, 1994.

Johnson, James Weldon. *Along This Way*. 1956. New York: Penguin Books, 1990.

Malcolm X. *The Autobiography of Malcom X*, with the assistance of Alex Haley. New York: Ballantine, 1965.

Marable, Manning. *W. E. B. DuBois, Black Radical Democrat*. Boston Twayne, 1986.

McDowell, Deborah E. "In the First Place: Making Frederick Douglass and the Afro-American Narrative Tradition." *African American Autobiography: A Collection of Critical Essays*. Ed.William L. Andrews. New Jersey: Prentice Hall, 1993. 36–58.

Muckley, Peter A. "Iceberg Slim: Robert Beck—A True Essay at a BioCriticism of an Ex- Outlaw Artist," *Black Scholar* 25 (June 1994): 18–25.

Patton, Phil. "Sold on Ice." *Esquire* 118 (October 1992): 76.

Pedersen, Carl. "Sea Change: The Middle Passage and the Transatlantic Imagination." *The Black Columbiad*. Ed. Werner Sollors and Maria Diedrich. Cambridge: Harvard UP, 1994. 42–51.

Schwenk, Katrin. "Lynching and Rape: Border Cases in African American History and Fiction." *The Black Columbiad*. Ed. Wemer Sollors and Maria Diedrich. Cambridge: Harvard UP, 1994. 312–24.

Sollors, Werner. *Beyond Ethnicity: Consent and Descent in American Culture*. New York: Oxford UP, 1986.

Smith, Valerie. *Self-Discovery and Authority in Afro-American Narrative*. Cambridge: Harvard UP, 1987.

Walker, David. "David Walker's Appeal." *The Norton Anthology of African American Literature*. Ed. Henry Louis Gates, Jr. and Nellie Y. McKay. New York: Norton, 1997. 178–90.

Wright, Richard. "The Ethics of Living Jim Cow: An Autobiographical Sketch." *Black Voices: An Anthology*. Ed. Abraham Chapman. New York: Mentor, 1968. 288–99.

CHAPTER TEN

Subject Positions in Elizabeth Bishop's Representations of Whiteness and the "Other"

ZHOU XIAOJING

Elizabeth Bishop scholarship recently has seen a significant shift from a focus on Bishop's formal and stylistic accomplishments to her treatment of gender, race, class, and sexuality, as well as to her portrayal of "underdeveloped" countries and their peoples. This shift has generated different views of Bishop and her poems, raising questions about the relationships between her subjectivity as a white woman and her poetics, between her lesbian sexuality and her authorial positionality. Although shedding new light on Bishop's poetry, some of these critical views collapse the difference of lesbian sexuality with the difference of race and class, while others regard the speakers in Bishop's poems as identical with Bishop herself. The former critical approach overlooks the irreducible categories of socially and historically constructed difference and their effects on Bishop's poetics; the latter forecloses the possibility of Bishop's critical representation of whiteness in terms of race, class, and culture. While it is crucial to recognize the fact that the subject position of Bishop as a white woman is implicated in a racially structured social order, it is equally important to understand that subject positions are also discursively produced. In other words, subjects can be positioned and repositioned differently in discourses, whereby subversion is possible. Overlooking this possibility in Bishop's poems may result in turning Bishop's racial identity into a fixed position that shapes almost all of Bishop's representations of images and characters into a binary opposition of white domination versus colored subordination, as Renée R. Curry's reading of Bishop's poems seems to do. Thus to examine Bishop's poetics as simply a reflection of dominant racial ideology of white supremacy is as reductive as equating difference of race and class with the difference of Bishop's sexuality.

167

Margaret Dickie, for instance, observes that Bishop's interest in the conflicts of "other classes and races" is related to her own "conflicted identity" as a lesbian, and that Bishop is "knowledgeable about the marginal, the exiled, and the dispossessed in society because she was one herself" (116–117). Dickie's view downplays the difference of race, class, culture, and nationality, while privileging the difference of Bishop's lesbian sexuality. Differing from Dickie, Deborah Weiner insists on reading Bishop's observations of a "Third World" culture and people in terms of her privileged position as a white American. Weiner contends that in her poems about Brazil, "Bishop sees difference in terms of binary oppositions, hierarchically ranked as superior or inferior, with clear separation between self and other [. . .]" (208). Like Weiner, Timothy Morris perceives a "patronizing curiosity" in Bishop's Brazil poems, arguing that they "make South America quaintly inferior and helplessly deficient in comparison to North America" (129). Curry goes further than both Weiner and Morris in her reading of Bishop's poems in terms of the latter's privileged racial identity. Detecting racial coding in Bishop's use of the color white in poems such as "A Cold Spring" and "Cape Breton," Curry claims that Bishop privileges the color white. In "A Cold Spring," Curry argues, Bishop's use of white "connotes a natural, fading type of change that does not remind us of death or aging, but rather remains (unnaturally) brilliant and pure in its transformation" (98). Curry finds in "Cape Breton," "[a]nother way in which Bishop expresses her whiteness and its whispering ideology [. . .] by using whiteness as the veil through which the rest of 'nature' struggles to exist" (100). Curry's reading of Bishop's poetry, like Weiner's and Morris's readings of Bishop's Brazil poems, challenges an idealized and universalized outsiderhood of Bishop's lesbian sexuality.

Nevertheless, it is reductive and misleading to read Bishop's poems as simply expressions of her whiteness and its ideology. This mode of reading assumes an unproblematic identification of the poet's subject position with that of the speaker in a particular poem. For instance, while exposing the power relations between the so-called developed and underdeveloped countries embedded in the speaker's observations about Brazil, Weiner and Morris insist on equating Bishop's authorial position with the privileged, superior position of the speaker in her poems. Such readings of Bishop's Brazil poems are based on a misleading assumption that the position of the speaking subject in Bishop's poems is always single and authorial. But the author, Michel Foucault points out, "is not in fact the cause," or "origin" of a statement. "So the subject of the statement," Foucault writes, "should not be regarded as identical with the author of the formulation—either in substance, or in function" (95). Foucault further contends that

> If a proposition, a sentence, a group of signs can be called 'statement' [. . .]
> it is because the position of the subject can be assigned. To describe a
> formulation *qua* statement does not consist in analysing the relations

between the author and what he says (or wanted to say, or said without wanting to); but in determining what position can and must be occupied by any individual if he is to be the subject of it. (95)

In this sense, the speaking subject's position in one author's work can be multiple, different, and unstable, for this position is assigned and the subject is constructed, rather than a straight forward expression of the author's identity or subjectivity.

I would argue that it is precisely because "the position of the subject can be assigned" that agency for perpetuating or subverting dominant ideologies is possible. My reading of Bishop's poems aims to reveal the complex relationships between Bishop's own subject position and her assignment of particular subject positions to her speakers, including the ideologies of specific subject positions and manners of articulation. In so doing, I hope to address two related issues which have emerged in Bishop criticism—the displacement of the difference of race and class to the difference of lesbian sexuality on the one hand, and, on the other, the dismissal of the possibilities of subversive agency in Bishop's poems by regarding the speaking subject as exclusively identical with Bishop herself. In taking issue with these two critical methodologies respectively, I seek to analyze Bishop's strategies for articulating whiteness and its "Other" while exploring their various, and even competing, possibilities of agency. Rather than focusing only on Bishop's representation of the "Other" from the position of a naturalized privilege, I will examine Bishop's use of the speaker's subject position to expose the privilege of normative whiteness even as the speaker articulates white superiority. Indeed, in exposing whiteness as such, Bishop accomplishes what Ruth Frankenberg calls "naming whiteness," which "displaces it from the unmarked, unnamed status that is itself an effect of its dominance." Frankernberg adds that white people's "seeming normativity, their structured invisibility" are among the effects of white dominance (*White Women* 6). Bishop's poems render visible her white characters' privilege as structured invisibility.

In the early period of her poetic career, Bishop showed an interest in the lives of African Americans and tried to represent them in her poems such as "Songs for a Colored Singer," "Cootchie," and "Faustina, or Rock Roses." The subject positions in these poems differ greatly, and so do critics' readings of the poems. Bishop's attempt to speak about an African American woman's life through the latter's voice in "Songs for a Colored Singer," however, becomes problematic because of her position as a white woman. Adrienne Rich in her 1983 review of Elizabeth Bishop's *Complete Poems, 1927–1979*, criticizes Bishop's attempt which she finds "respectful," but "risky." Explaining her objection to Bishop's risky attempt, Rich points out the relationship between whiteness and power:

The personae we adopt, the degree to which we use lives already ripped off and violated by our own culture, the problem of racist stereotyping in every white head, the issue of the writer's power, right, obligation to speak for others denied a voice, or the writer's duty to shut up at times or at least to make room for those who can speak with more immediate authority—these are crucial questions for our time, and questions that are relevant to much of Bishop's work. (131)

Rich's criticism of Bishop's attempt is provocative, raising a range of questions concerning the relations between power and knowledge, particularly about whiteness and its assumed authority to represent the "Other." At the same time, Rich's remarks pose the question about the possibility of white's women's agency. Can white women writers deal with issues of race and gender without denying black women a voice? What textual strategies must be employed in order to confront social issues without reinforcing dominant ideologies?

The first two songs in "Songs for a Colored Singer," which Rich singles out for criticism, reveal the problems and possibility of agency for white women to represent women of color. Reading the songs only in terms of Bishop's position as a white woman, Curry dismisses "Songs for a Colored Singer" completely, asserting that they simply reflect upon "Bishop's sense of white privilege as that which enables a white woman to narrate a fictionalized black woman's story" (95). Differing from Rich's and Curry's perspectives on the songs, Victoria Harrison notes that Bishop's songs "suggest a mixture of voices, each slightly different and together voicing the alienation fostered by gendered and racial oppression" (98). Harrison's reading of the first two songs in "Songs for a Colored Singer"emphasizes the influence of the blues of Billie Holiday and Bessie Smith on Bishop's treatment of gender and racial oppression. The speaker in those songs, Harrison writes, "is strident and playful by turns, her unbashful rhymes reflecting how basic these problems are: life is unjust for the black woman in the 1940s, stunted by both white and male supremacy" (99). But a close reading of the first two songs reveals no explicit evidence of the black woman as victim of "white and male supremacy." The speaker complains about poverty in her life, which she blames on her husband. The first song begins with the speaker describing the destitute condition of her life in comparison with her neighbors' riches. Then she quickly turns to her husband, Le Roy, to ask him to explain why they cannot seem to be able to accumulate any wealth because "the more we got the more we spend. . . .," telling him ironically that he is "earning too much money now." Le Roy takes his wife's indirect complaint in his stride, saying nonchalantly:

> "Darling, when I earns I spends.
> The world is wide; it still extends. . . .
> I'm going to get a job in the next town."
> Le Roy, you're earning too much money now. (Poems 47)

Although the speaker compares her poverty with her neighbors' wealth, it is unlikely that during the 1940s in the United States her neighbors are white. Therefore, the discrepancy between the speaker's and her neighbors' economic status is not implied as a result of racial difference. In fact, Le Roy is supposed to be responsible for the situation, as the speaker reveals, "What have we got for all his dollars and cents? / —A pile of bottles by the fence" (47). And Le Roy's own remarks further establish the fact that they are poor because he spends freely: "Darling, when I earns I spends." The refrain, "Le Roy, you're earning too much money now," enhances that fact. Thus the problems in this black woman's life are personalized within the domestic space.

A problematic personal relationship is shown to be at the center of the black woman's unhappy life, as the second song continues to suggest.[1] But a significant change takes place within the speaker in the second song. As Le Roy becomes even more irresponsible, compounding drinking with womanizing, the speaker decides to end her relationship with her husband. Speaking lightheartedly, she expresses her determination to take matters into her own hands by leaving Le Roy to start a new life. In her reading of these two songs, Harrison observes that "Like a Louis Armstrong trumpet accompaniment to Bessie Smith's blues, both songs have a lighthearted tone that refuses to take itself seriously, just as they are making the issues of inequity bluntly evident" (99). It is true that the lighthearted tone is typical of African American blues which uses humor to deal with apparently hopeless situations, but Bishop's two songs do not in anyway render "bluntly evident" the speaker's poverty and unhappy marriage as the result of racial and gender inequity. Rather, they suggest that Le Roy's personal irresponsibility is the cause, and that to change the conditions of her life, the black woman has to leave her husband. As the speaker says, "this occasion's all his fault," "I'm going to go and take the bus / and find someone monogamous" (*Poems* 48). While Bishop represents the black woman as assertive, independent, and capable of seeking happiness on her own terms, she provides no other voices in the songs to undermine or situate the speaker's blame on Le Roy's faults in a social context. This emphasis on personal relationships as the source of the black woman's poverty and unhappiness risks reproducing racial stereotypes, while displacing socially produced problems in African Americans' lives to the domestic space. Thus it is not surprising that Curry finds that "Bishop's attempt to get the Otherness right" in the songs "only results in trite stereotyping" (94).

However, to achieve a more complete understanding of the problem of racial stereotyping in Bishop's songs it is necessary to relate the songs not simply to Bishop's position as a white woman, but also to the generic characteristics of blues and their social contexts. According to Angela Y. Davis, "The expression of socially unfulfilled dreams in terms of individual sexual love" is characteristic, though "not peculiar to the African American experience" (236). Due to the "slave system's economic management of procreation, which did not generally tolerate—and often severely punished—the public exhibition of self-initiated sexual relationships," Davis points out, "love themes in slave music," in contrast to those of blues, are rare. Within this historical context, Davis notes, "the blues developed a tradition of openly addressing both male and female sexuality," and "reveals an ideological framework that was specifically African American" (232). In the songs performed by Gertrude 'Ma' Rainey, known as the "Mother of Blues," "the institution of monogamous marriage was often cavalierly repudiated with the kind of attitude that is usually gendered as male" (241). At the same time, her songs also warn women against being deceived by "romantic expectations associated with the bourgeois and patriarchal institution of marriage." Related to this major theme, but adopting a different perspective, Davis observes that "Bessie Smith's work poses more explicit challenges to the male dominance that ideologically inheres in this institution" (242). Bishop's songs have drawn these themes from traditional blues, including those that assert female freedom and an independence that challenges male dominance in love relationships. However, removed from the specific African American historical context and the traditions of blues, Bishop's songs can be easily read as reproductions of African American stereotypes, since most readers are not familiar with the historical context for or particular major themes of blues. Thus dehistoricized, the poverty and problematic love relationships of the racially marked African American man and woman in the first two songs of "Songs for a Colored Singer" are depoliticized as purely a personal matter. As Roland Barthes observes, the "*political*" must be understood "in its deeper meaning, as describing the whole of human relations in their real, social structure, in their power of making the world [. . .]" (143). The connection between personal relationships and social problems, then, needs to be established within the text in order to avoid reproducing racial stereotypes out of social and historical contexts.

Bishop's other poems about African American women's experience are more successful, for they illustrate the personal-social connections through socially structured subjective positions. In poems such as "Cootchie" and "Faustina, or Rock Roses," Bishop situates personal interracial relationships in their social structures, and explores their complexity with attention to historical context. In these poems Bishop achieves more than the agency for articulating issues of inequity; she is able to expose white women's privilege, dependency, and vulnerability through their relationships with women of color. By the time Bishop wrote "Cootchie" and "Faustina, or Rock Roses," she had lived for a few years in Key West, where she had close contact with some black women and learned about their experience of racism, which had a profound impact on her and her poems. In a letter written in 1965 from Brazil to her aunt, Bishop rebuked her aunt (Grace) for following white Southern opinion about Martin Luther King. In the same letter, Bishop told her aunt about the brutality and injustice African Americans in Key West had suffered:

> Don't forget I did live in the south—My dear old laundress's (black) son was murdered by the Key West police because one of them wanted his wife.—Everyone knew this and nothing was done about it. The

laundress was given her son's body in a coffin, straight from jail—She said "I looked at his arm—Miss Elizabeth,—it wasn't an *arm* anymore. . . ." (13 March 1965, qtd. in Goldensohn 77)

Bishop's first-hand knowledge of racism has led to her poems such as "Cootchie" and "Faustina, or Rock Roses," which are based on the lives of black women she came to know in Key West.

"Cootchie" portrays the relationship between a black maid, Cootchie, and her white mistress who is deaf. The poem first appeared in the September/October 1941 issue of *Partisan Review*. More than a year before its publication, after Cootchie had passed away, Bishop enclosed her manuscript in a letter to Marianne Moore. "Maybe you will remember Cootchie," Bishop wrote. "I don't know what Miss Lula is going to do without her. She had lived with her 35 years" (24 February 1940, *Letters* 88). In her poem, Bishop reveals not only Miss Lula's white privilege and her dependence on Cootchie, but also the irony of the inequality in their life-long relationship which reflects the irreducible difference of race and class in black and white women's lives:

> Cootchie, Miss Lula's servant, lies in marl,
> black into white she went
>   below the surface of the coral-reef.
> Her life was spent
>   in caring for Miss Lula, who is deaf,
> eating her dinner off the kitchen sink
> while Lula ate hers off the kitchen table.
> The skies were egg-white for the funeral
>   and the faces sable. (*Poems* 46)

The racially marked contrast in Cootchie's relationship with Lula indicates social inequality and racial alienation, which Bishop foregrounds through black and white images. By emphasizing the fact that all the faces at the funeral were black, Bishop indirectly points to the absence of whites, which is particularly ironic since Cootchie's life was spent in taking care of Lula, a white woman. Bishop places the inequality of class in Cootchie's life in the context of race relations; thus the personal is effectively related to the social and political through socially situated subject positions.

In the second part of the poem, Bishop further probes the meaning of the relationship between Lula and Cootchie. Immediately following Cootchie's funeral, the description of the burning of "the pink wax roses / planted in tin cans filled with sand / placed in a line to mark Miss Lula's losses" at the beginning of the second part raises the reader's expectation for a gesture of mourning or remembrance from Lula for Cootchie. But by the end of the poem, it has become clear that those pink wax roses carefully placed in a line to mark Miss Lula's losses do not include one for Cootchie. Rather, those roses for the dead indicate that Lula has been alone with only Cootchie to take care of her. The speaker suggests that Lula's loss of Cootchie now makes her other losses easier to bear: "Tonight the moonlight will alleviate / the melting of the pink wax roses/ [. . .]," "but who will shout and make her understand?"(46). Following the obvious class and racial inequity that marked Lula's relationship with Cootchie, the speaker's question suggests more than the fact that Lula does not know Cootchie is dead. It points to the absence of sympathy in Lula's feelings toward Cootchie, whose service Lula has taken for granted, and whose assigned inferior status in society Lula has maintained in her household. Bishop foregrounds Lula's insensitivity in her dehumanized relationship with Cootchie by displacing emotions to inanimate images:

> Searching the land and sea for someone else,
> The lighthouse will discover Cootchie's grave
> and dismiss all as trivial; the sea, desperate,
>   will proffer wave after wave. (*Poems* 46)

Through personified images of the lighthouse and the sea, Bishop refocuses the poem on Cootchie. The speaker's concern for Lula's helpless situation and her need for someone else to take care of her will seem "trivial" when the lighthouse's beam will "discover Cootchie's grave," while searching for another servant to replace her. By closing the poem with Cootchie's death and the sea's proffering of waves for her grave, Bishop emphasizes the injustice in the relationship of white and black women whose lives are bounded together by dependence on the one hand, and racial inequity on the other. The significance Bishop gives to Cootchie's life—all is dismissed as "trivial" in front of Cootchie's grave—at the end of the poem contrasts and resonates with Cootchie's life-long subservience to a white woman stated at the beginning of the poem: Cootchie's "life was spent / in caring for Miss Lula, who is deaf, / eating her dinner off the kitchen sink / while Lula ate hers off the kitchen table." The simplicity of the diction and imagery match the starkness of inequity in a black woman's daily life in service to a white woman. Situating white and black women's subject positions in a social structure shaped by racial hierarchy, Bishop undermines naturalized white superiority. More importantly, her treatment of the relationship between white and black women refuses to eliminate the difference of race and class.

In "Faustina, or Rock Roses," Bishop continues to explore black and white women's relationships and daily lives as these are conditioned by the difference of race and class. But the clarity of social and racial inequity in Cootchie's relationship with Miss Lula is replaced by complexity and ambivalence in Faustina's relationship with her white female employer. This poem, according to Brett Millier, is based on Bishop's selection "among many facts and anecdotes about a black Cuban woman, a familiar figure in Key West in the 1940s, and focuses on a single visit she made to Faustina at work, caring for an elderly white woman in her home"

(188–89). The first six stanzas of the poem are devoted to details of the room and the surroundings of the sick bedridden woman, who is holding "the pallid palm-leaf fan" which she "cannot wield." The visitor senses something hidden beneath the surface and is "embarrassed" by the false façade. But just what is withheld seems elusive. The speaker's description of and reflection on the interactions between the sick white woman and her black nurse probe beneath the surface of their relationship. Responding to the white woman's call which is no more than a whisper, Faustina appears on "bare scraping feet," bringing talcum powder, and pills, among other things. She requests for herself "a litte *coñac*," and complains and explains "the terms of her employment" (*Poems* 73). As she bends over the white woman,

> Her sinister kind face
> presents a cruel black
> coincident conundrum.
>   Oh, is it
>
> freedom at last, a lifelong
> dream of time and silence,
> dream of protection and rest?
> Or is it the very worst,
> the unimaginable nightmare
> that never before dared last
>   more than a second? (Poems 73–74)

The visitor's observation subtly depicts a complicated relationship between a white woman and her black nurse. Being a helpless invalid, the white woman who is dying relies completely on Faustina, whose complaint about "the terms of her employment" reveals her position as a hired nurse and her emotional detachment from the white woman. Their relationship is at once intimate and distant, the ambivalence of which is embodied in Faustina's "sinister kind face" that "presents a cruel black / coincident conundrum." By displacing the color of Faustina's face to that of the "conundrum," Bishop evokes questions about the possibilities of "freedom at last," or "a lifelong / dream of time and silence, / dream of protection and rest?" or "the unimaginable nightmare" for both the white woman and her black nurse. Bishop indicates that a racial barrier is intertwined in the white patient's intimate relationship with her black nurse—a relationship that is full of contradictions and possibilities. This intricate relationship embodied in the white woman's "conundrum" becomes a more overtly social issue in the following stanza.

The plural pronoun Bishop employs indicates that the questions raised with respect to the white woman's relationship with Faustina concern more than the two women in the poem:

> The acuteness of the question
> forks instantly and starts

> a snake-tongue flickering;
> blurs further, blunts, softens,
> separates, falls, our problems
> becoming helplessly
>   proliferative. (*Poems* 74)

By connecting the dying white woman's "conundrum" to "our problems," Bishop directs the unanswered questions to problematic race relations in the United States and to racially marked interpersonal relationships based on mutual needs and embedded in conflicts.

Critical readings of "Faustina, or Rock Roses" differ mostly on the implications of the ambivalent relationship between a white woman and her black nurse. Margaret Dickie suggests that the racial relationship in this poem serves as a means for Bishop to explore relationships of trust and protection. Dickie argues that this is "not a poem of rich and poor so much as a poem of trust and protection spelled out in racial terms, where trust has always been intertwined with exploitation [. . .]. The racial component of the situation marks an exploitation that works both ways" (119). Dickie's reading of the two women's relationship explains away its historical and social contexts of racial relations. To argue that racially marked exploitation "works both ways" in Faustina's relationship with her white patient, and to regard the racial dimension of this relationship as a means for discussing "trust and protection," result in what Barthes calls the "privation of history" in "myth" where "history evaporates," and socially produced problems are blamed on individuals' "irresponsibility" (151). By contrast, Adrienne Rich's reading of this poem insists on situating the racially marked relationship in history, attributing the legacy of racism to the ambivalence of the two women's relationship. She interprets the "conundrum" of the white woman in terms of "white power, the history of what whites have done to Black people, and the vulnerability of this particular dying old woman" (132). In addition, Rich emphasizes that the ambivalent possibilities of extreme situations in "Faustina, or Rock Roses" are "defined from a white woman's perspective," but the poem at least acknowledges the "acuteness of the question." Rich praises Bishop's treatment of race and class in the relationship between the two women. "I cannot think of another poem by a white woman, until some feminist poetry of the last few years, in which the servant-mistress dynamic between Black and white women has received unsentimental attention" (132). Differing from both Dickie's and Rich's respective readings of the poem, Harrison stresses the gender connection among Faustina, her white patient, and the visitor. Harrison notes that "the rapt attention to rose petals" in the closing lines of the poem "refocuses the poem on the women's intertwining" (105). She points out the implied connection among the women through the varied images of roses in the title and running throughout the poem—"The titular attachment of crystallized roses to Faustina, the enamel of the old woman's 'crazy bed' chipped in the shape of roses, and the 'wilted roses' of her sheets resonate in the visitor's 'rust-perforated roses.'" For Harrison, the rose petals "represent the delicacy" of Bishop's trust in "vital, daily emotions," which were Bishop's focus in locating "a voice that "challenged racial, national, and gender-determined barriers, a voice perhaps unavailable to her, were she to have taken a 'stand'" (105–106). Harrison's contention suggests that a situated voice attached to a particular subject position is not as politically subversive as an uncommitted voice. The voices in Bishop's poems, including "Faustina, or Rock Roses," reveal otherwise.

Although the speaker in "Faustina, or Rock Roses" assumes the position of an observer, the questions generated by "a cruel black / coincident conundrum" and "our problems" are, as Rich has noted, "defined from a white woman's perspective." Further, if Bishop's challenge to racial, national, and gender-determined barriers means nothing more than appealing to "vital, daily emotions" that can transcend those barriers as Harrison suggests, her challenge would, again, become what Barthes refers to as "myth" that "has turned reality inside out," and "has emptied it of history and has filled it with nature [. . .]" (Barthes 142). I would argue that rather than challenging the boundaries of race, Bishop exposes them in white and black women's daily, intimate interactions in "Faustina, or Rock Roses" as well as in "Cootchie." In this respect, Bishop deconstructs whiteness as "a privilege enjoyed but not acknowledged, a reality lived in but unknown" (Frankenberg, "Being White, Seeing Whiteness" 4). By identifying the white characters in her poems as a privileged racial category, and revealing what Frankenberg calls "the 'racialness' of white experience" (*White Women* 1), Bishop interrupts the predominant representation of whiteness as a naturalized norm.

In her later Brazil poems, Bishop locates the speakers' voices more explicitly in their respective positions determined by race, class, gender, and nationality. At the same time, Bishop's representation of the "other" is further complicated by cultural difference, particularly by Bishop's recognition of her own privilege and prejudice. Replying to a question about whether she had been able to get anything from Brazil besides visual material, Bishop said in a 1966 interview:

> Living the way I have happened to live here, knowing Brazilians, has made a great difference. The general life I have known here has of course had an impact on me. I think I've learned a great deal. Most New York intellectuals' ideas about "underdeveloped countries" are partly mistaken, and living among people of a completely different culture has changed a lot of my old stereotyped ideas. (Qtd. in Brown 290)

This shift of perspective on "underdeveloped countries," which results from her life in Brazil, enhances Bishop's keen awareness of the limitations and possibilities of the speakers' subject positions. With this changed perspective, Bishop finds new ways to articulate particular points of view through characters with specific social, cultural, and racial backgrounds.

In his praise of Bishop's accomplishments in her Brazil poems, David Kalstone regards the book "not so much as an indication of what has happened in American verse—its achieved grasp of conversational and colloquial idiom—but as something of a provocation for poets trying to find new ways of registering character in poetry" (310). Rich sees Bishop's achievements in her Brazil poems in a different light, stressing, again, Bishop's position as a white woman. "Some of Bishop's best Brazilian poems," Rich asserts, "are exercises in coming to terms with her location as a foreign white woman living as part of a privileged class in a city of beggars and rich people" (132). Rich's recognition of Bishop's awareness of "her location as a foreign white woman living as part of a privileged class" in her Brazil poems is extremely helpful in determining the functions of her speaker's agency. In fact, Bishop's accomplishment in registering characters and her awareness of her privilege as a white woman are inseparable from her development in linking voices to subject positions. In her Brazil poems, Bishop has found an effective way to employ the speaker's situated voice to reveal the speaker's personality, prejudice, and point of view as these are shaped by race, class, gender, and culture.

Although in poems such as "Arrival at Santos," "Brazil, January 1, 1502," and "Manuelzinho" Bishop locates the speakers' voices in a position similar to hers as a white woman of a privileged class, the speakers are not identical with Bishop. Rather, they represent particular subject positions which have been determined by race, class, gender, culture, and nationality in power relations. Thus, the speakers can function as agents who denaturalize normative whiteness even as they articulate white superiority. For instance, the opening poem of *Questions of Travel*, "Arrival at Santos," is written from the point of view of a white American tourist, who expresses value judgments about a third-world country from a privileged, superior position. After a sketch of the landscape and scenes, the speaker asks: "Oh, tourist, / is this how this country is going to answer you // and your immodest demands for a different world, / and a better life, and complete comprehension / of both at last, and immediately, / after eighteen days of suspension?" (Poems 89). Having established the speaker's position as a tourist with "immodest demands for a different world," the poem shifts to the speaker's responses to this foreign country:

> The tender is coming,
> a strange and ancient craft, flying a strange and brilliant rag.
> So that's the flag. I never saw it before.
> I somehow never thought of there *being* a flag,
>
> but of course there was, all along. And coins, I presume,
> and paper money; they remain to be seen. (*Poems* 89)

But the speaker finds, not surprisingly, the colors of their soap "unassertive," and their postage stamps "wasting away like the former, slipping the way the latter /

do when we mail the letters we wrote on the boat, / either because the glue here is very inferior / or because of the heat" (Poems 90). As the speaker's description of her voyage into a "Third World" country unfolds, the plural "we" replaces the singular "I," indicating a collective perspective which is marked by the tourists' race and nationality. Halfway through the poem, Bishop's persona introduces a "fellow passenger" from New York, named Miss Breen who is "six feet tall, / with beautiful bright blue eyes and a kind expression" (*Poems* 89). This image of an European American tourist becomes identical with white privilege and superiority when it is implicated in the speaker's statements about "us" and "them." As Frankenberg contends, racial identity is "relational, made through the claiming and the imposition of sameness and otherness [. . .]" ("Being White, Seeing Whiteness" 4). Bishop's persona's arrogant, condescending, and judgmental comments on the "backwardness" of Brazil simultaneously construct the identity of whiteness and its "Other." Even though the speaker reveals a "patronizing curiosity" about South America as Timothy Morris observes, her remarks about Brazil's flag being "a strange and brilliant rag," and its glue being possibly "very inferior" are too obviously prejudiced to be taken as statements of "truth." Indeed these outrageously condescending remarks parody, rather than support, what Bishop has referred to as her "old stereotyped ideas" and "Most New York intellectuals' ideas about 'underdeveloped countries.'" Thus Bishop undermines whiteness as the norm by allowing her speaker to perform whiteness in relation to its "Other." She achieves such subversive effects through deployment of tone, rhetoric, and subject positioning and impositioning, and by locating the speech and subject positions within specific social and historical contexts.

In her other poems about travel and "Third World" countries, Bishop's marking of whiteness takes on a global as well as local dimension when she associates whiteness with colonialism. In "Brazil, January 1, 1502," for instance, Bishop connects the tourists' attitudes and expectations to those of the colonialists. According to Ashley Brown, "New Year's Day of 1502 was the date on which the Portuguese caravels arrived at Quanabara Bay, which they mistakenly thought was the mouth of a great river—hence Rio de Janeiro (January)" ("Bishop in Brazil" 230). By using this historical date in the poem's title, Bishop draws the reader's attention to the colonial history of Brazil. The poem begins by relating the enchanting effect of Brazil's scenery on the tourists to that on the colonists:

> Januaries, Nature greets our eyes
> exactly as she must have greeted theirs:
> every square inch filling in with foliage—
> big leaves, little leaves, and giant leaves,
> blue, blue-green, and olive,
> [. . . . .]
>
> A blue-white sky, a simple web,
> [. . . . .]

> Still in the foreground there is Sin:
> five sooty dragons near some massy rocks.
> [. . . . .]
> The lizards scarcely breathe; all eyes
> are on the smaller, female one, back-to,
> her wicked tail straight up and over,
> red as a red-hot wire. (*Poems* 91–92)

Extended picturesque descriptions gradually reveal hidden threats amidst all this beauty in nature, and serve to link the landscape of Brazil to its colonial history in the last part of the poem. The impending male lizards' battle over the seductive female provides an implied parallel to the Portuguese and Spanish colonists' struggles over territory in South America:

> Just so the Christians, hard as nails,
> tiny as nails, and glinting,
> in creaking armor, came and found it all,
> not unfamiliar:
> no lovers' walks, no bowers,
> no cherries to be picked, no lute music,
> but corresponding, nevertheless,
> to an old dream of wealth and luxury
> already out of style when they left home—
> wealth, plus a brand-new pleasure.
> Directly after Mass, humming perhaps
> *L'Homme armé* or some such tune,
> they ripped away into the hanging fabric,
> each out to catch an Indian for himself—
> those maddening little women who kept calling,
> calling to each other (or had the birds waked up?)
> and retreating, always retreating, behind it. (*Poems* 91–92)

Bishop's abundant descriptions of nature in Brazil landscape resonates with European colonists' travel writings, in which detailed descriptions of African and American landscapes are "coded as resources to be developed, surpluses to be traded, towns to be built" (Pratt 61). The luxuriant land of Brazil in Bishop's poem is illustrated in terms of its seductive power over the Christian conquerors, whose violation and exploitation of it in pursuit of their dream of wealth is told along with their "brand-new pleasure" of pursuing the aboriginal women. Bishop exposes the irony in these Portuguese Christians' faithful observance of religious rituals and their greedy exploitation of the native people by describing how, "Directly after Mass," the Christians "ripped away into the hanging fabric, / each out to catch an Indian for himself" (*Poems* 92). These allusions to Brazilian history, charged with ironic exposure of the greed, hypocrisy, and arrogance of the Portuguese, provide the historical and cultural contexts in which Bishop situates her Brazil poems, including the speakers' subject positions. This historical context serves to denaturalize the norm of white superiority, situating white tourists' perspectives in the colonial history of Brazil.

While positioning her white characters in the context of colonialism, Bishop continues to explore the impact of class on personal relationships in poems such as "Manuelzinho." In this poem, Bishop revisits the master-servant relationship explored in "Cootchie" and "Faustina, or Rock Roses." But rather than an observer, the speaker in "Manuelzinho" is now the white mistress; Manuelzinho, a white tenant, is portrayed from her point of view. Bishop's representation of the relationship between a white female master and her white male servant in this poem illustrates the complexity of whiteness, revealing the gap between whiteness and whites. Through dramatic monologue, the speaker reveals Manuelzinho's dependence on her and her feelings about him and his family. Although benevolent and sympathetic, the speaker's social position prevents her from understanding the actuality of life's hardship for the poor. And her tone in describing Manuelzinho and his family is unmistakably condescending:

> Half squatter, half tenant (no rent)—
> a sort of inheritance; white,
> in your thirties now, and supposed
> to supply me with vegetables,
> but you don't; or you won't; or you can't
> get the idea through your brain—
> the world's worst gardener since Cain.
> [. . . . .]
>
> The strangest things happen, to you.
> Your cow eats a "poison grass"
> and drops dead on the spot.
> Nobody else's does.
> And then your father dies,
> [. . . . .]
> I give you money for the funeral
> and you go and hire a *bus*
> for the delighted mourners,
> so I have to hand over some more
> and then have to hear you tell me
> you pray for me every night! (*Poems* 96–97)

In her security and comfort, distanced from Manuelzinho's world by her economic and social status, the speaker does not comprehend Manuelzinho's behavior. In her eyes, Manuelzinho, though a middle-aged man and a father, is hopelessly incompetent, and the other people of his class ("the delighted mourners") appear to be strangely entertaining figures incapable of dignity or empathy.

However, there is one brief moment in the poem when the speaker and Manuelzinho seem to share some common ground: "In the kitchen we dream together / how the meek shall inherit the earth—," but the next line immediately marks the inevitable gap and conflict between them: "or several acres of mine" (*Poems* 98). The following passages enhance the irreducible class gap between the speaker and Manuelzinho's family. Despite her alleged kindness and generosity, Manuelzinho's children seem to be afraid of the speaker, keeping a distance from her, avoiding contact. As the speaker says, it is "impossible to make friends" with the children even though they would not hesitate to grab "for an orange or a piece of candy" (*Poems* 98). The timidity and estrangement in the children's behavior reflect a class barrier that cannot be eliminated by individual kindness. The speaker's recognition of the distance between her and Manuelzinho's family is accompanied by her realization of her condescension to Manuelzinho:

> Unkindly,
> I called you Klorophyll Kid.
> My visitors thought it was funny.
> I apologize here and now.
>
> You helpless, foolish man,
> I love you all I can.
> I think. Or do I?
> I take off my hat, unpainted
> and figurative, to you.
> Again I promise to try. (*Poems* 99)

Conditioned by her class, the speaker cannot escape her condescending attitude toward Manuelzinho and his family. Even though she acknowledges her patronizing humiliation of Manuelzinho, her efforts at humility are inescapably mixed with her sense of being the superior provider and protector. Her uncertainty about her professed love for Manuelzinho, and her promise "again" to try to change, contribute to the sense that the class barrier between them is impossible to overcome.

Bishop's portrayal of a benevolent female master as the provider and protector of her male gardener and his family also shows the complexity of gender relationship determined by class difference. By allowing the speaker in "Manuelzinho" to speak from an obvious position of privilege, Bishop achieves the effects of subversive agency that exposes, rather than naturalizes, the social conditions which have shaped the relationship between the speaker and her servant. Her representation of the relationship between people of different racial backgrounds and social status captures the complexity and contradictions of these relationships through the speaking subject's "socially localized and limited" speech manners, mediated by the speaker's social status (Bakhtin, *Dialogic* 287). In poems such as "Arrival at Santos" and "Manuelzinho," Bishop has found a way to portray characters and their attitudes through their socially and ideologically bounded utterances.

Bishop's strategy for exposing the speaker's subject position and attitudes through the speaker's own voice is especially effective in her prose poem, "12 O'Clock News." In this poem Bishop further develops her skill of revealing the speaker's prejudice against and stereotyping of the "Other," through parody of ideologically determined speech manners.[2] Although there are multiple speakers in "12 O'Clock News," they all speak in the collective voice of the Western world, supplementing, rather than challenging, one another's observations about an "underdeveloped" country and its people. Hence, the subversive effect of this poem, like that of "Arrival at Santos," comes from the obviously stereotypical remarks, the comic tone, and the condescending manner in which they are spoken. By having the speakers employ self-revealing mimicry, Bishop seems to have drawn from the Brazilian writer Clarice Lispector's strategy of parody in her story, "The Smallest Woman in the World," which Bishop has translated into English. Lispector's story exposes self-assumed superiority and racial prejudice through the characters' seemingly scientific interests and objective observations, and their utterances with regard to a tiny woman found in Africa.[3] The attitudes Lispector's story exposes and satirizes are characteristic of Edward Said's definition of "Eurocentrism" which is the result of colonialism and European imperialist expansion. In *Culture and Imperialism*, Said notes that, among other things, Eurocentric researchers "studied," "classified," and "verified" non-Europeans and banished their identities, "except as a lower order of being, from the culture and indeed the very idea of white Christian Europe" (222). Bishop parodies this kind of Eurocentric observation and impositioning of the "Other" in "12 O'Clock News," which, like Lispector's story, reveals the speakers' stereotypical ideas through their observations of a non-European country and people.

The speakers in Bishop's poem report in a matter-of-fact manner, giving what seems to be objectively observed facts. Bishop uses the Surrealist method of visual distortion to transform the objects on a desk into the landscape of a foreign country, which provides the material for the speakers' "news reports." Each speaker is identified with an object on the desk, functioning simultaneously as the thing observed and the observer, whose speech reveals more of himself than the thing he describes:

envelopes   In this small, backward country, one of the most backward left in the world today, communications are crude and "industrialization" and its products almost nonexistent. [. . .]

ink-bottle   We have also received reports of a mysterious, oddly shaped, black structure, at an undisclosed distance to the east. [. . .] The natural resources of the country being far from completely known to us, there is the possibility that this may be, or may contain, some powerful and terrifying "secret weapon." On the other hand, given what we *do* know, or have learned from our anthropologists and sociologists about this people, it may well be nothing more than a *numen*, or a great altar recently erected to one of their gods, to which, in their present historical state of superstition and helplessness, they attribute magical powers, and may even regard as a "savior," one last hope of rescue from their grave difficulties. (*Poems* 174–75)

These seemingly objective observations and speculations on the peculiar landscape and inscrutable objects of an alien country are undermined and ridiculed by their identification with actual objects on a desk—envelopes and an ink-bottle. As the reporters' observations and comments move on to give information about the people of this foreign land, mockery, seemingly directed at the journalistic jargon, expose these reporters' privileged position and superior attitudes toward an "underdeveloped" country and its people.

ashtray   From our superior vantage point, we can clearly see into a sort of dugout, possibly a shell crater, a "nest" of soldiers. They lie heaped together, wearing the camouflage "battle dress" intended for "winter war-fare." [. . .] The fact that these poor soldiers are wearing them here, on the plain, gives further proof, if proof were necessary, either of the childishness and hopeless impracticality of this inscrutable people, our opponents, or of the sad corruption of their leaders. (*Poems* 175)

The comic mimicry of extra-literary jargon and manners of speech punctures the inflated seriousness and superiority in the reporters' utterances, while undermining the content of the reports and calling the reader's attention to the speakers' attitudes toward the Other. But more importantly, Bishop's strategy of subversive mimicry calls into question the definition of otherness within a binary framework that reduces the Other to the opposite of the self-same. This binary construction of self and Other characterizes discourses of Orientalism, colonialism, and sexism.

However, critics in general do not read "12 O'Clock News" as a parody of a collective attitude. Adrienne Rich regards the poem as an example of the kind of Bishop poem in which "the poem-about-an-artifact [. . .] becomes the poem-as-artifact," the kind of poem that "owes too much to Moore" (125–26). Lorrie Goldensohn writes that "12 O'Clock News" is "notable [. . .] for the open interest it signals in writing as subject" (259). She adds that "the comedy of mistaken identity seems thin and unremittingly premised on the writer's insignificance and unproductivity: the 'joke' is too close to morose complaint" (260). Harrison's reading of "12 O'Clock News" seems so far the only one which recognizes that "Bishop reveals in layers the ways we silence and speak for the other," and notes that Bishop "mocks the superiority of her speaker" (202–03).

While mocking her speakers' superiority and their impulse to "speak for the other," Bishop also articulates her ambivalent feelings about Brazil in "12 O'Clock

News." She wrote to James Merrill from Brazil that she had almost given up going to the concerts in which artists from the so-called developed countries "play down so to the Rio audience, as a rule." And the Rio audience "resent it very much" (1 March 1955, *Letters* 303). Writing to Mrs. E. B. (Katherine) White, a fiction editor for *The New Yorker*, Bishop said that "after wading through ['a huge batch of American magazines'] I suddenly felt extremely happy to be living in an 'underdeveloped' country" (15 January 1963, *Letters* 414). But at times, she also dismissed the possibility of Brazil's capability and moral strength to fight against its backwardness and corruption, and occasionally disparaged Brazil as uncivilized. Writing to Robert Lowell, Bishop complained: "But I've had ten years of a backward, corrupt country, and like Lota, I yearn for civilization [. . .]" (26 August 1963, *Letters* 418). To Anny Baumann, Bishop wrote: "I wish Lota and I weren't so involved in the politics of this hopeless country" (17 November 1964, *Letters* 427). References to "the childishness and hopeless impracticality of this inscrutable people" and "the sad corruption of their leaders" in the closing line of "12 O'Clock News" can therefore be said to articulate Bishop's own prejudice.

But the attitudes expressed by the reporters in "12 O'Clock News" are not solely Bishop's own. Bishop has incorporated her ambivalent feelings about Brazil and the prejudices of her own and other people's into the reporters' observations. Thus the voices and their positions should not be considered as identical with Bishop's alone. As Bakhtin points out, by taking on "the flavor of someone else's language [. . .]" the comic style conceals "another's speech" or "a collective voice" (*Dialogic* 305). To locate Bishop's subjectivity as the exclusive source of meaning in "12 O'Clock News" overlooks the complex functions of double-voiced mimicry and self-mockery. "The expression of an utterance can never be fully understood or explained if its thematic content is all that is taken into account," Bakhtin emphasizes. He continues:

> The expression of an utterance always [. . .] expresses the speaker's attitude toward others' utterances and not just his attitude toward the object of his utterance. [. . .] The utterance is filled with *dialogic overtones*, and they must be taken into account in order to understand fully the style of the utterance. (*Speech* 92)

The speeches in "12 O'Clock News" are not self-enclosed, socially-detached utterances about the author's own feelings and thoughts. Rather, they are "double-voiced," orienting toward and incorporating the voices of others through parody, articulating culturally shaped values and attitudes.

Bishop's representation of the Other and of the relationships between people of different racial, social, and cultural backgrounds, is ambivalent and complicated, showing an acute awareness of the different positions of her speaking subjects. Rather than articulating viewpoints from a single and fixed subject position, her speakers are often double-voiced, at once performing and exposing racial, class, and cultural prejudice from the positions of privilege and power, or the positions of alienation and powerlessness. As Adrienne Rich notes, in a number of her poems, Bishop is "critically and consciously trying to explore marginality, power and powerlessness" (135). Discussing further the significance of Bishop's poetry, Rich adds "What I value is her attempt to acknowledge other outsiders, lives marginal in ways that hers is not, long before the Civil Rights movement made such awareness temporarily fashionable for some white writers" (131).

As we read Elizabeth Bishop's poems in light of Rich's compliment and criticism, it is crucial for us to recognize that the position of the speaking subject can be "assigned." Rather than merely questioning "the writer's power, right, obligation to speak for others," it would be fruitful to also investigate the necessity, limits, and possibilities of speaking *from* the positions of others and from the positions of power and privilege. This investigation will enable us to understand the ways in which Bishop's and other white women's work reproduce or subserve dominant ideologies of race and gender. Critics of whiteness are aware of the competing possibilities of agency in white women's works. Ruth Frankenberg, for instance, has noted the contradictory possibilities of discursive representation of whiteness in white women's writings. She observes that "The material and discursive dimensions of whiteness are always, in practice, interconnected. Discursive repertoires may reinforce, contradict, conceal, explain, or 'explain away' the materiality or the history of a given situation" (*White Women* 2). Like Frankenberg, Rebecca Aanerud in her discussion of whiteness in U.S. literature, points out the limitations and risks in naming whiteness, noting that power relations structured by racial hierarchy cannot be dismantled through discursive practices. She argues that "The act of situating whiteness on the part of either the critic or the author himself or herself does not lead to a quick and easy reshuffling of power relations. It can, in fact, result in reinscription of those power relations [. . .]." Both Frankenberg's and Aanerud's theories of discourses on whiteness help us understand the risk and limits in Bishop's representations of whiteness and racially marked otherness.

But our recognition of the limits of white women's discourses on whiteness must not lead to easy dismissal of white women's agency in exposing and critiquing the operations of racism. Aanerud's discussion on the naming and positioning of whiteness is extremely important for our reading of white women's discourses on race. Aanerud argues that when authors "name their white characters as white," the reader's critical practice should strive to "analyze the meanings assigned to or associated with whiteness by examining its representation and constructions and, if possible, to assess what significance a self-conscious narrative can have in challenging white supremacy" (44). Aanerud's proposition offers a useful methodology for our reading of Bishop's poems, which at once articulate and undermine whiteness as a naturalized norm through racially marked subject positions. Overlooking the subject positioning of racially marked speakers and characters in Bishop's poems, and ignoring the social and historical contexts for racially coded speeches and their various subject positions risk essentializing whiteness. In addition, to equate sexual difference with the difference of race and class, or to identify the speakers' positions with Bishop's own, will lead not only to reductive readings of the complexity of Bishop's work, but also to an oversimplification of literary discourses and their possibilities of agency. Bishop's representation of whiteness and the Other is situated in power relations embedded in subject positions. These voices and their subject positions must not be identified as transparent expressions of Bishop's white privilege. To assume such a straightforward, unproblematic relation between the author and the speaker's subject positions in a text prevents our full understanding of the discursive constructions of whiteness and its otherness. This assumption also forecloses the possibility of white women's intervention in the production of dominant racial ideology. Thus our modes of reading Bishop's poems have much larger implications than a single poet. My insistence on a nonidentical relation between Bishop's subject position as a white woman and the subject positions of the speakers in her poems seeks to investigate racial, gender, and cultural difference as a positioning, not an essence.

NOTES

1. I limit my reading of Bishop's "Songs for a Colored Singer" only to the first two songs because they are most relevant to the problems of the speaker's voice in terms of race and class. The third song is a lullaby, dealing with the reality of war. For an informative and sensitive reading of it, see Victoria Harrison, 99–101. The fourth song responds to "Strange Fruit," a song written by Lewis Allen for Billie Holiday, addressing the African American experience of racism.

2. A slightly different version of my reading of "12 O'Clock News" has appeared in my book, *Elizabeth Bishop: Rebel in "Shades and Shadows"* (New York: Lang, 1999).

3. Bishop translated and published three of Clarice Lispector's stories, including "The Smallest Woman in the World," in the *Kenyon Review* 26.3 (Summer 1964): 501–11.

WORKS CITED

Primary Sources

Bishop, Elizabeth. *The Complete Poems, 1927–1979*. New York: Farrar, 1987.
———. *Brazil* (with the editors of *Life* for the Life World Library). New York: Time-Life, 1962.
———. *One Art: Letters. Selected.* Ed. and introd. Robert Giroux. New York: Farrar, 1994.

————. "An Interview with Elizabeth Bishop." Ashley Brown, in Schwartz and Estess 289–302.

Secondary Sources

Aanerud, Rebecca. "Fictions of Whiteness: Speaking the Names of Whiteness in U. S. Literature." *Displacing Whiteness: Essays in Social and Cultural Criticism.* Ed. Ruth Frankenberg. Durham: Duke UP, 1997. 35–59.

Bakhtin, Mikhail M. *The Dialogic Imagination: Four Essays.* Ed. Michael Holquist. Trans. Caryl Emerson and Michael Holquist. Austin: U of Texas P, 1990.

————. *Speech Genres and Other Late Essays.* Trans. Vern W. McGee. Ed. Caryl Emerson and Michael Holquist. Austin: U of Texas P, 1992.

Barthes, Roland. *Mythologies.* Trans. Annette Lavers. New York: Noonday Press/ Farrar, 1990.

Brown, Ashley. "Elizabeth Bishop in Brazil." Schwartz and Estess 223–40.

Curry, Renée R. *White Women Writing White: H.D., Elizabeth Bishop, Sylvia Plath, and Whiteness.* Westport: Greenwood, 2000.

Davis, Angela Y. "I Used to Be Your Sweet Mama: Ideology, Sexuality and Domesticity in the Blues of Gertrude 'Ma' Rainey and Bessie Smith." *Sexy Bodies: The Strange Carnalities of Feminism.* Ed. Elizabeth Grosz and Elspeth Probyn. London: Routledge, 1995. 231–65.

Dickie, Margaret. *Stein, Bishop, and Rich: Lyrics of Love, War, and Place.* Chapel Hill: U of North Carolina P, 1997.

Foucault, Michel. *The Archaeology of Knowledge & The Discourse on Language.* Trans. A. M. Sheridan Smith. New York: Pantheon, 1972.

Frankerberg, Ruth. "'When We Are Capable of Stopping, We Begin to See': Being White, Seeing Whiteness." *Names We Call Home: Autobiography on Racial Identity.* Ed. Becky Thompson and Samgeeta Tyagi. New York: Routledge, 1996. 3–17.

————.*White Women, Race Matters: The Social Construction of Whiteness.* Minneapolis: U of Minnesota P, 1993.

Goldensohn, Lorrie. *Elizabeth Bishop: The Biography of a Poetry.* New York: Columbia UP, 1992.

Harrison, Victoria Gail. *Elizabeth Bishop's Poetics of Intimacy.* New York: Cambridge UP, 1993.

Kalstone, David. "All Eye." Rev. of *Questions of Travel* (1965), by Elizabeth Bishop. *Partisan Review* 37.2 (Spring 1970): 310–15.

Lispector, Clarice. "The Smallest Woman in the World." Trans. Elizabeth Bishop. *Kenyon Review* 26.3 (Summer 1964): 501–06.

Millier, Brett C. *Elizabeth Bishop: Life and the Memory of It.* Berkeley: U of California P, 1993.

Morris, Timothy. *Becoming Canonical in American Poetry*. Urbana: U of Illinois P, 1995.

Pratt, Mary Louise. *Imperial Eyes: Travel Writing and Transculturation*. London: Routledge, 1992.

Rich, Adrienne. "The Eye of the Outsider: Elizabeth Bishop's *Complete Poems, 1927–1979* (1983)." *Blood, Bread and Poetry: Selected Prose, 1979–1985*. New York: Norton, 1986. 124–35.

Said, Edward W. *Culture and Imperialism*. New York: Vintage, 1994.

Schwartz, Lloyd, and Sybil P. Estess, eds., *Elizabeth Bishop and Her Art*. Ann Arbor: U of Michigan P, 1983.

Weiner, Deborah. "'Difference That Kills' / Difference That Heals: Representing Latin America in the Poetry of Elizabeth Bishop and Margaret Atwood." *Comparative Literature East and West: Traditions and Trends*. Selected Conference Papers. Ed. Corneliar N. Moore and Paymond A. Moody. Honolulu: College of Languages, Linguistics and Literature, University of Hawaii and the East West Center, 1989. 208–19.

Zhou, Xiaojing. *Elizabeth Bishop: Rebel "in Shades and Shadows."* New York: Lang, 1999.

PART THREE

The Global "Memsahib"

CHAPTER ELEVEN

How Can a White Woman Love a Black Woman?

The Anglo-Boer War and Possibilities of Desire

PAULA M. KREBS

As with much work on pre-twentieth-century lesbian desire, this essay starts from a silence. In this instance, silence covers the desire of a white, Afrikaner woman not to be parted from her African servants when she and they are to be confined in concentration camps by the British army during the Boer War of 1899–1902. I don't want to make false promises—you will find no expressions of interracial lesbian sexual desire in the narrative I will be discussing. Instead, you will find a narrative of female relations that depends absolutely on there being *no* possibility of lesbian desire. This narrative from the concentration camps, examined in the context of other Boer War writing, shows the implications of the way a particular and significant antiwar discourse, the work of pro-Boer activist Emily Hobhouse, occluded the possibility of *desire* between Afrikaner and African women in order to promote an image of *sympathy*. Reading what is unspoken in the narrative of camp inmate Mrs. G allows us to see the ways in which the triangular South African political structure of Briton-Boer-African makes for a complicated, politicized sexual triangle as well.

Britain and the Dutch-descended Afrikaner settlers of Southern Africa fought the war of 1899–1902 for control of a land largely populated by Africans. Emily Hobhouse, a British philanthropist/social reformer who was working for the antiwar South Africa Conciliation Committee, traveled to South Africa in 1901 to investigate the conditions for Boer women and children in what were known as concentration camps (because the army had concentrated the populations of large areas into the camps). The British army had formed the camps of bell tents to house Boer women and children and African families whom it had deported from their farms. By early 1901 the camps had rapidly rising death rates from poor sanitation and nutrition, and Hobhouse's report on the conditions in the camps created a national scandal in Britain. Reports of her investigations appeared in the antiwar *Manchester Guardian* and were published in full as her report to the committee that had funded her trip and then issued as a book, *The Brunt of the War and Where It Fell*, after peace was signed.

Hobhouse tells of how a Boer farm woman, Mrs. G, complained that her "two old Kaffir servant-girls, who had been with her for years and years," had suffered at the hands of the same British soldiers who had burnt Mrs. G's house down. As Hobhouse retells the story in her report to British readers, the white and black inhabitants of the burned farms were carted off to the concentration camps:

> Back at Norval's Pont the little party was separated. The Kaffirs had to go into one camp and the white people into another. There was a strict rule against keeping any servants in the white camp, but they [Mrs. G's family] ventured to keep the two little orphan girls, as they had been brought up in the house and were like their own. . . . Mrs. G thereupon stated her case to the Commandant, saying, "They are orphans; I have had them ever since they were babies, and I am bringing them up as my own." He was very kind, and said he would give her a permit. . . . The only stipulation he made was that they should go back to the Kaffir camp at night. (262)

The story is one of dozens of such anecdotes recounted by Hobhouse in her effort to enlist British sympathy for the Boers. But this anecdote stands out in Hobhouse's writings because of its uncertainties, its blurrings of categories: Were the servants "old" or were they "little orphan girls"? Had they "been brought up" or was Mrs. G "bringing them up"? Were they "like [Mrs. G's] own" or were they her servants? And why were they permitted to stay all day in the white camp but not to spend the night?

We cannot answer these questions except to know, of course, that the "girls" were servants, not adopted children. The relationship that is to be understood from the narrative is a mistress-servant one, framed as a mother-daughter one. This displacement, of an economic relationship onto a familial one, is a common colonial trope. But I want to focus on how Mrs. G's relationship with her "girls" is presented, to the British reader of Hobhouse's pro-Boer propaganda, as maternal. Although the model for the relationship is maternal, and although the "one big happy family" metaphor for white employer-black domestic employee relations had been a cliché for generations, the Mrs. G story, I argue, cannot be certain of its reception in Britain and so must blur the answers to those questions with which I ended the previous paragraph. At the turn of the century, when British sexologists had already made lesbianism a visible possibility, the desire of a woman to have another woman living in close quarters (in a tent) with her must be legitimated for British readers. Thus, two orphan girls make a safer story than one would. Thus, the ages of the girls must be vague, for to count as daughter-equivalents the females cannot be seen as adults. Paternalism/maternalism demands infantilization. Hence nineteenth-century antislavery movements, in both Britain and America, focused on asserting the "manhood" of slaves: Josiah Wedgwood's famous image of a chained African asked "Am I not a man and a brother?" But Hobhouse's is not a "negrophilist" document—it is aimed at inspiring identification not with the servants but with the mistress. To inspire such connection, Hobhouse must demonstrate Mrs. G's power over and sympathy for her black servants. So, to be in a proper service relationship to Mrs. G, the girls must be both servants and loved children. The racial difference between Mrs. G and the girls precludes a solely affectionate bond, but the existence of an affectionate bond softens and qualifies a racial difference that virtually requires an economic bond. The shifting descriptions of the relations between these women are absolutely essential to Emily Hobhouse's project of winning British empathy for Boer women's lives.

Many historians locate the Anglo-Boer War of 1899–1902 as a key moment in British colonial relations, coming as it did after the scramble for Africa and before early twentieth-century decolonization. The war is often seen as marking the beginning of the British public's disillusionment with imperialism—it featured a good deal of antiwar organizing and propaganda, as many Britons began to question the motivation behind a war that seemed to be more about gold mines than about bringing the benefits of civilization to the Dark Continent. The war, however, is just as often seen as the occasion for the real arrival of jingoism in Britain, especially after the wild street celebrations that marked the relief of the besieged South African town of Mafeking. Imperialism was not the only dominant ideology that was in flux at the turn of the century, of course. The intersection of Boer War imperialism with changes in cultural ideology about women's sexuality makes for a complicated context in which Emily Hobhouse's report would be read in Britain.

Bram Dijkstra points out that popular late-Victorian theories of human evolution "held that in women signs of evolutionary progress were accompanied by a diminished sex drive" (119)—the highest-evolved woman, the middle-class European woman, had less natural interest in sex than just about any other cultural category you could name. At the same time (perhaps consequently), turn-of-the-century art and literature seems to have been fascinated with lesbianism, an interest that stemmed, at least in part, from Victorian sexologists' "scientific" study of homosexuality. Lesbianism was a Victorian possibility, as we know from numerous studies of sexology and of individual lesbians themselves, from Anne Lister to Radclyffe Hall. What had changed by the turn of the century was that lesbianism had moved from being a private possibility to being a more public phenomenon. Dijkstra's *Idols of Perversity* indicates that "around 1900 . . . the depiction of lesbianism became a popular and, among intellectuals, popularly accepted theme" (153). That

is not to say that lesbian *practice* became especially popular—but the representation of lesbianism was certainly spreading.

While lesbianism had a cultural presence in the metropolis, in the intellectual life of London and Paris and Berlin, it had no such presence in the rural Boer
republics of South Africa. Interracial sexual contact between men did feature in
narratives of imperialism, as such researchers as Christopher Lane, Ronald Hyam,
and Richard Phillips have pointed out. But interracial sexuality between women
held an entirely different place in the history of imperial discourse. In *Cities of the
Dead*, Joseph Roach discusses nineteenth-century drama and art in which black
women and white women are sexually linked, in both high cultural forms and low.
In his analysis of *The Victory of Faith*, a painting by Royal Academician St. George
Hare, Roach indicates that the image, ostensibly a scene of two Christian soon-
to-be-martyrs the night before their deaths, is in fact very sexual. The two nude
women, one black and one white, sleep next to each other. "The presence of the
(unchained) black girl, on which the grasp of the white girl's hand insists, insinu-
ates what the unrepresentability of pubic hair cannot: the pressure of sexual desire
from within even the whitest body. The sexualized virgin martyr rises transcendent from the flesh of her black double" (223–24), Roach writes. In such images,
as in the much-discussed Orientalist images such as Gérôme's *The Great Bath at
Bursa* (reproduced on the cover of Anne McClintock's *Imperial Leather*), black
women's bodies serve to code the sexuality of white women. *The Victory of Faith* is
no lesbian scene, argues Roach, but a use of the black female body to sexualize the
white. Roach differentiates between such uses of black women's bodies in relation
to white women's and another genre in which black and white women interact:
"[t]he implicitly lesbian coupling of two women, one fair, the other dark, proliferates
in the Victorian erotica of the circum-Atlantic exchange" (223), he says. The difference between the "implicit" lesbianism in the "erotica" (which is not documented
in Roach) and the image in *The Victory of Faith* remains a bit unclear, however.
Linda Nochlin's discussion of Orientalist painting is equally shifty on lesbianism.
For Nochlin, Orientalist painting's "sense of erotic availability is spiced with still
more forbidden overtones, for the conjunction of black and white, or dark and
light female bodies, whether naked or in the guise of mistress and maidservant,
has traditionally signified lesbianism" (49). The "tradition" in which lesbianism
is signified remains undescribed, as does, for Roach, the ways lesbianism comes to
be "implicit" in erotica or insignificant as lesbianism in *The Victory of Faith*. For these
critics, interracial lesbian images are not explored as lesbian—their meaning is elsewhere, or else it is self-evidently "signified." It is unlikely, of course, that the erotic
images of interracial lesbian sex that Roach and Nochlin cite were meant to correspond to an actual social phenomenon, a female equivalent of, say, Richard Burton's
experience in the East. But the images themselves are part of a public discourse
about race and homosexuality in the late-Victorian period.

If there is little or no traceable history of interracial colonial lesbian relations
in this period, there is, nevertheless, a place where one should have been. The

concentration camps, to which were deported the Afrikaner and African families who had been living on the farms in the warring districts, were racialized women's space. The British established separate camps for Afrikaners and for Africans, breaking up the social fabric of the patriarchal and paternalistic Boer farms. For white women used to the attendance of servants, the camp experience, despite the fact that the British army provided rations, must have been a shock in many ways (including, of course, the tremendous death rates from disease). For African servants used to wage labor, the camps, where they had to grow their own food and where death rates far surpassed those in the white camps, were a different kind of shock. The questions we have about Mrs. G's desire to have her "girls" with her in camp and the commandant's agreement that the two could stay in the Boer camp, but not overnight, force us to examine what Eve Sedgwick calls "a powerful unknowing *as* unknowing, not as a vacuum or as the blank it can pretend to be but as a weighty and occupied and consequential epistemological space" (77). In considering Mrs. G's case, we must do as Martha Vicinus does, and "argue for the possibilities of the 'not said' and the 'not seen' as conceptual tools for lesbian studies" (2).

Clearly Africans in the camps are segregated from Boers for reasons of race, but those reasons did not exist separately from factors of gender, sex, and South African British-Boer politics. In examining the questions left by Mrs. G's narrative, we begin to theorize a blank space—why is lesbianism not allowed as a discursive possibility in this particular colonial relation? If lesbianism can be spoken and seen in Europe, what prevents it as a possibility in South Africa or, in the case of Emily Hobhouse's writings for British readers, what prevents lesbianism as a possibility in the depiction of relations between black and white women?

Siobhan Somerville, in "Scientific Racism and the Invention of the Homosexual Body," calls attention to the "relationships between the medical/scientific discourse around sexuality and the dominant scientific discourse around race" at the turn of the century (243). Medical discourse about sexuality and about race, she shows, did not exist separately—definitions of homosexuality referred to racial concerns, and attempts to define race always included references to sexuality. In Boer War writing, discussions of Africans often invoke what had become the standard image of the hypersexualized African of either gender. But the European sexologists' interest in female homosexuality does not seem to have made the crossing to South Africa. Race (and in Boer War South Africa, race means the differences between African and English as much as the differences between African and either white nation) is the dominant framework for the discussion of the female-female relationships in Mrs. G's narrative. In the narrative, a relationship between African and Afrikaner women cannot be seen as sexual because the colonial context relies on that "powerful unknowing" Sedgwick describes. The space occupied by the unknowing, that refusal of interracial lesbian desire in Mrs. G's story, must be read through an understanding of the triangulation at work in South African race relations at the time of the Boer War—Boer relates to African through Briton; white woman relates to black woman through white man.

Mrs. G's story came to Britain as part of a larger picture of sexual relations and race relations during the Anglo-Boer War. At the turn of the century the image of black men as potential rapists of white women was certainly alive and well—in India, as Jenny Sharpe has shown, and in the United States. Both sides of the propaganda battles about the morality of the Boer War use the image of the black male rapist. Not surprisingly, the discourse of black men as potential rapists of white women posits a normative sexuality that would preclude any possibility that white women might actually desire black men.

The image of African men threatening to rape white women was used both to justify the concentration camps and to attack them. The British government claimed that the Boer women left on their farms without their men had to be brought in to camps because of the danger from "marauding natives" (Krebs, "The Last of the Gentlemen's Wars" 45). Such claims were countered by antiwar, or pro-Boer, assertions that the women were perfectly safe on the farms, surrounded by their own African servants. The pro-Boer version held that it was when the women were *removed* from the farms that they were in danger from African men. The natural order of Boer-African relations on the farms, the pro-Boers claimed, was disturbed when the British deported the whites, and the result was that African men were stirred up into resentment of the Afrikaners. In Hobhouse's report, the disruption of African-Afrikaner relations resulted in African men's sexual harassment of Boer women. Hobhouse quotes a petition from Boer women in the Klerksdorp camp citing the circumstances of their being brought in:

> On this occasion Kaffirs were used, and they equalled the English soldiers in cruelty and barbarity. The women knelt before these Kaffirs and begged for mercy, but they were roughly shaken off, and had to endure even more impudent language and rude behavior. . . . When the mothers were driven like cattle through the streets of Potchefstroom by the Kaffirs, the cries and lamentations of the children filled the air. The Kaffirs jeered and cried, "Move on; till now you were our masters, but now we will make your women our wives." (219)

The pronouns confuse: the story paints Boer women as the victims of "Kaffirs," but the "you" at whom the Africans jeer is not the Boer women—it is Boer men, who appear neither in the petition from the Boer women nor in Hobhouse's frame for it. The Hobhouse report creates an image of Boer women and children, unaccompanied by "their" men, under threat from hostile, predatory Africans. But the words the Boer women themselves attribute to the Africans in their petition seem to contradict the picture, for they assume a male auditor.

A male auditor is necessary for such a story of harassment to work, as the story depends on a notion of men insulting other men through "their" women. The Boer women's petition is the closest Boer War narratives get to the "Mutiny" writings Jenny Sharpe describes in *Allegories of Empire*—jeering, threatening black men assert their new power over their old masters by claiming sexual privileges over white women. In the stories Sharpe discusses, narratives (later disproved) of rebel Indian soldiers' atrocities against British women during the Sepoy Rebellion of 1857, the image for the rebellion itself becomes the image of Sepoys humiliating British men by sexually violating their wives and daughters. In the Boer War, the women who were "threatened" by black men were not English but the enemy of the English. It would appear from her quotes from the Boer petition that Hobhouse considered carefully what notes to strike to inspire sympathy for the Boer women. Surely the British would not approve of white women, even white women who had aided and abetted the enemy, being driven through the streets by black men and sexually taunted.

Nevertheless, the deportations continued. Hobhouse was not able to win support for Boers through her invocation of the sexually predatory African man, probably because the black rapist was already being called into service on the other side of the debate. The British army, after all, had claimed that it had deported the Boer women in the first place to protect them from African men. The British army claim was blunt—if we leave white women unprotected, of course black men will rape them. The pro-Boer use of the image was much subtler: Africans and Afrikaners live in harmony on South African farms. Breaking up the farms and stripping Afrikaner women of their power over African men gives those men reason to think that they could turn the tables on the whites. The ultimate expression of the reversal of power would be to "make your women our wives." Even Hobhouse, actively campaigning against British imperialism, invokes the spectre of black rule in South Africa as a horror, and she calls it up by positing interracial sex as its symbol. The language of the threat of interracial sex differs in very important ways, however, between the two uses of the image. While the British army indirectly (and occasionally directly) asserted the danger of African men raping white women, the Boer women report that the African men did not threaten to rape Boer women but to "make [them] our wives"—that is, to establish legitimate interracial unions, to create a civil society in South Africa in which black men could marry white women. To be sure, the story comes from Boer women rather than from African men, but whether from Afrikaner or African, the image is one that Boers would find horrifying. The threat, while undoubtedly a sexual one, is a threat of *legitimate*, not illegitimate, sex with white women.

War propaganda, government blue books, private correspondence, and newspaper coverage of the Boer War contain very few references to African women, whether the accounts are pro-war or pro-Boer. Occasionally African women are victims, as in Colonel Robert Baden-Powell's dispatches from the siege of Mafeking, in which he details Boer slaughter of African women who try to sneak out of the besieged city. One of the few direct mentions of African women in British newspapers during the course of the war was Arthur Hales's attempt at a literary sketch, "In a Boer Town," which appeared on 10 May 1900 in the *Daily News*:

> The girls are rather pleasing in appearance though far from being pretty.
> . . . The Kaffir girl is very dark, almost black. The bushman's daughter
> is dirty yellow, like riverwater in flood time. . . . But whether they are
> black, brown, or coffee-coloured, they are all alike in one respect—
> every daughter of them has a mouth that is as boundless as a mother's
> blessing, and as limitless as the imagination of a spring poet in love. . . .
> It is amusing to watch them flirting with the soldier niggers. They try
> to look coy, but soon fall victims to the skilful blandishments of the
> vainglorious warriors, and after a little manoeuvering they put out their
> lips to be kissed, a sight which might well make a Scottish Covenanter
> grin. (3)

Hales associates the African woman's mouth with "a mother's blessing" and "a
spring poet in love," but his metaphors do not emphasize the beauty of the feature—they emphasize the *size* of it, perhaps a bit sexually intimidating to the British
man. African women putting out the lips of those great mouths is a ridiculous sight,
for Hales, but the sight is a sexual enough one for the African men he describes.
The "soldier niggers," says Hale, "do enough love-making in twenty-four hours to
last an ordinary everyday sort of white man four months, even if he puts in a little
overtime" (3). The sexual anxieties of this British male observer, in relation to
African men and women, are not far below the surface.

Both African men and African women are heavily sexualized in Hales's account
as in much British writing on Africa. Afrikaner women, however, are generally
portrayed as fat, lazy, matriarchs in British writing on the war, unless they are shown
as sneaking spies. For Hales, however, Boer women are potential love interests for
British men. The *Daily News* correspondent sketched a picture of a young Boer
woman that was unlike either the monster usually seen in the British daily press
or the victim portrayed in antiwar propaganda. The narrator is captivated by the
youngest daughter of a Boer family:

> [T]he fourth had a face like a young preacher's first public prayer. A
> face that many a man would risk his life for. So much of my whole career
> has been passed amidst the rougher and more rugged scenes of life that
> a description of dainty womanhood comes awkwardly from me. But I
> have read so much about the ugliness and clumsiness of the Boer
> women in British journals that I should like to try and describe this
> daughter of the veldt, although only a farmer's daughter. I do not know
> if she was short or tall, but her cheek could have nestled comfortably
> on the shoulder of a fairly tall man. (3)

Her hands were the kind of hands that could "help a husband back to paths of
rectitude when all the world had damned him past redemption." This is not a woman
who appears often in accounts of the war—she is a Victorian woman with whom

an English man would fall in love. The series of possibilities of desire we can locate in this colonial setting thus comes to include, first, white male (both British and Boer, in the South African case) desire for African women, signalled by much anxiety about miscegenation. Next, we have the Boer women's petition, and propaganda on both sides of the war, positing African men's desire for Boer women. Now, Hales reveals the possibility of British men's desire for Boer women. While we don't find explicit male homosexual desire in accounts of the war, certainly a strong strain of male homosociality, male desire for other men, runs through Boer War accounts, as it does in much war writing. Histories of the period emphasize the "kindergarten" of young men with whom Lord Milner surrounded himself, and the Boer War superstar Baden-Powell, founder of the Scouts, is virtually a gay icon. Interracial male desire during this period in South Africa is under-explored. But I maintain the significance of the gap in Mrs. G's narrative: the refusal of lesbian desire in that setting is a powerful unknowing indeed.

If we speculate on what is behind the absence and, in Mrs. G's case, the inconsistencies, we find ourselves constantly confronted with the central impossibility of sexual desire between Afrikaner and African women. Here Siobhan Somerville's discussion of the connections between racial and sexual discourses at the turn of the century highlights the differences between the South African and the U.S. racial contexts. For while Somerville refers to the Saartje Baartman "Hottentot Venus" history as background for Victorian understandings of racial differences in sexuality, African female sexuality does not really come into play in her argument about female homosexuality and race. Somerville's most fascinating material is her discussion of a 1913 *Journal of Abnormal Psychology* article about interracial lesbian relationships in American all-girls' institutions such as reformatories and boarding schools. Somerville points out that the article's author, psychologist Margaret Otis, "characterized this phenomenon as a type of 'the homosexual relation' and not as a particular form of interracial sexuality" (251). Such a categorization would have been possible only in a country such as the United States, where what Otis called the "colored girls" were inmates in the institution on the same terms as the white girls. Such terms would have been impossible in a colonial context such as South Africa.

In her discussion of the connections between miscegenation and homosexuality as "perversions" in the early twentieth-century United States, Somerville draws important conclusions about the pathologizing of both kinds of desire. But the South African colonial context means a different relation between racial and sexual discourses from the relation in the United States. In the United States, interracial lesbianism could be seen as an interesting variation of the perversion of homosexuality. How was interracial sex seen in South Africa in the same period? Was it seen, as in the United States, as a psychological perversion? Or was it seen more directly in legal terms or as a violation of social or economic codes rather than psychological ones? If the latter is the case, then miscegenation and homosexuality were part of very different discourses in South Africa, not part of a shared medi-calized discourse, as in the United States. In the Britain that read Emily Hobhouse's report on the concentration camps, miscegenation was seen as a South African social problem, neither a domestic problem nor a psychological one.

Let us return to Mrs. G's narrative. To account for Mrs. G's petition on behalf of her servant "girls," we need to look at her story not in terms of sexual desire but in terms of sympathy. As Jenny Sharpe points out, "The trope of 'human sym-pathy' does not establish a common identity between colonizer and colonized so much as it identifies the racial superiority of the English" (52). In her writings for British audiences during the Boer War, Emily Hobhouse is making a double move in relation to this trope of sympathy. First, she is calling for British empathy with Boers, trying to persuade Britons to identify with Boers. This is difficult because the Boers are seen in Britain, even by such advocates as Olive Schreiner, as evolution-arily inferior to Britons—superstitious, backward agriculturalists whose insularity meant that they missed the entire Enlightenment. In Mrs. G's story and elsewhere, Hobhouse's report asks British readers to identify with the Boers: Boers have a class structure, just like us; Boers have good taste, just like us; and, above all, in Mrs. G's story, Boers treat Africans well, just like us. Here is the second strategy Hobhouse uses: she evokes that *empathy* for the Boers by showing Boer sympathy for Africans. If, as Sharpe argues, *sympathy* identifies racial superiority, then Hobhouse is equating the positions of Boer and Briton in her construction of Boer sympathy for Africans.

One of the reasons the British government had cited for entering the Boer War had been Boer mistreatment of Africans. This mistreatment was seen as an indicator of the lack of advanced civilization in the Boers. Boers, it was argued, could not see humanity in the lower races, were incapable of sympathy. For Hob-house to arouse empathy in British readers for the Boers, she had to show the Boers as roughly equivalent to a European nation. With the story of Mrs. G, Hobhouse is able to present a Boer woman who has a close, affectionate relationship with Africans. Boers are thus shown as sympathetic toward Africans just as the British saw themselves as sympathetic toward Africans. Boers, therefore, were colonizers in the same mold as the British.

To inspire British empathy with the Boers, Hobhouse was limited to citing relationships among females. Problems arose in showing Boer men demonstrating close affectional bonds for Africans: strong emotions of a white man for an African had a potential sexual component for a British reader. A white man expressing a desire to remain physically close to an African woman, man, or even child could be read sexually in late-Victorian Britain. Given the criticism of the mixed-race population in South Africa, Hobhouse could not praise Afrikaner male affection for African women. Given the discursive presence of the notion of male homo-sexuality by the turn of the century, even, or especially, in a colonial context, Hobhouse could not have used an image of an Afrikaner male's affection for his male African servant to illustrate the goodness or gentility of the Boer race.

Examinations of male interracial homosexuality in colonial contexts have focused primarily on India. But racial contexts in Africa are different from India. Even an anti-imperialist such as Olive Schreiner, for example, sees African sexuality as far lower down the evolutionary scale than European sexuality. In *Woman and Labour*, Schreiner says

> Were it possible to place a company of the most highly evolved human females—George Sands, Sophia Kovalevskys, or even the average cultured female of a highly evolved race—on an island where the only males were savages of the Fugean type, who should meet them on the shores with matted hair and prognathous jaws . . . so great would be the horror felt by the females towards them, that not only would the race become extinct, but if it depended for its continuance on any approach to sex affection on the part of the women, that death would certainly be accepted by all, as the lesser of two evils. . . . A Darwin, a Schiller, a Keats . . . would probably be untouched by any emotion but horror, cast into the company of a circle of Bushman females with greased bodies and twinkling eyes, devouring the raw entrails of slaughtered beasts. (248–49)

Miscegenation is degeneracy (Dubow). True "sex affection" cannot exist between white and black, for they are too far apart on the evolutionary scale. Lesbianism, too, had been an image of degeneration, from at least the eighteenth century, as Terry Castle has shown. In anthropological terms, too, lesbianism and male homosexuality were seen as degenerate, as practices of primitives for whom pleasure was the sole aim of sexuality. Arthur Hales's *Daily News* description of African sexuality participates in the British version of Africans as primitively oversexed. Degeneration is seen as a danger for whites who live amongst Africans, as Christopher Lane points out in his analysis of Richard Meinertzhagen's *Kenya Diaries* and the 1909 Crewe Circular, and degeneration's most concrete manifestation is sexual excess. If lesbianism is degenerate and interracial sexuality is degenerate, then it's no wonder that Hobhouse erases interracial lesbianism as a possibility in the narrative. While the British public thought of the war as a battle between British men and Afrikaner men, Hobhouse's use of Mrs. G's story makes the key dynamic the relationship between Afrikaner women and African women—that relationship reveals what Hobhouse presents as the true South Africa: a pastoral settler community in which the white colonizer lives in sympathetic harmony with the black indigenous peoples.

What are the options for one race loving another? Civilization demands that races come to love each other; religious rhetoric about imperialism reminds Victorians of that. But there is love and love. Sympathy, that love of the more powerful for the less, is the proper love of a white race for a black. Friendship, which demands a level of equality, is impossible. And, as Sara Suleri has noted, in a different context, "erotic exchange between cultures" is "a social impossibility." In the charged sexuality between British men and Indian men in Kipling or Forster or Scott, as Suleri says of Forster, "both race and body are subjected to an awareness of colonial chronology that allows for the signification of love even when it is at its most productively dismal depths" (148).

The three-"race" colonial context in South Africa produces a triangle of political as well as sexual significance in the Boer narrative we are examining. Rather than a woman forming the apex of the erotic triangle, mediating between men, as in Eve Sedgwick's discussion of Victorian literature, we have Mrs. G and her servants as the base of the triangle, with men mediating their desire, or, rather, failing to do so. For Emily Hobhouse, British male interference in the relationship between Boers and Africans, represented by the relationship between Boer and African women, is the tragedy of British imperialism. Hobhouse presents as ideal a sympathetic relationship between the Boer woman and her African servants. But what kind of desire can be present in such a relationship? There can be no denying that Mrs. G desires her servants' presence every day and night; it is the meaning of that desire that is in question. Desire between white women and black in this colonial context is always mediated by the third party of the white man, but it is also mediated by the conditions of colonialism itself. Colonialism offers the trope of sympathy to structure female-female desire. That trope produces a politically acceptable version of South African race relations for Emily Hobhouse's British readers, but it does so at the expense of a version of sexual relations that would, in the succeeding century, prove increasingly difficult to ignore or suppress.

WORKS CITED

Castle, Terry. *The Apparitional Lesbian: Female Homosexuality and Modern Culture.* New York: Columbia UP, 1993.

Dijkstra, Bram. *Idols of Perversity: Fantasies of Feminine Evil in Fin-de-Siècle Culture.* New York: Oxford UP, 1986.

Dubow, Saul. *Scientific Racism in Modern South Africa.* Cambridge, Eng.: Cambridge UP, 1995.

Hales, Arthur. "In a Boer Town." *Daily News.* 10 May, 1900: 3.

Hobhouse, Emily. *The Brunt of the War and Where It Fell.* London: Methuen, 1902.

Hyam, Ronald. *Empire and Sexuality.* Manchester: Manchester UP, 1992.

Krebs, Paula. *Gender, Race, and the Writing of Empire: Public Discourse and the Boer War.* Cambridge, Eng.: Cambridge UP, 1999.

———. "'The Last of the Gentlemen's Wars': Women in the Boer War Concentration Camp Controversy." *History Workshop Journal* 33 (Spring 1992): 38–56.

Lane, Christopher. *The Ruling Passion: British Colonial Allegory and the Paradox of Homosexual Desire*. Durham: Duke UP, 1996.

Nochlin, Linda. "The Imaginary Orient." *The Politics of Vision: Essays on Nineteenth Century Art and Society*. Ed. Linda Nochlin. New York: Harper, 1989. 33–59.

Phillips, Richard. *Mapping Men and Empire: A Geography of Adventure*. London: Routledge, 1997.

Roach, Joseph. *Cities of the Dead: Circum-Atlantic Performance*. New York: Columbia UP, 1996.

Schreiner, Olive. *Woman and Labour*. London: Unwin, 1911.

Sedgwick, Eve Kosofsky. *Epistemology of the Closet*. Berkeley: U of California P, 1990.

Sharpe, Jenny. *Allegories of Empire: The Figure of Woman in the Colonial Text*. Minneapolis: U of Minnesota P, 1993.

Somerville, Siobhan. "Scientific Racism and the Invention of the Homosexual Body." *Queer Studies: A Lesbian, Gay, Bisexual and Transgender Anthology*. Ed. Brett Beemyn and Mickey Eliason. New York: New York UP, 1996. 241–61.

Suleri, Sara. *The Rhetoric of English India*. Chicago: U of Chicago P, 1992.

Vicinus, Martha. Introduction. *Lesbian Subjects: A Feminist Studies Reader*. Ed. Martha Vicinus. Bloomington: Indiana UP, 1996.

CHAPTER TWELVE

From Betrayal to Inclusion

The Work of the White Woman's Gaze in Claire Denis's Chocolat

CÉLINE PHILIBERT

Racial and gender relations, as well as problems of origin and identity, are central to all of us who live within a postcolonial order which is being questioned and redefined. Gestures of confrontation and appropriation, destruction and construction, inform the ways we renegotiate the discursive streams of history and desire and re-member/re-appropriate our past. Claire Denis's film *Chocolat* (1986)[1] is a compelling illustration of the ways in which a narrative explores contemporary issues of identity and desire. Returning to Cameroon,[2] France Dalens (played by Mireille Perrier), a young French woman, is on her way to Mindiff, where she used to live with her parents when the country was under French rule. A black man, whom we know only as Mungo (played by Emmet Judson Williamson) at this point in the movie, offers her a ride to Limbé, the closest village where she is to catch an auto-bus to Douala. The car scene triggers a film-long flashback, in which France recalls fragments of the Dalens's life in troubled colonial times, by narrating the mother (played by Giulia Boschi) Aimée's desire for the family's servant, Protée (played by Isaac de Bankolé).

The French cinema has previously explored colonized West Africa,[3] yet never before has it offered such a different perspective upon colonialism as it does in *Chocolat*. Claire Denis's first full feature film[4] is the quasi-autobiographical recounting of the director's life as a preteen in colonial Cameroon.[5] Reluctant to include anything autobiographical, yet in need for ways to soften the screenplay, Claire Denis decides to ground her narration in the part of an eight-year-old girl like herself when she lived in Cameroon. As the present reflection of a white woman upon her girlhood, being part of the colonial power structures, and yet apart from them, the film stands at the juncture between colonization and postcolonization, between history and desire.

The focus of this paper is the white woman's gaze. Resituating and restructuring conventional representations and interpretations of colonizing structures, the white woman's gaze disrupts the social, cultural, ethnic, national, and familial identities, roles and relations that interdisciplinary gender analysis has been particularly adept at revealing. The white woman's return to memory and her intent to go back "home" operate in this motion picture against the traditional trajectory of colonial memory and against the mythic and collective memory the West holds about West Africa.

Typically, a return to the past works along a quest for identity and subjectivity. Yet, helping us "to conceive of human reality as a construction," the term "subject" has been examined as "the product of signifying activities which are both culturally specific and generally unconscious" (Silverman 130). As such, Teresa de Lauretis insists on a feminist critique as both "within" and "without" a culture (de Lauretis 119). Significant developments in feminist and postcolonial theories[6] have contributed to the definition of the gaze/point-of-view by grounding the exploration of "gender," "race," and "nation" upon the locality of culture. As a result of the cross-fertilization of contemporary research, film studies has developed a more acute preoccupation with diversity and multicultural considerations, and thus has witnessed the production of insightful works that incorporate national cinemas in theoretical discussions of nation-ness.[7] "The one most untheorized concept of the modern world" (Chatterjee 1993), "nation" has been explored and defined as having a "historical certainty and settled nature" that reveals the "Western nation as an obscure and ubiquitous form of living the '"locality of culture"'" (Bhabha, Nation 292).

Important steps have been made principally by feminist critics who have shifted their reflection from "the Other" to "I"—the one who theorizes, gazes, and speaks— and have examined the construction of "whiteness." Among them, Chandra Talpade Mohanty argues that the concept of "whiteness" is a racialized category which is nuanced or even contested by gender, class, ethnicity, religion, and sexuality, and that the white gaze can be defined by Western expectations and values "which possibly can be traced as a coherence of effects resulting from implicit assumption of the 'West' in all its complexities and contradictions, as the primary referent in theory and praxis" (Mohanty, Third World 51). Informing much recent theoretical discussion of national cinemas, a discussion of the shifting margins of cultural displacement that confound any profound or "authentic" sense of "national" culture clearly helps set the stage for a re-examination of the concept of the nation. I will focus on the connections made by Claire Denis between the exile of the white woman and her migration (outside French boundaries, the young woman France is on the road, crossing unknown territories), nationalism (what constitutes her French point of view), and new regionalism (both countries are not constructed as nations). Chocolat constructs, restructures, and transforms viewing strategies as well as gender and racial determinations, by producing both reifications of old gender biases and a new focus of resistance. The operations of construction and restructuring take place in a space which is charted by a shift in the nature of "hegemonic masculinity" as embodied by elite white men, displacing and transforming past "maleness" images to the "Other," the colonized, and by preventing the gaze from being tied to nation and subjectivity.

Although *Chocolat* has been applauded as a beautiful, enigmatic film—due to a great number of unexplained shots and scenes—it has also more specifically been considered as unsettling. The film opens up with the reification of traditional cinematic techniques that establish the white woman as the narrator and bearer of the gaze. An extradiegetically conventional appropriation of the cinematic gaze grants the character, France, narrative authorship and a white, heterosexual female point of view. A wide angle shot initiates the image-narrative and frames what seems to be the object of the woman's desire: the camera tracks 180 degrees clockwise from the view of Mungo and his son, Sawa, playing and resting in the ocean, to the sound of the waves that gently lap the contours of their bodies, to the figure of France looking at them, as she sits on the beach, with a Walkman. She gazes at the two bodies half-immersed in the gulf. Thus is established her gaze, bearer of racial and sexual differences. Sheltering her white skin from the torrid sun, and bearing a first world item, a Walkman, France faces the dark, sun-kissed bodies.

The initial panoramic camera movement is followed by the flashback technique that further secures the white woman's position as both narrator and spectator. In the car bound for Limbé, Sawa playfully identifies the different parts of his father's face in one of the twenty-four African languages spoken in Cameroon.[8] Such a sight transports the adult France back to her youth when she was in the company of the family servant, Protée. Framed from the car window, the shot of her face as she grips the father's travel journal is smoothly and beautifully substituted by that of the countryside, as she looks out to the green and lush lands. The camera lens becomes the occupant of the location of France's gaze. The view of the luxurious landscape dissolves into the dried and scorched scenery that France, as a little girl, her mother Aimée, and Protée enjoy from the pick-up truck driven by Marc, the father (played by François Cluzet).

An essential element of the narrative structure, the flashback functions as a temporal and spatial bridge that allows the white woman's gaze to tie two distinct periods—postcolonial and colonial Cameroon—and two different life stages—France as a young woman and as a preteen. Superimposing these two points of view, different yet similar, the flashback also leads us to reflect upon the intersections of time and place, and the encounter of nations and cultures. By means of the flashback, the white woman's gaze spans across time and spaces, creating an atmosphere which evokes both an era gone and a daydream. Upon the film's release, at a Paris press interview, Denis revealed that in order to create such an atmosphere "she needed to have images perceived from a certain distance" (Thomas 12), and for that reason, she had to blur the notion of time so that "one does not know if the film takes place in a minute or an hour" (Bishop 268).

Certainly contributing to the characterization of the film as enigmatic and unsettling, such distance generates a cinematic space which encompasses breaks, threats, and a plurality of points of view. Blurring traditional notions of time and space might appear threatening to the Western subject/spectator. This cinematic technique prompted some viewers to consider the landscape and cinematic spaces as "all devouring, sun-baked," filled with "scrubby expanses that eat away at the substantiality of figures in the landscape, and at the forms on which whites depend for emotional and social orientation" (Murphy 62). The introductory shot appears conventional in the ways it resembles a patriarchal/Western way of looking at the Other: the female gaze destroys and dismembers the dark bodies, in a gesture which reads as an affirmation of "white" subjectivity. Yet along with Homi Bhabha and Frantz Fanon, one can see in such a gesture how "the black presence ruins the representative narrative of Western personhood . . . the white man's [or woman's] eyes break up the black man's body and in that act of epistemic violence, its own reference is transgressed, its field of vision disturbed" (Bhabha, "Remembering" 139). Although at first both black bodies cinematically appear dismembered,[9] connoting disruption, they ultimately convey sensuality and harmony with the physical environment. The dark skin color blends with the deep blue of the gulf, creating a voluptuous and inclusive wholeness. This initial scene sets the tone for the entire film: landscapes and dark male bodies are conflated by France's remembering process and expression of desire. Reconstructing and unifying what has been disrupted, the woman's gaze helps the white spectators of the film "go beyond the chiasmatic intersections of time and place that constitute the problematic 'modern' experience of the Western nation" (Bhabha, *Nation* 292), in a dissolution of subjectivity and nation. If Denis names her female character "France," and positions her en route to revisit her "home" and find her "roots," it is to place the white woman in an apparent encounter between two nations. Yet, the notion of "nation" is challenged by the white woman's gaze that unravels the problematic re-presentation of French and Cameroonian identities and cultures. Instead of being tied to a personal experience, bringing out linearity and determinations, the film owes its existence to an accumulation of ideas, sensations, and memories that Denis calls the "great collective memory of colonizers." It is this atmosphere that succeeds in underplaying both the narration of "a particular story between a *houseboy*—a Cameroonese domestique—and a young French girl," and the significance of the stereotypes that have constructed Africa, meeting Denis's call for "removing colonizing glasses, and nourishing a simple relationship with a third world country living its own problems" (Gili 16).

The gesture of looking at the "Other" without colonizing glasses might raise the question as to what happens when the "Other" becomes the "same," thereby leading into arguments generated within politics of identity. Or, one might ask, does the gesture of looking at the "Other" with no power and privilege lead into the disruption of the image of "I," the white bearer of the gaze. Second, it might be interesting to reflect upon what it means "to have a simple relationship with a third world country." Such important questions about the cultural determinations imposed by colonization constitute the white woman's struggle in the film, which, in Chandra Talpade Mohanty's words "disrupts and challenges the logic of linearity, development, and progress which are the hallmarks of European modernity" and "suggests an insistent simultaneous, nonsynchronous process characterized by multiple locations, rather than a search for origins and ending" ("Feminist Encounters" 81).

The white woman's gaze encloses the relationships set between Aimée and Marc—the colonizers—on the one hand, and Protée—the colonized—on the other, and the interaction between marginalized people, Protée and France, excluded respectively from the white European world and the adult world. Encompassing the return of previously suppressed marginalized voices, the woman's gaze unsettles and disrupts the sense of static and unified conceptions of nation and identity, notions that France, as white narrator and spectator, appears to be ready to forge. To name the main character "France" indicates Denis's symbolic identification in the colonial configuration: France as the "mother country" to its colonies, that is to say, France in its authority and in its whiteness. Yet, instead of reading the film as a gesture of "returning home," and thus about possible nostalgia and longing for the colonial period[10] in a last gesture of clinging to colonial vestiges of power and privilege, but also determinations, I contend that the film narrative works precisely as a rejection of such reading. Supplanting the economic with the sexual, with what Denis calls "la chair" ("the flesh"), the film narrative confounds the colonial sociopolitical and hierarchical differences into a cinematic space whose "difference" resides in the ambiance created by the image and sound tracks. Instead of raising questions or answering them, *Chocolat* disrupts the cultural determinations of race and colonialism, developing along fluctuations and indeterminacies in the filmic space constituted by Denis's "certain distance."

Distance is first manifest in the white woman's exile, outside the French borders, transgressing Cameroon's national borders. "This exilic cinema trangresses boundaries through a self-narrativization informed by the deterritorialization of distance and loss" (Naficy 24). Such distance constitutes an impossibility for France, as a little girl, to cope with the sociopolitical situation in Cameroon, characterized or alluded to by the imminent decolonization movement. The atmosphere is created first by subverting the gender differences which have characterized classic film narratives: the man as the hero, the mover of the narrative, active principle of culture, the establisher of distinction, and the creator of differences; the woman as the space, resistance, matrix, and matter (de Lauretis 119). Protée and Mungo (who, we later discover, is an African American named William Parker) are looked at, as they stand still and strong, and are a boundary (to appropriation) and a space (which could be appropriated, but is not). Although they do not occupy positions of heroes, they offer a strong physical presence. Such reversal of the colonial configuration implies more of a sexual and voluptuous understanding of the film's narrative than a traditional socioeconomic reading that would consider Cameroon, the daughter country, freeing itself from France, the mother country. Such allegory identifies the film as postmodern, in that the very definitions adhered to by a modernist project can be subverted, or rather, redefined from a woman's point of view. Intrinsic to the reversal of the colonial configuration, and thus to the reversal of the power relations, are the sexual relationships, which are diverse: Jonathan Boothby (the family's old British friend) is attracted to Aimée, yet alludes to his sexual encounter with Aimée's husband; Delpich, a coffee planter, is flanked by his black mistress, Thérèse; Luc Segalen, an ex-seminarian, has had a sexual encounter with married Suzanne and is attracted to Aimée and Protée; married Aimée is attracted to Protée; and Protée, who has a girlfriend with whom he corresponds by means of a writing school teacher, is attracted to Aimée.

On the night of Jonathan's visit, having decided to dress up to match her guest's formal wear, Aimée asks Protée to help her with the dress. In a splendid scene, Protée stands behind Aimée as both face and stare at the camera for a few seconds, apparently looking at each other in a mirror. Aimée ends up looking down while Protée stares on. The scene reads the male gaze upon the woman as the expression of the white woman's desire for the servant, but also as a gaze which inverts the power relations of the colonial order. Protée stares on, thus taking over the colonizer's position, and Aimée looks down, in the position of the colonized.

The narration of fragmented images which refer to authentic African rituals signifies the collapsing of ethnic distinctions: Protée eats live ants, tells the young girl France Cameroonian riddles, teaches her his language, and takes her on walks across sun-dried territories to the sound of warrior chants, suggesting a harmony which conflates the boundaries drawn by gender and racial differences. But, although suggesting a possible harmony, these shots also connote disruption and signify the violence in which Cameroon will engage to free itself from the colonial grip.

Despite the fact that the presentation of the black male bodies is stereotypical—in that Protée is depicted as the handsome and hypervirile sexual male, foregrounded against radiant images of the African landscape—it is also contradictory. Unlike the traditional image that the Westerners have forged of Africans—as incompetent, amiable, lovable, childlike, immature, talkative, and smiling people who are not to be trusted with much responsibility—Protée remains stoic, and along with Mungo, appears responsible, intelligent, and in charge. Protée, with the young white girl, and Mungo, with his son, Sawa, embody the potential the future holds for new generations. Thus, the colonial configuration is subverted: the colonized becomes the teacher, and the colonizer becomes the child, the student. In the colonial and patriarchal conceptions, France learns about Cameroonian cultural elements, and Sawa practises African languages, although his father is American. The model for future generations can be described as teaching tolerance and exploring the plurality of cultures and languages.

Although the use of the stereotypical colonialist trope (that of hypervirility) may call our white attention to the "product of the enervated white man's unholy longing for a life and sensuality that has long since deserted his over-civilized homeland" (Kher 7), it may very well underpin the expression of the sexual desire of the woman who is gazing upon and coveting the "Other." In that sense, the white woman's gaze can be described within a colonialist/capitalist consumerist preoccupation. This consumerism is integral to the theme of sexual difference and alienation, argued extensively by Jean-Luc Godard as being endemic to capitalist/colonizing societies. It is the eye-pleasing stimulation that produces the subject as consumer, the source of an undifferentitated demand whose sole relation to the object is one of possession (MacCabe 41). The little girl, in the continuation of the adult France's gaze upon Mungo, faces Protée with ambivalence. Denoting strength and beauty, the dark-skinned male is initially framed at the back of the pickup truck in a position of being looked at, yet he neither meets her gaze nor looks down. Avoiding an encounter with our white spectators' gaze, he gazes instead at the horizon, upon the immensity of the land. The Cameroonian body is presented, perhaps in the representation of a vestige from the colonial order, as the colonizer attempts to appropriate it. Yet, contrary to what happens with the white male gaze upon the woman's body, the white woman's eyes on the dark body unsettle colonial and traditional certainties about "the Other." Although Denis has talked about the black servant being possessed by the colonizers, and being in a position similar to that of the preteen, she has reconstructed/redefined such a colonial gaze. At the 1996 Colloquium of the Cinema of the Second Millennium, Denis referred her audience back to a hundred years ago, when the Lumière brothers sent filming crews throughout the world. She indicated that among these motion pictures, which are ineluctable bearers of a colonial gaze, one documentary shows a lady throwing coins to Indochinese youngsters. She reads in such a gesture a testimony of a way of life one would call racist and a proof of people's domination of others. But what can be welcome is the opportunity that contemporary societies give us, that of "seeing films made by a young man or woman who was one of those children who picked up a coin." According to Denis, such is "the space where gazes meet."[11]

Chocolat operates a shift in the meaning of culture which no longer is reduced to a static and unimportant force but is strengthened by the conflictual and dynamic racial and economic forces at stake in the colonial space. Three specific events stir up controversies and questions: the visit of Jonathan Boothby; the emergency plane landing which leaves five Europeans and an African maid stranded on the Dalens's estate for a few days; and the intrusion of Luc Segalen (played by Jean-Claude Adelin) among the group of African workers who have been called on to build a temporary runway. Jonathan's visit occasions a surge of activity among the servants in and around the house, thus providing the spectator with insights into the Cameroonese social roles in a colonial epoch, and into the attending racial division between masters and servants. The presence of the Europeans generates additional racist comments that attest to a society structured upon the exploitation of racial and gender differences. Delpich (played by Jacques Denis), the coffee planter who was also aboard the plane, submits his black mistress, Thérèse, to the double racial and sexual colonial exploitation of the Other. Not only does she perform physical tasks usually reserved for males in a Western society, such as helping Delpich carry a heavy trunk to the Dalens's house, but she is also relegated to the master's bedroom: she sits on the floor, awaiting to be fed the leftovers of the dinner from which she has been excluded. The introduction of Luc Segalen triggers a controversy amidst the Europeans when he turns down their invitation for lunch, voicing his decision to remain with the African workers. Seemingly taking sides with the exploited men, he nevertheless finds himself in direct contradiction to his adopted African way of life when he provokes an incomprehensible racist treatment of the Africans, thus falling into a colonial point of view. In the scene where Mireille, a passenger from the distressed plane, is extremely sick, Luc verbally ill-treats Prosper, the village doctor who has been called on in the middle of the night, and thereby encourages Machinard, Mireille's husband, to vent the Europeans' doubts about the medical competence of African doctors.

Occupying a liminal and therefore pivotal position in the colonial formation, Luc embodies oscillation, indeterminacy, and ambivalence. As the agent of colonialism—in his previous role of seminarian—he endorses the Western colonizing mission, and as one who purports to subvert the colonial order—the hippie who sets out to walk across Africa—he stands against injustice and the unfair treatment of the Africans. Reading some of Marc Dalens's reflections from his travel notes, Luc expresses colonialist tropes which not only disclose a gaze on "the Other" but also a reflection upon the white gaze:

> Au milieu des visages Africains d'un noir bronzé, la couleur blanche de la peau évoque décidément quelque chose de pareil à la mort. Moi-meme, qui, en 1891 apres n'avoir vu pendant des mois que des gens de couleur, j'aperçus à nouveau près de la Bénoué, les premiers europeéns, je trouvai la peau blanche anti-naturelle a côté de la plénitude savoureuse de la noire. Peut-on alors blamer les sauvages autochtones de prendre l'homme blanc pour quelque chose de contre-nature, pour une créature surnaturelle, démoniaque.[12]

In contrast to the savory and deep dark skin color, the white skin appears unnatural, supernatural, and evil to the Africans. The quotation reveals the underpinnings of racial processes which, in turn, expose the risks of transgressing a sexualized and racialized gaze. Although the comparison evokes a paternalistic view of the Africans, it nevertheless endorses the expulsion of Westerners from African territories. Suggested in the initial images, the appeal of the dark skin is by now symbolically inscribed in the cinematic text and has transgressed the boundaries of the hetero-sexual gaze. Luc's reading alludes to his sexual desire for Protée.

Expressing perhaps a celebratory emancipation of the white woman's gaze that dissolves racial and sexual boundaries, *Chocolat* emphasizes also the complexities tied to a postcolonial gaze. Later in the film, Luc unveils the tabooed sexual inter-action between Africans and Europeans by making public the white woman's pri-vate realm—her desire for the "houseboy." One afternoon, as the ex-seminarian sits and eats among the servants, Aimée questions the improper place that he occupies. In an open provocation to both Aimée and Protée, Luc discloses the white woman's secret desire for the black servant. Such a public declaration generates two deci-sive actions which are crucial to the narrative development: Luc and Protée engage in a corporeal fight and Aimée makes a sexual invitation to Protée. The fight scene is the only scene in the film which shows an altercation between two men of dif-ferent races deteriorating into a physical encounter. Luc orders Protée to vacate the porch where he is busy with house duties. Protée responds by nonchalantly throwing Luc's sleeping set off the porch. Luc has provoked Protée since his arrival. As such, the growing tension and fight between the two men confirm the racist conception of the divide between the dominant and dominated—manifest in land distribution and territory—and also reiterate the conventional male dispute over the woman, considered as space and territory, and the common object of the men's desire. Protée comes out of the fight with an upper hand, and thus claims victory.

In a further challenge to the Western symbolic interpretation and its attendant differential configuration, the narrative explores the expression of the white woman's desire. Subsequent to the fight, Protée resumes his work. As he proceeds to draw the curtain, Aimée, who has hidden from the scene, sits on the floor, in a dark cor-ner of the room, near the glass door. When Protée draws closer to her, she grabs his ankle for a few seconds before releasing the grip. He continues his work, away from her, then comes back, squats, looks her right in the eye, and swiftly pulls her back to her feet. He leaves the room as quickly as he makes her stand up. Refer-ring to a full understanding of his position, the colonized stands firm and imper-turbable, and, in silence and full physical presence, rejects the colonizer.

Thus, if the Western male intervention in Cameroon produces the stressful sociopolitical climate of the waning years of colonial life—the fear and threat evoked by the potential destruction that Luc and the few visitors to the estate sym-bolize—the Western woman's narrative conveys the merging of the various con-flictual points of view in the presentation of a visual and auditory register of the African body. The young French woman remembers Cameroonian life by engaging in a sensuous depiction of Cameroon in the image track, suffused with sunlit and sensual images of radiant landscapes, beautiful male bodies, and authentic indige-nous rituals, and in the sound track: Cameroonian languages and music, and the sounds of insects, vultures, and hyenas. Yet, the image track and the sound track suggest both harmony and disruption. The initial soothing sound of the waves is opposed by the threatening scream of vultures. The African music itself has a rhythm that evokes both comradeship and sensuality and, simultaneously, sends off a radical and rebellious edge. In such an atmosphere, France expresses her detachment from white cultural determinations. Suggested in various images and sounds, harmony constitutes France's attraction to the African continent. Yet, the sudden and intermittent break of continuous images and sounds evokes France's anxiety and fright before the intolerable socioeconomic present and its forthcoming colonial violence, and ultimately her rebellion. Unfolding along the intricate meanderings of her memory, Denis/France's narrative is not that of safety, identity, and meaningfulness, but rather, that of insecurity and a difficult search for identity and meaning. Fallible, the memory process merges France's initial feelings for the African body (as she gazes upon Mungo's and Sawa's bodies) and her reminiscence of the tensions among the Europeans with her own struggle to distance herself from the location/the political and personal understanding of what constitutes "home."[13]

Raphaël Basan considers *Chocolat* to be an illustration of the "present tendency in European cinema which reveals a certain fascination for the colonial era, serving as a romantic backdrop for the presentation of the feelings of drifting Westerners"—états d'âme d'Occidentaux à la dérive (32). I contend, however, that Denis's film is not only the expression of Westerners deprived of harbor or shore, but that it is also a film which renegotiates the gesture of revisiting colonization by means of a cinematic gaze which, instead of speaking "for," speaks "with" the colonized. In Leslie Roman's words, "Speaking with refers to the contradictions of voices engaged in dialogue with one another, without suggesting that they are reducible to the same voice or epistemic standpoint" (82). Applying the argument to the cinema, Catherine Portuges includes Denis among "the generation of women directors bearing witness to the dynamism of an arena of memory, the 'colonial féminin' in which border crossings translate into a mise-en-scène that destabilizes traditional assumptions of ethnicity, rationality, sexuality, and the family" (88), and in that respect, open the space for other voices.

The white woman's gaze encompasses flatlands and removal of boundaries. This is tied to the loss of the symbolic modality and the displacement of the authorial voice. In the absence of boundaries, spaces become devouring and threatening to the white viewer; in Mungo's words, "they could eat you up." If spaces are devouring, the mother's gaze and that of the young girl are also devouring of colonial and patriarchal determinations. Their gaze represents a public resistance to the socioeconomic and political system imposed by French colonialism. The traditional male-embedded voice of authority effaces itself: Mungo speaks English, a language that France and the Cameroonese do not understand; Marc is most of the time away on excursions, bivouacing across his land, and thus silences himself; Luc, as I have shown, holds an ambivalent voice; and Protée's silent voice stands against the Western logos. The only authorial voice in the diegesis is that of the mother.

Among the most present elements of authority and order, as understood in a modernist project, is the mother's voice. Aimée wields authority in her interaction with all the servants and, more particularly, in her communication with her daughter, as she commands her to study ("travaille, toi!"), cautions her not to go too far away ("ne t'éloigne pas trop"), and corrects her pronunciation of the German names that she reads off the tombs' wooden crosses. Instead of playfully interacting and engaging in an intimate and loving conversation with her daughter, the mother comes across as harsh and bossy. Her commanding tone of voice might translate into unhappiness. Indeed, life on the estate is oppressive: the country suffers from sizzling heat, the soil is hard and dry, and the place is infested with threatening wild animals. Yet, it constitutes the focus of the daughter's memory: taking over the initially established daughter's point of view, the mother's voice takes on the relay in the narrative of the woman's desire. Haunting, the mother's voice and desire fill the space created by the film-director. The phallic authority attached to the mother's behavior is granted to little France who acts out the mother's colonial role in her relationship with the "Other." The relationship between the "houseboy" and the little girl emulates that which exists between the mother as the dominant partner and the daughter as the dominated one, as well as that which exists between the mother as the "master" and Protée as the servant. Established in the opening shot of the flashback, the interaction between France and Protée can be considered to be that of a master/servant relationship. The servant falls under little France's gaze—and by substitution, via the lens of the camera, under the mother's and the spectators' gazes—right at the inception of the diegetic narration which introduces France and Protée. A later scene reiterates their respective socioeconomic positions: overseeing little France's lunch, Protée subjects himself to her whimsical demands. He squats down to the table level and opens his mouth, so that she can feed him; thus, in a playful manner the scene evokes tyrannical behaviors forged by colonialism.

Revealing the break of the symbolic and the modernist project—the colonial context—distance is rendered by unexplainable or paradoxical shots. The introductory shot of the flashback evokes both a sense of destruction and disruption: Protée prepares a sandwich with live ants and trades it with France for a piece of fruit. France looks at him with awe and disgust, yet she starts eating. With such a gesture, France accepts the "Other" by embracing the culture of the "Other." Later on, while France appears fascinated by the insects crawling across the tablecloth, Protée picks up a few ants off the table and eats them. She tells him, "You disgust me." This screen representation of the abject/horror which marks their cultural "differences" is further continued with the presentation of blood and corpse, elements that constitute horror, from a white person's point of view, in that they "constantly remind the subject of death" (Kristeva 9). In the scene where Aimée, France and Protée pay a visit to their Norwegian friends, Nansen and Martha, a bloody and dismembered donkey and livestock lie dead outside the house. (Nansen informs us that they have been attacked by hyenas.) Protée picks up a hen's leg, and in a caress, smears blood on France's forearm. Such rituals read as the "abject" of an idealized Western culture. Blood also represents both the narrator's desiring and threatened self. Nourishing, assassin, and fascinating, France's self evokes that which escapes language, colonialism, and the symbolic modality (Kristeva 15).

The white woman's gaze is further characterized by France's experience of both her fall as a subject and the loss of the object of her desire. This is manifest in terms of the narrative deprivation of the woman's gaze. The last scene diminishes the woman from her powerful and privileged gaze. At the airport, three Cameroonian workers are framed with their backs facing both France and the spectator, as a melodious African musical score is played against the heavy rain. France finds herself in the same position as that which she occupies in the film's opening scene: she is looking from a distance, while the Cameroonese are oblivious to her and excluded from her experiences. At the beginning of the film, the Walkman and torrid sun deprive her of the sensual water-lapping experience Mungo and Sawa enjoy, and at the end of the film, the heavy rain curtain obliterates the view that seems to please the three Cameroonese.

The white woman's colonizing gaze has transformed itself throughout the diegesis. Although she has been sketched early in the film as the main character who is to relive her past and rediscover Cameroon, France finds herself positioned outside the signifying process. At the closure of the flashback and by the end of the film, Mungo's words ostracize the white woman from Cameroon. She loses her gaze, that of the Western subject upon history and desire. Mungo examines her hands and cautions her to leave the country as quickly as possible: "elle est drôle ta main, pas de passé et pas de futur" ("it's odd, your hand has neither past nor future"). "Repars vite, avant qu'ils te mangent" ("go back home quickly, before they eat you up"). All traces of past and future have been symbolically erased: the female subject is absent from both the signified—the narration of a story in location, as a specific Cameroonian experience—and from a signifying position, being unsuccessful at recovering her roots and reliving her past. Absent from the signified— the historical Cameroonian consciousness—she does not belong, and wanders about. Displaced and decentered, she has lost her apparent object of desire, and in the same thrust, her relation towards the symbolic mode and history.

Embodying appropriation and construction, confrontation and destruction throughout the film, Protée's and Mungo's characters work as resistance to the colonial system. In the woman's gaze, Protée stands as "Other"—desiring and resisting, in lieu of what is to constitute the young narrator's "self." In opposition to France, who does not belong and is thus displaced and drifting, Protée belongs, desires, and resists. He symbolizes victorious gestures in territorial disputes, and yet, unlike territories, he remains unappropriated. Protée's resistance to colonization is affirmed by the fight he has with Luc, and sustained when he challenges Aimée's gaze. Unlike the conventional white male gaze that takes possession of the woman's body and territories, Protée's gaze conveys mixed meanings: economic, political, and sexual.

Embodying Cameroonian pride and resistance to colonialism and imperialism, Protée stands as a challenger to the dominant gaze. Face to face with vulnerable Aimée who is unable to sustain his gaze, Protée challenges the white female gaze. Rejecting Aimée's sexual invitation, Protée restores her "proper" socioeconomic position and reminds her of the impossible appropriation of the "Other."

Protée's resistance is further displayed through an effective use of images that foreground physical pain. Subsequent to his fight with Luc and his rejection of Aimée's sexual invitation, Protée is reassigned to work in the garage, on Aimée's demand. By now, being the only one free to cross the new, racially and sexually determined territorial boundaries, little France visits Protée in the garage. In a response to her inquiry about how hot the generator pipe is, Protée grabs it. Imitating his body language, France burns her little palm. A reverse shot reveals a close-up of her burned palm, and then Protée's clenched hand. Responding to Aimée's previous ambiguous position—considered socially and politically improper, when she was at his feet, in an expression of desire for him—and to France's challenging visit (transgressing the newly established territorial boundaries), Protée rejects both his roles, as object of desire and surrogate father, with pain. By inflicting severe burns on his hand, he signs with blood the end of a white woman's narrative of desire, and the continuation of Cameroon's resistance to the servitude imposed by colonialism. Protée's sexual and racial desire has now turned into pain, burns, and blood, signalling the end of French colonization in Cameroon and his personal distancing from France and Aimée.

Like Protée, who has previously turned down Aimée's sexual invitation, and has annulled the white woman's potential desire/identity in Cameroon in the context of Cameroon and France together as one nation, Mungo refuses France's invitation for a drink, and thus declares the expulsion of the French woman from Cameroon. Both black men reject the white woman's desire for them and abort her search for identity: not yet "at home," she finds herself at the airport, a place already symbolic of transnationality and border crossings, cheated in her quest for identity. As Claire Denis mentions, while the prologue (which is in the present) seems to echo the ending in the scene of Sawa learning a native language, the film's closure shows us that we mistook the narrator's and her interlocutor's identities. Thought to be a tourist, France turns out to be perhaps a Cameroonese, and while Mungo was thought to be "native" to Cameroon, he turns out to be American. The subversion of conventional roles retrospectively challenges their affirmations, which read as searching for their identities in the colonial narration. Such affirmation has an ironic element, with the names of the characters positioning them so as to be believed as conventional white cultural determinants, "d'autant plus que cette affirmation avait un caractère excessif, implicitement ironique, bien attestée par les noms des personnages: Aimée (la femme aimée), France (la fillette), Protée (le boy aux multiples talents), Védrine (l'aviateur)" (Bourget 68).

All such traditional associations of names with identities, and physical make-up with cultural and geographical determinations are shattered. While Mungo discloses his name and the name of his son, thus symbolizing fitting in a place and having an identity, he rejects a reading of France's past and future, barring her from identity, and estranging her. Yet, Mungo's gesture is quickly subverted in the following shot when he deprives himself of a set identity: "They've no use of my being here. Here I am nothing, a fantasy." The American mistakenly thought he could find his roots in Africa, but the brotherhood he sought was not of interest to the inhabitants of the country. In this sense, Mungo has been cheated. In Nikki Stiller's words: "the condition of estrangement—France has neither past nor future—is not limited to whites" (Stiller 56). Both the white woman and black man have been cheated, at different points in their lives, and Protée and France carry traces of such betrayal in their flesh because, as Kathleen Murphy says: "food and the way this black man and his white charge share it, both mocks and frees them from their designated places in the social order—to have dark skin and to be cheated" (Murphy 63).

As the expression of a Western white heterosexual woman's desire, *Chocolat* interweaves the description of a colonial context—characterized by a looming sociopolitical and racial conflict—with the disclosure of the taboo desire of a French woman/master for a Cameroonian man/servant. Via an intricate working of the gaze that is both sexual and racial, the film foregrounds the narrative links between a private and public consciousness of the past in an imbrication of sexuality, race, and economics. Both a recollection of the memories of colonial French life in Cameroon and the narration of a white woman's desire, the film invites the spectator to experience a complex and intricate personal and public sense of history. With the conflicts and tensions created by the intrusion of Jonathan Boothby, Delpich, and Luc Segalen into the Dalens's life, the film accounts for gestures of confrontation and destruction, and with the disclosure of Aimée's desire for Protée, the film presents gestures of appropriation and construction.

Chocolat is a work of self-consciousness about the paradoxes and problems of the historical representation of colonization and the difficult self-representation of the white female subject. Despite the lack of sociopolitical stability rendered occasionally by enigmatic shots and disruptive comments to account for the turbulent period of time, the film shows, via Protée's character, a strong and surviving Cameroonian culture. Interrogating, deconstructing, and even discarding old identities while creating and playing out new identities, images, and social possibilities, Denis's film reveals that in a postcolonial expression, the white female narrator is absent from both the signified—the historical Cameroonian consciousness—and the signifying process. Although from the start the narrative has been about the telling of France's experience in Cameroon, *Chocolat* turns out to be a different account as well; it offers a series of impressions about Cameroon that point more specifically to the expression of the white woman's desire, in the presentation of a plurality of possibilities.

Claire Denis makes a successful attempt at unveiling the existing tensions between many points of view/gazes. On the road, searching for her past and roots, France ultimately finds herself at the point of departure: off to Mindiff, Northern Cameroon, location of her parents' estate, or perhaps back to France. The film thus expresses an unrevered and unresolved past. Some thirty years after the decolonization movement, the representation of a specific historical period, such as Cameroon's colonial epoch, is virtually rendered impossible. But what is important in *Chocolat*, to borrow Stuart Hall's words, "is not what happens but what doesn't. It is a film of refusals, of barred intimacies, of turnings away, of meetings that don't come off, of relationships in the past that cannot be recovered, of a colonial world that is gone for ever" (50). It is also a film about the impossible reconciliation between colonizer and colonized. "[T]he film problematizes the impossible desire for reconciliation between colonizer and colonized, suggesting that the latter has invisibly been transformed, no longer defining the self in silent desire, as did the faithful Protée, not in terms of marginalized dependency" (Portuges 88).

Seemingly at the keyhole, looking at the male/capitalist engineering of the fissured colonial order, the white woman holds a gaze which effects cinematic displacements from the sociopolitical to the sexual, from the self to the community, from homogeneity to pluralism, from identity to coalition; she is looking from the colonizers' side but also along with the "Other," with Protée and Mungo. As appropriately conveyed by the film, "the question is not only who or what is on either side of the keyhole, but also what lies between them, what constitutes the threshold that makes representation possible" (Mayne 9). Being at the keyhole and staring might suit women perfectly. As Mary Ann Doane says, "[W]omen would seem to be perfect spectators, culturally positioned as they are outside the arena of history, politics, production—'looking on'" (2). Yet, today, as full participating agents of representation, women not only speak "for" Cameroon and/or France, but speak "with," annulling all obstacles, limits, hierarchies, and opening a space where there is a plurality of voices and gazes which allow a questioning of "whiteness" in the locality of its gaze. The film disengages itself from a nostalgic, melodramatic memory of colonization, and positions itself as an inclusive expression of pains, scars, and victimization.

NOTES

1. *Chocolat*, written by Claire Denis and Jean-Paul Fageau, music by Abdullah Ibrahim, photography by Robert Alazrahi, produced by MK2 Marin Karmitz, released in 1986, with Isaach de Bankolé, Giulia Boschi, Cécile Ducasse, Jean-Claude Adelin, Mireille Perrier, Emmanuelle Chaulet, Emmet Judson Williamson and François Cluzet.

2. Located on the west coast of Africa, Cameroon occupies 475,000 square kilometers of land, and is inhabited by 11 million people who represent about 200 ethnic groups. The Bamileche, the largest ethnic group, lives in the Western mountainous region, and the Fulani live in the North. The Douala, the Eurondo, and the Fang inhabit the Southern and Central regions. Great Britain and France ruled Cameroon from 1929 to the early 1960s. From the late 1400s to late 1800s many Europeans flocked to West Africa principally because of the flourishing slave trade. Great Britain abolished its slave trade in 1807. Over the years, Britain, France and Germany struggled for control of Cameroon. In 1884, two local Douala chiefs signed a treaty with Germany that made Cameroon a German protectorate. Germany lost control of Cameroon to Britain and France during World War I (1914–1918). In 1922, Britain and France divided Cameroon; the British section included two independent parts along the Western border. In 1946, Britain and France pledged to eventually grant Cameroon self-government or independence. On January 1, 1960, French Cameroon became the Independent Republic of Cameroon. In 1961, the British Parliament voted for the country to become either Nigeria or Republic of Cameroon. From 1961 to 1972, East and West Cameroons were part of a federation. Finally in May 1972, a new constitution eliminated the two separate states. English and French are Cameroon's official languages, but most Cameroonese speak one of the country's twenty-four identified African languages. About 45% of the people practice traditional African religions, 35% are Christians, and 20% are Muslims. Yaoundé is the capital of Cameroon, Douala is its largest city. For further information, see Harold Nelson's *Area Handbook for the United Republic of Cameroon* (Washington: Foreign Area Studies, U.S. Government, 1994) and Mark Delancey's *Cameroon: Dependence and Independence* (Boulder: Westview, 1989).

3. In "Le cinéma et l'histoire: l'Afrique noire coloniale," Didier Thouart provides us with a list of French films made about West Africa. Documentaries include Léon Poirier's *Amours exotiques* (1925), which is half documentary, half fiction, *La Croisière noire* (1926), and Marc Allégret's *Voyage au Congo* (1927). Fiction includes René Le Somptier's *La marche vers le soleil* (1928), Léon Mathot's *Bouboule ler le roi nègre* (1933), Jacques de Baroncelli's *L'homme du Niger* (1939), Georges Régnier's *Paysans noirs* (1947), Claude Vermorel's *Les Conquérants solitaires* (1949), André Haguet's *Il est minuit Docteur Schweitzer* (1952), Maurice Cloche's *Un missionnaire* (1955), and Robert Darène's *La Bigome, caporal de France* (1957). Jean Rouch's 1958 documentary *Moi, un Noir* was followed by Jean-Jacques Annaud's *La victoire en chantant* (1976). Before Denis's film, Bertrand Tavernier's *Coup de torchon* (1981) and Serge Gainsbourg's *Equateur* (1982) dealt with West Africa. In 1989 Raymond Rajaonarivelo made *Tabataba*. In most of these films, the point of view has unfailingly positioned the colonized as the "Other" by focusing on the white point of view.

4. Claire Denis also directed *S'en fout la mort* (1990), *U.S. Go Home* (1994), and *J'ai pas sommeil* (1994). Denis's cinema shows a deep concern for the

construction of "race" and for the presentation of its properties. Also interested in the issue of integration and racial difference, she has further explored the public and private sense of history in all of her films subsequent to *Chocolat*, in which she investigates the secret rituals and mores of clandestine immigrants in France, and their lives on the margins.

5. Claire Denis was raised in a French colonial family in West Africa. She was two months old when she moved from her native France to Africa. Denis's family stayed in Cameroon for three years after its 1960 independence. Her father set up a radio station for the new government. However, polio-stricken in 1963, Denis, her sister and their mother were sent back to France. After a prolonged stay in the hospital, Denis fully recovered, but her sister was left with a slight limp. Information gathered from the interview with Kevin Thomas, staff writer at the *Los Angeles Times*, "Denis Offers a Taste of Her Own Past with *Chocolat*."

6. For a review of postcolonial theory, see Homi Bhabha's analysis of the contradictions and complexities of colonial discourse in "The Other Question— The Stereotype and Colonial Discourse" in *Screen* 24.6 (1983):23; and Frantz Fanon's *A Dying Colonialism* (New York: Grove, 1965), *Black Skin, White Masks* (New York: Grove, 1967), and *The Wretched of the Earth* (Harmondsworth: Penguin, 1967). For feminism and postcolonialism, see Gayatri C. Spivak's "Can the Subaltern Speak?" in *The Post-Colonial Critic: Issues, Strategies, Dialogues*, ed. S. Harasym (New York: Routledge, 1990) 271–313; *Feminist Genealogies, Colonial Legacies, Democratic Future*, ed. M. Jacqui Alexander and Chandra Talpade Mohanty (New York: Routledge, 1997); *Third World Women and the Politics of Feminism*, ed. Chandra Talpade Mohanty, Ann Russo, and Lourdes Torres (Bloomington: Indiana UP, 1991); *After Colonialism: Imperial Histories and Postcolonial Displacements*, ed. Gyan Prakash (Princeton: Princeton UP, 1994); *Social Postmodernism: Beyond Identity Politics*, ed. Linda Nicholson and Steven Seidman (Cambridge: Cambridge UP, 1995); Mary John, *Discrepant Dislocations: Feminism. Theory and Postcolonial Histories*. (Berkeley: U of California P, 1996).

7. Over the past ten years, film studies have incorporated more studies of "nation." For a very insightful analysis of "nation" and postcolonialism in the media, see *Unthinking Eurocentrism: Multiculturalism and the Media*. Ed. Ella Shohat and Robert Stam (London: Routledge, 1994).

8. All information and data about Cameroon were gathered from Harold Nelson's *Area Handbook for the United Republic of Cameroon*, and Mark Delancey's *Cameroon: Dependence and Independence*.

9. In a similar fashion to the white male's gaze, the white female's gaze disassembles the "other's" body. I am referring to Bhabha's article "Remembering Fanon." Bhabha articulates ways in which the white man performs visual violence, and how in that gesture one can read a process of the (de)construction of colonialism.

10. Most newspaper articles, movie reviews, and magazines analyze the film within its colonial context and/or from a postcolonial point of view, such as Nikki Stiller's "*Chocolat.*"

11. Interview with Claire Denis in *Le cinéma vers son deuxième siècle*. Ed. Jean-Michel Frodon, Marc Nicolas and Serge Toubiana, International Colloquium, March 20 and 21, 1995, Odéon-Théâtre de L'Europe (Paris: Le Monde Editions, 1995) 198-201, qtd. on 199.

"Dans l'envie de faire du cinéma il y avait le désir d'aller vers les autres, de sortir d'une forme d'autisme, de manière physique et presque violente. Parce qu'à la différence d'autres formes d'art, le cinéma saisit des corps en mouvement, de la chair . . . En commençant à faire des films, je me suis aperçue qu'en définitive, derrière cette envie d'aller vers les autres, il y a d'abord qu'on parle de soi. Peut-être qu'on peut parler de soi dans le désir des autres, ou avoir une réponse qui vient des autres, ou un regard qui vient croiser le vôtre."

"With the desire to make films, there was the desire to go toward others, to leave behind a kind of autism, in a physical and nearly violent manner. Because unlike other art forms, the cinema captures moving bodies, and flesh . . . When I started making movies, I realized that in fact, behind this desire to go toward others, there was first a desire to speak about oneself. Perhaps one can speak about oneself in the desire of others, or obtain a response that comes from others, or a gaze that meets yours" (my translation).

12. "Among the African bronze-colored faces, the white skin color evokes something akin to death. Even I, who, after seeing only colored people for months and months, noticed the first Europeans in 1891 near Bénoué, found white skin unnatural next to the delicious fullness of dark skin. Then, who can blame the natives for believing the white man to be an unnatural, supernatural, and devilish creature?" (my translation).

13. For a helpful contribution to analyses of the contradictions between home and identity, see "Feminist Politics: What's Home Got to Do with It?" co-authored by Chandra Talpade Mohanty, et al., in *Feminist Studies/Critical Studies*, ed. Teresa de Lauretis. (Bloomington: Indiana UP, 1986): 191–212.

WORKS CITED

Basan, Raphaël. "*Chocolat.*" *La revue du cinéma* 439 (1988): 32.

Bhabha, Homi. *Nation and Narration*. New York: Routledge, 1990.

———. "Remembering Fanon, Self, Psyche, and the Colonial Condition." *Remaking History*. Ed. Barbara Kruger and Phil Mariani. Seattle: Bay, 1989.

Bishop, Kathy. "In and Out of Africa, First-Time Director Claire Denis Rediscovers the Heart of Darkness." *Vogue Magazine* 129 (Mar. 1989): 268.

Bourget, Jean-Loup."Aimée et les Camerounais." *Positif* 328 (Paris: Nouvelles Editions Opta, 1988): 67–68.

Chatterjee, Paratha. *The Nation and its Fragments: Colonial and Postcolonial Histories*. Princeton: Princeton UP, 1993.

Delancey, Mark. *Cameroon: Dependence and Independence*. Boulder: Westview, 1989.

De Lauretis, Teresa. *Alice Doesn't: Feminism, Semiotics, Cinema*. Bloomington: Indiana UP, 1984.

Denis, Claire. *Le cinéma vers son deuxième siècle*. Ed. Jean-Michel Frodon, Marc Nicolas and Serge Toubiana, International Colloquium, Mar. 20–21, 1995, Odéon-Théâtre de l'Europe. Paris: Le Monde Editions, 1995.

Doane, Mary Ann. *The Desire to Desire: the Woman's Film of the 1940s*. Bloomington: Indiana UP, 1987.

Gili, J. A. "Aimée et les Camerounais." *Positif* 328 (Paris: Nouvelles Editions Opta, 1988): 14–16.

Hall, Stuart. "European Cinema on the Verge of a Nervous Breakdown," *Screening Europe: Image and Identity in Contemporary European Cinema*. Ed. Duncan Petrie. London: British Film Institute, 1992.

Kher, Dave. "*Chocolat*, a Picturesque, Unsettling Mood Piece." The *Chicago Tribune* May 12, 1989: 7, A, D.

Kristeva, Julia. *Les pouvoirs de l'horreur: essai sur l'abjection*. Paris: Editions du Seuil, 1980.

MacCabe, Colin. *Godard: Images, Sounds and Politics*. Bloomington: Indiana UP, 1980.

Mayne, Judith. *The Woman at the Keyhole: Feminism and Women's Cinema*. Bloomington: Indiana UP, 1990.

Mohanty, Chandra Talpade. "Feminist Encounters: Locating the Politics of Experience." *Social Postmodernism: Beyond Identity Politics*. Ed. Linda Nicholson and Steven Seidman. Cambridge: Cambridge UP, 1995.

———. "Under Western Eyes: Feminist Scholarship and Colonial Discourses." *Third World Women and the Politics of Feminism*. Ed. Chandra Talpade Mohanty, Ann Russo, and Lourdes Torres Bloomington: Indiana UP, 1991.

Murphy, Kathleen. "*The Color of Home.*" *Film Comment* 28.5 (Sept., Oct.1992): 62, 63.

Naficy, Hamish and Teshone, Gabriel, ed. *Otherness and the Media: The Ethnography of the Imaged and the Images*. New York: Harwood, 1993.

Nelson, Harold. *Area Handbook for the United Republic of Cameroon*. Washington: Foreign Area Studies, U.S. Government, 1994.

Portuges, Catherine. "'Le Colonial Féminin': Women Directors Interrogate French Cinema." *Cinema, Colonialism, Postcolonialism: Perspectives from the French and Francophone World*. Ed. Dina Sherzer. Austin: U of Texas P, 1996.

Roman, Leslie G. "White Is a Color! White Defensiveness, Postmodernism, and Anti-Racist Pedagogy." *Race, Identity and Representation in Education*. New York: Routledge, 1995.

Silverman, Kaja. *The Subject of Semiotics.* New York: Oxford UP, 1983.

Stiller, Nikki. *"Chocolat." Film Quarterly* 44 (Winter 90/91): 52–56.

Thomas, Kevin. "Denis offers a taste of her own past with Chocolat." The *Los Angeles* Times 20 Apr. 1989, col.1, 12.

Thouart, Didier. "Le cinéma et l'histoire: l'Afrique noire coloniale." *Historia* 509 (1989): 110–13.

CHAPTER THIRTEEN

The Imperial Feminine

Victorian Women Travellers in Egypt

MELISSA LEE MILLER

In April of 1863, approximately five months into her seven-year stay in Luxor, Egypt, Lucie Duff Gordon writes to her mother, "I have a black slave—a real one" (*Letters from Egypt* 51). The eight-year-old girl, Zeynab, has come to her from the American Consul-General and Gordon initially takes great pleasure in the "poor little savage," though she adds that "the utter slavishness of the poor little soul quite upsets me; she has no will of her own" (53). Within a month, however, Gordon makes the curious note that Zeynab has "grown fatter, and, if possible, blacker" (62) and by December of that same year, following accusations of religious intolerance resulting from Zeynab's fear of pork, she prepares to rid herself of the girl:

> She is very clever and I am sorry, but to keep a sullen face about me is more than I can endure, as I have shown her every possible kindness.[. . .] She waits capitally at table, and can do most things, but she won't move if the fancy takes her except when ordered, and spends her time on the terrace. One thing is that the life is dull for a child, and I think she will be happier in a larger, more bustling house. (83)

From 1500 to 1821, there were a total of four books written by European women on the Middle East. By 1911, after a peak which was reached in the 1890s, that number had swelled to 241 (Melman 31), and one needs look neither long nor hard to find sentiments similar to Gordon's. What is rare is critical treatment of such attitudes. In his 1993 review essay of a number of new books on Victorian women and the empire, what James Buzard calls a "selective critical generosity" (447) has resulted in the creation of a Victorian heroine who, presumably unlike her male counterparts, displays a greater sensitivity to difference and reluctance to dominate. It has also, of course, resulted in the careful excision of certain voices from the research field. While such critiques do reflect the accurate realization and acknowledgment of the alternative subjective experience of an oppressed group—here, British women—the move to representations of them as somehow free from gendered, racialized Western ideologies or engaging in the seemingly effortless sub-version of those ideologies is both optimistic and unnecessary. The ultimate pro-clamation that women are simply innocent bystanders of the social systems which envelop and guide them leads directly to the status of victim, a position as power-less as it is blameless. Buzard asks, "What if the neglected voices which the critic allows us once more to hear, and the neglected agency she allows us once more to see, turn out to speak and serve racism and domination?" (444).

My aim in this essay is twofold: first, to illustrate the ways in which three dif-ferent British women travellers—Lucie Duff Gordon, Emmeline Lott, and Amelia Blandford Edwards—represent racial and cultural Others within the context of Victorian gender roles and attitudes, and second, to inquire as to how the genre of travel narrative operates for women as autobiographical text. While these writers do not present their work as autobiography—their purposes range from informing loved ones at home of their experiences abroad to the writing of scientific trea-tises—the nature of travel writing itself necessitates a certain autobiographical function. For, regardless of the desire to "merely represent" experience, that expe-rience is always refracted through the changing identity of the writer.

Critics such as Patricia Meyer Spacks, Carolyn Heilbrun, and Estelle Jelinek have done much to illustrate the issues of form versus content, feminine style versus masculine style, and the "nature" of feminine self-expression and interpretation as they relate both to the history of autobiography and the status of specific texts themselves. Spacks's study on autobiography and the eighteenth-century novel argues that "to read an autobiography is to encounter a self as an imaginative being" (19) and that,

> to turn lives into words—whether those words claim to render fiction or fact—involves some act of the mind that discovers the logic of hap-penings in memory or imagination, although such logic seldom emerges in immediate experience. Putting a life into words rescues it from con-fusion, even when the words declare the omnipresence of confusion, since the act of declaring implies dominance. (21)

In reference to women's travel narratives and their representation of the racial Other, this confusion is quite palpable. It shows itself most clearly through the contradictory attitudes which cause these women at one moment to embrace and romanticize difference and then, in the next, to vilify and mock it. The system of logic, I argue, is one which is intimately related not to gender connections between women of different cultures, but a variety of attempts made by these women to do two things: support the British way of life and attitude, and find some way to support that way of life through Victorian gender codes immediately threatened when practised within the context of the Other. The ways in which they succeed at these goals is perhaps best defined by Mary Louise Pratt's term "anti-conquest," which, "refer[s] to the strategies of representation whereby European bourgeois subjects seek to secure their innocence in the same moment as they assert European hegemony" (7).

The incorporation of this group of travel narratives—beyond Martineau's much-studied *Autobiography*—into the ongoing discussion of the genre adds a particularly important racial dimension—one which gives us the opportunity to witness and analyze the construction of a racialized *and* gendered female self through writing. These women, through letters sent from overseas, novelistic accounts compiled upon their return to Britain, and texts written for the furthering of scientific inquiry, all include important portraits of their own personal difficulties with the experiencing of difference.

All travellers experience a certain degree of subjective disruption. For these travellers, the social designations of "woman," "white," and even "British" are loosened—a loosening which provides the potential for individual reinterpretation. As Victorian women found themselves outnumbered, surrounded, even, by the difference of Arab culture, gender issues were quickly overridden by racial and nationalistic interests. In the resultant struggle for stable subjectivity, Victorian women identified themselves with the roles which had been taught them in Britain, but then enacted those roles in unique ways to include and dominate the Arab Other. In this fashion, they performed "cultural duties" for the empire which shored up the ideological climate back in Britain through the publication and impact of their many collections of letters, diaries, journals, and essays. Their activities and attitudes can only be termed "feminine," although the results of their encounters are, of course, anything but "feminist."

David Spurr's *The Rhetoric of Empire* argues that, "the ultimate aim of colonial discourse is not to establish a radical opposition between colonizer and colonized. It seeks to dominate by inclusion and domestication rather than by a confrontation which recognizes the independent identity of the Other" (32). Here, voice is given to a potentially systemic approach to women's travel narratives. First, if we acknowledge that the climate of gendered behavior during this period included, as it does still, the requirements that women avoid open confrontation, demonstrations of power and control, and that they must strive to maintain private and public calm, then this form of imperialist action is particularly well suited to feminine ideology. Second, the inherently private nature of the writing act, as well as the "free space" between lived experience and imaginative demonstration of that experience (which has proved so troubling to the defining of autobiography as a genre), combine to suggest that the travel narrative is a unique site for the interpretation of one's own subjectivity insofar as it is defined through and against the racialized Other.

THE MOTHER

In her explanation of the metaphoric significance of the Family of Man in the Victorian evolutionary imaginary, Anne McClintock writes:

> The family image came to figure hierarchy within unity as an organic element of historical progress, and thus became indispensable for legitimizing exclusion and hierarchy within nonfamilial social forms such as nationalism, liberal individualism and imperialism. The metaphoric depiction of social hierarchy as natural and familial thus depended on the prior naturalizing of the social subordination of women and children. (45)

Significant in this passage is the fact that women, too, are dominant with regard to the child figure of the metaphor. Through the behavioral codes of motherhood, the Victorian woman typifies a variety of gendered and, when overseas, racial attitudes. "Mothering" becomes a way in which she could simultaneously enact previously held beliefs and teachings specific to women *and* seek to create, or recreate, the Other in the British/parental image.

References to racial Others as children are not rare, and are found quite regularly in the collection of letters published by Lucie Duff Gordon as *Letters from Egypt*. What is of greater significance here, though, is the actual representation of Gordon as mother to Arab children, both in England and Egypt. Much support is given to the idea that Gordon did not suffer from racist tendencies because she accepted into her household in England a Nubian boy, Hassan el Bakket, nicknamed "Hatty," in the 1840s (Shereen 161), but her attitude in Egypt is more problematic. Mothering overseas is more fully a conscious choice than any enactment of a "natural" or "biological" expression. Gordon's letters suggest that white women in relation to children in foreign nations make decisions—some conscious, some not—about whom they wish to mother, and there ensues a kind of selection process which is based on several criteria—the attractiveness of the child, the attention it pays to the mother-figure, and its ability or lack of ability to mirror that mother-figure. And maternal functions are simultaneously political functions: "[. . .] the West seeks its own identity in Third World attempts at imitating it; it finds its own image, idealized, in the imperfect copies fabricated by other cultures" (Spurr 36).

Gordon writes of her experiences with two Arab children: Zeynab and Achmet. Zeynab is the slave given to her by the American Consul-General. And although she anxiously writes that she may be forced to bring the girl home with her because "she has set her whole little black soul upon me" (52), Zeynab is eventually abandoned by her. Gordon shows little sympathy for Zeynab's plight and once the young girl has been removed from her home, she writes no more about her. She is happily tempted, however, to adopt Achmet. The explicit reason Gordon gives for passing the eight-year-old slave Zeynab to another household is that she has become "sullen." But the evolution of her attitude toward the child is more complicated than this. It is an evolution of perception made possible by the temporal immediacy of her letters, which are published as they were written, in historical sequence. Gordon decides to abandon Zeynab only after she has begun to define herself as Arab and behave in a fashion independent of Gordon. Once Zeynab moves from pathetic child to Arab "woman," she is quickly pushed out of Gordon's care. Gordon first writes to her mother,

> I looked at her little ears wondering they had not been bored for rings. She fancied I wished them bored (she was sitting on the floor close at my side), and in a minute she stood up and showed me her ear with a great pin through it: 'Is that well, lady?' the creature is eight years old. The shock nearly made me faint. What extremities of terror had reduced that little mind to such a state. (52)

The simultaneous feelings of power and revulsion Gordon expresses create a kind of interest in Zeynab for her, but it is short-lived. When Gordon travels to Alexandria in May of that year, she leaves Zeynab with her daughter, Janet Ross, but returns in October to find her changed:

> Zeynab is much grown and very active and intelligent, but a little louder and bolder than she was owing to the maids here wanting to christianize her, and taking her out unveiled, and letting her be among the men. However, she is affectionate as ever, and delighted at the prospect of going with me. (71–72)

Two months later, in a letter to Janet, Gordon expresses the desire to be rid of Zeynab, noting that "the Berberi men have put it into her head that we are inferior beings" (83), and that "I think she despises Omar for his affection towards me" (83). (Omar Abu-el-Halaweh was the servant Gordon hired upon her arrival in Egypt.) Whether the latter comment refers to a sort of jealousy based on a sexual agency attributed to the child or a cultural bond Zeynab holds with Omar, which excludes Gordon, is unclear, although both hold potential significance. That Zeynab has repeatedly demonstrated loyalties to her "own" cultures rather than Gordon's is problematic enough to dissolve Gordon's interest in her and create a desire to send her to "a household of black Mussulman slaves" (83). Her hostility toward the child is further demonstrated when she writes that if she does not "do" at such a household, "they must pass her on to a Turkish house" (83). Given the fact that previous entries relate that Zeynab has described her former Turkish master as "batal (bad)" (62) and that he called her "Salaam es-Sidi (the Peace of her Master)" (62)—perhaps a reference to sexual molestation and/or rape—Zeynab's refusal to mirror Gordon would, in Gordon's mind, warrant a return to such a state.

Twelve-year-old Achmet, however, does not suffer the same fate. He is the perfect, imperfect copy of the British presence. Achmet appears in Gordon's writing as something more than "the most merry, clever, omnipresent little rascal, with an ugly little pug face, [and] a shape like an antique Cupid" (27) when he proclaims that he is "sick of love" (216), for Baroness Kevenbrinck, one of Gordon's visitors. Gordon writes,

> The fact is the Baroness was kind and amiable and tried to amuse him as she would have done to a white boy, hence Achmet's susceptible heart was "on fire for her." He also asked me if I had any medicine to make him white, I suppose to look lovely in her eyes. He little knows how very pretty he is with his brown face—as he sits cross-legged on the carpet at my feet in his white turban and blue shirt reading aloud— he was quite a picture. (217)

Just as Zeynab's expressed desire for her own culture distances Gordon from her, Achmet's desire to be white allows Gordon to proclaim his beauty in being dark.

The autobiographical significance in *Letters From Egypt* is primarily displayed through their form as an historical sequence, and therefore presentation, of the evolution of her attitudes as well as the contradictions contained within them.

THE GOVERNESS

> Pray, kind reader, just picture yourself surrounded by such a motley group of beings, gabbling, chattering to me in their unknown tongues (for at that moment I did not understand either Arabic or Turkish), and making grimaces like monkeys from four o'clock in the morning until ten at night incessantly; and then you may form some idea of life in the Harem— that myth-like Elysium of the fertile imagination of both western and eastern poets. (*Harem Life* 107)

Unlike Gordon, Emmeline Lott traveled to Egypt for work. She went to serve as governess to the Viceroy's five-year-old son, Ibrahim, in 1861, but information about her life before and after her trip is sketchy. Michael Wojcik's essay in *The Dictionary of Literary Biography* is perhaps the most complete and, as he writes, "her moment in the public eye was too brief to be recorded in the usual public sources" (235). What *Harem Life* itself illustrates quite vividly, though, is a Western, feminized vision of the Arab harem which revolves not around sexual objectification of the Arab female body and its concomitant sensual excesses, but a predominantly racialized space wherein the British woman herself is objectified, demeaned, and placed at serious physical risk. Through a series of pseudo-syllogistic depictions, *Harem Life* explains and "proves" the fact that just as the white British woman is at the mercy of her racialized counterpart, so will the world eventually be at the mercy of the effect these women have on the present and future rulers of Egypt. Not even twenty years prior to Lord Cromer's return to the country and installment as

British consul-general, *Harem Life* appears with the message that not only is the eroticism of Egypt and the Arab harem a lie, but that at the heart of the (in her mind) culturally aggressive and politically crippled Egypt lay, as its creator, the Arab woman.

Lott authored three books about her five-month stay: *The English Governess in Egypt, Harem Life in Egypt and Constantinople* (two volumes, 1866), *The Mohaddetyn in the Palace of Ghezire, or Nights in the Harems* (two volumes, 1867) and *The Grand Pascha's Cruise on the Nile in the Viceroy of Egypt's Yacht* (two volumes, 1869). Billie Melman's *Women's Orients* offers several extended considerations and Judy Mabro's *Veiled Half Truths* remarks upon her enough to give evidence of Lott's racism, but the texts themselves remain obscure. The ferocity with which Lott demeans her subject may play a part in this. But her almost complete isolation from European companions in *Harem Life* (her only references to contact with other Europeans appear in the form of complaints about being forced to take her meals with the German laundrymaid) inevitably gives her a unique voice. That isolation creates for her a more involved, and even violent, culture shock, and invests her writings with a richer potential for analysis of how Victorian women provided specific, experiential reasons for oppression and control of the Arab Other. Simply put, Emmeline Lott hated Egypt. But how and why she hated it illustrate more vividly, perhaps, the nature of feminine imperialist ideology than those writings of women who never experienced such close contact with the Arab Other in the first place. She did not have the luxury of ideological distance and British social support which may have allowed other writers to find their surroundings "charming," "fascinating," or "unusual."

Lott's initial moments within the harem prefigure the difficulties she experiences as she jostles subjective positions in search of stability. While critics such as Margaret Strobel have described European women within indigenous cultures as "the inferior sex within the superior race" (xi), Lott cannot establish her white superiority with any real confidence. She describes her arrival in Stanley-and-Livingstone-like rhetoric, writing that she is surrounded by slaves who squat at her feet, kiss her hands and knees, and shout in unison that she is "Pretty! Pretty!" (47), but at other moments, she describes herself as a "bundle" which was brought into the harem "like a bale of merchandise" (69). She writes, "upon seeing me the whole of them [slaves helping with luggage] stood by while I arranged my things, staring at both myself and luggage as if I had just been imported from the Gold Coast" (49). Later, she attempts to force her position by explaining that, "in short, the whole of the inmates of the Harem soon began thoroughly to appreciate my European ways and habits" (131) without any textual corroboration whatsoever. She is not dominant, although she is white. And she does not belong, although she is female.

Lott's confusion and anxiety become localized in her dealings with Ibrahim's nurse, whom Lott will only name "Shaytan" (Satan) throughout the narrative. This ongoing relationship illustrates an "equal" one between a white British woman and a woman of color. Although Shaytan is a slave of Ethiopian origin, the role she plays in *Harem Life* is one of aggression and treachery, and is important because although she is a royal slave, as nurse, she maintains special accesses and privileges. Her status in connection to Ibrahim rivals that of Lott, as does her existence, and their relationship becomes a greater metaphor which represents Lott "battling" Satan for control and access to Ibrahim, the symbolic future of Egypt.

Lott insists on calling the nurse "Shaytan" before and after she explains to her readers that it means "devil" or "Satan" and offers the following description of her rival:

> her countenance was one of the most artful, cunning, and malicious it is possible to conceive: she was, in fact, an admirable type of the lowest caste negress to be found in Ethiopia. She was afflicted with a most ungovernable temper. Revenge and hatred seemed to be depicted in her face, and it was an enigma to me how the Viceroy, or my Princess, could possibly have selected such a creature to nurse my pupil. (49)

Lott regularly assumes the possessive position when discussing Shaytan (*my* princess, *my* pupil) and she goes even further by representing the nurse as a kind of fairy-tale witch in relation to the innocent governess:

> I knew that the head-nurse hated me, simply because more respect was paid to me than was shown to herself. On one occasion that negress offered me an apple; but looking round I perceived a slave, who had been one of the Viceroy's favourites, fix her large blue eyes upon the nurse, who changed colour—for, "although black as ebony as she was," still she blushed—and recalling to my mind [an incident of the attempted poisoning of the Viceroy with dates] I declined the fruit and after that Shaytan ever afterwards abstained from offering me any more. The vile wretch had betrayed herself by her own countenance, and henceforth I was on my guard. (107–108)

For all of the fears and anxieties that Lott expresses, she is unable, because of the sheer power of her employers, to direct her rantings at them. And so the nurse-figure becomes the site for the fuller expression of all she perceives of her surroundings: racial anxiety, class resentment, and gender confusion.

However, it is not just Lott, but Western culture and Britain specifically, that has much to fear from the Arab woman. About her perceived treatment, Lott writes, "Is not all this natural to the heart of Eastern women? especially in marble halls, where many a Lucretia Borgia abides her time to turn to account her intuitive knowledge of poisons and acts of cruelty" (310). In this way, the Arab harem operates on two ideological levels: first, as a nexus of feminine power structures, and second, as a demonstration of those structures as articulated through a discourse of racial and cultural difference. Egypt is ruled, via Lott's extension, not just by *women,* but by the racialized harem women she is describing with such fear and loathing. Lott makes quite clear the fact that hers is not an isolated representation of racial and gendered relations between a governess and a nurse (which could in some way be interpreted as the story of *one*), but that it is indicative of far greater political imperatives—a story which will affect *many.*

Her writing designates the English, and English women in particular, as targets for Arab aggression. She comments that Turks, Arabs, and Egyptians treat all Europeans with "apathy and absolute indifference," (69) but adds, "I know not why, but my countrywomen are not, as a general rule, very great favourites with any foreigners, especially those residing in the East, unless they have a well-lined purse" (176). During a description of the size of her room she complains,

> But as I was one of mother Eve's daughters, all of whom they looked upon as handmaids and slaves, born to be bought and sold, anything was good enough for me; [. . .] Perhaps had I been a Frankfort lady, or a denizen of the lovely village of Oppenheim, on the banks of the beautiful Rhine, my comforts would have been better cared for, and I should have found my position much more endurable; but I was a Kopek, "a dog" of an Englishwoman, a Howadjee [traveler], an unbeliever, a Pariah, whom both Moslems and Jews despised and spat at [. . .]. (156)

Lott's tone in this passage is quite passionate, but nowhere in the text does she represent specific scenes where such statements were made. Hers is an experiential resentment expressed through the rhetoric she brought with her from England.

What Lott ultimately provides for her British audience is an Arab woman at once so powerful and so corrupted that she is responsible for a vast array of political ills:

> The downfall of a Minister, the spoilation of the goods and chattels of an Egyptian Prince, the removal of a hated rival, the substitution of one infant for another, the sending of an heir apparent to his last home, the poisoning of the reigning Sultan or Viceroy, in short all crimes are hatched in the lower regions. (309)

The harem symbolizes weak, "petticoat government" (308), where,

> The inmates are surrounded by rivals, always watched, for the surveillance surpasses even that of the secret police in Russia, where the very walls have ears, and spies, most emphatically termed by our own neighbors the French *les mouches,* buzz about as thick as mosquitoes in India and Egypt. (309)

Not just the white woman, but, by extension, the world, is a potential victim to this image of the Arab female which conflates racial and gendered anxieties into an agent of "trickery, subtlety, and artifice" (309).

Throughout *Harem Life*, Lott swings widely back and forth between descriptions of the life she led, which may generally be considered "true" or "accurate," and prophesies for the future like that above. In this way, she repeatedly crosses the line between fiction and autobiography. Without the established progression gained by the publication of dated letters, her text is more fully a reinterpretation and re-presentation of her experiences in the harem, but created once she has returned to Britain. It has a temporal linearity which is indicative of writers who begin and end their narratives with their arrival in and departure from the country in point, but it is fashioned so that the start of the text introduces a character by the name of Mr. Xenos, who serves as a guide for her. In those beginning pages, Lott prefigures all that is to come in the remaining ones and one quickly suspects Xenos's literary construction.

Mr. Xenos is a Greek cotton merchant whom Lott meets on the train from Alexandria to Cairo and he offers little but warnings. He tells her to avoid the "petty intrigues of the court cabals" (5), and adds that as she may attempt to procure for herself special amenities necessary for an English lady, the harem's "entire ignorance of your habits will make them regard such trivial attentions on the part of their liege lord and master as signs of his too pointed wish to become on terms of familiar intimacy with you" (6). He even foretells her troubles with Shaytan with a suspicious specificity, "the loose and uncleanly habits of the attendants, more particularly those of the Arab nurses, will disgust you" (8).

But insofar as Mr. Xenos is Lott's own imagined guide, he functions very differently from the "real" men who created the orientalist fantasies which helped bring her to Egypt in the first place. She concentrates most upon Thomas Moore's *Lalla Rookh*, but also mentions articles from *Once a Week*, Dr. Abbott's Egyptian Antiquity Exhibit, and DeQuincey's *The Confessions of an Opium Eater*. More so than the other women considered in this essay, Lott consciously and repeatedly references what she read and heard in Britain before her departure, and the stark contrast between that and what she finds upon her arrival contributes to her hatred of the latter. In this way, *Harem Life* offers a kind of feminine orientalism, a set of perceptions which results from the differences between her lived experience and the representations she had learned at home. After describing the bathing ritual of harem members, she writes, "this only occurs when they have visited the Viceroy, and not daily, or even at any other time, as so many authors have erroneously stated. The bath of the poets is a myth" (38). She states her point more clearly in the following:

> Brilliant as are the pen-and-ink sketches that our poets have painted of Harem life, I have visited and resided in three of them, which ought to have been, and most undoubtedly are, the most magnificent of all those gilded cages, and I have no desire to visit or live in a fourth. I did not set my foot in the second with the same interest which my ignorance of daily life therein had inspired me on entering the first. (HL 307)

Carolyn G. Heilbrun argues in *Writing a Woman's Life* that "The expression of anger has always been a terrible hurdle in women's personal progress" (25). It evidently wasn't difficult for Lott to express her anger in *Harem Life*, but it may have contributed to its reception, for "Lott's books brought her little profit or recognition" (Wojcik 235). Ultimately, Lott fails miserably at providing her reading public with an exciting, exotic account of travels abroad. Instead, she shows her readers a woman struggling to assume her position as governess, lonely for companions who are like her, complaining about perceived insults and disrespect, and, finally, expressing sheer hatred of and unjustified accusations about all that is different, frightening, and foreign, the impact of which she attempts to explain:

> It was not the feeling of what we Europeans call ennui which I experienced, for that sensation can always be shook off by a little moral courage and energy; but it was a state bordering on that frightful melancholy, that must, if not dispelled, engender insanity. And my experience of such feelings is not to be wondered at, if my position in the Harem is thoroughly examined. (103–04)

It is at moments such as these, it seems, that she re-crosses the boundary from fiction to reality—a reality which interests no one.

THE SCHOLAR

Because orientalism and Egyptology were such young topics of study in English academic life in the nineteenth century, scholars who travelled and studied abroad had little or no prior training in their fields. The new orientalist sciences of archaeology and Egyptology "emerged outside the universities and, until [the last decade of the nineteenth century] were barely incorporated in the curriculum" (Melman 255–56). As Billie Melman notes,

> the archaeologist or Egyptologist, like the evangelical ethnographer, culled his or her expertise from an informal individual experience, not from any formal training. Moreover, in a science particularly shunning theory and speculation and condemning deduction, that very experience was actually superior to theoretical *a priori* knowledge. (Melman 256)

As a result, the field of study was a particularly available one for women, who wouldn't have been allowed to earn such degrees had they even been offered.

Amelia Ann Blandford Edwards, author of *Pharaohs, Fellahs and Explorers* (1891), *A Thousand Miles Up the Nile* (1877), various fictional works, a multitude of published articles, and co-founder of the Egypt Exploration Fund, is one of these women, and an important component of her work stems directly from this diverse background. After having written, for a number of years, purely fictional works, her move to more scientific texts did not mean the abandoning of her "literary eye." In fact, her wish to represent the difference between "her own emotional and 'romantic' brand of archaeology and the emotionless writing of her close associates, Flinders Petrie and Llewellyn Griffith," caused Samuel Birch, Director of Egyptian Antiquities at the British Museum to oppose, in 1882, her plans for the EEF "on the basis of her promotion of what he dubbed 'emotional archaeology'" (Melman 257–58). Edwards herself comments on the matter as follows:

> the Egyptologists do not write a picturesque and popular style like that of A.B.E., who had thirty years of literary work in the romantic school, and who has especially cultivated a style—worked at it as if it was a science—and mastered it . . . style is an instrument which I have practised sedulously, and which I can plan upon. But our Egyptologists, etc., what do they know of that subtle harmony? They have never flung themselves into the life and love of imaginary men and women; they have never studied the landscape painting of scenery in words . . . It is not their vocation. I am the only romanticist in the world who is also an Egyptologist. (Qtd. in Melman 258)

But while Edwards's romanticist style may be argued about in relation to her descriptions of both landscape and archaeological findings, it is her pseudo-literary representations of the Egyptian people themselves which are of interest here. In *A Thousand Miles Up the Nile*, while creating for her scientist audience a material commodification of Egyptian relics and areas, she simultaneously fashions a commodified Egyptian person through the rhetoric of theater. Although Melman argues that *A Thousand Miles* is not autobiographical and that "Edwards's obliviousness to life and people in 'modern' Egypt is striking" (262), Melman's own observation that during descriptions of Egyptians Edwards "lapses to the narrative 'I' [and] reveals her own feelings" (263) suggests that much more, in fact, is going on in such passages.

The autobiographical underpinnings of *A Thousand Miles* reveal Edwards as a woman struggling to define herself through both literary and academic methods. At the same time that her literary style threatens her scientific standing, her scientific interests, along with their stylistic requirements, threaten her own vision of Egypt. One explanation of how this conflict is made manifest in the text is offered in Billie Melman's chapter on Edwards in *Women's Orients*. She points out that "the narrator/traveller in *A Thousand Miles* is androgynous" and that "Edwards plays down gender and almost obliterates her female identity" (259). Perhaps such a persona allows Edwards the freedom to shift between discourses more comfortably. But androgyny is also *both* genders, and in that, the text reveals an academic rhetoric painted masculine and a literary rhetoric painted feminine, the former of which addresses science and the latter which addresses Egyptians themselves.

Egyptians in *A Thousand Miles* appear most regularly *en masse*. They appear in carnival and procession form. The following exerpt, though lengthy, is demonstrative of this:

Meanwhile, the crowd ebbs and flows unceasingly—a noisy, changing, restless, parti-coloured tide, half European, half Oriental, on foot, on horseback, and in carriages. Here are Syrian dragomans in baggy trousers and braided jackets; barefooted Egyptian fellaheen in ragged blue shirts and felt skull-caps; Greeks in absurdly stiff white tunics, like walking pen-wipers; Persians with high mitre-like caps of dark woven stuff; swarthy Bedouins in flowing garments, creamy-white with chocolate stripes a foot wide, and head-shawl of the same bound about the brow with a fillet of twisted camel's hair; Englishmen in palm-leaf hats and knickerbockers, dangling their long legs across almost invisible donkeys; native women of the poorer class, in black veils that leave only the eyes uncovered, and long trailing garments of dark blue and black striped cotton; dervishes in patchwork coats, their matted hair streaming from under fantastic head-dresses; blue-black Abyssinians with incredibly slender, bowed legs, like attenuated ebony balustrades; Armenian priests, looking exactly like Portia as the Doctor, in long black gowns and high square caps; majestic ghosts of Algerine Arabs, all in white; mounted Janissaries with jingling sabres and gold-embroidered jackets; merchants, beggars, soldiers, boatmen, labourers, workmen, in every variety of costume, and of every shade of complexion from fair to dark, from tawny to copper-colour, from deepest bronze to bluest black." (5).

Not only Edwards's punctuation, the use of semi-colons which creates a lengthy flow of visual images across the page, but her specific reference to Portia, comment on the theatrical nature of the scene.

CONCLUSION

One of the issues which surfaces repeatedly in scholarship on imperialism and imperialist action is that of blame. Do we, as critics, benefit from, or, perhaps more accurately, feel the need to absolve those we analyze from their racism and desire to control and dominate groups of people who now are able to express just what that control and domination meant? What they continue to mean? And, if we do lend ourselves to historical relativism and focus on context, do we in any way inadvertently condone racism? In his essay on the connections and disconnections between colonial educational policy and imperialist goals, Clive Whitehead argues that, "British policy was not a synonym for cultural imperialism in the pejorative sense. [It was] more like an expression of the confused nature of British colonial education in the 1920s than a blueprint for the perpetuation of British rule" (212). I admit, [this view is] a very hard sell. But it reflects, I believe, a certain reality that, although uncomfortable, is important. If the ways in which Victorian women involved themselves in imperialist acts are glossed over because they are in some way "unseemly" to feminist goals, then, by extension, so too may be our own national and global perceptions of race and cultural relations. The fact that such attitudes and behaviors do *not* show themselves through the guise of a metaphoric "boogey-man" but, instead, through average, unassuming, and even unnoticed social codes is far more disturbing to some than the proclamation of hatred itself. I am aware, as I write this essay, that I could be perceived as being less than vigilant in my treatment of the negative impact the racist discourses discussed had on the Arabs they were directed at, as well as the precedents they set which remain with us still. But the lack of explanation that such discourses do, in many ways, result from confusion and fear on the part of those who write them strikes me as the most unseemly act of all.

WORKS CITED

Buzard, James. "Victorian Women and the Implications of Empire." *Victorian Studies.* 36.4 (1993): 443–53.

Edwards, Amelia Ann Blandford. *A Thousand Miles Up the Nile.* London: George Routledge and Sons, 1877.

Gordon, Lucie Duff. *Letters from Egypt.* 1865 London: Virago, 1983.

Heilbrun, Carolyn G. *Writing a Woman's Life.* New York: Ballantine, 1988.

Jelinek, Estelle C. *The Tradition of Women's Autobiography: From Antiquity to the Present.* Boston: Twayne, 1986.

Lott, Emmeline. *The English Governess in Egypt: Harem Life in Egypt and Constantinople.* Philadelphia: T. B. Peterson, 1866.

Mabro, Judy. *Veiled Half-Truths: Western Travellers' Perceptions of Middle Eastern Women.* NY: I. B. Taurus, 1991.

Martineau, Harriet. *Eastern Life, Present and Past.* London: E. Moxon, 1850.

McClintock, Anne. *Imperial Leather: Race, Gender and Sexuality in the Colonial Contest.* New York: Routledge, 1995.

Melman, Billie. *Women's Orients: English Women and the Middle East, 1718–1918, Sexuality, Religion and Work.* Ann Arbor: U of Michigan P, 1992.

Pratt, Mary Louise. *Imperial Eyes: Travel Writing and Transculturation.* New York: Routledge, 1992.

Shereen, Faiza. "Lucie Duff Gordon." *Dictionary of Literary Biography.* Vol. 166. Detroit: Bruccoli, 1996.

Spacks, Patricia Ann Meyer. *Imagining a Self: Autobiography and the Novel in Eighteenth-century England.* Cambridge: Harvard UP, 1976.

Spurr, David. *The Rhetoric of Empire: Colonial Discourse in Journalism, Travel Writing, and Imperial Administration.* Durham:Duke UP, 1993.

Strobel, Margaret. *European Women and the Second British Empire.* Bloomington: Indiana UP, 1991.

Whitehead, Clive. "British Colonial Educational Policy: A Synonym for Cultural Imperialism?" In 'Benefits bestowed'? Education and British Imperialism. New York: Manchester UP, 1988.

Wojcik, Michael. "Emmeline Lott." Dictionary of Literary Biography. Vol. 166. Detroit: Bruccoli, 1996.

CHAPTER FOURTEEN

Chinese Coolies, Hidden Perfume, and Harriet Beecher Stowe in Anna Leonowens's *The Romance of the Harem*

SUSAN MORGAN

"The road of excess leads to the palace of wisdom"
—William Blake

In *The Romance of the Harem*, Anna Leonowens's second memoir of her more than five years as a governess in the royal harem of Siam, there is a moment which invokes American slavery and the American Civil War, and the reference is both veiled and bold. It comes near the end of the book, in an eclectic and anecdotal chapter called "Stray Leaves from the Schoolroom Table." Anna, as the governess-narrator, turns again, as she had both earlier in this 1873 narrative and in her 1870 memoir, *The English Governess at the Siamese Court*, to the topic of sexual slavery in the royal harem of Siam. But unlike the other moments, this one is not an explicit statement condemning the practice of sexual slavery. Instead, Anna introduces her readers to her friend, Sonn Klean.

Inside and outside the narrative, for Sonn Klean was an actual person, this lady had great stature in the royal city of women and children called Nang Harm. She was one of the approximately three dozen out of the many thousands of women imprisoned there who, as one of the king's concubines, had produced a child with the King, and one of the even fewer ranked as having noble blood. Best and rarest of all, and the ultimate source of the historic Sonn Klean's continuing status, she had produced a son, Prince Kreta. The actual prince would have an internationally distinguished public career, including, among many achievements, service as the Siamese Ambassador to London. At the time the narrative was written, less than a decade after the time in which it is set, that Prince was still young. The single image of him in the book highlights his narrative insignificance. When Anna and her son go to dinner at his house, the little prince and little Louis are crammed into a single chair, in the margins of this narrative about women.

The focus of the section is on Sonn Klean. The narrative introduction to her is remarkable in its eloquence and, I believe, radical in its implications: "Among the ladies of the harem, I knew one woman who more than all the rest helped to enrich my life and to render fairer and more beautiful every lovely woman I have since chanced to meet"(246). Sonn Klean's power to enrich Anna's life can be understood quite conventionally. Less conventional is her power "to render fairer and more beautiful every lovely woman" Anna has since met. How she has done that, and what it might mean, is the focus of the brief memories that follow. First, this powerful lady's name may be translated into English, and Leonowens assures us that "no other name could ever have been so appropriate," as Hidden Perfume. Whatever Sonn Klean's power "to render fairer and more beautiful," that power is located within, as a force for bringing out what is hidden. The beauty she has enhanced is not a matter of physical sight. But only a few paragraphs after offering this assurance of the perfect appropriateness of Sonn Klean's name to describe the deep affections and hard-won strength of her spirit, the narrator moves on to reveal that Hidden Perfume is not Sonn Klean's only English-language name. Sonn Klean has herself rejected this given name in favor of another, one she has chosen for herself and which she uses as a signature for all of her correspondence. That second name is Harriet Beecher Stowe. After this sudden and startling announcement of Sonn Klean's willed metamorphosis into Harriet Beecher Stowe, the narrator offers an explanation. Sonn Klean chose the name in order to "express her entire sympathy and affection for the author of 'Uncle Tom's Cabin.'" Moreover, this "entire sympathy and affection" had developed because "her favorite book was 'Uncle Tom's Cabin,' and she would read it over and over again, though she knew all the characters by heart, and spoke of them as if she had known them all her life" (248).

The little section on who Sonn Klean is and what she calls herself constitutes an extraordinarily rich moment in this narrative, one in which three central motifs of this book—slavery, imperialism, and women's power—are intertwined. Hidden Perfume is characterized by a series of polarized identities, as American and Siamese, Christian and Buddhist, free woman and enslaved concubine, author and character in a book. The complexities of these dualistic constructions of Hidden Perfume are created at the point when Leonowens names Harriet Beecher Stowe. In that moment, the narrative overlays its vision of the evils of slavery in Siam with a suddenly invoked glimpse of another narrative of the evils of slavery in America. That overlaying, that doubleness, of the two places and the two women, is the critical problem, or rather the creative phenomenon, I want to take up in this essay.

The reference to Stowe in an 1873 book published in the eastern United States may, at least for American critics, immediately invoke the familiar American context, and the enormous resonances of Stowe's name in the writings of her American contemporaries. Rather than turn to this cultural and rhetorical locale, I bring two opening questions to the process of offering a reading of the Sonn Klean piece.

If the reference to American slavery à la Stowe and her novel provides the hermeneutic frame within which Siamese slavery can be judged, what provides the hermeneutic frame within which American slavery can be understood? And what does gender matter? My initial assumption is that signs or icons such as "American slavery" and "Harriet Beecher Stowe" are just that. They have local meanings, which cannot be generally presumed. The richness of the Hidden Perfume passage in *The Romance*, with its startling moment of metamorphosis from Siamese royal concubine to American author, has everything to do with some historically specific locations not in the United States which provide the rhetorical contexts for reading it.

The American slavery question in public rhetoric outside America occurred primarily in journalistic coverage of the American Civil War. What people talked about when they talked about American slavery in the 1860s and up through the early '70s was the war. And in public discourse the Civil War was a trope, which could function in a range of ways. For Leonowens, the discursive frame in which she would have heard/read the talk about the war was produced in Southeast Asia. *The Romance* belongs with public discourses published in English in Singapore and Bangkok. Each of these two forums uses the Civil War in ways and for reasons unique to the demands of its own political geography. Yet the ways and reasons of both places are similarly regressive: one to hide its own system of slavery and the other to argue for the hegemony of Christianity over Buddhism. In Leonowens's book the trope functions quite differently, as a vehicle for revealing the inequalities and the freedoms of a gendered understanding of identity.

THE CIVIL WAR

What the Civil War was, what happened in it, how to understand it, how to judge it, what to call it: such issues have occupied historians of American history for well over a century. I am concerned first with the war as it was represented during the 1860s in Singapore, the British island colony that was the major metropolitan center of British imperialism in the region now known as Southeast Asia. Singapore was where I suggest Leonowens predominantly heard about the War, and rhetoric in Singapore initially directed Leonowens's knowledge of and views about American slavery. Leonowens appeared in Singapore sometime after May 7, 1859, when her husband died in Penang (another Straits Settlement further north). She lived in Singapore until March 1862, when she moved to Siam to be the governess to the royal harem, staying until June 1867. After returning to Singapore for a few months, she moved to the United States some time between late 1868 and late 1869, with a stay in England to pick up her daughter and drop off her son. In other words, Singapore was the particular location which provided Leonowens with a public perspective on events in America for almost a decade, including the years just before, during, and just after the Civil War. It was through the representations published in the Singapore papers that Leonowens, like the rest of the foreign population of Singapore, learned about—which is to say, had her views shaped about—the American Civil War. And, to a significant extent, it is in relation to the particular meanings of that imperialist discourse that her own antislavery rhetoric belongs.

The first point I want to emphasize is the sheer significance of the topic during that decade. Singapore boasted several English-language newspapers. The business of Singapore was commercial shipping, and the initial and continuing major function of its newspapers was to publish shipping news. Extending out from that base, and inseparable from its interests, were a wide variety of other topics. The dominant newspaper was the *Singapore Straits Times and Singapore Journal of Commerce*, which came out every Saturday. In its early years, the *Straits Times* filled its front page with advertisements, with the following pages offering shipping news (arrivals, departures, nationalities, ports of origin, goods, significant passengers disembarking at or embarking from Singapore), always the results of the opium sales in Calcutta, and, at the back, what we now call news articles. By 1861 the ads had shifted to the back pages and the prose to the front. The *Straits Times* functioned as the major paper in the central imperial city in the South Seas, and used much of its space to carrying articles, some reprinted, some by "correspondents," about events in the region. This regional coverage included the other Straits Settlements, the various islands, usually Dutch or Portuguese, of the East Indies, Siam, Burma, and even India. There were also, of course, pieces from Europe and London. And starting in 1861, the paper routinely offered articles about the conflict in America. Representations of the war were of enormous interest to the foreign communities in Singapore, judging by the extensive coverage in English-language papers of events that preceded it, of so-called "actual battles," and of projections of the possible outcomes. In a decade when a great deal was happening locally, regionally, and in Europe, which the foreign communities in Singapore would see as important world news, it is notable how many articles on that war between faraway states did appear.

The second point I stress is that these representations of the war consisted of two clearly opposed positions, in two clear categories of articles. The first was a series of reprints from the *Evening Mail* edition of the *London Times*, appearing about once every three months, and representing a very popular view of the war in England. These were vituperatively anti-North, anti-Lincoln and anti- the Emancipation Proclamation. Thus, in November 1862, on Lincoln's making the Emancipation Proclamation: "powerful malignity is a dreadful reality, but impotent malignity is apt to be a very contemptible spectacle" (Nov. 22, 1862); and in December 1864, on the victories of the Union forces: "Some physiologists have asserted that the Americans have gradually acquired something of the Red Indian cast of countenance. Can the spite of the savage have also entered into them?" (Dec. 17, 1864).

The second kind of article is the more interesting. Some reprints from other English papers and some written by Singaporeans, they are self-consciously contrapuntal, eschewing the florid style of the *Evening Mail* for a declaredly "moderate" tone (Jan 18, 1862). These articles suggest that they are offering the local, the rational, and the real view. Thus, on the blockade of the South which hurt the British production of cotton goods, the paper argues that raw cotton had been overproduced anyway and what is needed in London can be supplied by India, so the blockade was actually good for colonial business (Mar. 22, 1862). While explicitly neutral, and even having "Southern sympathy," these articles are self-represented as pro-Emancipation, arguing the "realistic" case that in terms of the institution of slavery, Americans should accept that the war has already permanently "undermined its foundations" (Jan. 18, 1862). The writers assert matter-of-factly that Negroes are human because they are hard workers who learn quickly, and that slavery is inhuman. Finally, any "Southern sympathy" is explained away as just a matter of admiration for courage in adversity. Moreover, that sympathy is to be understood as odd, as something that needs to be accounted for. It can be labeled "remarkable because there was nothing whatever in common between us and the Southern States." And the reason for that lack of commonality is explicitly given: the South was in the war to protect "human property"(Jan 30, 1864).

1860s SINGAPORE

Why should this group of issues and events generate such interest and the American Civil War function as a common trope in the public, semiofficial, discourse of 1860s Singapore? Quite conventionally for a trope, this one had everything to do with events and issues in Singapore and very little to do with what was happening in America. Much like DeQuincey's "Malay" in his *Confessions of an Opium Eater*, Singapore's "American Civil War," while seeming to refer to a real historical something somewhere else, had its own life and its meaning in a quite localized frame. There were practical and personal reasons why the war and emancipation rhetoric was a regular feature in the newspapers. Many people among the foreign community had extensive family and business ties with people and companies in the northern United States. The Singapore newspapers were generally edited by men like John Cameron, who would have labeled themselves as British. They often had immediate business reasons, including dealing with American commercial shipping lines whose main offices were in the American Northeast, for leaning to the Northern side. But along with these sorts of practical reasons, there were ideological ones as well.

I have recreated elsewhere a kind of history of nineteenth-century Singapore, but I offer here a brief image. Singapore was a British possession, virtually a British creation, and the premier port for international travel and trade in Southeast Asia from the 1820s through the rest of the nineteenth century. The key definition of Singapore among its foreign and merchant class population was that it was a free port, a place which was founded and prospered on the laissez-faire principle that anyone with industry and initiative could make a good life for himself there. The commitment to private enterprise and individual possibilities, to what I may as well call "life, liberty, and the pursuit of happiness," was at the heart of Singapore's public image and its public language during the middle and later decades of the nineteenth century.

Colonial administrators in India had run Singapore since the island's "founding" as a British trade station for the East India Company in 1821. Singapore-governing officials and businessmen had long called for its independence, an odd term used to signify that the settlement should be governed directly from the Colonial Office in London rather than control being routed through India, another colony with its own agenda. In the decade following the Rebellion in India in 1857 and the abolishing of the East India Company in 1858, rich merchants and administrators in Singapore increased their volubility about their need for and rights to direct rule from London. This debate, which was in fact about which forms of colonial governance were best for business, was cast in the language of independence and self-rule, with the Singaporean governing classes taking the role of the freedom fighters. In both its terminology and in its reasonable and practical style, this Singaporean public rhetoric about administration of the colony paralleled the rhetoric about the American North, borrowing its language from that about emancipation in America. The "struggle" for a free Singapore continued through the years of the American Civil War, with victory coming in 1867 when the Colonial Office finally accepted control of the Settlement.

In contradistinction to its rhetoric, Singapore was in practice neither a free port nor a place that allowed individual freedoms and opportunities. Yet that doubleness exactly characterized its peculiar form of government. The city financed the infrastructure, which sustained it as a free port through opium, through an extensive and highly profitable system of coerced addiction that enslaved the tens of thousands of Chinese coolies who were building Singapore's economic success. The government sold opium licenses, at fabulous fees, which provided operating revenues in lieu of taxes. In turn, rich businessmen paid their workers partly in opium, in lieu of wages. The discourse of freedom, continually represented in its newspapers as well as in government papers, allowed the British government of Singapore to ignore not only its utter complicity with and dependence on Chinese coolie slavery but even the very fact of that slavery. Emancipation rhetoric in 1860s Singapore was not about slavery in America but about slavery in Singapore, about a discursive absence that functioned to erase its material presence. Every acknowledgment of the rights of the Africans in America, every expression of distance from the values of the American South through Singapore's self-representation as a place which valued the rights and humanity and basic freedoms of its people, functioned as a claim to the innocence of the coolie system. It was a silent proclamation. And what it proclaimed was, "there is no slavery in Singapore." Because, of course, there was.

1860s SIAM

A second localized discourse that used reporting on the American Civil War as a trope for its own imperialist project was produced in 1860s Siam. The international politics of Siam were different from those of Singapore. First, in spite of the enormous concessions to British rights in Siam which had been established by the Bowring Treaty in 1857 (John Bowring being at the time the governor of British Hong Kong), Siam remained an independent state. It had a complex system of slavery, involving debt-slavery, polygamy, and the capture of state enemies, all of which had evolved through centuries in terms of the religions and the political and social practices of the peoples in the region. Unlike the practice of addicting coolies to fund the running of Singapore, slavery in Siam was not part of the economy of British imperialism. It was indigenous and it was a public, legal, and virtually universal practice.

Though an international port through river access, Bangkok did nowhere near the trade of pre-eminent Singapore, and had many fewer English-language publications. But Bangkok was only a few days by ship from the great hub of Singapore and foreigners regularly received their newspapers from there as well as, less regularly, papers from Europe and the United States. It would be fair to say that the regular newspaper for the foreign community in Bangkok was the Singapore *Straits Times*. Bangkok did have the annual *Bangkok Calendar* and the bimonthly *Bangkok Recorder*, but this last didn't appear in English until 1865. The two Bangkok publications can be compared in some significant ways to the *Straits Times* in their views on the American Civil War. There were no "Southern sympathy" articles and *London Times* reprints. There was only the other side, support for the North, and images of the war as a fight against slavery. This Bangkok rhetoric made no claims to being practical or "moderate." It was presented in the language of the high Christian purpose of emancipation.

The differently positioned rhetorics on the war in America in these two imperial locations reflect clear differences in political geography. The *Straits Times* was the unofficial voice of the British government and merchant interests in the region, and committed to representing that government and those interests as nonrepressive. Opinions on the war and slavery were part of the effort to justify and support British business interests in Singapore. The Bangkok publications were American and Christian rather than British and business-oriented. The American Missionary Association, a press run by Reverend Dan Beach Bradley, an American medical missionary from Ohio, published both the *Calendar* and the *Recorder*. The Bangkok papers were outside commentators on the state. Part of their function as Christian voices for imperial interests and against Siamese culture, was to attack slavery, specifically as a means to attack Buddhism. The imperial discourses in both Singapore and Siam, one economic and official and the other religious and unofficial, used the emancipation rhetoric of the American Civil War to serve their own efforts for greater power and influence in their respective locations. I would say that merchant and missionary both shared a project of domination, the goals of which were to foreclose the very values their rhetorics claimed to uphold.

HIDDEN PERFUME AND
THE EMANCIPATION PROCLAMATION

These two public discourses were the venue within which English-speaking residents of Singapore and Bangkok in the 1860s received public representations of the American Civil War. Yet Leonowens's writings do not fit neatly with either of these discourses of Southeast Asian imperialism. *The Romance* does not take its positions from the rhetorics of colonial Singapore and Christian Bangkok to offer a narrative of the royal harem that paints Siam as backward, uncivilized, and primitive. The Sonn Klean episode does not function as a claim that "they" need to learn from "us," from the enlightened British teacher and the books of Harriet Beecher Stowe. It transforms the trope of the Civil War in quite a different way, creating a structure in which the antislavery position functions not to demonstrate the hegemony of an imperialist culture but to subvert the basic dualism of subject and Other on which that hegemony is based.

Like the public discourse about the war in both Singapore and Bangkok, the narrator's attacks on slavery in *The Romance* do imply that she is a citizen of a free world offering "life, liberty, and the pursuit of happiness." The question is, where does the narrative suggest that such a world is located? Where is the narrator of *The Romance* from? Or perhaps, where did Anna and also the other characters get enlightened? What does the narrative itself imply about the origins of enlightenment? Reading the public discourses against slavery in Singapore and Bangkok, and the lies of political and religious superiority and moral innocence those discourses functioned to support, requires attention not only to issues of imperial hegemony but also to issues of gender. These two propaganda machines of big business and big religion, with their concomitant claims that they respect the rights of each and every one of the people on whose backs they stand (even as they campaign for more and more power over these people), were, after all, run not only by imperialists but by men. A reading of the Sonn Klean section of *The Romance* which simply places it as a version of the repressive imperial discourses of English-speaking Singapore and Bangkok during the 1860s ignores gender. The passage offers a dynamic process of constructing identities, which shift into and change places with and influence each other in various ways. Does it matter to our understanding of the play between American slavery and Siamese slavery in this passage that the players—Anna and Sonn Klean, as Hidden Perfume and as Harriet Beecher Stowe—are women? Yes.

After the opening description of Sonn Klean as the woman who had most helped to enrich the narrator's life, Anna begins her account of their relationship with what at first seems quite the typical imperialist view. "Our daily lessons and talks had become a part of her happiest moments. They gave her entrance into a new world . . ."(246). However, the examples which follow this reference to "daily lessons" contradict any assumption that the foreign governess is the teacher who brings enlightenment to the cloistered and less progressive Siamese. Surely one lesson for the reader is that what constitutes the "daily lessons" cannot be taken for granted, that imperialism lives more in the cultural ideology that drives the reader's hermeneutic expectations than actually *in* these sentences.

Anna's first anecdotal memory is that she drops by at the house of Sonn Klean, who shows her some new wallpaper. Commenting that "I see you do not understand the meaning of it" (247), Sonn Klean becomes Anna's teacher and "proceeded to explain the allegory" (247) in Buddhist terms. Next, after watching Sonn Klean pray, Anna as unenlightened student falls back on the key imperial claim of Christian American publications in Bangkok, a critique of the backwardness of Buddhism: "I said . . , 'You were praying to that idol?' But the Buddhist is neither passive nor silenced nor otherwise displaced from her authority here. She turns aside Anna's attack in a lesson that reveals that attack's narrow intolerance. Sonn Klean, "laying her hand gently upon my arm, said: 'Shall I say of you, dear friend, that you worship the ideal or image which you have of your God in your own mind, and not the God? Even so say not of me' (248).

In both these moments Anna errs, first in not having the perspicacity even to notice, let alone interpret, the allegory painted on the wallpaper, and second in not having the breadth of vision to understand the significance of Sonn Klean's forms of worship. In both cases Anna is marked by her own narrative as a bad reader, unable to see other than on the surface. And in this book, which insists on the possibilities both of learning and of teaching, once Anna has been taught, she willingly and gratefully learns. In the spiritual hierarchy established at the very beginning of the passage, in the introduction to Sonn Klean, she is the enlightened teacher and Anna the admiring student.

These two anecdotes, about the wallpaper and Sonn Klean's prayer in front of a statue of Buddha, function to set up the most important recollection of this section, the special dinner party Sonn Klean gives for Anna. At the end of that party Sonn Klean makes an announcement. She tells Anna that she is "wishful to be good like Harriet Beecher Stowe" (249) and, in a reenactment of Lincoln's 1862 Emancipation Proclamation, calls all of her household slaves into the room and declares their freedom. This moment does not simply imitate history, but improves upon it. Unlike the American male president, who, as the Singapore papers extensively pointed out, did not at the time of the proclamation actually free a single slave, and unlike Stowe's novel, which directly freed no one, the Siamese concubine, immediately and in everyone's presence, frees 132 slaves. She even goes into precise detail about the practical arrangements.

The direct effectiveness of Sonn Klean's emancipation proclamation in contrast with Lincoln's speech and Stowe's novel is not the only way her speech as action forestalls a simple reading of *The Romance* as an argument for European or American hegemony. Immediately after describing the proclamation, the narrator once again offsets her own perspective with the perspective of Hidden Perfume, "quoted" as speaking directly in her own voice: "Her sweet voice trembled with love and music whenever she spoke of the lovely American lady who had taught her, 'even as Buddha had once taught kings,' to respect the rights of her fellow-creatures" (249).

This is partly a conventional moment of displacement in imperialistic discourse, with the evil of slavery in America now being rewritten as the evil of slavery in Siam. America is the land of the free and operates, through Stowe's relocation in Sonn Klean, as the inspiration to the still less civilized Siam. There are some obvious biographical reasons for Leonowens to invoke Stowe. Leonowens had arrived in the eastern part of the United States sometime in late 1868 or 1869. At that time she became friends with Annie Fields, wife of the publisher and editor of the *Atlantic Monthly*, James Fields. The most famous contributor to the *Atlantic Monthly* in the 1860s, and deeply admired by both James and Annie (who was to be her first biographer), was Harriet Beecher Stowe. Moreover, the *Atlantic* significantly helped Leonowens's reputation as a writer by publishing excerpts of both her books on Siam just before they came out as well as publishing favorable reviews of the books themselves. It would be easy to dismiss Sonn Klean's self-identification with Stowe as an inserted tribute to Leonowens's well-connected literary patrons. But I am arguing that the narrative context here is crucial, and that the preceding two anecdotes along with Sonn Klean's reference to Buddha preclude any rush to such a judgment.

With her references to Buddha and to Stowe, Sonn Klean is offering the foreign teacher yet another lesson, another whiff of hidden perfume. Himself a teacher rather than a god, Buddha was the teacher of kings. In the female world in which Sonn Klean lives, spiritual lessons become a matter of transcultural transmission: as Sonn Klean learns from the "lovely American" lady's words, takes on the identity of that lady without denigrating or abandoning her own identity as Sonn Klean, and in turn teaches the "British" teacher the lesson yet again. If one must look for origins to this chain of transmissions and metamorphoses, the origin would be Buddha, explicitly refuting the claims of Christianity both in American missionary discourse in Bangkok and in Stowe's novel. But central to Sonn Klean's lesson is that origins, and the hegemonic values carried by such attention to being the teacher or knowing and being first, are precisely not the point. Those values belong in a male-governed world, where enlightenment is defined by precedence and authority, where scholars argue about sources, and where Buddha teaches kings (presumably Siamese kings), who still keep slaves.

Sonn Klean and Stowe and Anna belong in a feminine universe, where boundaries of identity are permeable, where insights and understandings and "daily lessons" are fluid and really do move between characters, where the presumed power of teaching continually crosses borders, shifts shapes, and is willingly passed back and forth. For the American missionaries in Bangkok the Buddhists are damned, and for Singapore businessmen the coolies are not even there. Sonn Klean's hidden perfume is her sympathetic power, hard won through being "deprived of her opportunity of loving as a wife and a woman" (246). Responding to the "sorrow" of her life as a slave and a concubine, Sonn Klean has learned to enter into other people, to "respect the rights of her fellow-creatures," to read Anna's feelings so as to teach her, to become a Buddhist Harriet Beecher Stowe. Moreover, Sonn Klean can move through time as well as space, not only becoming Stowe but also, as yet another implication of that eloquent introduction to her is here revealed, able to reach into the future and transform other women that Anna has still to meet.

The location of Leonowens's *Romance* is not Bangkok but Nang Harm, the royal city of enslaved women and children. This is not a place of fixed subjects or established identities, with all the clarity of masculine power such fixity entails. Nang Harm is, of course, framed by the power of the king, who is in turn framed by the power of Buddha. Sonn Klean, owner of slaves, is herself a slave, while Anna is a liberated British woman who can pass out of the gates of Nang Harm every night. But the landscape of power, built in part with rhetorical materials supplied through the rhetoric of the American Civil War, and contained in the Christian representations of slavery in Bangkok and the government representation of the freedom in Singapore, remains a landscape built by men. Even in Leonowens's fantastic narratives, that imperial landscape, decorated with tall stone obelisks to Truth and Selfhood and Reality and Knowledge, cannot be escaped from. But it also, for all its proclamations, cannot—or, in terms of the rulers of Siam and of Singapore—perhaps, will not, free its slaves. That power and that choice the narrative locates in some small and feminine-gendered ₁laces, where there are what Leonowens called "Stray Leaves" from the table, where selfhood shrinks and expands and transmutes, and where nationality need not utterly dominate either identity or location. In those places a Siamese woman can speak, can proclaim, can liberate, and can teach.

PARTIALITIES

My larger hope in writing this essay is to suggest that the question of who it is that speaks, far from being critically or politically or morally simple, is perhaps the most vital and complex question I can bring to a reading of this memoir. In thinking about how to read the Hidden Perfume section of *The Romance*, it doesn't seem to me adequate to interpret this moment as a typical strategy of an imperializing rhetoric, neither as an erasing of the particulars of an "Eastern" situation by reference to a defining "Western" situation nor as a transposing of the evils of American culture to the discursive site of Siam. One reason an interpretive grid of oppressor/oppressed does not seem compelling is that the concepts of West and East are themselves the language of imperialism, a familiar point but one which actually means to me that we should avoid those terms or the strategic polarity they imply. The narrator of the passage certainly sees with imperial eyes. But her eyes, and the I that sees with them, have many subject positions in this narrative, few of which are particularly easy to label or to judge, and none of which can usefully be called "Western."

I find it particularly compelling that in *The Romance of the Harem* other characters as well as Anna take up various subject positions at various moments in the story, none of which can be taken as self-defining and final. One result is that power, national and social, does not flow consistently in any one geographic or cultural direction in this narrative. As a feminist reader interested in how international policies of domination are enacted in literature, I am drawn to those places in this text (and other texts) when gender works to suspend, or perhaps just to lift temporarily, the veil of imperialist assumptions which drive the narratives of so many nineteenth-century British travel memoirs.

That those assumptions are so often cast in the language of literary realism is, I think, an important reason why Leonowens's startlingly nonrealistic "romance" has been so neglected in the Victorian canon. A vivid feature of its nonrealism is precisely that its female characters don't stay put in their given social identities. They are represented in multiple subject positions, occasionally even by their own power of choice. Their abilities to shift location, sometimes minor, sometimes—as with Sonn Klean—quite radical, allow moments in the book when the conventional hierarchies of nineteenth-century imperialism and gender not only don't drive the narrative but also become themselves objects of critique. There are, it seems to me, many kinds of narrative conflicts which work in nineteenth-century British travel narratives to challenge a seamless imperialism, and gender is only one. If these books are to teach us, as, I have been arguing, Sonn Klean so variously taught Anna, we might consider the value of a politics of metamorphosis rather than a politics of identity.

WORKS CITED

Alatas, Syed Hussein. *The Myth of the Lazy Native: A Study of the Image of the Malays, Filipinos and Javanese from the 16th to the 20th Century and its Function in the Ideology of Colonial Capitalism*. London: Frank Cass, 1977.

Blunt, Alison and Gillian Rose. *Writing Women and Space: Colonial and Postcolonial Geographies*. New York: Guilford, 1994.

Edney, Matthew. *Mapping an Empire: The Geographical Construction of British India, 1765–1843*. Chicago: U of Chicago P, 1997.

Bowring, Sir John. *The Kingdom and People of Siam*. 1857. 2 vols. Reprint, Kuala Lumpur: Oxford UP, 1969.

Bradley, William L. *Siam Then: The Foreign Colony in Bangkok before and after Anna*. Pasadena: William Carey Library, 1981.

Bradley, Dan Beach. *The Bangkok Calendar*. Bangkok: American Missionary Association, 1859–69.

Bristowe, W. S. *Louis and the King of Siam*. New York: Thai-American Publishers, 1976.

Chula Chakrabongse, Prince of Thailand. *Lords of Life: The Paternal Monarchy of Bangkok, 1872–1932*. London: Alvin Redman, 1960.

Feltus, George Haws, ed. *Abstract of the Journal of Rev. Dan Beach Bradley, M.D.* Published by Rev. Dan F. Bradley. Cleveland: Pilgrim Church, 1936.

Frankfurter, Dr. O. "King Mongkut." *Journal of the Siam Society*. I (1904) : 191–206.

Gikandi, Simon. *Maps of Englishness: Writing Identity in the Culture of Colonialism*. New York: Columbia UP, 1996.

Great Britain, Foreign Office in Siam. *Correspondence, 1867–1948*. Microfilm. Kew, Richmond, Surrey: Public Record Office, 1984.

Griswold, A. B. *King Mongkut of Siam*. New York: Asia Society, 1961.

Knight, Ruth Adams. *The Treasured One: The Story of Rudivoran, Princess of Siam*. New York: Dutton, 1957.

Kukrit, Pramoj, M. R. *Si Phaendin, Four Reigns*. Trans. Tulachandra. 2 vols. Bangkok: Duang Kamol, 1981.

Kukrit Pramoj, M. R. and Seni Pramoj, M. R. *A King of Siam Speaks*. Bangkok: Siam Society. 1987.

Landon, Margaret. *Anna and the King of Siam*. New York: John Day, 1943.

Leonowens, Anna Harriette. *The English Governess at the Siamese Court; Being Recollections of Six Years at the Royal Palace in Bangkok*. Boston: Fields, Osgood, & Co, 1870.

———. *Life and Travel in India: Being Recollections of a Journey Before the Days of Railroads*. Philadelphia: Porter & Coates, 1884.

———. *The Romance of the Harem*. 1873. Ed. Susan Morgan. Reprint, Charlotte : U of Virginia P, 1991.

Mills, L. A. *British Malaya, 1834–67*. Kuala Lumpur: Oxford UP, 1966.

Mills, Sara. *Discourses of Difference: An Analysis of Women's Travel Writings and Colonialism*. London: Routledge, 1991.

Mohanty, Chandra. Rev. of *European Women and the Second British Empire* by Margaret Strobel and *Waging Change: Women Tobacco Workers in Nipani Organize* by Datara Chaya. *Signs* (1995): 1058–61.

Moffat, Abbot Low. *Mongkut, the King of Siam*. Ithaca: Cornell UP, 1961.

Morgan, Susan. *Place Matters: Gendered Geography in Victorian Women's Travel Books about Southeast Asia*. New Brunswick: Rutgers UP, 1996.

Pratt, Mary Louise. *Imperial Eyes: Travel Writing and Transculturation*. London: Routledge, 1992.

Radhakrishnan, R. *Diasporic Mediations: Between Home and Location*. Minneapolis: U of Minnesota P, 1996.

Rose, Gillian. *Feminism and Geography: The Limits of Geographical Knowledge*. Minneapolis: U of Minnesota P, 1993.

Smith, Malcolm. *A Physician at the Court of Siam*. 1946. Reprint, Singapore: Oxford UP, 1982.

Stoler, Ann. "Sexual Affronts and Racial Frontiers: European Identities and the Cultural Politics of Exclusion in Southeast Asia." *Comparative Studies in Society and History: An International Quarterly* 34.3 (1992): 514–51.

Tarling, Nicholas. *British Policy in the Malay Peninsula and Archipelago, 1824–71*. London: Oxford UP, 1969.

Thomas, Nicholas. *Colonialism's Culture: Anthropology, Travel and Government*. Cambridge: Polity, 1994.

United States Consulate in Bangkok. *Records. 1856–1912*. Washington: National Archives and Records Service, 1962.

Young, Ernest. *The Kingdom of the Yellow Robe: A Description Of Old Siam*. 1898. Reprint, Singapore: Oxford UP, 1982, 1986.

Vikrom Koompirochana. "Siam in British Foreign Policy 1855–1938: The Acquisition and Relinquishment of British Extraterritorial Rights." Ph.D. Diss., Michigan State U, 1972.

Wyatt, David K. *The Politics of Reform in Thailand: Education in the Reign of King Chulalongkorn*. New Haven: Yale UP, 1982.

———. 1982. *Thailand: A Short History*. New Haven: Yale UP, 1982.

About the Contributors

Elizabeth Ammons is Harriet H. Faye Professor of Literature at Tufts University. She is the author of *Conflicting Stories: American Women Writers at the turn into the Twentieth Century* and *Edith Wharton's Argument with America*, as well as the editor or coeditor of a number of volumes.

Peter A. Chvany is an ex-academic, an LGBT (Lesbian Gay Bisexual and Transgendered) community author and activist (especially in the bisexual community), a sometime antiracist agitator, and currently works as a computer systems administrator at Harvard Law School. His writing has appeared in the *Washington Blade*, *The Slant* (Marin County, California), and the *minnesota review*, and his analysis of the racial and cultural politics of representation of *Star Trek*'s Klingons is forthcoming in a collection from Duke University Press. He has presented at the annual Creating Change conference sponsored by the National Gay and Lesbian Task Force and the first Gay Men's Health Summit. His monthly column on bisexual issues appears in *The Slant* (www.theslant.org). He lives near his nondomestic partners in the Boston area.

Delia Caparoso Konzett holds a Ph.D. in English from the University of Chicago. She is the author of the forthcoming work, *Ethnic Modernisms: The Aesthetics of Transnationalism and Displacement in Anzia Yezierska, Zora Neale Hurston, and Jean Rhys* (St. Martin's/Palgrave Press), and has published essays in *American Literature*, *Journal of Film and Video*, and *The Journal of Caribbean Literature*. She is currently working on American World War II films and the relationship between orientalism and multiethnicity. Konzett teaches at Yale University.

Susan Koshy is Associate Professor in the Asian American Studies department at the University of California, Santa Barbara. Her articles on globalization and neocolonialism, diasporic feminist narratives, post-civil rights articulations of whiteness, Asian American literature, and racial identity in silent film have appeared in the *Yale Journal of Criticism*, *boundary 2*, *Differences*, *Diaspora*, *Social Text*, *Transition*, and in several anthologies. She is currently completing work on a book-length manuscript on Asian/American miscegenation and the national imaginary.

Paula M. Krebs is Associate Professor of English at Wheaton College, in Massachusetts. She has published on Olive Schreiner; colonialism and *Wuthering Heights*; feminist pedagogy; and other topics. Coeditor of *The Feminist Teacher Anthology: Pedagogies and Classroom Strategies* (Teachers College Press, 1998), she is the author of *Gender, Race, and the Writing of Empire: Public Discourse and the Boer War* (Cambridge University Press, 1999).

Melissa Lee Miller recently completed her Ph.D. in English literature at Kent State University and is currently an Assistant Professor of British Literature at Notre Dame College in Cleveland, Ohio. The selection here is taken from her dissertation, *The Imperial Feminine: Victorian Women Travellers in Egypt*. Her most current research project is a study of race, masculinity, and father-son bonds in the nineteenth-century American South.

Susan Morgan's books include *In the Meantime: Character and Perception in Jane Austen's Fiction*; *Sisters in Time: Imagining Gender in Nineteenth-Century British Fiction*; and *Place Matters: Gendered Geography in Victorian Women's Travel Books about Southeast Asia*. She is the author of many articles, has edited two travel memoirs—Anna Leonowens's 1873 *The Romance of the Harem*, and Marianne North's 1892 *Recollections of a Happy Life*, Vol. 1—and has recently finished editing a third: Ada Pryer's 1892 *A Decade in Borneo*. Her current project is a biography of Anna Leonowens. Morgan is Professor of English and Women's Studies Affiliate at Miami University of Ohio.

Samina Najmi received her Ph.D. from Tufts University and teaches gender studies, cultural studies and multiethnic American literature at Babson College, in Massachusetts. She has published essays on whiteness and gender in Asian American and African American fiction, edited the reprint of Onoto Watanna's 1903 novel, *The Heart of Hyacinth* (U of Washington P, 2000), and coedited *Asian American Literature: Form, Confrontation, and Transformation*, a volume highlighting Asian American writers' appropriations and transformations of mainstream genres. Her current projects include a book manuscript, titled *Gendering Whiteness: White Women as Image and Audience in Asian American and African American Literature*, and a booklength study of Asian American women's war narratives.

Terri Hume Oliver is Assistant Professor of English at Bryant College, and a visiting fellow at Harvard University's Du Bois Institute. With Henry Louis Gates, Jr. she coedited and coauthored the preface to the Norton Critical Edition of Du

Bois's *The Souls of Black Folk* (New York: W. W. Norton, 1999). She has also published reference entries on Cynthia Ozick, Susan Cheever, and Robert Beck.

Diana R. Paulin is Assistant Professor of American Studies and English, with secondary appointments in African American Studies and Theater Studies, at Yale University. She received her Ph.D. from the English Department at Stanford University in 1999. Her articles and essays on race and representation have been published in *Cultural Critique, Theatre Journal, The Journal of Drama Theory and Criticism*, and *African American Performance History: A Critical Reader*.

Céine Philibert is Assistant Professor of French at State University of New York at Potsdam. She received her Ph.D. in French Literature and Cinema from Ohio State University. She has worked and published on French cinema and feminism, and women directors from the Maghreb, and is currently researching and writing on contemporary French male-directed cinema, which she identifies as a "new cinema of cruelty."

Vijay Prashad is Associate Professor and Director of International Studies at Trinity College, Hartford. He is author of *Everybody Was Kung Fu Fighting: Afro-Asian Passages and the Myth of Cultural Purity* (Beacon, 2001), *Karma of Brown Folk* (University of Minnesota Press, 2000), and *Untouchable Freedom: A Social History of a Dalit Community* (Oxford University Press, 2000). With Biju Mathew, he edited *Satyagraha in America: The Political Culture of South Asian Americans* (a special issue of *Amerasia Journal*, 1999–2000), and with Janet Bauer he edited *Dilemmas of the Border* (Cultural Dynamics, 2000).

Kanishka Raja was born in Calcutta, India in 1969. He lives and works in Boston, MA. His work can be seen at Allston Skirt Gallery in Boston and LFL Gallery and Bellwether Gallery in New York.

Monali Sheth is currently a graduate student in Nationalism and Ethnicity at the London School of Economics and Political Science. In May 2000, she completed her undergraduate honors thesis in the Ethnic Studies Department at University of California Berkeley. Titled "Class, Transnationalism and Political Mobilization in South Asian America: The Community Response to the Manjit Basuta Case," the thesis has become the basis for two publications; aside from her contribution to this volume, she has published in *Amerasia Journal* (Spring 2001). Her research interests include South Asian American identity politics, and portrayals of South Asians in Western media.

Rajini Srikanth teaches in the English Department and Asian American Studies program at the University of Massachusetts Boston. She is coeditor of

Contours of the Heart: South Asians Map North America, an award-winning anthology of fiction, poetry, essays, and photography by first- and second-generation South Asian Americans and Canadians; coeditor of *A Part, Yet Apart: South Asians in Asian America,* a multidisciplinary collection of essays that examine the ambiguous position of South Asians in Asian America, and coeditor of *Bold Words: A Century of Asian American Writing,* an anthology of fiction, poetry, memoir, and drama by over sixty-five writers from the early years of the twentieth century to the present. Her other interests include race and performance studies, Southern literature, and diaspora studies.

Zhou Xiaojing is Associate Professor of English at the University of the Pacific. She received her Ph.D. in English from Memorial University of Newfoundland, Canada. Author of *Elizabeth Bishop: Rebel "in Shades and Shadows"* (1999), her publications have appeared in various journals and anthologies. She is coeditor of *Asian American Literature: Form, Confrontation, and Transformation,* a volume of critical essays emphasizing the dialogic relationship between Asian American- and mainstream literatures. She is currently working on book-length studies in Asian American poetry and Asian American women's autobiographical writings.

Index of Names

Index of Terms

Ramakrishan Mission, 78
rap music, 147–148
   contemporary rap music, 148
   old school rap music, 148
rape, 199, 153
   rapists, 198–199
Reaganism, 76
Reconstruction, 106, 114–116
redemption, 115
reggae, 41
regionalism, 208
Retake, 41
Rolling Stone magazine, 147

Samaritans, 127
savage, 98
Savings & Loans fiasco, 76
Savoy Ballroom, 161
scientific discourse, 197
Scouts, 201
Scribner's, 134
Second Vatican Council, 73
Sepoy Rebellion, 199
September 11, 43
servant-mistress dynamic, 176
sexism, 184
sexologists, 194–195
sexual:
   anxieties, 200
   harassment, 198
   hegemony, 157
   identity, 137
   orientation, 4
shaken baby syndrome, 63
Shawnee Indians, 92
Shelter Now International, 99
Sikhism, 52, 55, 57
Sioux Indians, 92
Sisyphian labor, 78
slavery, 150
slaves, 195
slave narrative, 151–152
Sleeping Beauty, 93
Snow White, 93
soap opera justice, 58

social constructionist, 7
social Darwinism, 110
social identities, 143
social inequality, 173
Society of Jesus, 72
soul, 41
South Africa, 193–205
South Africa Conciliation Committee, 193
Southall Black Sisters, 41
South Asians, 18, 45–46
   British South Asians, 18, 52, 62
   South Asian Americans, 6, 29–48, 52, 58–59, 62
   South Asian American Invisibility, 18
   South Asian Journalists Association, 24
   South Asian American Leaders of Tomorrow, 24
   South Asian masculinity, 44
Southerness:
   Southern blacks, 141
   Southern culture, 144
   Southern race relations, 143
   Southern racial hierarchy, 142
   Southern racial etiquette, 140
   Southern racial relations, 133

Taliban, 99
Templeton Prize, 71
Texas Pacific railroad, 113, 115–116
The New Yorker, 185
The Simpsons, 37
   Apu, 37
Third World, 1, 19, 55, 168, 178–179
Third World Feminists:
   hooks, bell, 14
   Lorde, Audrey, 14
   Minh-ha, Trinh T., 14
   Mohanty, Chandra Talpadale, 14
   Moraga, Cherrie, 14
transnationality, 219
travel narrative, 228, 229, 254
Treasury Department at Washington, 93
Tuskegee Institute, 150